CONVICT VOICES

BECOMING MODERN
New Nineteenth-Century Studies

SERIES EDITORS

Sarah Way Sherman
Department of English
University of New Hampshire

Janet Aikins Yount
Department of English
University of New Hampshire

Janet Polasky
Department of History
University of New Hampshire

Rohan McWilliam
Anglia Ruskin University
Cambridge, England

This book series maps the complexity of historical change and assesses the formation of ideas, movements, and institutions crucial to our own time by publishing books that examine the emergence of modernity in North America and Europe. Set primarily but not exclusively in the nineteenth century, the series shifts attention from modernity's twentieth-century forms to its earlier moments of uncertain and often disputed construction. Seeking books of interest to scholars on both sides of the Atlantic, it thereby encourages the expansion of nineteenth-century studies and the exploration of more global patterns of development.

For a complete list of books available in this series, see www.upne.com

ANNE SCHWAN

Convict Voices

Women, Class, and
Writing about Prison in
Nineteenth-Century
England

UNIVERSITY OF NEW HAMPSHIRE PRESS

Durham, New Hampshire

UNIVERSITY OF NEW HAMPSHIRE PRESS

www.upne.com/unh.html

© 2014 University of New Hampshire

Manufactured in the United States of America

Library of Congress Control Number: 2014935035

5 4 3 2 1

Für Rudolf und Brigitte Schwan

CONTENTS

ACKNOWLEDGMENTS

Many people and institutions have helped me on the path toward completion of this book. I am especially indebted to my former supervisor, the late Sally Ledger, whose intellectual curiosity, positive attitude, and sense of humor continue to inspire my research and work with my own students. Without her warm and generous support, I would not be who I am today. I also thank the following individuals who have assisted me professionally, through constructive feedback, words of encouragement, or acts of friendship, at different stages of my career: Jan Alber, Isobel Armstrong, Maurizio Ascari, Philip Barnard, Joseph Bristow, Laura Coffey, Ella Dzelzainis, Carrie Etter, Edith Frampton, Hilary Fraser, Gill Frith, Holly Furneaux, Regenia Gagnier, Laurie Garrison, Michelle-Marie Gilkeson, Michael Gliddon, Walter Göbel, Jenny Hartley, Ann Heilmann, Tim Hitchcock, Marcelo Hoffman, Tobias Hug, Anne Humpherys, Susan Hyatt, Louise Jackson, Tobi Jacobi, Frank Lauterbach, Andrew Lawrence, Katherine Lebow, Tara MacDonald, Andrew Maunder, Josephine McDonagh, Rohan McWilliam, Ellen O'Brien, June Purvis, Amber Regis, Helen Rogers, Saskia Schabio, Joanne Shattock, Robert Shoemaker, Sarah Turvey, Ed Wiltse, Sue Wiseman, Joanne Woodman, and Heather Worthington. For inspiring conversations and good collaboration, I thank my colleagues at Edinburgh Napier University; the participants of my conference "Reading and Writing in Prison" at Edinburgh Napier in June 2010; Fife College, HMP Edinburgh, and the Scottish Prison Service; and my students on the option module "Crime in Text & Film" over the past three years.

Thanks are due to the following libraries and their staff: Bodleian Library, British Library, Cambridge University Library, Edinburgh Napier University Library, Edinburgh University Library, Library of the Society of Friends in London, Museum of London, National Archives London, National Library of Scotland, Rochester University Library, San Diego State University Library, University of London Library at Senate House, Women's Library London (now at the London School of Economics). I gratefully acknowledge funding from the Arts and Humanities Research Council (AHRC) in the form of an Early Career Research Fellowship (January–August 2011) and doctoral funding in the earliest stages of this project. I am similarly indebted to the Heinrich Böll Stiftung for a doctoral scholarship. The University of London Central Research Fund and a travel grant from the Carnegie Trust for the Universities of Scotland enabled me to visit specialist libraries and archives at different moments of this research. A British Academy Overseas Conference Grant facilitated important networking opportunities at the 2006 College English Association (CEA) Conference in San Antonio, Texas, which were crucial for the further development of my work. A British Association for Victorian Studies (BAVS) award for conference organization allowed for valuable networking at my "Reading and Writing in Prison" conference. My current and previous employers—Edinburgh Napier University, Birkbeck College, Keble College, University of Hertfordshire, University of Warwick—and my host institution in autumn 2010, San Diego State University, have given institutional support in various ways, which I appreciate. I thank the University Press of New England—especially Phyllis Deutsch and the series editors—for their interest in this project, and the editorial team for efficient and thoughtful support during the final preparation of the manuscript.

I am eternally grateful for the backing of my family: my parents, Rudolf and Brigitte Schwan, for their unflinching support, both moral and material, and for never suggesting, during the long years of postgraduate training, that I get a "proper" job; and Franziska Horn for taking an interest in academic life during long phone conversations. Finally, I thank Stephen Shapiro for his love, companionship, and conversation over the years and for sharing the ups and downs throughout this long process.

NOTE ON ABBREVIATIONS

PP   Parliamentary Papers

RCHL   *Reports from Select Committees of the House of Lords*

RDCP   *Reports of the Directors of Convict Prisons*

RI   *Reports of the Inspectors of Prisons*

The volumes of Parliamentary Papers used are those at the British Library. My citation format for Parliamentary Papers is as follows: title of paper, year of publication, report number in parentheses, volume number, printed page number. If a handwritten page number is given, it is added in square brackets after the printed page number. The page reference provided in the list of works cited refers to the handwritten start page of the document in question, within the bound volume.

Introduction

Approaching Female Prisoners' Voices

What does the past tell us? In and of itself, it tells us nothing.
We have to be listening first, before it will say a word; and even
so, listening means telling, and then retelling.

    Margaret Atwood, *In Search of Alias Grace*

This is a book about women's voices in the penal sphere and the difficulty of uncovering them. In 1985, criminologist Pat Carlen published *Criminal Women: Autobiographical Accounts*, a collection of female offender life narratives. Designed to give female (ex-)prisoners a sense of agency and the chance to "destroy the mythology which inseminates contemporary stereotypes of criminal women" (13), the pioneering work aimed to counter the ramifications of "monocausal and global" (9) models of female criminality by drawing attention to the diversity and complexities of women prisoners' experiences through their stories. *Convict Voices: Women, Class, and Writing about Prison in Nineteenth-Century England* pursues a similar agenda by tracing historically earlier efforts to give voice to female offenders. By demonstrating how such articulations covertly or explicitly intervened into debates around gender and class relations, I aim to complicate our understanding of women's imprisonment in the nineteenth century and, in turn, to provide critical strategies for approaching female prisoners' voices at other historical moments, including the present day.

    In the broadest sense, I see this book as part of the unfinished interdisciplinary project of feminism, what Julia Swindells has described as "a widespread commitment within the women's movement, commonly understood in terms of the retrieval of absent or silent women's 'voices'" ("Conclusion" 205–6). Despite being dedicated to such a feminist recovery project, *Convict Voices* highlights that this "retrieval" can never be unproblematic, especially with a view to historical, nonelite prisoners' perspectives, which are typically subject to multiple levels of submergence. This book explores the processes of mediation at work in the representation and recovery of convict voices, while acknowledging that I, too—a white, middle-class academic with no personal experience of imprisonment—am inevitably implicated in this practice of mediating.

Encompassing different textual forms, the book's methodology draws inspiration from a range of academic disciplines—from feminist criminology, auto/biographical studies, the history from below, law, and literary studies—to offer original insights for the burgeoning interdisciplinary field of prison studies and to contribute to Victorian studies' renewed interest in the "hidden lives" of socially marginalized groups.[1] I analyze a variety of mostly British primary sources, including gallows literature, prison narratives by metropolitan journalist and popular fiction writer Frederick William Robinson, mid-Victorian novels by George Eliot and Wilkie Collins, late nineteenth-century prison autobiography, and the secret diaries and letters of incarcerated suffragettes, before concluding with a postscript on two late twentieth-century historical novels about women in prison. The study begins in the early nineteenth century, at a moment when female philanthropists such as the Quaker Elizabeth Fry were raising public awareness around women's imprisonment; the historical part of my analysis ends with a chapter on the suffragettes' writings right before the First World War, because it is here that many of the debates around female lawbreaking and its wider social contexts culminated in particularly unequivocal and often self-conscious ways. To briefly interrogate historical differences and continuities, the book concludes with reflections on more contemporary attempts at recovering or imagining female prisoners' voices in the late twentieth and early twenty-first centuries—a period in which there has been a steep increase in female prison populations in the West, which has made considerations around such women's experiences and their representation more urgent.[2] While it is beyond the scope of this book to include a discussion of material from the intervening years, such as Joan Henry's best-selling *Who Lie in Gaol* (1952), based on her time in English penal institutions, or her slightly later *Yield to the Night* (1954), a fictionalized first-person account of a woman awaiting execution, it is hoped that some of the insights from *Convict Voices* will inspire further work on these, and other, writings about prison.[3]

The chapters' roughly chronological order does not suggest a teleological development from a less to a more "advanced" understanding of women's offending behavior and incarceration. Similarly, I am not contending that influence is necessarily at work between these different sources, although I will establish such connections when they occur. In this book, I wish to open up a conversation between what, on the surface, might seem like disparate textual forms that would typically not be read together, to illustrate the presence of a cultural problematic across different discursive sites and historical periods—namely, a sustained interest in women's crime and punishment and female prisoners' perspectives as a platform for interrogating broader social concerns, such as gender and class relations. These diverse articulations evoke a contested, and often contradictory, (proto) feminist consciousness that emerges through the prism of nineteenth-century penal debates.

While acknowledging the complex and contested nature of the term *feminist*, I use the concept loosely to denote an interest in gender equality and women's right to a life of opportunity without fear of deprivation, oppression, stigma, and emotional or physical harm, within and outside prison walls. The texts, writers, and historical moments under scrutiny here do not offer a uniform approach to matters of gender inequality or women's rights, thus illustrating that feminism's history, as much as its current manifestation, is diverse and contingent.[4] Imprisoned suffragettes, for example, unmistakably called for political rights and fuller civic involvement for women; others, such as the spiritualist and alleged fraudster Susan Willis Fletcher and Florence Maybrick, serving time for the supposed murder of her husband, bemoaned a sexist bias in the criminal justice system, while shying away from overtly formulated feminist demands. Yet their narratives, like many of the other sources studied in this book, need to be situated within a broader cultural context that witnessed emerging debates around gendered expectations and women's changing roles in society in general and in the penal system more particularly.[5] Where a concern with gender-specific conditions is implicit rather than explicit—for instance, in execution broadsides hinting at the gendered contexts for women's crimes—I employ the term *protofeminist* to indicate that gender critiques may be contained but not fully articulated. The concept of intersectionality implicitly motivates much of my analysis, that is, an understanding that a prisoner's gender identity is to be considered in conjunction with other categories of identity, with a particular focus on class and its impact on female prisoners' voices and their mediation.[6]

Prisoners' Voices and Life-Writing |
Critical Contexts after Foucault

Not least because of a surge in Western countries' prison population over the past three decades, recent years have seen a rise in critical concerns with prison narratives, prisoner life writing, and the perspectives of (ex-)prisoners more generally—inside and outside the Anglophone academy—if not always necessarily with a gendered focus.[7] Even criminology, traditionally a subject dedicated to the production of scientific models *about* offenders, has begun to accept the prisoner viewpoint as a necessary element for theoretical thinking about crime and punishment, partially thanks to the self-reflexive work of feminist criminologists such as Carlen, Carol Smart, and Anne Worrall.[8] As Judith Scheffler suggests in her introduction to *Wall Tappings: An International Anthology of Women's Prison Writings, 200 to the Present*, though, "historical writing by imprisoned women is especially difficult to identify and locate, and this gap constitutes a cultural loss of undetermined scope" (xxii). I aim to begin redressing this cultural void, while remaining conscious of the limitations of such recovery work.

The knowledge and experiences of the vast majority of women in nineteenth-century prisons remain unrecorded, owing to a number of factors—illiteracy and the generally low cultural capital among female offenders, who mainly came from disadvantaged socioeconomic backgrounds, but also the cultural sanctioning of certain forms of knowledge over others.[9] My sources include what can be assumed to be genuine self-expressions—typically by middle- or upper-class women with the relevant literacy skills, access to writing material, and means of publication—as well as staged or fictionalized prisoners' voices, such as those in execution broadsides' "last lamentations," which purported to be written by the convict and predominantly featured the voices of nonelite women. I do not claim that these and other representations—no matter how "authentic"—offer us unproblematic or direct access to female prisoners' experiences. While I am sensitive to differences in textual form and publication history, my primary interest here lies less in the question of the texts' authenticity, factual accuracy, or representativeness than in how their representational acts *construct* and *authorize* the female convict's perspective as a way of imagining and commemorating otherwise hidden or lost knowledge.[10] My emphasis on "voices" acknowledges the fragile, ephemeral nature of this knowledge and serves as a reminder of prisoners' limited literacy, which, in most cases, prevented them from leaving a written record for posterity with their own pen.

In literary and cultural studies, the lasting influence of what could be termed Michel Foucault's disciplinary thesis as a theoretical paradigm has made it difficult to take notice of prisoners' voices. The overemphasis on "discipline," control, and silencing over prisoner agency and self-expression is less Foucault's fault than the result of a reductive reception of his work. Although, as Helen Rogers rightly notes, "inmates never speak in *Discipline and Punish*" (75), Foucault's project as a whole demonstrates personal and political commitment to "the insurrection of subjugated knowledges," that is, "historical contents that have been buried or masked in functional coherences or formal systematizations," including the perspectives of offenders (*"Society"* 7).[11] Post-Foucauldian readings have often risked perpetuating rather than challenging such "formal systematizations" by highlighting particular forms of discourse or obliterating the complexity of voices in texts.[12]

Responding to one-sided receptions of Foucault's work, recent research on the Frenchman's role as founding member of the Groupe d'Information sur les Prisons (GIP), which provided French prisoners with a platform for complaints against prison conditions in the early 1970s, uncovers the interplay between Foucault's theoretical work and his prison activism, ultimately dedicated to bringing about change in the penal system and the entire social structure.[13] Similarly, my own readings of nineteenth- and early twentieth-century attempts to give voice to female prisoners are interested in these articulations' relationship with social change within and beyond the penal sphere, including, in some cases, their negotiation of concepts of female citizenship and nationhood. Foucault's idea of knowledges historically "kept in the margins" (*"Society"* 8) clearly resonates in the context of such feminist recovery work, even if he famously neglected gender as an analytical category himself.[14] My method here combines Foucault's approach aimed at the "insurrection of subjugated knowledges" with a feminist agenda to reinstate "a whole series of knowledges that have been disqualified" (Foucault, *"Society"* 7). As I will go on to demonstrate, such knowledges include not only "the knowledge of the delinquent" (7) but also the historically subordinate knowledges of female prison staff or prison visitors who, in the examined texts, help restore prisoners' stories.

Rather than dismissing the significance of earlier post-Foucauldian studies that focused on the ways in which nineteenth-century discourses and genres such as the novel participated in objectifying offenders and "disciplining" socially transgressive voices, this book complements such critical accounts by giving thorough attention to spaces that allowed for a more sustained interrogation—and occasional celebration—of female prisoners' voices. Such textual representations were not always and automatically counterhegemonic. My readings are informed by a view of culture as a contested space, recognizing that containment and resistance are always in interplay with each other, that texts often celebrated and constrained convict voices simultaneously, not least owing to social and generic conventions. Instead of reducing the effects of textual representations of prisoners' voices to either containment or resistance, the subsequent chapters illustrate the complicated cultural work of these articulations. For example, my interpretations of "last lamentations" in execution broadsides place female convicts' voices in a larger context of production and reception to show that broadsides primarily targeted female audiences, opening up a space for exploring women's transgression, while also drawing on social and generic conventions that limited female self-assertion. Similarly, Robinson's prison narratives combine seemingly conservative conventions of confession or conversion narratives with more unusual efforts to uncover the hidden experiences of women prisoners and prison matrons with a view to advocating change in the criminal justice system and wider social organization.

In *The Self in the Cell: Narrating the Victorian Prisoner*, an analysis of literal and symbolic imprisonment, Sean Grass argues that Victorian novels participated in prison authorities' desire to construct individuals' awareness of their identities by subjecting incarcerated characters to self-inspection through the use of letters, diaries, autobiographies, and confessions.[15] Furthermore, Grass shows how prison chaplains such as H. S. Joseph and John Clay edited and used prisoner self-narratives strategically to legitimize regimes of reformation.[16] By contrast, my readings of different sources, which did not have an institutional investment in a particular kind of penal policy, expand and recalibrate our understanding of historical prisoners' self-expressions in two ways. First, by suggesting that these self-representations—be they fictionalized or "authentic"—cannot merely be reduced to the disciplinary strategy of "turning human subjectivity into the object and product of the penitentiary's power" (Grass 11), the following analyses explore how such stories often moved beyond concerns with individual psychology and redemption, instead becoming emblematic of *inter*subjectivity and collective experiences. For instance, I examine nonelite women's voices in execution broadsides and their relevance for communities of working-class females, while also interrogating middle- and upper-class prisoners' attempts to give voice to the experiences of "common" convicts besides their own. Second, I illustrate how some ex-prisoners' autobiographical accounts self-reflexively engaged with both the potential and pitfalls of self-expression. Susan Willis Fletcher's *Twelve Months in an English Prison* discusses enforced silence and the significance of public speech as a form of empowerment, while Florence Maybrick, examined in chapter 5, articulates anxieties over turning herself into a case study for public consumption through her life narrative *My Fifteen Lost Years*. Regenia Gagnier's twofold definition of autobiography as an "arena of empowerment to represent oneself in a discursive cultural field as well as the arena of subjective disempowerment by the 'subjecting' discourses of others" (41) is useful for my understanding of prisoners' voices here, since life narratives afforded those who had been previously silenced an opportunity for entering the "discursive cultural field," while simultaneously locating them within already existing—often damaging—discourses about women convicts.

Female prisoners' voices in this context had to contend with the constraints of generic conventions, which dictated narrative closure marked by remorse, reformation, and redemption. Exploring the relationship between the totalizing effect of genre and penal institutions in the contemporary moment, Dylan Rodríguez rejects the category of "prison writing," for it allows "the prison [a]s a political and intellectual apparatus" to "validat[e] and benefit[] from the existence of a literary genre which foregrounds the prison's pedagogical capacities" (409). With an awareness of this critique, my study resists attempts to define a supposedly coherent genre of "prison writing," examining a variety of loosely connected writings *about* women in prison that do not always fully endorse the prison's reformatory (what we would now call "rehabilitative") potential. This allows for an analysis of prisoner-authored texts as a complex "cultural production that is both *enabled* and *coerced* by state captivity" (Rodríguez 410) alongside outsiders' efforts to offer platforms for prisoner perspectives.

In a nuanced discussion of present-day reading practices of incarcerated African American women, Megan Sweeney suggests that despite the prescribed normalizing functions of reading in US prisons—what in the mid-twentieth century became known as *bibliotherapy*—reading materials simultaneously facilitated unintended "radical" reading practices (37). Likewise, for the Victorian period, Rogers has argued that reading and writing allowed inmates at Great Yarmouth Gaol to use such opportunities creatively, suggesting a relationship defined by "negotiation and not just domination" (80). Similarly, I demonstrate that we should read nineteenth-century female (ex-)prisoners' self-expressions, as well as their staged, fictionalized voices, as articulations that often, if not always, exceeded dictated agendas of punishment and reformation. Prisoners' voices and their reception played a significant role in the cultural field, battling over the meaning of convict experience.

Scholars from a range of disciplines have examined female offenders' stories in literature and popular culture from a historical perspective, beginning with women's voices in early modern street literature.[17] Robert Shoemaker's work on print culture and self-representations of female offenders in the late seventeenth and early eighteenth centuries notes how such women benefited from a range of cultural spaces to express their viewpoints and share their personal histories, from criminal biographies and novels such as Daniel Defoe's *Moll Flanders* (1722) to the Ordinary of Newgate's Accounts.[18] Shoemaker argues that subsequently, "changing cultural understandings of femininity and the emergence of a 'humanitarian narrative' of suffering [which] meant that female deviants increasingly elicited sympathy as passive victims rather than as active agents," led to a "decline of the female criminal voice" (87). Similarly, Nicola Lacey's *Women, Crime, and Character: From Moll Flanders to Tess of the D'Urbervilles* describes a shift from the eighteenth to the nineteenth centuries and from representations of vocal, transgressive literary heroines such as Moll to Tess as "an image of female powerlessness" (5). My study complements and complicates such critical narratives by tracing the existence of the "female criminal voice" in a diversity of nineteenth-century textual forms, beyond the novel. While an appeal to sympathy for women convicts is key to many of the texts investigated in the following chapters, these writings offered opportunities for staging voices and self-assertion that went beyond a construction of women offenders as passive recipients of the readers' goodwill. My project thus builds on Philip Priestley's *Victorian Prison Lives*; but while Priestley's social history of the prison fuses "hundreds of personal narratives of life in the nineteenth-century English prison into a single, collective account" (xix), including the voices of prisoners, warders, and other officials, I consider more carefully the textuality, genre conventions, implied audiences, and strategic functions of my sources rather than reading them as evidence of historical "fact" in an unproblematized way.

A key context for my readings of prisoners' voices is a transformation in the nineteenth-century legal system, which aggravated the problem of convict agency. Before the end of the eighteenth century, the vast majority of prisoners made their own defense in English courts. Eighteenth-century court transcripts contain fascinating records of female convicts speaking on their own behalf, such as the case of Sarah Malcolm, accused of triple murder and burglary in February 1733. Fighting for her life at the Old Bailey in London, Malcolm faced an all-male jury and court, including the lawyer acting for the prosecution. As Tim Hitchcock and Shoemaker note in their detailed discussion of the trial, Malcolm's was "an impressive performance by a woman who had been universally convicted and traduced in the papers and who faced a courtroom full of unsympathetic men" (128–29).[19] Malcolm "stuck with her story throughout" and, even though she had confessed to the theft, "refused to admit, for even a moment, any participation in the murders themselves" (129). Malcolm may have been unusual in her persistent and rhetorically skilled defense, given her social position as a poor woman and her lack of training, but, as Hitchcock and Shoemaker suggest, "the opportunities she took advantage of in her trial to present her side of the story are evidence of the substantial role defendants could (and indeed were expected to) play in eighteenth-century trials, even if the odds remained stacked against them" (130).

By contrast, from the late eighteenth century onward, it became more common for legal counselors to speak *for* the convict, especially in serious cases, thus erasing the defendant's right to tell his or her own story.[20] In 1836, the Prisoners' Counsel Act formalized the growing convention of having felons defended by a counsel or attorney.[21] In practice, most prisoners were unable to afford legal support, but in serious cases, they would often be assigned counsel at the discretion of the judge.[22] This change was in theory designed to help defendants make a more effective case through a legal professional—it was rightly assumed that most lacked Malcolm's verve (even *she* was eventually convicted and executed)—but it also precluded possibilities for self-defense from the start. This threat of obliteration of speech had particular resonance for women in a broader cultural climate hardly conducive to female self-expression in public. Some defendants, such as the articulate spiritualist Susan Willis Fletcher in the 1880s, saw such silencing as an additional form of disempowerment. She used her autobiography as a substitute for the speech that she had been denied in court.[23]

Recent scholars working on women and the law, such as Christine Krueger, have noted "the beginnings of a concerted feminist assault on women's legal handicaps" in the mid-nineteenth century—handicaps that had served as extensions of women's wider disempowerment in a patriarchal society ("Witnessing Women" 338). According to Krueger, the 1836 act "effectively eliminated the only occasion in which women spoke in court in their own defense" (340). She illustrates how women writers from Charlotte Elizabeth Tonna and Elizabeth Gaskell to George Eliot interrogated "the exclusion of women's voices from public speech through mechanisms symbolized by the law" (338). Jan-Melissa Schramm argues similarly regarding Victorian literature's engagement with the legal context, investigating how realist writers such as Eliot or Charles Dickens sought "to recover those stories which the law ignores as inadmissible or irrelevant" (*Testimony* xii). My study suggests that the prisoners' voices staged across a *range* of nineteenth-century textual forms fulfill a similar function in that they offer an alternative forum for the prisoner's own story and thus act as expressions of discursive agency denied to female defendants in the criminal justice system. I am not arguing for a simple causal relationship between a change in the law and cultural responses, or even the rise of new genres as a consequence of a shift in the legal system, as critics interested in the relationship between law and literature have sometimes tended to do.[24] What I do suggest here is that at that particular historical moment, the cultural role of "giving voice" to prisoners took on a new significance, and that a perusal of related representational strategies across my chosen sources enables us to reconstruct a nineteenth-century history of women's imprisonment that considers the function of prisoner perspectives in ways that have not been possible before. Extending our evidentiary basis beyond canonical authors to popular texts such as execution broadsides allows us to see how responses to the law—and the threat of excluding women's voices from the law and wider public arena—were staged across a diversity of genres, including those traditionally marginalized in the literary canon, from midcentury street literature to late Victorian and early Edwardian life narratives of former prisoners.

Gendering the Prison Reform Debate |
From Elizabeth Fry to Mary Gordon

Before undertaking a more detailed discussion of prisoners' voices, I will begin with a contextualization, illustrating how public awareness of gender identity in the penal sphere experienced a boost at the beginning of the nineteenth century. An interest in penal institutions and prison reform emerged as a field of activity for Christian reformers in the second half of the eighteenth century, with women from dissenting religions such as Methodism and Quakerism at the forefront of these developments.[25] In the first half of the nineteenth century, Elizabeth Fry followed the path laid out by fellow Quaker reformer John Howard, the "founding father of penal reform" (Forsythe, *Reform* 18), but initiated a specifically gendered response to prison conditions. Emerging from this context, new policies were implemented, including the separation between male and female prisoners, gendered models of treatment, and female staff to look after women in prisons.[26] An individualized approach was seen as crucial to female reformation, gaining more weight as the century moved on.[27]

Fry institutionalized her own activities with the foundation of the Ladies' Association for the Reformation of the Female Prisoners at Newgate in 1817, followed by the national organization of the British Ladies' Society for Promoting the Reformation of Female Prisoners in 1821, which subsequently opened branches throughout the country, as well as abroad.[28] Benefiting from influential links with the worlds of commerce and parliamentary politics through her Quaker networks, she began to enjoy a reputation throughout Britain and Europe and is even credited with inspiring female prison visitors in North America.[29]

The work of women such as Fry illustrates how prison reform became an important platform for middle-class women's claims to public-sphere activities. As Annemieke van Drenth and Francisca de Haan, drawing on Foucault, have argued, involvement in philanthropy enabled women to participate in "a mode of power that operates through care, that is, a commitment to the well-being of others" (11). This "caring power" contributed to "a new sense of collective gender identity" and "would lead to the first all female organizations, and to the beginning of the (middle-class) women's movement" (12). Women's public engagements in the penal realm brought about significant improvements for female convicts, who came predominantly from lower-class backgrounds, while simultaneously opening up opportunities for middle-class women to fashion themselves as modern subjects of the bourgeois public sphere within a clearly defined social hierarchy. Humanitarianism thus provided a valve for middle-class women's genuine desire to help the socially disadvantaged but also formed part of a larger social tactic to improve relations between the classes and thus guarantee social order and stability.

After a first visit to Newgate Prison in London in 1813, Fry launched her regular attendance and reform efforts at Christmas 1816, beginning with the provision of basic clothing for the inmates and their children.[30] In 1827, after ten years of experience with women's prisons, Fry presented her vision for women's penal institutions in *Observations on the Visiting, Superintendence, and Government of Female Prisoners* (1827). The treatise advocated the project of reclaiming female prisoners as "useful" members of society, advertising women as particularly suited to assist "the helpless, the ignorant, the afflicted, or the depraved, of *their own sex*" (Fry, *Observations* 3). Promoting a model of gentle control presented as participatory and democratic, Fry imagined the initial encounter between benevolent visitors and female prisoners in the following way:

> They [the lady visitors] will express their sympathy with them [the female prisoners] under their circumstances, soothe them with words of gentleness and kindness, and endeavour to hold up, in strong colours, the danger and misery of vice, the beauty of holiness, and the innumerable advantages which attach to a life of sobriety, industry, honesty, and virtue. When the attention of the prisoners has been thus engaged, and their better feelings excited, it will be necessary to propose a series of rules for their future conduct. To these rules they may be expected, in the first place, to give their deliberate and voluntary assent; and secondly, to consider themselves firmly bound to adhere to them, during their continuance in prison. Experience has amply proved, that when prisoners are tenderly treated, there is a general willingness to submit to such regulations as the ladies who visit them may propose for their conduct and improvement. (15–16)

Inviting prisoners to embrace and internalize the rules presented to them, the model of "voluntary assent," as outlined by Max Weber, followed Quaker principles based on "voluntary submission" rather than the "authoritarian moral discipline" characteristic of the established churches (Weber 152). According to Fry, the central object of the visitors' work was "the *reformation* of the prisoners" through "useful elementary knowledge," "practical acquaintance with Holy Writ," and training in "habits of cleanliness, order, and regular industry" (20). In order to achieve this aim, Fry implored her colleagues to proceed with "kindness, gentleness, and true humility," combined with "serenity and *firmness*" (21). Aside from recommendations for penal reorganization, Fry also suggested models for the "continued kind superintendence" (66) of female prisoners after release—for example,

FIGURE 0.1 Elizabeth Fry reading to the female prisoners at Newgate in 1816 (after Jerry Barrett). Reproduced by permission. © Religious Society of Friends in Britain

through placement in a temporary refuge until a respectable situation could be found.

Prison matrons and other female officers in the women's section of prisons became a key element of Fry's vision; hence, they had to act as positive examples "of feminine propriety and virtue" for the prisoners (Fry, *Observations* 30). For the office of matron, Fry recommended women who knew their own station well and were willing to submit to orders from above. Although she wanted them to have some basic education to be able to instruct the prisoners, she insisted that they should not be "*greatly* elevated above [their] charge, yet in a station of life so far superior to their own, as to command their respect and obedience" (29). In her evidence before parliamentary committees in 1832 and 1835, Fry envisioned lady visitors as supervisors of female prison staff to "keep[] the female officers in their places" (*Report from the Select Committee on Secondary Punishments*; PP 1831–32 (547) vii, 117 [675]). Carving out more space for middle-class women's influence, she suggested analogies between prison matrons and servants, advertising the skills of lady visitors—who were "in the habit of hiring Female

Servants"—as employers and recommending ladies as consultants to magistrates in charge of appointing female prison staff (*Second RCHL*; PP 1835 (439) xi, 333 [521]). The first matron at Newgate was indeed introduced by the newly formed Ladies' Committee and "regarded as their servant" (K. Fry and R. E. Cresswell qtd. in Fry, *Memoir* 1:269). While matrons received a regular salary from the authorities, they were paid an additional annual amount from the funds of the Ladies' Association (1:269).

Despite having exceptional drive, Fry was mindful of the need to avoid "interference" (*Observations* 23) with the gentlemen in authority, urging her lady visitors to be "at once *wise as serpents, and harmless as doves*" (25), not least because she had run into trouble herself after her attempt to rescue a woman from the gallows.[31] The initiatives of the Ladies' Association were recognized and valued by men in power, but an increasing conflict between the ladies' ambitions and official penal authority is noticeable in the parliamentary papers of the period. The *Report from the Select Committee on Secondary Punishments* for 1831–32, incorporating Fry's own evidence, commended the work of prison visitors. However, a few years later, the *First Report of the Inspectors of Prisons* in 1836 expressed reservations over the ladies' practice of classifying prisoners, appointing wardswomen, and having outsiders attend their religious reading sessions in prison (see figure 0.1, which shows some ladies and gentlemen observing Fry preach to the female prisoners at Newgate). While acknowledging the general success of the ladies' work "in a miserable prison like Newgate," the Inspectors alluded to concerns that such ambitious women might become a disruptive element in "well-regulated gaols" (*First RI*; PP 1836 (117) xxxv, 18–19 [20–21]). Fry's idea of gentle reformation and crime prevention by means of religious teaching and employment was increasingly supplanted by the rise of stricter and centralized prison regimes.[32] From around 1835, as June Rose notes, an "official policy of harsher, more deterrent sentences had replaced Mrs Fry's vision of prisons that would regenerate prisoners," weakening the influence of Fry's model of reform (158). We may speculate that Fry's extensive travels across continental Europe in the late 1830s and early 1840s occurred partly in response to her loss of influence at home.

In 1843, Fry's appeal to Colonel Joshua Jebb, surveyor general of prisons and chairman of the Directors of Convict Prisons in England, regarding the new model prison Pentonville—she was shocked after a visit to its dark solitary cells—was ignored, and she found herself having difficulties getting into Newgate, thirty years after she had first set foot in this prison.[33] As

Lucia Zedner's research has shown, this trend of restricting the influence of women philanthropists became even stronger in the second half of the nineteenth century, particularly when Sir Edmund Du Cane headed the penal administration beginning in 1869, as his regime emphasized uniformity and deterrence over individual reform. Prison visiting subsequently ceased to be organized voluntarily and "became integrated as formal, institutional provision," leading to the foundation of a National Association of Lady Visitors in 1901, presided over by Adeline, Duchess of Bedford (Zedner 124).[34]

The decline of philanthropists' influence from the mid-nineteenth century concurred with the rise of penology as a science, which dismissed voluntary reformism as amateurish. In a letter to the editor of the *Manchester Guardian* in 1848, Joseph Adshead, author of *Prisons and Prisoners* (1845), countered the popularity of Fry's recently published memoirs with an accompanying letter from Professor Lieber of Columbia, South Carolina, which constructed male penology in contrast to female religious philanthropy and rejected Fry's opposition to solitary confinement:

> "We, I mean *men*, who have attentively occupied themselves with the psychology of criminals, and not women, who cannot dive into all the loathsome depths of crime, know that the darkest plans of extensive crime are concerted in the jails; and that criminals of a certain degree of criminality, if brought into contact, will criminalise (if you will permit me the word) each other still more. It is the law of all crime and all virtue, the law of moral reduplication, as I have called it." (*Prison Discipline* 7)

Despite such attempts to claim penological science as a masculine domain, new female reformers such as Bristol Unitarian Mary Carpenter rose to the fore in the 1850s by combining Fry's earlier model of amateur managerialism with a scientific register, the concerns of social science, medicine, and imperial capitalism. Carpenter, like her predecessor, gave evidence before a select committee of the House of Commons, which played a key role in the introduction of reformatory schools for delinquent boys and girls. Carpenter's magnum opus, *Our Convicts* (1864), followed a series of publications on young offenders in the 1850s. Unlike Fry, who had focused on the reformation of female prisoners, Carpenter examined the social circumstances and prison treatment of adult male and female offenders. But similar to the Quaker in the 1840s, Carpenter found herself at odds with official penal policies by the beginning of the 1860s. Convinced that the authorities had a particularly poor understanding of female prisoners' specific needs, which she saw as underrepresented in official documentation, she did not shy away from bold criticism of the convict system as a whole, which she thought had "totally failed" and must therefore be "radically wrong" (*Our Convicts* 2:218). Like Fry, who traveled to continental Europe at the age of sixty, Carpenter spent the last phase of her life concentrating her energies abroad, with four visits to India and publications such as *Suggestions on Prison Discipline and Female Education in India* (1867).[35]

Prison reform at home and abroad afforded women from Fry and Carpenter to lesser-known prison visitors such as Matilda Wrench opportunities for professionalization.[36] As scholars such as Anne Summers have suggested with regard to middle-class women's philanthropy, such "initiatives were [therefore] both progressive *and* reactionary: progressive in that they were reaching out for more power for women; and reactionary in that they sought to prevent that power from passing from a restricted social group to a wider one" ("Home from Home" 60). Aside from genuine humanitarian motivations, women's philanthropic activities in the eighteenth and nineteenth centuries were partially driven by larger strategic interests, such as "the insatiable demand for reliable servants" (Prochaska 148) who might be molded through benevolent schemes.

In contrast to these philanthropic reform agendas, commentators on the English prison system, such as the French socialist Flora Tristan, who visited Newgate, Coldbath Fields, and Millbank Prisons in London in 1839, at exactly the same time when Fry was traveling through France, attacked philanthropy and religion as mechanisms of control, designed by the elites to subdue the recipients of charity into servile roles in capitalist society. Although *Flora Tristan's London Journal* acknowledged Fry's "love of humanity" (110) and the introduction of employment for female prisoners, it challenged religious education as a supposedly effective remedy. Tristan's critique of the prison system went deeper, attacking the very basis of social organization as the root cause of crime. Rather than suggesting regimes of reformatory discipline, Tristan pleaded for a reconstruction of society instead: "Legislators, statesmen and you to whom God has entrusted the destinies of nations, before you think of reforming the guilty, make it your first concern to eliminate the causes of crime so that there may be no guilty" (97). Speaking of female offenders specifically, Tristan examined women's structural inequality, identifying dominant gender ideologies as a factor behind unlawful behavior: "It is a fact that the barbaric and fanatical prejudice brought to bear against the unwed mother sometimes drives her to crime.

Finally, since women are excluded from almost all the professions, when their children have no father to earn their bread, they find themselves faced with infanticide, prostitution or theft" (97). Illustrating her arguments with the example of one particular prisoner at Newgate, a single mother who had stolen to be able to feed her children, Tristan decries social conditions and the law, which lead to what she regards as the unjust incarceration of such women:

> I was struck with admiration . . . and it grieved me to think that her life was going to be blighted and ruined: that there would be judges incapable of *feeling*, of *understanding* the sacredness of a mother's duty! Judges who, with eyes only for property . . . would sacrifice maternal devotion to respect for property; and unable to distinguish between the *heroic mother* and *professional thief* would sentence her to the same punishment. I cursed the laws of man which make no distinction between crime and virtue! I cursed Property which must be defended from the hungry by means of imprisonment and suffering! And it seemed to me that the luxury enjoyed by owners of property was bought with the blood of the poor! (102)

With such a fierce attack on society's social and economic organization, Tristan's language anticipates many of the concerns of Karl Marx and Friedrich Engels, while elsewhere her writing foreshadows later scientific models of female criminality as she draws on discourses of physiognomy, phrenology, and mesmerism, connecting physical with moral characteristics.[37] Although the latter is problematic from today's point of view, Tristan's polemical critique of English society and its prison system offers a powerful insight into alternative ways of nineteenth-century thinking about crime and its causes, beyond the religious reform agendas of other lady visitors.[38] In many ways, her approach also anticipated some of the materialist critiques of women's offending behavior offered by feminists in the late twentieth century.[39]

Despite the class-based limitations of the pioneering work of female prison reformers such as Fry, it had a lasting legacy, shaping subsequent understandings of the significance of gender in the penal context. The Quaker became an icon, inspiring future generations of women, including those who found themselves convicted prisoners during the women's suffrage campaign at the beginning of the twentieth century.[40] It was in this context, in 1908, that the first female inspector of prisons, Mary Gordon, was appointed. Trained as a physician, she reported annually on women's prisons in England and Wales, as well as on inebriate asylums.[41] According to Zedner,

Gordon, unlike her amateur predecessors, "became highly disillusioned with the philanthropic, reformist spirit, which she saw as masking the profoundly damaging impact of imprisonment" (129). The female inspector stressed the need to foster prisoners' independence as a basis for social responsibility. After her retirement, *Penal Discipline* (1922) laid out her theories on women offenders and penal organization. As Deborah Cheney has shown, in the book's concern with female offenders' poverty, histories of maltreatment, low self-esteem, substance abuse, mental health problems, and tendency toward self-harm and suicide, Gordon identified many of the issues still recognized today as factors shaping the life experience of female prisoners. Gordon's pioneering work was long neglected, however. A suffragette sympathizer who refused to publicly renounce her political leanings, Gordon fell afoul of the Home Office and Prison Commission, thus suffering a fate not unlike that of previous generations of female prison reformers.

Voices from the Nineteenth-Century Prison

While female reformers from Fry onward played an important part in gendering the prison-reform debate, their focus typically did not lie with providing platforms for prisoners' perspectives. An early exception was author and philanthropist Felicia Skene, who acted as professional prison visitor at Oxford Gaol and published *Scenes from a Silent World, or, Prisons and Their Inmates* (1889) under the pseudonym Francis Scougal.[42] Skene's writing style echoes other representations of penal institutions and prisoners in nineteenth-century literature and culture. Her introduction, which states the author's desire to interest "the large majority" of the population "in the Silent World and its inhabitants" (xiv), is reminiscent of Dickens's motivation in his *Sketches by Boz* to jolt his readers out of their "force of habit" by drawing their attention to the hidden lives of people behind prison walls (Dickens, "Visit to Newgate" 234). Similarly, Skene's insistence that "prison revelations" (xvii) are valuable and ought not to be "tabooed in polite society" (xvi–xvii) mirrors Dickens's defense in the 1841 preface to the third edition of *Oliver Twist* arguing that his attempt to tell offenders' stories constituted a necessary "service to society" (Dickens, "Author's Preface" liv). *Scenes from a Silent World*, in its claim to authenticity, also recalls Robinson's narratives *Female Life in Prison, Memoirs of Jane Cameron*, and *Prison Characters Drawn from Life*, published in the 1860s under the anonym of "A Prison Matron." Like Robinson, Skene mixed investigative journalism with an imaginative writing style, elements of melodrama, and sensationalism. Her account of the history of a young woman convicted of infanticide, in the form of reported speech running over several pages, evokes literary representations of imprisoned child murderers from Walter Scott's *Heart of Midlothian* (1818) to George Eliot's *Adam Bede* (1859). Like Hetty Sorrel in *Adam Bede*, who breaks her silence in response to her Methodist cousin Dinah Morris's implorations in the prison cell, the self-representation of Skene's prisoner begins as she commands her visitor's/reader's attention: " 'Listen!' she cried—'I will tell you all' " (72).

While Skene's text, like those discussed in the following chapters, is unusual in its desire to create a relatively extensive platform for this prisoner's tale, the "tell-all" nature that such writings advertise points to their ambivalent status, caught between a genuine wish to increase public visibility and understanding of the experiences of the convicted, on the one hand, and authors' or publishers' pursuit of commercial gain through the sale of prisoners' stories, on the other hand. The following chapters investigate some of these tensions between giving voice to the socially marginalized and issues of mediation, appropriation, and exploitation.

CHAPTER 1

"Shame, You Are Not Going to Hang Me!"

Women's Voices in Nineteenth-Century
Street Literature

Street literature, including execution broadsides, provided one of the main textual spaces for representing the voices of female convicts up until the last third of the nineteenth century. Regardless of the truthfulness of these texts, the ways in which many of them claim a platform for female convicts mark them as significant cultural interventions, allowing prisoners to express remorse, shame, and suffering in view of impending punishment, to provide reasons for committing a crime, or conversely, to declare innocence and defiance toward the formidable force of the law, as in the case of Priscilla Biggadike, who, on the verge of her execution for murdering her husband, reportedly refused to admit her guilt in "a firm voice," alternately exclaiming, "All my troubles are over" and "Shame, you are not going to hang me!" ("Execution of Priscilla Biggadike" broadside).[1] After establishing a context for the production and distribution of street literature and providing a brief history of critical debates on crime and execution broadsides as a genre, this chapter considers examples of female convict voices in gallows literature and their function for the predominantly female target market. Such texts not only created a platform for female offenders' perspectives; they also constructed a space for a female public voice more generally, allowing nonelite women audiences to engage with and debate popular ideas around female transgression and its containment.

Gallows Literature and Its Publishing Context

Execution broadsides and chapbooks detailing crime, legal proceedings, and punishment formed a highly popular and profitable subcategory in the street-literature industry—the so-called gallows literature.[2] Street literature had developed from folklore, with broadside ballads serving as a cheap, accessible, and "popular literature of ordinary people" from the early modern period onward (Shepard, *History* 14).[3] In the nineteenth century, the street-literature trade experienced a final wave of popularity, exercising, in Henry Mayhew's estimation, an "influence on masses of the people" (1:220), before giving way to the rise of more widely affordable books and newspapers. The center of the street-literature trade was the shabby Seven Dials area in Central London, where the most famous printer and publisher, James ("Jemmy") Catnach, had his business.[4] Broadsides were distributed by "patterers" or "street-orators" who prided themselves on being more educated than ordinary street sellers and would recite or sing the stories printed on paper or have them sung by an accompanying "chaunter," not least for the benefit of illiterate members of the audience (Mayhew 1:213, 1:226).

Gallows literature around an individual's arrest, trial, and execution came in a variety of forms. Many broadsides provided a detailed account of the events leading up to the crime and conviction, followed by a copy of the verses—in ballad form—containing the alleged "confession" or "last lamentation" of the convict from the prison cell or scaffold. In other cases, the verses were formulated from an observer's perspective, written in the third person.[5] The pairing of court proceedings and execution with the convict's first-person lamentation highlighted the existence of different perspectives on crime, trial, and punishment. Verses and accounts of court proceedings were often accompanied by an image of the convict on the gallows. For economical reasons, such illustrations generally drew on a so-called stock-block, a generic image for repeated use, so that sometimes images bore little relationship to the subject matter discussed in the text. Illustrations were not individualized, but women were distinguished by the cutting of a square at the level of the knees to represent a skirt.[6] Printers also used set pieces to illustrate murder scenes and the condemned cell. At times, accompanying images pictured the convict as a literate, even artistic, reading and writing subject, leaving behind his or her legacy in poetical words. "Life, Trial, Confession and Execution of Martha Browning for the Murder of Mrs. Mundell at Westminster" offers a visually elaborate example, with the image of a tearful but reading prisoner at her writing desk in the prison cell, paired with another woodcut of the convict on the scaffold, bordered by the prisoner's verses on each side. A framed sheet titled "The Lamentations of a Sinner" is shown attached to the prison wall, and writing paper is spread out on the

FIGURE 1.1 "Life, Trial, Confession and Execution of Martha Browning" (1846). Reproduced by permission from The Bodleian Libraries, The University of Oxford, John Johnson Collection; Broadsides: Murder and Executions Folder 10 (21)

desk next to a fountain pen, drawing attention to the woman's own viewpoint and suggesting the prisoner/poet's creative productivity (see figure 1.1).[7] Such broadsides underscored the convict's own subjectivity by framing descriptive third-person accounts of the proceedings and preparations for the execution with first-person verses and illustrations of the prisoner.[8] Pamphlets and chapbooks on crime and punishment presented similar kinds of information but were visually less opulent, with chapbooks usually consisting of several small sheets of paper, bound together as a little booklet.[9]

The layering of text and image and of different narrative agents in broadsides, including the convict herself, suggests a multiplicity of perspectives. Broadsides and other street literature typically drew on various sources, such as newspaper reports and legal proceedings, but they also relied heavily on the industry's collective imagination. Mayhew notes how some of the broadsides' "authors and poets . . . refer regularly to the evening papers, [and] when they hear of any out-of-the-way occurrence, resort to the printer and desire its publication in a style proper for the streets" (1:220). Conversely, "if there be no truths for sale—no stories of criminals' lives and loves to be condensed from the diffusive biographies in the newspapers—no 'helegy' for a great man gone," writers and traders made them up (1:228). Insider accounts of the life styles of patterers—who enjoyed drink, entertainment, and light reading, with the Chartist and proponent of female emancipation Eliza Cook, the Newgate novelist William Harrison Ainsworth, and early Charles Dickens listed as favorites (Mayhew 1:250)—suggest that broadsides were also implicitly informed by intertextual engagement with other contemporaneous material.

Female prisoners as the subjects of broadsides are thus constructed at the intersection of different viewpoints: those of the authors (anonymous male hacks who were typically paid a shilling for their work), those of their sources, the voice of the law, the (alleged) voice of the convict herself, and the voice of the crowd as audience.[10] This multiplicity leads to contradictions and tensions in the representations of women's criminality and punishment, resulting in texts that combine contrary impulses—to warn, control, and contain, as well as to critique and explode. As Miriam Jones suggests in her study of the subgenre of child-murder broadsides, this type of text is "something very akin to a genre: it is inscribed with its own internal logic and its own set of rules for reading . . . even *across* the generic markers of poetry and prose, tragedy and comedy that coexist, and compete, within it" (136). Broadsides arguably capitalized precisely on this generic hybridity and multiplicity of voices—conflicting viewpoints that they sought to display and play against one another through a range of rhetorical and generic features.

The crimes committed by women recorded in broadsides ranged from petty theft to murder. Killings often involved poisoning but sometimes more physically violent methods. The victims were usually close relatives of the female convict—children, husbands, or parents—lovers, or employers. While some of the texts speculate about the prisoner's motives for the deed, others leave this question unresolved, occasionally promising more details in a forthcoming update as a marketing strategy. The execution broadsides were sold just after the hanging took place. They were distributed not only to the audience but also to the general public, after the event. However, it is worth pointing out here that the executions described in broadsides had not always taken place;[11] the accounts printed in street literature, including the alleged "confessions," are not uncomplicated depictions of convicted women's motivations and feelings either. Rather than an authentic account of the actual experiences of prisoners, "last lamentations" are stylized and relatively formulaic representations of these experiences, which *may* contain some autobiographical elements picked up from other textual mediations of prisoner experience, such as newspaper reports.

While I will provide a wider context of individual trials and executions where such information is available, my interest here lies not in the question of the texts' authenticity and factual accuracy but rather in how the representational acts of the broadsides construct and authorize the female convict's perspective. What makes "last lamentations" formally and thematically transgressive in the nineteenth-century context—regardless of whether they involve an overt attack on law and state—is that they give a voice to the female convict at all. The controversy surrounding the criminal subject matter of Dickens's *Oliver Twist* (and the "Newgate School of fiction" more broadly speaking) serves as a useful reminder that such themes, let alone the portrayal of an offender's viewpoint, were not taken for granted by many middle- and upper-class readers at the time. In the 1841 preface to the third edition of *Oliver Twist*, Dickens felt compelled to defend his decision to depict the criminal milieu in detail, including prostitute Nancy's life among thieves, and insisted that this story "needed to be told" (lvii). Broadsides shared the impulses of Newgate novels such as *Oliver Twist* and, in the widest sense, claimed visibility for and commemorated the otherwise hidden or lost forms of embodied knowledge of female offenders. Because broadsides, like Dickens's novels, were read across different social classes of society, this was an effective way of making such perspectives available to a broad audience, even though the broadsides' primary target audience were nonelite women, as discussed in more detail shortly.[12]

As Richard Altick has pointed out, "sorrowful lamentations" told from the convict's perspective were rare before 1836. A legal requirement before that date stipulated that condemned offenders be executed within two days of their conviction, whereas afterward, writers and printers were able to exploit the longer interval between conviction and execution more extensively (Altick 49).[13] However, 1836 also marked a shift toward advocacy, so that felons were increasingly defended by legal representatives, rather than making their own defense.[14] In this context, we can think of "last lamentations" as attempts to maintain, or reclaim, the discursive agency for (women) convicts that was increasingly being eroded in the legal system. In rendering different voices, mid-nineteenth-century broadsides covertly explored the cultural problematic of speech power and conflicting truth claims that was also debated across a range of other narrative forms following the institutionalization of the adversarial system. Whereas novels such as Elizabeth Gaskell's *Mary Barton* (1848) explored women's roles as witnesses in court, street literature highlighted the position of female offenders—surely, in part, a reflection of these different genres' implied audiences and their imagined subject positioning in relation to crime. Writers such as Gaskell targeted the "respectable" working classes and middle-class readers, whereas broadsides were primarily produced for the semiliterate "lower orders." Broadsides, then, enacted similar concerns to those addressed in Victorian novels but from a different angle, with particular consideration of nonelite voices.

A "Voice of and for the Poor"? | Critical Approaches[15]

The ideological functions of crime broadsides have been a subject of critical debate for several decades. While some early popular-culture critics such as Altick considered the moral frame of Victorian broadsides merely as a rhetorical strategy or regarded these texts as primarily subversive (Elkins), others, such as Beth Kalikoff, read the "last confessions" printed on these sheets as didactic, reinforcing the authority of the law and the state. Similarly, Judith Knelman's study of representations of female killers in the nineteenth-century English press emphasizes the punitive function of broadsides when she interprets them as "moral levers in the social system" and texts that "were particularly satisfying [for contemporaneous audiences] because they taught a moral lesson" (*Twisting* 34). My own readings are especially indebted to Ellen O'Brien's recent attempts to reclaim broadsides from "critical dismissals of them as vulgar, sensational, and morally unsophisticated" (*Crime in Verse* 23). O'Brien makes a case for these texts' discursive and generic complexity, interpreting the "layering of affective tropes and legal discourse" in execution broadsides "as skeptical readings of state authority and ambiguous readings of individual transgression" and the "oft-noted poetic inferiority" of such texts "as performances of working-class challenges to cultural authority and artistic propriety" (19). Whereas critics such as Knelman imply that popular genres such as broadsides provided crude moralizing while other textual forms, such as the middle-class novel, offered more sophisticated psychological insights into offenders' motivations, broadsides in fact also contributed psychological perspectives (for instance, on the punishment's effects on offenders) alongside sociological interrogations of authority and the causes of crime. As this book as a whole illustrates, some of the most interesting explorations of female convict voices and psychology can indeed be found in noncanonical literary forms.

O'Brien's important reconceptualization of crime broadsides as a complex and potentially "resistant cultural and textual space" ("Every Man" 322), rather than simply a force of social containment, needs to be balanced against the recognition that popular textual forms may not be either exclusively subversive or restrictive in effect. Theorizing popular culture as an "arena of consent and resistance," Stuart Hall writes that "we should always start here: with the double-stake in popular culture, the double movement of containment and resistance, which is always inevitably inside it" (239, 228). Juliet John makes a similar claim regarding the popular-cultural form of nineteenth-century melodrama, a genre often dismissed for its perceived emotional "excess." She notes that "melodrama is not simply excessive" but characterized by an "excess/restraint dialectic" reflected formally and thematically, in that passionate and transgressive actions are "momentarily contained" within stock characters, tableaux, and narrative solutions in which poetic justice is reestablished (31).[16] John rejects the notion that such conventions are simply ideologically conservative, contending that excess and constraint are in constant interplay with each other and that melodramatic happy endings are marked as "both reassuring and fragile" (31). Although execution broadsides obviously lack a happy ending, they similarly oscillate between transgression and containment and, with their stock images, depiction of the convict's suffering, and appeals to audience identification and sympathy, share some of the stylistic devices, the emotional "excess," and the "communal, anti-individualist agenda" of the melodramatic genre as defined by John (30).

Within this context, then, broadsides constituted a terrain where the meaning of female criminality and its causes, and the legitimacy of crime and punishment, were interrogated, "a sort of battleground," in Foucault's words, "around the crime, its punishment and its memory" (*Discipline* 67). Foucault notes that such texts are best understood as "two-sided discourses" which collectively, at times simultaneously, "justified justice, but also glorified the criminal" (68). As V. A. C. Gatrell has shown, public hangings were always met with a diversity of responses, rather than one uniform reaction by an undiscriminating mob, depending on the nature of the crime and the identity of the convict. This range of reactions is reflected in the execution broadsides' contradictory impulses, which leave scope for different community interpretations of female deviance and its punishment.

Although some executions and related broadsides potentially helped justify justice, nineteenth-century commentators, including Dickens and William Thackeray, were unconvinced by the intended moralizing influence of public executions and condemned such events—during which the broadside trade flourished—as socially corrupting.[17] Even writers of broadsides explicitly addressed these concerns, such as the one detailing Margaret Cunningham's execution for the murder of her husband in Edinburgh in 1807, which deplored public executions' "baneful effect on the mind" in that they "harden the social feelings, [rather] than . . . terrify or deter offenders." The text acknowledged that spectators did not necessarily give much thought to "the breach of morality which has brought [the convict] to such a deplorable end" ("Treason & Murder" broadside).

Some commentators perceived broadsides as part of the problem, because they belonged to a wider culture of popular reading for the poor that many members of the "respectable" classes viewed with suspicion. Such anxieties typically centered on the question of whether popular representations of criminality evoked identification and might invite imitation.[18] Similarly, Mayhew remarked on "the morbid sympathy and intended apology for the criminal" expressed in "last lamentations" (1:281). Reflecting on the convicted murderer Mary May's verses, Mayhew recognized that these simple lines might appear "crude to all educated persons" but that they are "well adapted to enlist the sympathy and appreciation of the class of hearers to whom they are addressed" (1:282). A review of a broadside in the *Town* in 1839 complained "that the poet makes his hero speak of his offence rather too lightly" and that the use of a playful pun reduced the verses' "plaintive-ness" (qtd. in Hindley, *History* xiii).

As O'Brien has suggested with regard to murder broadsides, "the per-sona of the criminal poet" in first-person lamentations "destabilized ethical commonplaces and legal fictions by linking the sentimental poet and the violent murderer, thereby challenging a practice of capital punishment predicated upon the irremediable monstrosity of the condemned and the unimpeachable righteousness of the state" (*Crime in Verse* 24). In the case of female convicts, such processes were potentially even more transgres-sive, as the first-person accounts undercut the monstrosity associated with female deviance in particular and humanized those whom many people of the time considered as more difficult to reclaim than male offenders.[19] Broad-sides, especially verses detailing the convict's first-person perspective, pro-vided a space where the mundane and more unusual experiences of (female) prisoners were interrogated, performed, and aestheticized, bringing about, in Foucault's words, an "insurrection of subjugated knowledges" (*"Society"* 7) and elevating such knowledge to a new position of visibility and cultural value through its inscription in poetical form. While similar textual strate-gies can be found across gallows literature detailing the cases of female *and* male offenders, the material examined here indicates an interest in gender-specific experiences impacting on women's crimes and punishment, themes which include the vulnerable position of female servants; the risk of gender-specific (sexual) exploitation; women's living conditions and lack of social welfare provision, particularly child care; social stigma pertaining to ille-gitimate children; and the role of men as inadvertent enablers or more im-mediate causes of women's offending behavior. The writers' willingness to engage with such gender-specific themes is arguably directly related to con-siderations about audience expectations. As the following section will dem-onstrate, gallows literature especially appealed to female customers, who would look for opportunities of identification in representations mirroring the life experiences that characterized their own female communities.

Target Market and Female Audience Identification

The significance of broadside literature goes beyond its role of providing a discursive space for the recovery of women offenders' culturally submerged perspectives. Broadsides served a wider social function in that they also gave, by extension, a public voice to nonelite women in the audience, who may have shared similar living experiences with the convict.[20] As Martha Vicinus has suggested with regard to nineteenth-century broadsides and other cheap literature such as penny novels, these melodramatic texts were "rooted in a reader's daily concerns," offering "forms and language for understanding the daily violence of one's own life" and giving the reader/listener "a means of interpreting and managing violence" (16). Violence was only one aspect of lived experience that these popular texts dealt with, however; they also encompassed courtship, romance, betrayal, family relations, employment, and material hardship. Taken together, broadsides' rhetorical strategies, in their portrayal of recognizable aspects of experience, point to popular constructions of a female public voice that evoke a collectivity, so that the prisoner becomes a female prototype and source of identification for women in the audience, inviting watching or listening women to draw parallels to their own lives, even if they were not accused of crimes themselves. While Knelman has argued that the broadsides' dual function was simply to deter potential offenders and to impose "accepted norms of behaviour" (*Twisting* 34), the tales of the extraordinary deeds of ordinary women—such as the killing of a husband—simultaneously offered a titillating way for female audience members to catch a glimpse of transgression without actually committing it.

Such a function is particularly pertinent given the popularity of executions and related popular literature among female spectators. Writing on the infamous public hanging of Maria Manning and her husband in 1849, popular writer Robert Huish claimed, "It is certain that the female sex preponderated over the male in the ratio of ten to one" (819).[21] One of Mayhew's interviewees, a "running patterer" selling broadsides in different parts of London and the country, similarly noted, "Mostly all our customers is females" (1:222). According to Mayhew's informant, female clients preferred stories that spoke most closely to their own living situation, with young women displaying a strong interest in tales of seduction, illicit pregnancy, and infanticide, whereas older women found cases such as an elderly mother's filicide more suitable to their taste (1:223). The patterer's commentary on his female customers' tearful responses to such tales suggests that sentimental identification was a significant response to street literature's representations of female offenders, which coexisted with, or even superseded, purely judgmental assessments of these criminal cases.

The notion of a collective, if not necessarily homogeneous, women's "voice" and identification is reinforced by the fact that verses were experienced communally through shared reading practices or song, which was performed by ballad peddlers in the streets according to a tune that was specified on the broadside and could then be imitated by consumers. As O'Brien, drawing on Foucault's writings on "The Songs of Murder" in *I, Pierre Rivière*, notes, this exchange challenged "notions of an essential or distinguishable criminal identity by rendering it performative and transferable" ("Every Man" 322). The textual and oral form of the crime broadside thus served as a commemoration of nonelite female subjectivity in the broadest sense, expressed through the prism of female convict experience.

"Within a Dark and Gloomy Cell / In Anguish Now I Lie" | Condemned Women's Voices

The chapbook titled "Full Particulars of the Life, Trial, and Sentence of Mary Ann Hunt" (1847)—a servant convicted of killing and robbing her elderly landlady—illustrates how street literature juxtaposed different perspectives on female crime and punishment, including the defendant's viewpoint.[22] The book publishes Hunt's lamentation alongside a description of the proceedings in court, including the witnesses' testimonies. The very pairing of different forms of portrayal and narrative perspective within the text draws attention to the act of offender (self-)representation. The prisoner's lamentation in the form of verses here supplies a missing perspective by granting Hunt the authority to tell her tale at some length, whereas the account of the court proceedings merely states that "after the indictment has been read, the prisoner in a firm voice, pleaded Not guilty." Hunt's verses address her own suffering while she anxiously awaited her public execution ("Within a dark and gloomy cell / In anguish now I lie") and a gruesome account of the crime ("Her old grey locks I bathed in blood, / As she lay on the floor, / And my aged victim left, / Weltering in her gore"). The seven stanzas combine a remorseful account of her case ("Oh! what could ever possess me / Upon that fatal day"), in which Hunt depicts herself as "borne down with grief and woe," with a sentimental "adieu" to parents and friends and appeals for mercy to God and other women lest they should commit similar mistakes ("You females all a warning take, / By my untimely fate. / And shun all thoughts of wickedness / Before it is too late"). Two chorus lines, to be sung collectively, further encourage audience identification among young women: "In youth and bloom I am doomed to die / For murder, on the gallows high." Although Mary Ann Hunt confesses her crime of murder, the text's structure and content allow her to appeal to the audience's empathy and to draw attention to her suffering, loneliness, and repentance. These representations challenge us to refine existing critical narratives, such as Knelman's claim that "at mid-century, public revulsion at murder by women was palpable" (*Twisting* 19), suggesting instead a more complex negotiation of female guilt and its consequences in some of these popular texts.

It is likely that the verses on Hunt's situation were published immediately after her conviction, because they do not pay detailed attention to the further development of the case. Hunt's conviction became a subject of debate across numerous newspapers for several months, because—after much toing and froing—it was finally established that she was indeed pregnant, as she had claimed when receiving the verdict, and her death sentence was ultimately commuted to transportation for life.[23] Hunt's verses place emphasis on sentiment and audience identification rather than a debate around capital punishment, especially the execution of potentially pregnant women (the focus of many newspapers reporting her case). Yet the verses illustrate how such popular treatments formed part of a wider media culture of critical interrogation around women's crime and punishment that contributed a unique angle by highlighting—*in contrast to* newspaper accounts—the convict's own perspective on her initial sentence.

Hunt's verses appeal to the audience despite the convict's admission of guilt, whereas other lyrics address the compassionate listener on the basis of wrongful conviction. Mary White's lamentation before her execution at Exeter for the murder of her master and mistress begins, "Oh! you that have no hearts of stone, / Attend to what I say, / For Death has seal'd my early doom, / And summon'd me away" ("Life, Trial, and Execution of Mary White" broadside).[24] In contrast to Hunt, White's plea is accompanied by an insistence on her innocence, a position ultimately confirmed in the final stanza of the verses, which switches to a third-person perspective to report that only after Mary's "ignominious death," the true murderer confessed the crime. Although the broadside avoids an explicit attack on this miscarriage of justice, the choice of language clearly implies a critique: the convict's execution is described as "ignominious," which ambiguously suggests shame and humiliation not only for the convict on the scaffold but also for those who brought her there. The lamentation's first stanza alludes to the guilty power of a state that has the legal authority to punish by death its young women ("Although as guiltless of the crime / As is the babe unborn"), thus hinting at the dangers of the death penalty as a nonreversible form of punishment. The broadside provides the convict with an imaginative platform to speak out against the insurmountable power of the state in order to draw attention to injustice and to rescue her reputation. Thus, Mary White—whose very name underscores the idea of purity and innocence—resolves,

> Before the knot is tied,
> My innocence I will declare,
> To all the world wide.
> . . . .
> Before my eyes are clos'd I pray,
> And Heav'n my prayers hear,
> My innocence may be reveal'd,
> And be as noon-day clear;
> And bring the real hand to light,
> Who did the horrid deed,
> That all may know poor Mary White,
> Was innocent indeed.

Mary White's case echoes the infamous execution of Eliza Fenning in 1815, which became a cause célèbre and cultural reference point for many decades to follow.[25] Fenning had been a servant convicted on circumstantial evidence for attempting to poison her employers, but she insisted on her innocence to the last.[26] Writers such as the satirist William Hone defended her reputation and used her death as a vehicle for criticizing the class bias of the legal system.[27] A pamphlet on the hanging of "the fair and beautiful Eliza Fenning," titled "The Heroes of the Guillotine and Gallows, or, the Awful Adventures of Askern, Smith and Calcraft," attacked the hangmen and their regime of death. The description of the execution scene, in prose, casts Eliza as a virginal martyr "in a new white dress," threatened by the hangman's impurity and "vile hands" (6).[28] The pamphlet also exposes the presumed culprit, the son of Fenning's master, who allegedly wanted to take revenge because she had refused to "submit to his embraces" (7). Even though historical evidence on the man's guilt is less than conclusive, street literature used such opportunities to implicitly problematize the class bias of the law and the precarious position of female servants.[29]

"Valiant" Women | Female Violence and Revenge

If the language used in the Fenning case relied on the assumption of the maid's innocence, other street literature explored the vulnerability of servants by featuring crimes by such women as a response to gender-specific forms of oppression. The chapbook account titled "The Full Particulars of the Examination and Committal to Newgate of Annette Myers [*sic*], for the Wilful Murder of Henry Ducker, a Private in the Coldstream Guards," based on an actual case in 1848, draws attention to a "valiant" woman's reaction to "the shameful depravity and corrupt habits of that body of men to which the deceased belonged" (3). Meyers, a Belgian woman, was convicted at the Old Bailey in February 1848 but was "strongly recommended to mercy by the Jury, on account of the extraordinary provocation and ill-treatment that she had been the subject of" (Trial of Annette Meyers, Old Bailey Proceedings).[30] Ducker had not only abandoned Meyers for another woman but also tried to coerce her into prostituting herself for his own financial advantage. The press widely condemned Ducker's conduct; "xxxiii" in the conservative *Morning Post* called him "the vilest of the vile—a pest to society." Although careful not to endorse murder, the paper portrayed Meyers as a martyr "who, in the very wreck of her honour, showed a certain nobleness, and preferred to brave the utmost penalties of the law rather than prostitute herself for lucre." The *Times* criticized laws that only recognized Meyers's offense even though "hers was not the larger share of outrage against right" (14 Feb. 1848). Letters to the editor warmly sympathized with the convict, including eyewitness reports from the courtroom which claimed to have seen the judge "burst into tears" during the process of passing the death sentence (H.R.D.). Opponents of capital punishment used the case as an opportunity to appeal for the abolition of the death penalty and to secure a commutation of sentence for Meyers. As in Mary Ann Hunt's case, the Belgian's sentence was ultimately converted into two years' imprisonment, followed by transportation for life, and she became a minor celebrity, having a wax figure modeled after her that was even displayed at provincial exhibitions.[31]

The "Full Particulars" of Meyers's case describe how Ducker, the murdered man, had a "habit of extorting money" (4) from his many girlfriends, mainly servant girls, and had warned Meyers that he would turn to another woman if she refused to give him anything. A transcript of the witnesses' testimony during the trial reports that the defendant then acquired a pistol at a shop, pretending it was for shooting a Newfoundland dog "that had bitten several of her friends" (7), shot Ducker from behind, and confessed immediately when overtaken at the scene. The account of the court scene describes Meyers as "a person of strong determination, wholly abandoned to her fate in the consciousness that she had been justified in the dreadful act which she had committed" (4). The "Full Particulars" also contain a letter by the accused to Ducker in which she announces her female independence: "You had the face to tell me one day that I could not do without you or other men. I have done before, and I can do now; but I am sure you cannot do without a woman" (9). The report presents Meyers as a strong woman, whose murderous act signifies not only individual self-assertion but also female working-class solidarity, revenging the exploitation by Ducker of "several of her friends," that is, other servant girls. The attached verses ask the audience to honor the prisoner's memory: "One pitying tear in tribute pay / To poor Annette Myers, / Who now does dwell / In Newgate's cell" (11). Subsequent stanzas tell Meyers's story from her first-person perspective, attributing her deed to "jealously" and "dark revenge" while interrogating to what extent the crime was premeditated or an act of passion ("Then frenzy fill'd my / brain / . . . With fevered brow I waited / there, / Determined not his life to / spare"). The ballad alternately shows the woman blaming herself ("I have brought myself to grief / and shame, / Althrough this sad affair") and hints at the man's shared responsibility for the tragedy, as a consequence of his duplicitous behavior ("So noble he appear'd and gay / That he stole the virgin heart / Away, / From poor Annette Myers").

While the ballad uses a moralistic frame—it ends with a warning to other women to "always bear the fate in / mind, / Of poor Annette Myers"—the chapbook as a whole leaves room for interpreting the female convict as a protofeminist icon, whose action and self-expression become a mouthpiece for other females with similar experiences of seduction, betrayal, and jealousy. Joining in a wider public debate around this crime and its punishment, the "Full Particulars" combine a critique of the male victim of the crime, rather than the convict, with a call for sympathy for the female offender, although the chapbook's attack on Ducker is less pronounced than complaints against his behavior found elsewhere, in the daily press. Yet, as the ballad explores both Meyers's motivation and perspective and the third-person response to her crime, it subtly interrogates criminal responsibility and gender relations.

Complementing perusals of gender relations, some broadsides, in the form of both third-person reports and first-person lamentations, function as a subtle critique of women's living conditions, social welfare provision, and the role of men as covert enablers or the direct cause of women's crimes. As Miriam Jones has illustrated in her detailed analysis of child-murder broadsides—an important subcategory—public discourse around this crime, including broadsides, "was full of contention and contradiction" (112). She rightly notes that many child-murder broadsides are not particularly sympathetic to the female perpetrators but that such examples do exist. Although most of these texts—similar to the majority of newspaper accounts—do not explicitly attack society's structural inequalities that lead to crimes, their subtexts allow for these hidden causes of women's criminality to come to the fore and thus open up spaces for sympathy or audience identification.[32]

Some accounts of child murder convey complex circumstances resulting in such killings, from material, practical causes to mental instability or a combination of the two. The broadside "Awful Depravity: Dreadful Account of Anne Graham"—about the wife of a Cumbria blacksmith who killed two of her children in 1824 and tried to commit suicide afterward—explains that the woman "was naturally of a gloomy disposition, and had latterly formed the idea that her children would come to poverty."[33] According to the broadside, Graham received a verdict of insanity from the coroner's jury. Similarly, a publication on the 1837 case of Ann Colley—a mother of five in Staffordshire who murdered three of her children, cut her own throat, and confessed when found—prints the woman's justification. She explains that she had committed the deed "from dread of want," following her husband's dismissal as superintendent of police, "which had subjected the family to great privation" ("Dreadful Murder of Three Children" broadside). Like Graham, Colley was found not guilty on the grounds of insanity.[34]

While child murders such as Colley's were reported in daily newspapers in more or less the same terms as those printed on broadsides, including information on the woman's (fear of) poverty, broadside ballads on infanticide dedicated space to a more detailed exploration of the female offender's condition, motives, and viewpoint.[35] As Vicinus has argued with regard to Mary Ann Brough, an infanticide who murdered her six children in 1854, broadside ballads on such cases "portray a state of mind which many readers must have recognized—overcrowded housing, excessive hours of work and poor health were common enough to working mothers" (16).[36] "The Sorrowful Lamentation of Sarah Baker: Who Was Found Guilty of Wilful Murder at Stafford" contains many of the usual tropes found in infanticide ballads, beginning with the convict's appeal to the sympathetic listener and the agony she suffers in Stafford Prison. Baker describes the murder of her little boy, whom she had thrown down a pit, her reason for doing so, and her subsequent regret:

> On the 12th, of June 1853,
> I took its precious life away,
> All in a sad and brutal way;
> He by my hands did bleed,
>
> > 'Twas poverty,
> > that caused me,
>
> its precious life to take away,
> Which now upon my mind does prey
> And causes me to rue the day,
> I did the fearful deed.

Though the long ballad ends with a warning and has the infanticide ask for God's mercy, rather than social justice, it also spells out poverty as the underlying motivation for the crime. By offsetting the two lines addressing material deprivation from their surrounding stanzas, the writer attributes particular visual prominence to them. Whereas reports on Baker in daily newspapers offer more detailed information on the woman's background— how she was abandoned by the illegitimate child's father, gave birth at a workhouse, and, being homeless, supported herself through a combination of working for one shilling a day and a parish allowance—the ballad explains the crime's root cause in an easy-to-convey core message of two lines that would effectively capture the popular audience's attention.[37] Such examples illustrate that *some* broadsides engaged with reasons behind criminal offenses, challenging Jones's assertion that there is a "startling lack of consideration given to the question of women's motivations to commit infanticide" in these texts (125).[38]

Aside from poverty, other causes alluded to indicate that child-murder victims were seen as obstacles and a sign of disgrace. Cases of women murdering children from previous relationships were not uncommon in the nineteenth century. In 1873, the charwoman Ann Orton was accused of drowning her illegitimate six-year-old daughter, after the aunt taking care of the child had abandoned the girl. The broadside on the case powerfully conveys events from Orton's perspective in a double way—while newspaper reports stuck to a third-person description of what had happened, the broadside prints the mother's own reaction to her arrest alongside a first-person lamentation.[39] When taken into custody,

> the prisoner said, what could I do? and began to cry . . . , what could I do with the child? My aunt had run away, and left it at Ashby. I went over to try and get it into the workhouse but could not, and I wanted one or two women to take the child, but they could not; they had got enough of their own. I did not know what to do with it. My husband did not know that I had had this before I was married, I dare not tell him. I did not know what to do with it, so I threw it into the water, I have been miserable ever since. ("Murder of a Child Near Measham" broadside)

To complement this prose account, the verse lamentation addressed to sympathetic listeners, especially other mothers, offers an unusually detailed description of the (now married) mother's desperate attempts to find a solution for her child:

> To the workhouse I went with my child,
> But they would not it take,
> With sorrow almost driven wild,
> My poor heart near to break;
> I sought some mothers living near,
> To find my child a home,
> But no shelter could I find it there,
> They'd enough to mind their own.
> The slur that lay upon my name,
> Prey'd on my distracted mind,
> Led me, I confess to my shame
> To contemplate this crime

The convict's own voice does not reject responsibility and confesses the crime; the verses also make a statement about the complex causes of infanticide, from poor state provision and lack of community cohesion to mental instability. The ballad spells out social stigma ("The slur that lay upon my name") as Orton's final motivation for the killing. References to her "wild" and "distracted mind" hint at temporary insanity—Orton was found "not guilty" on those grounds ("Midland Circuit"; "Measham Murder").

Broadsides such as these interrogate infanticide and its causes in the context of practical living conditions and material deprivation, mental health, and communal pressures. While the verses recognize the possibility of unfavorable responses toward the prisoner ("For sympathy on you I call, / When my sad tale you hear; / And though you all may me blame, / My sufferings none can tell"), they actively encourage collective identification through their chorus lines: "For the murder of my darling child, / Her age was but six years, / Mothers, pity take, on my sad fate; and shed, oh! shed a tear." The lamentation thus opens up spaces for identification and sympathy as well as critique among female audience members familiar with similar circumstances.

Although Orton addresses the role played by new partners in (unintentionally) driving women to kill children who had been kept secret from the new relationship—she recounts her fear of discovery and abandonment ("But I did not dare to tell him, / It is the truth I own, / Lest he should turn, and on me spurn, / And drive me from my home")—the illegitimate child's father is not mentioned. Likewise, in the case of infanticide by young unmarried women, the role of the father is often silenced in broadsides, such as the "Shocking Case of Child Murder!" by Mary Rule, who had killed with her mother's assistance. Told from Mary Rule's perspective, the verses on the occasion merely concede and warn, "I've brought myself to scandle, grief, and shame, / I've lost my virtue and an honest name / By murder, a crime of blackest dye."

By contrast, the ballad describing Mary Hardcastle's story in 1824—like Rule, she had been condemned to death for the murder of her illegitimate child—slightly shifts agency in the crime away from the convict. Although the broadside presents the verses "as a caution to young women," the lines that follow, spoken in the first person, clearly draw attention to the key role of the man who helped to bring about Hardcastle's downfall and descent into criminality ("Account of the Execution of Mary Hardcastle"). Whereas Rule's lines suggest that she had brought *herself* to "scandle, grief, and shame," Hardcastle insists, "I'm brought to scandal, grief and shame, / By putting trust in a false young man." Although Hardcastle does not deny responsibility for her crime, she traces her deed back to the young man's advances:

My sins are great I must confess,
From time to time I did transgress,
To this young man I became a prey,
I cannot rest neither night nor day

As Hardcastle reflects on her impending execution, she implicitly suggests that she is not "the vilest sinner" after all, even if she has to pay for her crime:

Lord when that dreadful day is come,
And I on earth receive my doom,
Good people I hope you'd pray for me,
The vilest sinner may yet be free.
When I am brought to the fatal tree,
Young women take advice from me,
If by false men you deceiv'd should be,
From cruel murder God keep you free.
(emphasis added)

Hardcastle's lines are ambiguous, suggesting that the "vilest sinner" could be either another unsuspecting young female or another male tempter or indeed her own tempter, all of whom are "yet free." Significantly, while far from condoning the woman's crime, the broadside creates a more sympathetic portrayal of the infanticide, implicitly ascribing a share of the blame for the catastrophe to the man's "falseness"—presumably his refusal to marry his pregnant lover. At the same time, as the convict renders her story in a first-person narrative, the ballad allows her to claim agency as an autonomous subject. The text keeps an equilibrium between Hardcastle's ultimate responsibility for her behavior ("From time to time I did transgress") and the criminal deed, and her victimization at the hands of an irresponsible man ("To this young man I became a prey"). The 1824 broadside thus paints a more complex and balanced picture of the crime than do some later, Victorian portrayals of female infanticides in criminal law that characteristically refused to treat women as "rational, autonomous agents" (T. Ward 269).[40]

Conclusion

This chapter has argued that broadsides and chapbooks had the potential to undercut straightforwardly punitive conceptions of female convicts by addressing the causes of women's criminality—such as poverty, ill mental health, social stigma, or betrayal by men—and by invoking sympathy and identification with the convict, even when the prisoner's guilt was not questioned. These texts addressed the disempowerment, as well as resistance, of prisoners and opened up a representational space for the convict's own perspective, typically rendered in verse form. More broadly speaking, street literature dealing with women's crimes gave an insight into nonelite females' living conditions and thus functioned, by extension, as a public platform for voicing the concerns of a larger constituency of women, beyond the group of female offenders. By drawing attention to competing stories around the crime and by giving a voice to convict subjectivity, street literature rehearsed and made available conflicting perspectives around women's criminality and punishment and provided alternatives to "official" stories, as represented by the law, for example. By offering a platform for female prisoners' voices, some of these texts thus anticipated the agendas of late nineteenth- and early twentieth-century prison autobiographies—illustrated in chapters 4 and 5—which explicitly presented themselves as legitimate acts of reclaiming the right to talk back to judicial power. Even if street literature did not formulate explicitly gendered critiques, in its interrogation of the plights of female offenders—including poverty and lack of child care, sexual exploitation, and betrayal—it subtly raised protofeminist concerns which were to be explored more overtly in other representations of women convicts' voices.

CHAPTER 2

The Lives of Which "There Are No Records Kept"

Convicts and Matrons in the Prison
Narratives of Frederick William Robinson
("A Prison Matron")

Written during a period when the broadside trade was already in decline, the commercially successful prison tales by the little-known Victorian popular-fiction writer Frederick William Robinson served as one of the channels in which popular interrogations into women's crimes and punishment continued in the 1860s, albeit with a different target audience in mind. Published in two volumes, rather than cheaper installments, Robinson's *Female Life in Prison* (1862), *Memoirs of Jane Cameron: Female Convict* (1863), and *Prison Characters Drawn from Life with Suggestions for Prison Government* (1866)—all written under the anonym of "A Prison Matron"— were pitched at a more educated readership. This chapter reads Robinson's prison trilogy and his later story "Daisy March, the Prison Flower," serialized in 1881, as an early social history approach that validates the marginalized experiences of women in prison. *Memoirs of Jane Cameron* in particular constitutes a deliberate and self-reflexive attempt to reinstate not only the voices of female convicts but also those of prison matrons. Although these prison narratives also employ and reinscribe conventional notions of gender and class familiar from other writings on women's criminality and punishment, Robinson explicitly constructs his tales of female imprisonment in opposition to other, institutionally legitimized, modes of representation, such as parliamentary reports, thus posing a political challenge. The narratives' ideological position is ultimately an ambiguous one, oscillating between pro-working-class statements, Christian paternalism, and the use of familiar stereotypes and colonial tropes in relation to female convicts. Yet, as this chapter will demonstrate, Robinson's paternalism is counteracted by the recording and affirmation of aspects of offenders' lives not usually given a space in reformist writings or official documentation.

While various critics have drawn on the Prison Matron's narratives, they have typically used them as a source of empirical evidence, without much consideration for the textuality of these sources.[1] By contrast, questions of narrative construction and authorship within the prison narratives are one of my key interests here, including Robinson's use of and metareflexive comments on competing genres of penal inquiry and the limits of representing female convict subjectivity. In this context, the relationship between Robinson, male popular-fiction writer, and the Prison Matron, as well as the impact of that relationship on the depiction of female life in prison, needs close critical examination. Robinson constructs the Matron as a female narrative persona whose first-person narrative voice at times coincides with, and at times diverges from, the voice of the implied male author.

As I argue in more detail elsewhere, Robinson drew on the literary traditions of Daniel Defoe and Charles Dickens while sharing mid-Victorian social-problem fiction's desire to offer, in Mary Poovey's words, "an explicit alternative to the abstract aggregations with which political economists appealed to readers' rational judgment, . . . in order to engage [their] readers' sympathy" (133).[2] Through the occasional use of free indirect style for the representation of fallen woman characters such as Jane Cameron, Robinson's work both looks back to eighteenth-century literary techniques and gestures toward quasi-modernist ones—similar to those found in later writings, such as the internal focalization in George Moore's *Esther Waters* (1894)—allowing him to draw attention to the inner life world of nonelite convict women, which is rarely presented elsewhere. Despite the formulaic nature of some of his writings, Robinson's metareflexive commentary, in combination with these literary strategies and thematic concerns, offers a distinctive generic variation which brings into focus issues of gender and class in the context of women's imprisonment. His tales are protofeminist in content and technique, then, in that they problematize the living conditions of poor women who end up in jail while also intervening into debates around women's employment—especially the working lives and salaries of prison matrons—through a relatively complex deployment of women's voices. In creating platforms for such voices, Robinson anticipates more contemporary appreciations of women's contributions in the penal sphere as well as the significance of offender viewpoints.[3]

Literary Cross-Dressing | Authenticity, Narrative
Voice, and Audience in the Prison Matron's Tales

Robinson's popular fiction typically led its readers into the world of romance, with strong religious overtones.[4] As the *Dictionary of National Biography* notes, though, "Robinson was also a pioneer in novels of low life" (Norgate), writing about society's outcasts, such as abandoned children, although these tales, too, usually included a love interest.[5] In a review of Robinson's life, fellow writer and long-term friend Theodore Watts-Dunton commented on the tremendous success of the first book in the prison series, *Female Life in Prison*, suggesting that contemporaneous audiences never doubted that it was the authentic account of a prison matron. Prison reformer Mary Carpenter, for instance, in *Our Convicts* (1864), referred to the Prison Matron's narratives repeatedly, assuming the publications' authenticity and using textual examples as evidence to support her own arguments.[6] Watts-Dunton also claimed that the tales were indeed "based in part upon the personal record of a real prison matron" (813), but it is hard to verify this statement; Watts-Dunton's primary purpose here may well have been to protect the moral integrity and legacy of his friend, similar to his claims that changes in prison conditions were an immediate result of Robinson's publications. The *Bookman* even asserted that the series of prison narratives "attracted so much attention that a Royal Commission was the result" and that "it was urged at the time that Mr. Robinson should be offered the first vacant directorship of prisons" ("Late F. W. Robinson" 555). These contentions lack credibility from hindsight, considering that Robinson's contemporaries largely believed the texts to emanate from the pen of a real prison matron.

Robinson's decision to write the three prison books as A Prison Matron was more than the choice of a pseudonym (or anonym); it was part of his narrative and marketing strategies.[7] The use of A Prison Matron as alleged author helped fuel the illusion of authenticity, as well as the curiosity of potential readers interested in "racy," entertaining accounts of crime and imprisonment, promising an all-female prison context and the possibility of same-sex romance—a romance that indeed develops in *Memoirs of Jane Cameron* most explicitly. The Prison Matron as literary and social agent can furthermore be seen as a nod to an emerging trend at the time, indicating a thirst for female perspectives on crime and punishment, in which women adopted the roles of commentators and investigators, rather than solely those of victims or perpetrators. Alongside journalistic and reformist writings on criminality by Carpenter, Harriet Martineau, M. E. Owen, and others, the late 1850s and 1860s also witnessed the rise of the female (amateur) detective in fiction, with Wilkie Collins's *The Diary of Anne Rodway* (1856), Andrew Forrester's *The Female Detective* (1864), and William Stephens Hayward's *Revelations of a Lady Detective* (1864). As Joseph Kestner has suggested, the rise of such fictional characters highlighted "the insertion of women in heretofore patriarchal institutions like the courts, law and criminal investigation" (*Sherlock's Sisters* 24). Robinson's Prison Matron both mirrored and made for a unique and original addition to this broader cultural trend.

All of the "Prison Stories," as Robinson called them, were commercially successful (Watts-Dunton 813). *Female Life in Prison* and *Memoirs of Jane Cameron* received many approving reviews, with the *Examiner* calling the former "probably the best 'woman's book'—of the year" ("Female Life in Prison"). Within the first two years of its publication, *Female Life in Prison* went through three (revised) editions—including a cheaper version in Low's Favourite Library of Popular Books, with an image of Elizabeth Fry reading to the prisoners at Newgate in 1816—and through a total of four editions between 1862 and 1888.[8] While Robinson's romance novels were most likely targeted at a female readership, his prison narratives appealed to women and men alike. In an advertisement for *Female Life*, the *Athenaeum* insisted that the book "should have many readers among our social reformers of both sexes" ("Advertisement" 6 Sept. 1862).[9] That women took heed of these publications is evidenced by Bessie Rayner Parkes's long lead article on *Female Life* in the *English Woman's Journal*, a monthly committed to promoting women's education and employment (Parkes, "Female Life in Prison").

Unlike the street literature dealing with the experiences of female convicts, largely written for and available to the working classes, Robinson's multivolume works primarily reached middle- and upper-class readers—like those of the *English Woman's Journal*—wealthy enough to afford subscription to a circulating library, although it is not impossible that his narratives were read by lower-class people as well.[10] Robinson's prison narratives, like his other novels, were advertised in the press targeted at an educated audience, giving another clue to his likely middle- and upper-class readership.[11] *Prison Characters* claimed that "many high and illustrious personages" had responded to the first in the series, *Female Life* (1:2).[12] The prison tales were widely reviewed, from the *Quarterly Review* ("Ticket of Leave System") to the *Edinburgh Review* ("Convict System in England and Ireland"), which discussed a number of official reports on the prison system and the Reverend John Clay's memoirs (*The Prison Chaplain*, edited by Walter Clay) together with *Female Life in Prison*. Harriet Martineau examined *Memoirs of Jane Cameron* for the *Edinburgh Review* in 1865, alongside Carpenter's *Our Convicts* ("Life in the Criminal Class").[13] This suggests that Robinson's prison narratives reached a middle-brow audience that read these accounts together with other, official and reformist, writings that were less commercially oriented. Although reformist accounts such as Carpenter's *Our Convicts* were successful too, they were unlikely to appeal to an audience that was after entertainment. Robinson, by contrast, pitched his prison narratives cleverly, and we can assume that he attracted readers concerned with social questions *and* those interested in entertaining accounts. The *Publishers' Circular* indeed expected *Female Life* to "be read by a large class" and, praising it for its originality, commended it to "the social philosopher" and "the general reader" alike (qtd. in "Advertisement," *Athenaeum* 28 June 1862).

Memoirs of Jane Cameron acknowledges the assistance of "the principal public functionaries of Edinburgh and Glasgow" (1:5) as well as members of prison boards, governors, chief constables, superintendents, detective officers, the secretary of the Prisoner's Aid Society, and "those good Christians and kind friends who have helped to throw a light upon the after and better life of Cameron" (1:6). Whether Robinson actually met with all these alleged informants or whether he simply uses them as another authenticating device, apart from the Prison Matron, is difficult to determine. While I have no evidence that Robinson actually visited women's prisons himself, a chapter on visitors in *Female Life in Prison* is suggestive in this regard. The narrative alludes to the "steady and incessant stream of visitors [to Millbank and Brixton Prisons], furnished with orders from Parliament-street or the Secretary of State," maintaining that "scarcely a week in the year occurs without some one from the outer world passing by order through the gates and being conducted from pentagon to pentagon, and ward to ward, by a matron of the establishment" (2:159). In what sounds like a self-reflexive statement, the writer—hidden behind the identity of A Prison Matron—refers to "the poet or novelist, in search of a new idea, which the wild lives of prisoners may suggest," as one type of visitor to women's prisons (*Female Life* 2:160). Robinson's contemporaries and fellow metropolitan writers Charles

Dickens and Henry Mayhew—two explicitly acknowledged sources of inspiration—had also visited prisons; hence, it is conceivable that this path was open to him as well.

An acknowledgment in the first volume of *Memoirs of Jane Cameron* also implies that Robinson did indeed research prisons and criminal life on a personal basis. Here his Prison Matron thanks the Scottish functionaries: "gentlemen who, partly ignorant of the object which took me and a valuable co-operator to Scotland, were yet most anxious, by every means in their power, to show me the interior of their prisons, the working of their criminal law, the darkest secrets of their streets" (*Memoirs* 1:5–6). A review of *Female Life* in the *Times* ("Female Life in Prison"), noting the narrator's depictions of well-known, incarcerated offenders, similarly indicates that Robinson may have seen them firsthand, although it is possible that he invented details of these portraits.

In a metafictional comment at the end of the first volume of *Female Life in Prison*, the writer foreshadows more comprehensively the task he was to complete two years afterward, with *Memoirs of Jane Cameron*. Relating some incidents of "prisoners' freemasonry" (*Female Life* 1:291) at Millbank, which, the narrator promises, "take[] us to the world of romance" (1:300), Robinson's tale suggests that female prisons harbor a plethora of ideas for the fiction author: "If the hearts of these prison women could be laid bare, there would be found a story in each which has hitherto escaped the poet and the novelist; the matter for a thousand books is floating amidst the desolate wards that echo to these women's sighs, or ring with their defiance. Theirs have not been quiet lives, and from the elements of life's discord spring the incidents to interest mankind" (*Female Life* 1:301). Illustrating the problematic status of Robinson and his prison fiction, the author's call to record the lives of female convicts validates the experiences of such women and gives them a voice to a certain extent, while also exploiting their stories for his own economic benefit—the sale of his books. In this regard, his fiction shares the commercial impetus central to other popular narratives of crime and punishment, such as execution broadsides, which ventriloquized, yet simultaneously profited from, the experiences of nonelite women in similar ways.

The fact that Robinson writes disguised as A Prison Matron—"one retired from Government service" (*Female Life* 1:1)—deploying gender strategically to feign authenticity, further complicates his position. The writer's agenda to "convey to the reader some idea of what prisoners are, and what prison life really is" is two-sided (*Female Life* 2:34). If it presents itself as an explicit attempt to rectify misrepresentations of women convicts, it is likewise not free from (unacknowledged) biases and misconceptions regarding the biographies, behavior, and treatment of incarcerated offenders, not least because the author is not the insider he pretends to be but a commercial writer.

Robinson's claims to authentic representation, however, are embedded in interesting broader reflections on which discursive forms can adequately render a truthful account of prison life. In the introductory chapter of *Female Life in Prison*—which can also be regarded as a mission statement for the two later prison narratives—Robinson's Prison Matron expresses her belief that she offers "for the first time, a true and impartial chronicle of female prison life" (1:3). The Matron legitimizes her project by pointing to her inside view, contrasting her woman's perspective, and her more immediate access to the prisoners' feelings, with that of male officials: "Directors may issue their annual reports, the governors of prisons may write their ponderous tomes upon the question, the chaplains may preach, and pray, and visit, but their opportunities of judging fairly and honestly are few and far between, and they are misled and deceived every week in the year. In men's prisons I believe it is the warder, and in female prisons I am convinced it is the matron, who alone has the power to offer a true picture of prison life" (1:6). Promising to provide a more balanced account, the Matron suggests she has a better insight into more positive aspects of the prisoners' character: "And of that better side to prison character which a Matron has the greatest chance of observing, of that evidence of affection for some kind officer who has screened offenders from a trivial punishment, or has listened to some little story in impulsive moments, about a mother, sister, brother, child, they loved once, the great report books utter not a word" (1:7). When Robinson's Matron promises to give an insight into prison life beyond official reports and statistics—"the life within the outward life that Blue Books speak of, and Parliament agitates concerning," the life of which "there are no records kept" (1:7)—she offers a social history that aims to note down formerly unknown aspects of the lives of female convicts (and prison matrons).

Robinson's agenda here converges with Foucault's concern to insurrect "subjugated knowledges . . . buried or masked in functional coherences or formal systematizations" (*"Society"* 7). Robinson's tale makes the struggle between different social voices explicit, decenters the linguistic and social authority of official documentation, and reinstates the authority of formerly peripheral agents.[14] In this context, the narrative also works in support of women's professional roles and validates the matrons' labor and their perspective within the penal system, attributing to it a special status and power. Robinson's project not only argues for the improvement of matrons' working conditions (*Female Life* 1:36–37) but also aims to recover the delegitimized knowledge of minor female employees in the penal system, contrasted with the institutionally sanctioned knowledge of male directors, governors, and chaplains. The fact that this female "subjugated knowledge" is—at least partially—fictionally mediated through Robinson's narratives detracts from the more radical potential of this act of recovery, of course. Nevertheless, there is evidence that contemporaries read *Memoirs* as a daring and powerful attack on the penal establishment and dominant theories of crime and punishment, which typically sought to classify (female) offenders as categorically different from the rest of society and increasingly emphasized physical punishment and deterrence over reform.[15] A reviewer of Jane Cameron's life history in the *Spectator* commented on the Prison Matron's alternative vision:

> No one who reads it will doubt for a moment that he has before him the actual life of a recently living woman, a life worth for all purposes of instruction whole columns of Parliamentary talk. We, at least, never read such an answer to the theory now prevailing, which denies that criminals are human beings actuated by precisely the same impulses as the people who are not criminal, and considers them simply evil animals, to be lashed, and starved, and frightened into an endurable attitude towards the respectable classes. Jennie Cameron throughout her whole life was just an ordinary woman, governed by the emotions of all other women, and doing precisely the things they do under circumstances which made the doing an offence against society. ("Jennie Cameron")

Underlining Cameron's similarity to "ordinary women," the reviewer underscores the value of Robinson's narrative in presenting criminality as circumstantial, rather than innate, while implying that such a convict life narrative is *as*, or even *more*, effective than "whole columns of Parliamentary talk." The commentator here picks up on the Prison Matron's own ambition to substitute ineffectual official documentation with a more authentic form of representation that humanizes convicts; the review thus endorses the narrative's textual strategies and its political vision, challenging harsher regimes of punishment promoted by the political establishment at the time.

Robinson's prison narratives explicitly draw on other contemporaneous writings on criminality and the penal system, thus situating the tales within a larger cultural context of discourses on crime.[16] Similar to the authors of sensation fiction, or the slightly earlier generation of writers for execution broadsides, Robinson pursued an eclectic method, obtaining ideas from a range of contextual material while ensuring topicality for his readers through (coded) references to real-life cases. Accordingly, Parkes noted in her review for the *English Woman's Journal*, with reference to the Prison Matron's biographical sketches of prisoners, that "many of those whose names were once familiar in the newspapers re-appear here under their own or assumed names" ("Female Life in Prison" 5). For example, one of the Prison Matron's chapters was dedicated to Celestina Sommer, a woman convicted for murdering her ten-year-old stepdaughter in 1856. After successful petitioning, Sommer's death sentence was commuted to transportation for life; she ended up in a lunatic asylum before being released in 1876. The *Times* referred to the case on a number of occasions. While Robinson's Prison Matron calls Sommer's crime "peculiarly bold and cruel" (*Female Life* 1:94), she approves of the commutation of sentence and the woman's removal to a mental institution (1:100).[17]

Although Robinson's prison narratives argue in favor of a new and different perspective on women's criminality, the accounts are complicated by the fact that in writing this social history—however authentic or inauthentic it may be—he appropriates women's voices in multiple ways, both those of female offenders and that of A Prison Matron, which is problematic from a contemporary feminist viewpoint. The fact that Robinson's Matron explicitly insists that no other matrons know she is speaking on their behalf (*Female Life* 1:41) indicates some awareness of the implications of this rhetorical move on Robinson's part, although it does not mitigate entirely the appropriation of a prison matron's perspective. Female prisoners and matrons themselves have no unmediated voice in his writings; yet his recording of their allegedly authentic experiences in itself ascribes a different, more positive cultural value to them, which acts as a protofeminist gesture.

Voices from Prison | Genre, Mediation, and Self-Reflexivity

Similar to the crime broadsides analyzed in chapter 1, Robinson's prison narratives follow a formulaic pattern, with regard to both form and content. *Female Life in Prison* and *Prison Characters* have a comparable structure, alternating between chapters containing general information on women's prisons and mini case studies of specific female convicts, mainly organized around little anecdotes, presumably to break up the dryness of the narrative and to keep his readers amused. The narratives hence offer both education and entertainment. *Memoirs of Jane Cameron* fuses all these elements into one life narrative—a conversion tale—starting with Jane's childhood in neglect and then showing her fall into criminality, repeated incarceration, and eventual death after successful reformation. Many of the elements in *Female Life in Prison* and *Memoirs of Jane Cameron* overlap suspiciously— prisoners turn bad due to neglect but are really good inside; they take a fancy to a particular matron, who becomes their mentor and reforms them. Robinson arguably recycled much of the information collected for *Female Life in Prison* and transformed it into a more vivid, personalized account in *Memoirs of Jane Cameron*, centered around the life of one female offender.

The lack of unmediated speech power for convicts manifests itself most obviously in *Memoirs of Jane Cameron*, which is not the autobiographical account the title suggests. The title, rather, serves as a marketing device by harking back to the eighteenth-century literary tradition, in which *Memoirs* (and variations of this title) frequently indicated a tale narrating the (sexual) adventures of a woman, ranging from the sentimental to the bawdy. Some of Robinson's readers might have secretly hoped for the kind of saucy, articulate heroine familiar from *Moll Flanders* (1722). Implicitly substantiating this point, Watts-Dunton's obituary indeed placed Robinson in the literary lineage of Daniel Defoe (and Dickens).[18]

While *Memoirs of Jane Cameron* is not an extensive first-person account like *Moll Flanders*, the narrative is occasionally intersected with passages that record Jane's train of thought, such as her feelings about her first theft, instigated by her jealousy and desire to join her unfaithful lover at a dance (for which she needs some money). Reporting the young girl's nervousness in the process of stealing some items from a haberdasher's shop, the Matron says, "'I thought my heart would burst,' was her comment upon this incident,

'I was sae afeard o' bein' foond oot—naethin' else. I didna think o' anythin' but my Johnnie dancing with the Frazers, and if I could ony get at the ribbons or the gloves and mak' awa' wi' them!'" (*Memoirs* 1:56). Although the narrative gives Jane a voice and quotes her at various points in her local Glaswegian dialect, authorial control ultimately rests with the Prison Matron, that is, Robinson. Jane's Scottishness also operates in an ambivalent way throughout the narrative; her marked otherness serves as an additional distancing device for middle-class readers in the English metropolis, while offering them an air of exoticism and romance through this "Scotch story" (1:7). On the other hand, Jane's tale becomes exemplary for others closer to home, when the Matron asserts that it could be "a story of our own city" (1:7), with Glasgow functioning as the Scottish equivalent of "Whitechapel and Drury Lane" (1:8).

Robinson creates the illusion that it is Jane herself who stands behind this "faithful chronicle of a woman's fall and rescue" (1:5), as the Matron begins *Memoirs of Jane Cameron* by asserting that she is rendering "an authentic record of a female criminal's career" (1:7), on the basis of nothing but "this woman's word" (1:4). Quotations from Jane are inserted into chapters again and again, often to back up the "moral" of the narrative, thus resembling the use of convicts' testimonies in conversion tales and other writings authored by prison chaplains in support of their own ideological argument. John Field's *Prison Discipline* (1846), for instance, contains the "evidence of prisoners" extracted from testimonies given to the Inspectors of Prisons in 1837 (32–39). Generally, these statements are deployed in order to back up the message intended by the reverend, confirming the disadvantages of association in prison.[19] Similarly, the Prison Matron records Jane's admiration of her prison cell during imprisonment in Scotland, which, according to the narrator, "tells its own moral": "If we all had a room to our ainsel' like this, we should na get into half the trooble, and many o' us would ne'er gae bad at a'" (*Memoirs* 1:233–34). While this statement draws attention to the material conditions at the root of women's criminality, it can also be instrumentalized in the service of an agenda of social control, aiming at the sanitizing of the lives of the poor.

Even if the narrative does not provide an unmediated prisoner's perspective, Robinson's Matron unusually draws attention to this very act of mediation and the problematic task of giving an insight into and a "truthful" transcript of Jane's thoughts and feelings, thus going beyond a mere appropriation of the prisoner's voice in support of a particular ideology—the latter a method characteristic of Field's account, for example. Toward the end of *Memoirs of Jane Cameron*—Jane in the meantime has left prison to take up a position as servant but is seduced into leaving through a chance encounter with a former prison "pal"—the Matron gives a record of Jane's decision-making process in the form of free indirect style, subsequently commenting on her own writing:

> No; she could not write her warning, or give warning in any fashion. She could not remain another month in that house with her mistress wearying her with well-meant advice. . . . She could not wait a month, she could not endure service a week longer, she must go away at once!
>
> I do not attempt to say that this was exactly the train of thoughts or their sequence in the mind of Jane Cameron that night, but I believe that she had all these thoughts, and that they beset her and kept her restless till the morning. In that confession of her conduct, made at a later period of her life, she explained forcibly and simply the motives which led her to go, and the reasons which urged her to adopt this course, and they approximate to that analysis which, in the preceding pages, I have attempted to set before the reader. (2:205–7)

Through free indirect style, Robinson's Matron here explicitly tries to gain an insight into Jane's thoughts and emotions in order to paint a more sympathetic and complex picture of the servant's escape. As John Bender notes in his study of eighteenth-century narratives, including prison tales, "The device of free indirect discourse creates the illusion that the unvoiced mental life of fictional personages exists as unmediated presence" (211). Importantly, though, while Robinson's tale employs such a device to create a sense of immediacy, the narrative draws attention to the limits of representation, a self-reflexive gesture uncommon in other writings on female convicts in the mid-nineteenth century. Although *Memoirs of Jane Cameron* draws on the conventions of confessional tales and conversion narratives, it moves beyond the ideological constraints of these genres by including such a metaperspective, thus offering a distinctive generic intervention into the depiction of female prisoners in this period.

The attempt to access personal motivations of an offender in itself constitutes a departure from other, positivist representations of women prisoners as objects of inquiry or mere repositories of the failures and advantages of a particular "system," rather than subjects with an emotional, intellectual, and social agenda. At the beginning of the second volume of *Memoirs of Jane*

Cameron, the Matron renders an account of Jane's reflections after being arrested for her involvement in a robbery:

> In the cell at Glasgow Prison, awaiting her sentence, she was left to reflect upon the fate that lay before her in the future. Would it be four years, seven years, ten years—how many years taken from her life? How many years set aside from the streets which had been life to her, and confinement apart from all that had constituted "*happiness*," would be fixed upon her? The thought and the suspense were horrible, and, as her trial did not come on at once, she begged for work to relieve her from the monotony which preyed upon her, and seemed to drive her mad. . . .
>
> She felt bewildered by the importance and gravity of her trial, by the judge on the bench, and the state and solemnity surrounding her. In the midst of her suspense, her incertitude of the sentence which would be passed upon her, there came at times a little spasm of pride to think that all the pomp and parade of justice were for her, that all those people before her were interested more or less in her case, and that the crowd representing the public had come to hear about her, and would go home talking about her. (2:24–25)

In passages such as this, and similar to execution broadsides' last lamentations, Robinson's narrative provides the reader with a history of emotion from below—a history of the experiences (imagined but not necessarily that far from actual, lived experience) of an incarcerated individual rarely recorded elsewhere.[20] Although some of the ideas put forward here overlap with arguments made by prison authorities and reformers—such as the need for prison labor to counter the effects of solitary confinement—the passage also gives room to Jane's transgressive sensations during the trial. The description humanizes Jane during the process of imprisonment, implicitly inviting a better understanding on the reader's part of the challenges faced by the prisoner.

At various other points, the narrative makes an attempt to depict and account for the emotional life of the convict. For instance, the Matron reports Jane's changing moods during imprisonment, her desperation in her cell with "the old monotony of labour" and "nothing to look at but the four walls," as well as her desire for change, resulting in the refusal of food and the carrying out of "all the evil arts which are in vogue at prisons" (2:33). Again, the Matron quotes Jane, reflecting on the anxiety-ridden period in Glasgow Prison before her transfer to Millbank Prison in London: " 'I ken that I was hardenin' fast eno' at that time,' were her remarks; 'that I ne'er felt a warse woman in a' my leef. The fourteen years made me care for naethin'; I had the fancy that I should die lang afore my time was up, and that I was na gude warking hard for a character' " (2:34). Thus, the narrative describes the psychological aspects of incarceration in a more nuanced way than other sources, such as official reports, which may record prisoners' moods but do not usually offer convicts an opportunity to explain themselves in detail. Robinson's analysis replaces the quantitative approach of official documentation with a qualitative one, more attuned to the representation of individual prison lives and convict experience, anticipating the more contemporary recognition of offender perspectives.

Although Robinson's narratives encourage readers to pity rather than condemn people like Jane, they do not consider convicts as equals. The narratives' paternalism manifests itself in the language employed by the Prison Matron to describe her prisoners. Robinson's Matron repeatedly draws analogies between the prison inmates and children or describes them as irrational, diseased, or physically abnormal, hence identifiable by the observer. In *Female Life in Prison*, the Matron expresses paternalistic pride, contradicting "the satirist" who critiques the management of prisoners and their release as "a paternal government" (1:64). She insists instead that the government "*has* a fatherly interest in its misguided children—and the satirist is not always in the right" (1:64–65). Reflecting on violent behavior by female inmates, the Matron concludes, "Hurried as by a will beyond their own—impelled by a force that seems bestowed upon them to work evil in the hour of their desperation—we can but wonder, pity, pray for these wild natures" (1:145). If individualized treatment, characterized by special attention from the prison matron, and reformation succeed, however, the Matron maintains that convicts—like "Macklin" in *Female Life in Prison*—develop an attachment to their matron that is "almost the fond, faithful attachment of a dog to its mistress" (1:235–36). The narrative alternates between such patronizing images of these women's ultimate docility and images of their total lack of restraint, suggesting the need to supervise them at all times.

Yet there is another side to Robinson's representations of female prisoners, which complicates his accounts and distinguishes him from other commentators such as Carpenter who deployed similar, often colonial, tropes to describe them.[21] Although Robinson's Matron uses a whole catalogue of jungle creatures to refer to female convicts—lionesses, tigresses, hyenas, panthers, and elephants, among others (*Female Life* 1:108, 1:213; 2:58, 2:60,

2:63)—the depictions occasionally seem to bear the traces of gleeful admiration (and simultaneously provoke such in the reader) for the strength, agility, and grace of these powerful women. The same is true for Robinson's desire to record the secret alliances, communication, and romantic attachments between female prisoners. Although, arguably, this keenness serves as a strategy to render his prison narratives "racier" and hence more commercially profitable—*Memoirs of Jane Cameron* offers a popular mixture of crime and romance, detailing Jane's early involvement with men alongside her criminal career—the stories also acknowledge aspects of convicts' lives not usually given much attention in official publications or reformers' writings.

"Palling-In" | Hidden Romance and Relationships between Women

Rather predictably, the narrator in *Memoirs* codes Jane as highly sexualized and "precocious" from a young age (1:19). While Robinson avoids plain language, he has the Matron insinuate that Jane was subject to an abusive father ("a brutal, morose, drunken vagabond"; 1:17), who may have forced her into prostitution at the age of ten. Jane roams the streets at night, with other neglected children who display no "innocence of childhood in their midst" (1:36), ending up with a first sweetheart, a thief, at the age of twelve. As a teenager, the young woman's oversexed nature is depicted as both the cause of her final fall and the major turning point in her life, when she is facing a long sentence after she "trade[s] on a man's passions" (2:3), lures him to her house, drugs him, and robs him.

More unusually, though, Robinson also chooses to depict the "palling-in," the formation of romantic bonds, between women convicts, recovering a hidden lesbian history in nineteenth-century prisons that is rarely found elsewhere.[22] The Matron draws attention to the value of these attachments, despite the problems and quarrels they cause in penal institutions, because they "indicate[] in most cases that craving for affection, that wish to be loved, and to find some one to love, which is the natural instinct of woman, however low in the scale of humanity" (*Prison Characters* 1:31). A sense of voyeuristic sensationalism certainly plays a role in these instances of desire between women, occurrences which the Matron occasionally describes in medicalized terms as "strange, morbid fancies" (*Memoirs* 2:46) and "spasmodic liking" (*Memoirs* 2:176). Telling the story of Jane's prison romance with another woman, though, the Matron's words acknowledge the nature of same-sex desire in penal institutions more forcefully:

> But she *fell in love* with this woman; I know no phrase that can more truly convey my meaning. And women do fall in love with each other in prisons; exhibit for each other at times strange passionate and unselfish attachments, lasting, as a rule, nine or twelve months, and then ending in a whirl of rage and jealousy, a desperate quarrel, and a new "pal." I have known one woman leave her baby to a stranger's care, and fight her way to the dark, where she knew her "pal" was confined. (*Memoirs* 2:93–94, emphasis in original)

Although this passage is not an unambiguously positive endorsement of desire between women, it highlights female prisoners' ability to form intense and "unselfish" bonds. The Matron's positive evaluation of these ties as "love" competes against a distancing assessment of such feelings as "strange." While the specific example of one woman here emphasizes the convict's sense of loyalty to another woman as a positive feature, it may also have alienated readers, considering that this devotion resulted in the abandonment of a child. The Matron's comment on the transient and turbulent nature of female prison romance further undercuts the positive affirmation of these affective bonds between prisoners.

Aside from such depictions of the deep emotional attachments among convicts, Robinson's Matron alludes to the possibility of strong connections between convicts and matrons, noting Jane's "strange attachment, almost devotion" for Miss Weston, the Brixton prison matron who begins to take a special interest in her. Jane's "love" for Weston is described as "intense," and the Prison Matron's narrative is highly suggestive of secret moments of intimacy between officer and inmate, with an added flavor of fetishism: "She [Jane Cameron] had a strange habit of crouching on the floor of her cell, and watching the dress of Miss Weston pass her. . . . Cameron would lie extended along the floor of her cell, watching for the matron, occasionally reaching forth her hand, and touching her foot gently, if she approached too near" (*Memoirs* 2:125–26). When Jane Cameron's release from prison is imminent, the women's relationship is sealed with another breach of rules and a secret encounter:

> The preceding night, let it be confessed, to the amazement of disciplinarians, Miss Weston had found her way to the ward—adjacent to her own at that time—

and whispered her "good-bye," and heard the woman call God's blessing on her head for all the interest she had taken in her.

Matron and prisoner touched each other's hands beneath the door, and then the interview had ended—a fugitive interview, that the rules would have punished by a fine for Miss Weston, and for the matron who had allowed her to pass in, and Cameron flung herself on the bed and covered her head with the clothes to stifle her sobs. (2:147–48)

Robinson, prolific writer of romance fiction, here cannot resist his impulse to embellish the "couple's" separation with dramatic and sentimental detail. According to the Prison Matron, the eventual parting between Jane and Weston in the outside world—after Weston, sought out by Jane, successfully assists in restoring the former prisoner's servant position with the employers she had abandoned, now about to move their household to America—constitutes "a trial" for both of them (2:297).

The regime promoted by Robinson's narratives thus relies on occasional subversions of official institutional rules, manifesting themselves in close alliances between individual matrons and prisoners and their conversations that are "not in the books" (*Memoirs* 2:113). This advocacy of female-female coalitions, occasionally with erotic undertones, is at times combined with an explicit critique of governmental policies. With reference to Miss Weston, Robinson's Matron notes, "In my time, she was even a critic of the Government under which she held office, and had Colonel Sir Joshua Jebb or Captain O'Brien condescended to have solicited her opinion upon many requirements of the prison service, it is just possible that her practical opinions would have shaken their faith in the wisdom of a few of the 'Rules'" (2:115). Robinson's narrative skillfully packages the critique of government "Rules" by reporting it as another's opinion. (Interestingly, the earlier prison tale, *Female Life in Prison*, was dedicated to O'Brien, the director of convict prisons, who here does not receive more than a snide comment.) The narrative presents the occasional alliances of nonelite women—the matron Weston is characterized as a woman "who had known trouble and seen better days" herself so that "the trouble of others always drew her towards them" (2:282)—as a more effective alternative to the strict disciplinary regime instituted by influential men. Robinson's tales explicitly support the subversion of discipline in some cases and present secret bonds and emotional attachments as potentially helpful elements in the process of convict reformation.

"That Hard-Worked Class" | Reevaluating the Labor of Prison Matrons

The description of secret bonds and moments of intimacy between matrons and prisoners goes hand in hand with a detailed depiction of the matrons' labor. A report of the daily routine in *Female Life* comments on the duties of the night matron: "Slow, weary hours of prison service are these hours on night duty; pacing dimly-lighted wards, and listening for a breath or murmur that may be significant of one ill at ease within the cells; checking at times artful signals on the wall between one prisoner and another, or pausing, perhaps for company's sake, to whisper a 'good night' to some one as sleepless as herself" (1:26).

Although *Female Life* declares that its focus is on female convict life, it is also an account of the working lives of female officers and of women more generally. Robinson's Matron takes great pains to illuminate the working conditions of women officers, with the first few chapters in *Female Life* devoted to a detailed description of their role and duties. The *English Woman's Journal* recommended the chapter on the matrons' work to all its readers "who may be interested in the organization of the higher and more responsible kinds of female labor" (Parkes, "Female Life in Prison" 5), noting that the officers' salaries and pensions "are far more favorable than women usually secure in their work" (4) while acknowledging that "the duties are heavy" (4). Parkes's extensive review for a feminist periodical indicates that Robinson's narratives of female imprisonment served as platforms for problematizing larger issues around women's position in society, including salaried employment.[23] In celebrating the Matron's professional knowledge, skill, and experience, Robinson's writing echoed prior feminist demands to increase employment opportunities for women with (at least some) education, which had also been endorsed by newspapers such as the *Times*.[24]

Robinson takes care to emphasize the harder aspects of female officers' duties. In the spirit of Mayhew's reevaluations of physically demanding labor in *London Labour and the London Poor*, Robinson's narratives acknowledge the achievements, both physical and mental, of prison matrons. The Prison Matron insists, "it is as well that the world should know there are these useful, humble servants doing its hardest and most unthankful work" (*Female Life* 1:42). *Female Life* points to the monotony and tediousness of the matrons' tasks, suggesting that officers are incarcerated alongside their convicts: "The hours are the same to prisoners and prison matrons at Brixton as Millbank" (1:26). Robinson's Matron furthermore draws attention to the physical challenges that come with the officer's job and have the matron "shivering in her bear-skin cloak during the winter months, and struggling against the heat in the summer," during her duty of watching the prisoners' daily exercise in the yard (1:23).

Robinson's *Female Life*, then, provides a different perspective on prison matrons than do the writings of earlier prison reformers such as Elizabeth Fry, which considered female officers predominantly as servants who needed to be controlled by lady supervisors. *Female Life*, through the power of the narrator's first-person account, instead aims to "awaken the reader's interest and sympathy" (1:31) for the lives and labor of "that hard-worked class" (1:28) and hopes to "secure the attention of all thoughtful men with power to speak for [these women] in Parliament, or in newspapers and magazines" (2:293). The text thus conducts tactful political lobbying on behalf of female employees.

Although Robinson still portrays matrons as servants to the government, his descriptions give them a new kind of dignity when he defends their status as workers in their own right. The narrative of *Female Life* criticizes the exploitation of female officers during excessively long working days due to understaffing and calls for the recruitment of additional employees (1:36–37), as opposed to "a few more gentlemen, with large salaries" at the top (2:292). A reviewer in the *Examiner* nodded approvingly: "Strict economy at the expense of the weak is too much the bad system of our Government under Ministries of every complexion, and there is no Ministry that would not earn credit to itself by spending the few pence that in a few directions justice asks of it" ("Female Life in Prison"). *Female Life* also attacks a government policy that refuses matrons the right to be promoted to deputy or lady superintendent and allows such posts to "be filled from without by lady friends of the direction" (1:34). Here, Robinson's narrative is notably antiestablishment and sides with the female prison workers—generally members of "that large class which has seen better days and known happier times therein" (1:31)—against the Board of Direction and upper-class women who access prestigious positions in the penal system through personal connections with male officials, rather than long-term service.[25] Contemporaries such as Dickens enjoyed such antiestablishment diatribes; his *All the Year Round* printed Eliza Lynn Linton's long, approving review of *Female Life*, which ended by acknowledging the hard lot of female officers who "suffer almost as severely as the criminals" and whose case was therefore "to be looked into" (Linton 493).[26]

Robinson's later narrative *Prison Characters* speaks less favorably of prison matrons. Although the Prison Matron still maintains that "a clever matron is a wonderful instrument in the proper machinery of a female prison" (1:16), she also complains in more drastic language that there are "not a few" officers "who are no more judges of character than they are judges of horseflesh" (1:12), asking for the standard of matrons to be raised (1:24). Siding with the model promoted by Fry earlier in the century, the narrative asserts that the "task of supervision of matrons" by a lady—apart from the lady superintendent and deputy, who already have other duties—would be a good idea (1:14). In contrast to Robinson's earlier work, which had challenged the male establishment and its employment strategies, his later book reaffirms the position of elite women over nonelite matrons. Robinson's classist views here can be read as a concession to his middle- and upper-class female readers, many of whom would have sympathized with professional opportunities for *educated* women but might have felt piqued by the relative independence of lower-class prison matrons and their comparatively "favorable" working conditions, as noted in Parkes's review for the *English Woman's Journal* ("Female Life in Prison" 4).

"Why, We Must Help Ourselves" |
Capitalism, Working-Class Communities,
and Christian Paternalism

Robinson's contradictory representations of prison matrons are indicative of the ambivalent depictions of nonelite people in his narratives. At various points, the Prison Matron explicitly takes a pro-working-class position against other, culturally hegemonic representations of this section of society. In a chapter on "prisoners' friends," the Matron comments on the forgiving character of working men and husbands in relation to their wives, contradicting Lord Alfred Tennyson's poetic lines that such men are the "worst of public foes" (qtd. in *Female Life* 1:174). The Matron insists on the inappropriateness of this characterization, maintaining that "it is a harsh assertion, and, in some cases, this 'worst of public foes' may be the best of Christians and the most forgiving of men. And working men do not read Tennyson to any extent, and have much to consider, and were not thought of when the Laureate wrote those lines" (1:174). The narrator's rejection of "high" art as ineffective in addressing the realities of working people's lives also implicitly reaffirms Robinson's position as a popular-fiction writer.

In a similar spirit, *Memoirs of Jane Cameron* points to the friendships and strong bonds that exist among poor communities. After giving birth to an illegitimate child—the baby later dies—the young, weakened Jane is supported by her friend Mary, also a thief, and the community of Irish beggars sharing their building:

> The Irish who thronged that unhealthy dwelling-place knew her condition, and did their best for her. . . . The feminine portion, callous as they naturally were, felt their womanly sympathies aroused by the young girl's miserable position. . . .
>
> They pitied her position, and ignored the shame of it, and did their best to support her by their humble contributions. (1:190)

The passage illustrates once more that female members of the underclass, while unrefined, are capable of mobilizing "womanly sympathies," disregarding sexual transgression, and offering practical help, thus becoming a model for middle-class philanthropists.

Robinson's Prison Matron also joins in the debate around cheap female prison labor and its dire consequences for needlewomen in the outside world who, she suggests, are forced into crime because of "this obnoxious policy" (*Memoirs* 1:120). Aligning herself with the popular radical poetry of Thomas Hood, the Matron predicts that "there will be living illustrations to Hood's 'Song of the Shirt' to the end of time, if some better and more just system be not presently adopted" (*Female Life* 1:185; see also *Prison Characters* 1:94). In strong language, the Matron blames both the city firms that are seeking out prisons as an alternative market—"shame on the City firms who seek so cheap a market as our Government prisons!" (*Female Life* 2:275)—and the government for selling to them: "it is an unnatural expedient to reduce prison expenditure, that in moral and enlightened England, with a thoughtful, feeling Lady on its throne, should be cried down by every honest soul with power to raise a voice against its glaring inconsistency" (*Female Life* 2:292).[27] In these passages, Robinson's passionate voice fuses with that of his persona, the Prison Matron, in an evident way.

Robinson's Matron repeatedly points to the economic causes at the root of crime and female criminality more particularly. In a chapter on circumstances encouraging criminal activities, the Matron criticizes the regulation of street trade and insists that "to throw difficulties in the way of the huckster is to add to his difficulties of living honestly" (*Prison Characters* 2:239). Similarly, the narrative in *Memoirs of Jane Cameron* traces Jane's misfortunes back to economic difficulties. After her alcoholic mother has kicked her out of the apartment to have more space for paying lodgers, Jane is befriended by a couple in the building, who take her in at night. They are mat makers but disappear after prices for mats fall so that they cannot sell them anymore and are forced to move out (1:26–30).

Despite such critiques of the economic system, Robinson's narratives shy away from endorsing an explicitly materialist attack on the distribution of wealth, familiar from earlier socialist accounts such as Flora Tristan's *London Journal* (1840), which identified flawed government policies "based on privilege," unfair taxation of workers, and misspending as the cause of crime and predicted a warlike antagonism, involving governments that would have to "resort to mass deportation, erect scaffolds everywhere and arm half the population to shoot down the other half when it asks for bread" (96).[28] In *Memoirs of Jane Cameron*, it is the character of Elizabeth Harber, a cell mate of Jane's—portrayed in a rather unsympathetic light as a "crafty, hypocritical prisoner" (1:131)—who formulates this critique of the unequal distribution of wealth most clearly: "If people will see us starve rather than give us money, why, we must help ourselves. If anybody would give you and me a hundred a-year and a house to live in, why, we should be honest people, and go to church every Sunday" (1:140). Although the Prison Matron's call for Christian philanthropy supports this statement to a certain extent—the Matron formulates the desire to awaken the interest of philanthropists as one of her original aims in the writing of these stories (*Prison Characters* 1:1–2)—the portrayal of Harber as Jane's temptress who gives her advice and "whispers" to her throughout the night, against Jane's will (*Memoirs* 1:138–39), suggests that Harber's cynical twist on Samuel Smiles's notion of "self-help," legitimizing crime as a response to social inequality and the only way toward self-improvement, goes too far. Nevertheless, the fact that Robinson offers a narrative space for this voice in itself suggests that he is willing to allow for different perspectives, offering a balanced picture beyond a coherent, socially conservative message.

The transformation of Jane's criminal career is exemplary of the kind of reformation promoted by Robinson's narratives. The former convict leaves Britain, sailing toward "the new world and the new life" with her employers (*Memoirs* 2:299). Her mistress, Mrs. Evans, an "energetic" and "Christian woman, with a great and undying interest in the progress of the weak and the erring to repentance" (2:291), sees "evidence of a new religious feeling, without which, perhaps, no reformed prisoner ever kept strong to the last" (2:299–300). Jane's health declines only a few months after she starts service with her family in America, and she dies. The narrative concludes with a letter from Mrs. Evans to Jane's old prison matron, Miss Weston, and a comment by Robinson's Matron: " 'To the last she was a good servant and a faithful friend—she died truly penitent for all past sins, and truly thankful for the mercies which had been vouchsafed to her.' This was the last news of Jane Cameron—the last and the best!" (2:301).

In this account, the "good" news of Jane's complete reformation and penitent death outweighs the bad news of her demise. Implicit in this eventually successful conversion of the former convict, so close to a relapse, is the wider rationale behind Robinson's prison tales—a call to other "Christian men and women," like the Evanses, "who may read this book," to support organizations such as the "Discharged Prisoners' Aid Society" (2:155) and to discreetly take on former prisoners like Jane "at a fair salary" (2:159). Although Robinson's Matron criticizes patrons who take women into service and do not pay "fair" wages (2:159), the general class structure of society remains intact in these narratives. As in earlier models of reform, initiated by the Quaker Fry and other prison visitors, reformed female prisoners are advertised as a valuable resource for wealthy households, because, as the Prison Matron insists, "there are no servants so thoroughly industrious as a discharged prisoner" (2:167). It is only for a brief moment that we get a glimpse of the secret discontent that some of these women might have been experiencing simultaneously. Describing Jane's servant existence shortly before her decision to escape, the Prison Matron reports that her life "was very still and quiet and *prison-like*—not much resembling freedom, or what she had once believed freedom to consist of" (2:169). It is her "wild desire to have less restraint upon her actions, to be her own mistress in any way" (2:195), which ultimately leads to her decision to break out. Although Jane returns and her servant discontent is dissolved into penitence at the end, the fact that Robinson acknowledges her dissatisfaction and prison-like living conditions in a wealthy household at all demonstrates that the narrative's ideological agenda is ambivalent.[29]

Happy Endings? | Reformation and Marriage in "Daisy March, the Prison Flower"

Unlike *Memoirs of Jane Cameron*, which follows literary conventions in that it concludes with the fallen woman's death, after successful redemption, Robinson's later serialized story "Daisy March, the Prison Flower" ends on a cautiously optimistic note, with the prospect of a happy marriage for reformed convict Daisy.[30] "Daisy March" was published in London in June 1881 as part of the *Crystal Stories*, monthly publications sold for one penny at booksellers and railway bookstalls.[31] It was Robinson's answer to what he, through the voice of his Prison Matron, and many other concerned commentators in the mid- to late nineteenth century, saw as "the curse of the thieves' literature" (*Prison Characters* 2:246)—penny serial tales glorifying criminal life with particular appeal to young, lower-class readers.[32] As the first number of the *Crystal Stories* explained, this illustrated supplement to the *British Workwoman* was pitched as "a new series of original tales for family reading" (2) targeted at working-class families, especially women and girls.[33] It promised "a high moral tone and pure teaching" by "writers of considerable eminence in their profession," in contrast to "the cheap and sensational literature now circulating throughout the country under the name of NOVELETTES." Hoping "to offer true pictures of English homes and hearts, and of those life-trials, temptations and victories, which make up the sum of human existence," the publishers aimed to provide moral education and entertainment. The publication called for the "hearty co-operation of all those interested in disseminating healthy literature amongst the masses" (2), from religious societies and temperance associations to mechanics' institutes and clubs for working men and women.

A month later, in July 1881, "Daisy March" appeared across the Atlantic, in the weekly New York–based magazine *Harper's Bazar*, a "Repository of Fashion, Pleasure, and Instruction" for well-to-do women which, from 1867 onward, had presented a mix of serialized fiction—including well-known authors such as Mary Elizabeth Braddon, Wilkie Collins, and Charles Dickens—and reportage on topical issues such as "art, morals, education, hygiene, housekeeping, 'Home and Foreign Gossip'" (1.1 [2 Nov. 1867]: xii).[34] With "Daisy March," Robinson consolidated his reputation as a writer on women's issues, while proving his ability to address audiences across the boundaries of class and nation. The story revisits many of the themes familiar from his earlier prison tales, constructing women's delinquency as a result of the environment, lack of positive role models, and "neglect" (423) rather than innate depravity. The fiction of authorship by A Prison Matron was maintained for "Daisy March," which was not associated with Robinson's name but was presented as the work of the author of *Female Life in Prison* and *Memoirs of Jane Cameron*. The publishers of the *Crystal Stories* capitalized on Robinson's earlier success, printing positive reviews of his existing prison narratives alongside the advertisement for the forthcoming "Daisy March" (*Crystal Stories* 1.3 [1881]: 38). Unlike his earlier prison trilogy, this story is told in third person rather than first person, with occasional focalization, reported conversations, and a barely literate, secretly composed prison note (a so-called stiff; 443) to bring in prisoners' perspectives.

After an early criminal career, Daisy March is sent to prison at age fourteen and becomes an unruly inmate, before developing a strong attachment for Patience Greenwood, a new officer with "imagination," "strong religious feeling," and "a deep sympathy with the unfortunate" (423). Robinson contrasts Patience with her older sister, Kate, who is also a matron, disliked by many inmates, including Daisy. When Patience dies, she passes on "the kindly Christian virtues" and "the lesson of true sympathy for the poor humanity about her" as a "legacy" to her sister (454). After Kate and Daisy enter a pact to honor Patience's dying wish, Daisy improves her conduct and reforms: "She awoke to penitence; she learned diligently to read and write now; she became one of the most promising of the prison school; she read and presently she understood, her Bible. . . . She grew up a fair young woman, with a very sad and thoughtful face—they called her the Prison Daisy, or the Prison Flower" (454). Robinson, as in his earlier tales, promotes strong personal alliances between matrons and prisoners as the best recipe for reformation. Such women's practical religious efforts are contrasted with futile attempts by male officials, such as the prison chaplain, when Daisy comments, "The parson's been a-tryin' to make me know a bit, and I've been a tryin' to understand him; but, lor bless you, there's no making him out, miss, try as hard as you can" (442).

In contrast to such failed communication, Robinson celebrates cross-class relationships between women as a way of reconstructing former offenders' lives; after seven years, when Kate comes into property bequeathed by her aunt, Daisy becomes her servant and friend—"for more of a companion than a lady's maid, and more of a friend than either, had this prison waif become"—exchanging the corrupting influence of the city for Kate's home and "old-fashioned garden" in Essex County (454). Robinson's paternalistic idea of a personalized employer-employee relationship in wholesome rural surroundings, modeled after family rather than market relations, anticipates similar concepts suggested in later fiction, such as George Moore's *Esther Waters* (1894), in which the fallen woman Esther is eventually reunited with her former mistress in a communal life of simple comfort and harmony.

Daisy and Kate's friendship, and Kate's practical compassion, facilitates another union in the end, when the former prisoner overcomes her feeling of shame and unworthiness to reconsider a marriage proposal from a "stalwart young farmer" (470). After Daisy's initial refusal, her suitor coincidentally discovers the truth about her past, when fellow convict Janet Finlanson returns to tempt Daisy back into her old life among her criminal clan in Liverpool. However, Janet, previously described as "violent as a man" but "with an infinitesimal amount of brain, and some semblance of a heart left" (423), retreats in awe when she overhears Daisy and Kate praying together, before confessing everything to the farmer after she suffers an accident. The power of the Bible and Kate's "extensive knowledge of the Scriptures" (470) thus function as the key to Daisy's reformation and the means of averting recidivism.

While "Daisy March's" conclusion is open-ended, it is strongly implied that the reformed convict will enter a happy marriage. Such a move would not have been uncontroversial, with the desirability of marriage for former convicts a matter of debate across the nineteenth century. Dickens, for instance, had welcomed marriage for the reformed women of his "Home for Homeless Women" as possible and desirable, whereas others, including his sponsor, philanthropist Angela Burdett-Coutts, did not (Tomalin 86).[35] Robinson aligns himself with Dickens's vision for reformed prisoners, while breaking with literary conventions; he offers Daisy hope for a brighter future, without implying an unrealistically positive picture for female offenders overall. For example, Daisy's older sister, Mary Wilton, meets with a different fate, dying in prison as "a poor, weak, willful woman to the last, and resisting to the last all efforts to amend" (454). Robinson's point here may be that it is the young who stand the best chance of successful reformation, provided they receive individual attention by sympathetic women and support from a "stalwart" man who is not too far removed from their own class.

"Daisy March" suggests role models to working-, middle-, and upper-class readers, promoting strong bonds between females across classes as the nucleus of a well-functioning society. Although Robinson's tale ultimately assigns women a place in domesticity, the story hints at the good that can be achieved through their employment in the public sphere, which explains why the tale might have appealed to the aspirational female readers of *Harper's Bazar*. Despite the fact that Patience dies—which in itself constitutes an interesting reversal of literary convention, as it is the reformer rather than the reformed who dies—her impact offers a compelling case, for it is her commitment as a prison officer that marks the turning point in Daisy's life. Like Robinson's successful matrons in the earlier stories, Patience, an "eccentric" and "inquisitive young woman" (442) with a zest for preaching, likes to challenge authority a little, not taking prison regulations too seriously. Daisy's reformation is *her* legacy, rather than the prison system's or the chaplain's. Like the earlier prison narratives, "Daisy March" commends a pinch of independent-mindedness to women, inviting them to use their own good sense of judgment—in their working and private lives—to help reconstruct society and to offer new perspectives on and for female offenders. It is this gesture that makes Robinson's prison writings as a whole protofeminist in outlook and purpose.

Conclusion

The overall vision of Frederick William Robinson's prison narratives may not be a politically radical one. Rather, it calls for Christian benevolence and an organic relationship between the different classes of society in order to halt an increase in crime in "the richest country in the world" (*Prison Characters* 2:248). *Female Life*, *Memoirs of Jane Cameron*, *Prison Characters*, and "Daisy March" offer some sympathetic, humanizing portrayals and an insight into the challenging living conditions of female prisoners—as well as nonelite people more generally—even if more positive representations are counteracted by descriptions typifying offenders as animalistic, irrational, childlike, and physically deviant creatures. Some of the stereotypes and narrative conventions used by Robinson might have been employed to satisfy audience expectations. We could speculate whether, in the case of *Memoirs of Jane Cameron*, the conventions of confessional or conversion tales served a strategic function, to detract attention from the more radical aspects of the narrative, similar to the moralistic frames of execution broadsides.[36] But the ideological contradictions in Robinson's narratives may also be a result both of his own ambivalence—and that of his readers—with regard to female crime and punishment and of the constraints of the marketplace, which called for some recognizable tropes and generic formulas.

Although the voices of female prisoners themselves are mediated in multiple ways in Robinson's stories, they do exist. Akin to representations of offenders in gallows literature, these narratives—*Memoirs of Jane Cameron* especially—open up a space for readers to take notice of the convict's story. It is here that an analysis of Robinson's work can contribute to the "insurrection of subjugated knowledges . . . buried or masked in functional coherences or formal systematizations" that Foucault had in mind (*"Society"* 7). As I have argued, it is not only the prisoner's "subjugated knowledge" that Robinson's narratives reinstate—if in a limited way—but also the delegitimized knowledge of prison matrons. Robinson's narratives thus constitute a polyphonic pastiche of different voices expressing the experience of women's imprisonment. By deploying strategies such as metacommentary and focalization, Robinson presents thematic as well as formal interventions into midcentury depictions of nonelite women, particularly incarcerated women.

While the Prison Matron makes carefully pitched complaints against society's structural inequalities as a cause of crime—from the meager salaries of needlewomen to inadequate housing for the poor—Robinson's focus lies on an appeal to his readers' *compassion* for convicts. Implicitly aligning himself with George Eliot's view of art as a necessary complement to "generalizations and statistics," of art as facilitator for "the extension of our sympathies" (Eliot, "Natural History of German Life" 270)—in this case with regard to female offenders—Robinson uses Eliot's first novel, *Adam Bede* (1859), as an explicit intertextual reference. His Prison Matron tells the story of the prisoner Sarah Featherstone, a story, she says, "not unlike Hetty's in 'Adam Bede,' from which, perhaps, Hetty's character was conceived—for novelists are quick at piecing the fragments of stern truth into a story that may touch all hearts" (*Female Life* 2:272–73).[37] With this metareflexive comment, Robinson once more covertly draws attention to his own literary method—his wider reading, which, alongside real-life cases, had provided him with inspiration.

Robinson's emphasis on an author's ability to "touch all hearts," while powerful, precluded a more thorough, structural critique of the material conditions at the root of women's criminality. Even the reviewer of *Female Life* for *Chambers's Journal* advised readers of the limits of sympathy, concluding that financial support for the Discharged Prisoners' Aid Society would constitute a more effective response: "Over her [the Prison Matron's] volumes many a tear will be dropped from sympathising eyes; but would it not be better for some of us to drop a subscription?" ("Female Felons" 314). Yet, as I have argued, Robinson's mode of representation, including his metacritical comments, departed in important ways from other, institutionally sanctioned ways of portraying women in prison, complementing parliamentary statistics with a personalized account, albeit with a tendency toward the sensational and sentimental at times. The following chapter turns to other fiction writers' attempts to bring female prisoners' stories to the attention of a broad audience, from Robinson's point of reference *Adam Bede* by Eliot, with its tale of the convicted infanticide Hetty Sorrel, to Collins's *The Moonstone* (1868), which confronts its readers with the fate of the reformed thief Rosanna Spearman.

CHAPTER 3

The Limits of Female Reformation

Hidden Stories in George Eliot's *Adam Bede* and Wilkie Collins's *The Moonstone*

Although the most visible and sustained representations of female convicts and their perspectives in early to mid-nineteenth-century Britain can arguably be found in popular, noncanonical forms of writing, such as the staging of female offenders' voices in execution broadsides or Frederick William Robinson's *Memoirs of Jane Cameron, Female Convict*, more recognized Victorian novelists also made efforts to give voice to the life histories of such marginalized women. This chapter analyzes George Eliot's depiction of the infanticide Hetty Sorrel's imprisonment in *Adam Bede* (1859)—an explicit reference point in Robinson's *Female Life in Prison*—alongside Wilkie Collins's narrative of the former thief and ex-prisoner Rosanna Spearman in *The Moonstone* (1868). Whereas Robinson's *Memoirs*, discussed in detail in the previous chapter, moves the life narrative of the "female convict" center stage, underscored from the start through the book's title, Hetty and Rosanna are not eponymous heroines; yet, although Hetty and Rosanna appear secondary to the novels' principal characters, at least on the surface, both Eliot and Collins challenge their audiences to take heed of the two offenders' submerged biographies. As I will demonstrate, Collins thematizes this submergence in formal terms, through narrative construction and use of gothic convention, while contextual evidence on *Adam Bede*'s inception and Eliot's motivations suggests that she saw the prison scene with Hetty's confession as the core of her narrative.

"I Will Speak . . . I Will Tell" | Confession
and Female Prison Ministry in *Adam Bede*

In Eliot's first full-length novel, *Adam Bede* (1859), we find one of the rare
moments in nineteenth-century realist fiction dealing with female imprisonment in a literal sense. It has been suggested that the novel is primarily
concerned with the eponymous hero's development of sympathy—kind and
intelligent, carpenter Adam learns to question his unforgiving attitude toward his alcoholic father after the latter's death, only to be confronted with
a new moral dilemma when his seventeen-year-old fiancée, Hetty Sorrel, a
simple but pretty maid, is convicted of infanticide following an illicit liaison
with the local aristocrat Arthur Donnithorne. Condemned to death, Hetty
is rescued at the last minute by a reprieve and commutation of sentence,
before dying on her way back from transportation several years afterward.[1]
While the exploration of Adam's sympathy toward Hetty, and, by extension, evoking a similar response from the reader, is certainly one of Eliot's
aims, interpretations that emphasize Adam's character development risk
obliterating the significant role of Hetty's story.[2] Furthermore, without dismissing the gender- and class-based limitations in Eliot's work and the justified critical discomfort with Hetty's demise—the conventional death of
the fallen woman—moving away from a purely plot-based analysis, which
inevitably must read Hetty's banishment and passing as a kind of "spiritual
cannibalism," to use Jennifer Uglow's phrase, and the girl as a "sacrificial
victim" (113), allows us to complicate the tale that the novelist wants to tell.[3]
In this chapter, I argue that the scene of Hetty's imprisonment—in which
the convict confesses under the ministry of her Methodist cousin Dinah
Morris and which Eliot regarded as the "climax" of her narrative (*Journals*
297)—allows the author to create a platform for the experiences of female convicts as well as pioneering women in prison visiting. Focusing on the prison
chapter as the novel's core, a moment that, in Christine Krueger's words, constitutes the "principal scene of female empowerment in the novel" (*Reader's
Repentance* 251), enables us to engage with some of the more transgressive
gestures in Eliot's text, beyond the constraining mechanisms of established
literary devices—arguably the novelist's nod to convention at a moment
when she was anxious to establish her reputation.

Eliot famously obtained inspiration from her Methodist aunt's anecdote
of a visit to a condemned infanticide in 1802 and regarded this family prison
tale as "the germ of 'Adam Bede'" (*Journals* 296). Her aunt Elizabeth

Tomlinson Evans, born in 1776, attended to Mary Voce, a young woman convicted of poisoning her child, in Nottingham jail, accompanied by another female visitor. The women prayed early in the morning before the impending execution, until Voce finally confessed, and then they went together in the cart to the scaffold.[4] Evans was part of a generation of women coming of age in the relatively progressive climate of Wesleyan Methodism. From a modest background, she felt encouraged to become a preacher after listening to a sermon by the revivalist William Bramwell, who challenged more women to be actively involved (Lloyd 42). The movement's leader, the Reverend John Wesley, promoted charitable activities such as visiting people who were sick or in prison and explicitly endorsed women's equal right to pursue such tasks (Chilcote, *John Wesley* 72–73).[5]

The Methodist tradition of prison visiting started in Oxford, when Wesley and others sought out condemned prisoners in the castle prison. Early female Methodists working with prisons were Hannah Ball, who visited three sailors in March 1769, and the Countess of Huntingdon, who lent money to people imprisoned for debt. During the early years of the revival, Sarah Peters had called on John Lancaster, imprisoned at Newgate for robbing a Methodist chapel, thus pioneering activities at this London prison that later were conducted more famously by the Quaker Elizabeth Fry (E. Brown 72–73). Finding Lancaster incarcerated alongside a group of six other condemned prisoners, including one woman, Peters accompanied the convicts for nineteen days, singing hymns, reading from scripture, and praying. Having converted several of them before execution, Peters paid the ultimate price herself, dying of "gaol fever" (typhus).[6]

Elizabeth Evans built on such a rich tradition, before an increasingly conservative atmosphere after Wesley's death created obstacles for Methodist women's public engagement until the mid-nineteenth century. A year after the 1803 Methodist Conference, the religion's governing body, imposed restrictions on women, Evans married the fellow Methodist and preacher Samuel Evans, the younger brother of George Eliot's father. The Evanses subsequently ignored official regulations when Samuel sent his wife to preach in his place on occasion—a transgression for which he was disciplined. Following further restrictions on women in 1832, the couple joined the new sect of Arminian Methodism, which allowed women to preach, but eventually rejoined the Wesleyans. Elizabeth continued to preach at the local level, with official permission, until 1844, a few years before her death (Lloyd 43). It has been suggested that, alongside a number of other women, she served as an important female mentor figure for Eliot, inspiring the writer's interest in "women's discursive power" (Krueger, *Reader's Repentance* 241).

In the wake of *Adam Bede*'s publication, Eliot dismissed claims that Dinah Morris constituted an exact portrayal of her aunt, insisting that Evans's personality and story had "suggested Dinah" but no more (*Letters* 176).[7] Although it has been argued that Eliot had a tendency to cultivate the idea of the "female genius" (Krueger, *Reader's Repentance* 235) over a commitment to the achievements of women as a group, the author's contention that Dinah functioned as a "generic resemblance" rather than an individual "portrait" suggests that the character also serves as a broader acknowledgment and celebration of Methodist, and other dissenting, women's contributions to public charitable work in prisons (Eliot, *Letters* 176). The repeated references to Dinah's "Quaker-like" dress (*Adam Bede* 21) not only operate as a realist description of Methodist style but also evoke the image of Elizabeth Fry, which would have been familiar to many of Eliot's readers in 1859. Whereas Quakers such as Fry came from wealthy middle-class families, female Methodist preachers were usually from a working-class background—Evans worked in a lace factory, and the fictional character Dinah Morris is employed at a cotton mill.[8] Alongside echoes of the Quaker tradition of prison visiting, then, Eliot's novel reinscribes the charitable prison labor of *lower-class* women into her country's cultural memory.[9]

If the anecdote of Evans's prison visit served as the "germ" of the novel, an experience that had "affected" Eliot so "deeply" that she "never lost the impression of that afternoon" and the women's "talk together" (*Journals* 296), Hetty's confession to Dinah in the condemned cell constitutes the short but significant kernel of the narrative. Aside from Eliot's real-life model for Dinah, the chapter "In the Prison" recalls the encounter between half sisters Jeanie and Effie Deans—the latter awaiting her trial for infanticide—in Walter Scott's *Heart of Midlothian* (1818) as an intertext. As Josephine McDonagh has argued convincingly, Eliot's tale of child murder drew on an array of literary sources, Scott's novel being one of them.[10] Some editions of *Heart of Midlothian* printed Charles R. Leslie's frontispiece depicting the two women in close embrace in Effie's cell, with the guard, holding an oversized key, looking on. The image pictorially reflects Scott's language of tactile sentimentality, which describes the sisters as they are "throwing themselves again into each other's arms" and then "lifted up their voices and wept bitterly" (*Heart of Midlothian* 210).[11]

Eliot echoes Scott's emphasis on physical touch, with Hetty "clasped in Dinah's arms" moments after the visitor's arrival, "clutching the hand that held hers, and leaning her cheek against Dinah's" (*Adam Bede* 430). It is the bodily as much as the spiritual support from Dinah that finally enables Hetty to break her silence and tell her story as she is "throwing her arms round Dinah's neck" (433). In a speech running over three and a half pages, the convict shares her thoughts, emotions, and motivations during her lonely wanderings after leaving home and her desperate decision to abandon her newborn child in the woods. Eliot's decision to imagine a lengthy first-person account of a female prisoner's experiences not only is noteworthy given the general lack of such self-representations in the mid-Victorian novel but is also unusual within the novelist's oeuvre. As Courtney Berger notes, "Quite uncharacteristically, Eliot withholds an omniscient account of the events leading up to the child's death, instead leaving Hetty herself to describe and account for her actions" (314). Hetty's story depicts the act of burying her baby as a last resort following her aborted suicide attempts and as a consequence of her fear of becoming "a beggarwoman," of social stigma, and of rejection by her family: "I daredn't go back home again—I couldn't bear it. I couldn't have bore to look at anybody, for they'd have scorned me" (434). Moreover, though Hetty admits that she abandoned the child ("I did do it, Dinah. . . . I buried it in the wood"; 433), her confession complicates what appears to be a ruthless crime, when she offers an insight into her confusion and hesitation at the time: "But I thought perhaps it wouldn't die—there might somebody find it. I didn't kill it myself. I put it down there and covered it up, and when I came back it was gone" (434). Hetty's speech furthermore conveys a sense of her guilt-ridden conscience, as she describes being haunted by the baby's cries and visions of "the place in the wood" (437). The themes and wording of Hetty's confession here echo the tropes of child murderers' last lamentations in execution broadsides (discussed in chapter 1), which quite possibly served as another source of influence for Eliot.

Hetty's tale, shared with another woman, contrasts with her "obstinate silence" (419) in the courtroom, where, frozen and muted by overpowering fear, "she stood like a statue of dull despair" (418).[12] Although the courtroom is symbolically male, Eliot also problematizes class privilege to complicate her narrative of gendered oppression, spatially aligning the "foolish women in fine clothes, with gewgaws all up their arms and feathers on their heads, sitting near the judge" (411), with unsympathetic masculine authority, while implicitly juxtaposing this curious, gossipy audience of affluent women who "stared and whispered" (411) with Dinah's simple style and "gentle, mild" (408) femininity, which succeeds in drawing Hetty out of her shell.

What Eliot celebrates in Dinah and Hetty's prison encounter is a model of working-class women's intersubjectivity, which facilitates spiritual and physical comfort for the condemned prisoner, who begins to cling to the "human contact" offered by Dinah (430). The chapter demonstrates in detail how Dinah's exhortations gradually win over Hetty's trust, transforming her from an "animal"-like creature "that gazes, and gazes, and keeps aloof" (429) to a woman emphatically declaring, "I will speak. . . . I will tell" (433). Dinah's success in eliciting Hetty's confession confirms Adam's earlier endorsement that "the Methodists are great folks for going into the prisons" but also underlines the significance of informal *female* ministry in contrast to the work of male officials, for, as the Anglican rector and friend of the family Mr. Irwine concedes, "the jail chaplain is rather harsh in his manner" (408). Such a tribute to the positive influence of charitable women echoes Fry's evidence before a select committee in 1832, evidence which acknowledged the preference of female prisoners for unpaid visitors, as opposed to the chaplain.[13] Similar to Robinson, who, in his later story "Daisy March" (1881), celebrated the beneficial effects of two prison matrons' religious teachings over those of the parson, Eliot privileges the impact of female solidarity over that of institutionalized reformatory power, which is gendered masculine.[14]

Though Krueger is right in noting a critical distance between the (implicitly male) narrator and the woman preacher, there is arguably an identification at work between Eliot the novelist and Dinah, especially at the intense moment of the prison scene. Such identification is signaled by Eliot's comments in her letter to Sara Sophia Hennell, in which she records surprise at suggestions that she had directly plagiarized from her aunt's materials: "How curious it seems to me that people should think Dinah's sermons, prayers, and speeches were *copied*—when they were written with hot tears, as they surged up in my own mind!" (*Letters* 176). Through Dinah's ability to help Hetty express her feelings and actions, then, Eliot illustrates the value of pioneering women's work in prison visiting, but she also makes a covert statement about the role of the female novelist (albeit one disguised under a male pseudonym) in constructing public platforms for prisoners' voices.

Scholars such as Susan David Bernstein, building on the work of Michel Foucault and Sigmund Freud, have analyzed confession as "a discourse of power" in Victorian culture (1), which, typically within the gendered "dyadic structure of confession" between female confessant and male confessor (3), largely functions as "a site of coercion" (1). But Bernstein also notes moments of "contradictions, . . . inconsistency and ambivalence" (1) in this relationship, with women inhabiting "a kind of dubious or constraining agency" (1–2). Eliot's prison scene, with its model of working-class female intersubjectivity, challenges the traditional structure of confession, while Hetty's role as speaking but condemned prisoner is emblematic of confession's tension between agency and constraint. Hetty's role here, indicating transformation from formerly muted prisoner in the courtroom, is certainly more complex than merely that of "an *object* of confession and conversion," as Raymond Williams would have it (173, my emphasis). By making space for Hetty's voice, through the admittedly conventional generic device of the confessional narrative, Eliot creates a channel for covertly bringing the convict's concerns to public attention. Confession, then, acts as a potentially transgressive tool, permitting Hetty, in Krueger's words, "to disclose her oppression and exploitation in the guise of a confession" (*Reader's Repentance* 243).

Despite this momentarily empowering speech act, not only is Hetty's character silenced again when she is written out of the narrative at the end, but, as others have noted, Dinah's position as active preacher is also ultimately undermined, when she marries Adam and agrees to follow new Methodist rules prohibiting women from public ministry.[15] Eliot's choices in telling these histories are both enabling and limiting at the same time, then. Dinah's fate becomes representative of the struggle for influence that faced many nineteenth-century women who had tried to effect social change by public activities, such as preaching and prison work.[16] Hetty's story— which stands for the larger histories of fallen women and female convicts— mirrors the challenges posed to such women by social and literary conventions. Furthermore, despite providing a platform for these women's stories, Eliot does not pursue a more systematic critique of the fate of female offenders. Although Hetty is enabled to tell her tale, these words remain contained within the private sphere of the condemned cell, employed with a view toward personal salvation rather than overt social critique. Yet, by the rare move of allowing readers a glimpse into a female prisoner's thoughts and motivations, which arguably sum up the worst fears of a whole class of women, Eliot elicits her audience's sympathy for Hetty's fate, which, in turn, might become the seed for larger social critique and philanthropic activism.

While readers of *Adam Bede* primarily consisted of people wealthy enough to afford subscription to a circulating library, Eliot also received positive responses from working people who, beyond identification with the habits and customs of laboring folk, may well have seen Hetty's story as a tale painfully familiar from—or at least imaginable in—their own community's experience.[17] Some of Eliot's more refined readers struggled with the novel's honesty in this context. For instance, a rather squeamish, if overall positive, unsigned review in the *Saturday Review* clearly found the story of Hetty's fall, conviction, and punishment unpalatable, complaining that the novelist "knows and cares nothing about trials, scaffolds, and pardons," while associating the final volume of *Adam Bede* with the popular form of melodrama and "the hackneyed region of sham legal excitement" (Feb. 1859, in D. Carroll 75). The popularity of the novel defied this reviewer's judgment, as did the response of readers such as Dickens, who was already keenly aware of the plights of fallen women and former female prisoners through his work at the "Home for Homeless Women."[18] In a letter to Eliot, full of glowing admiration, Dickens reacted to Hetty's story with particular fervor: "The conception of Hetty's character is so extraordinarily subtle and true, that I laid the book down fifty times, to shut my eyes and think about it. I know nothing so skilful, determined, and uncompromising. . . . And that part of the book which follows Hetty's trial (and which I have observed to be not as widely understood as the rest), affected me far more than any other, and exalted my sympathy with the writer to its utmost height" (July 1859, in D. Carroll 85). Surely, Dickens here saw an attempt, akin to his own, to give voice to the socially disadvantaged and to experiences at the margins of society, including fallen women and other offenders, which perhaps explains his otherwise oddly jarring comment that the novel inspired his "sympathy with the writer," rather than with Hetty's character.

Dickens's case also illustrates how readerly and writerly sympathy and reformatory work (in Dickens's case with former female prisoners) can mutually enable and reinforce each other in a constructive way. Eliot herself was not involved in such practical activities and may not have pursued an overtly feminist agenda in her depiction of Hetty. Krueger notes that Eliot responded reluctantly when her friend Barbara Leigh Smith Bodichon, a campaigner for women's social and legal emancipation and cofounder of the

English Woman's Journal (1858–64), applauded what she had interpreted "as a feminist defense of outcast women" in the novel (*Reader's Repentance* 252). But Eliot's choice to write about, and briefly give voice to, this female prisoner (perhaps inadvertently) created potential incentives for her readers to follow Dickens's example and become actively engaged in, or at least more aware of, necessary efforts for improving the condition of vulnerable and socially excluded women.

"Justice to the Girl's Memory" | Decriminalizing Rosanna Spearman in *The Moonstone*

Wilkie Collins, like his mentor, friend, and collaborator Dickens, as well as other writers of sensation fiction, demonstrated a sustained interest in female criminality, its causes, and its punishment throughout his career. His exploration of women's motivations for crime ranged from an insight into governess Lydia Gwilt's diary, with its reasoning for her repeated murder attempts, in *Armadale* (1866) to a debate about criminality as either hereditary or circumstantial through his pairing of sisters Helena and Eunice, the latter adopted from a female prisoner, in *The Legacy of Cain* (1889).[19]

The Moonstone explores the events surrounding the disappearance of a diamond from an English country house and the multiple suspects thought to be implicated in the case. Although the three Brahmins who appear on the scene to restore the precious stone to its point of origin—an ancient shrine in India—are initially suspected of stealing the moonstone from the Verinders' residence, they are found to be "as innocent as the babe unborn" (119). Despite the fact that the foreigners ultimately succeed in reclaiming the diamond, the real thieves are revealed to be three Englishmen: John Herncastle, whose illicit acquisition of the gem during a battle in India sets the action in motion; Franklin Blake, who unconsciously removes the stone from his cousin Rachel Verinder's boudoir under the influence of opium; and fraudulent philanthropist and "Christian Hero" Godfrey Ablewhite (239), who secretly takes possession of the diamond to repay his exorbitant debt.

Contesting D. A. Miller's seminal reading of *The Moonstone* as a classic example of the supposedly disciplinary features of the Victorian novel, more recent critics such as Lillian Nayder and Upamanyu Pablo Mukherjee have interpreted Collins's novel as a socially subversive, or at least ambivalent, text that criticizes the foundations of imperialist ideology and simplistic conflations of foreign with criminal identity by "annulling the empowering distance between the self and the Others" (Mukherjee 167).[20] Aside from the criminalization of foreigners—in the form of the three Indians traveling to Britain to restore the moonstone to its point of origin—the novel also interrogates social prejudice around the supposedly criminal propensities of the working class and female servants, by uncovering the history of the life and death of the former convict Rosanna Spearman, now employed as a housemaid in the Verinder household, at the center of the intrigue around the disappearance of the moonstone. As an ex-prisoner, incarcerated for theft, Rosanna becomes one of the first suspects after the moonstone's disappearance; as she later reveals, she had nothing to do with the stone's removal but discovered gentleman Blake's involvement while folding his nightgown, stained with fresh paint from Rachel's bedroom door. Collins employs the sensation-fiction trope of the secret knowledge of servants to interrogate class relations, false prejudice, and the morals of the supposedly respectable to make visible Rosanna's unhappy life history.[21] In the process, he not only offers "a sympathetic and admonitory portrait of the sufferings of a lower-class woman who transgresses class boundaries by becoming infatuated with her social superior Franklin Blake," as Lyn Pykett suggests (118), but also explores social barriers that obstruct the lives of former prisoners.

Beginning the story of the loss of the diamond, the house steward Gabriel Betteredge cites Franklin Blake—himself now cleared of malicious intent after the biracial doctor Ezra Jennings's scientific experiment demonstrates that the gentleman had been administered laudanum without his knowledge—and his motive for asking eyewitnesses to give accounts of the events leading up to the discovery of the truth: "The characters of innocent people have suffered under suspicion already. . . . The memories of innocent people may suffer, hereafter, for want of a record of the facts to which those who come after us can appeal" (Collins, *Moonstone* 39). Although Rosanna's name is not mentioned here, she is one of those "innocent people" unjustly accused during the investigation. With such a mission statement in place, Collins's narrative slowly unravels how easy targets of suspicion, such as a reformed convict, become vindicated, while the supposedly respectable are revealed to be the true culprits—the latter a familiar trope in the genre of sensation fiction.

Rosanna's story is, literally speaking, hidden away in the Shivering Sand, where she buries herself alongside the evidence that Blake took the moonstone and her explanatory narrative in the form of a letter. Blake's efforts in digging up this material allow Collins to draw attention to the archaeological process required for unearthing the hidden stories of the socially marginalized *and* the complicity of gentlemen such as Blake in the former convict's fate. Blake arguably functions as an alter ego for Collins himself—the publication of stories such as that of Rosanna relies to a large extent on privileged men such as Blake/Collins who have compiled the different narratives that make up *The Moonstone*. But Collins also underlines the role of working-class solidarity in this process of excavation—"Limping Lucy" Yolland is the guardian of Rosanna's memorandum that provides clues as to how the letter hidden in the Sand can be recovered; the fellow servant Betteredge urges for "justice to the girl's memory" (361) and demands she be allowed to "speak for herself" (362).

Analyzing women's voices in *The Moonstone*, Tamar Heller has noted that the novel's "radical elements" are transformed "into a subtext" and that Collins "buries his social criticism so deep that the reader can only with difficulty dig it out again" (156). Whereas Heller primarily interprets the "buried writing" of the novel's social outcasts, such as Rosanna, as "a synecdoche for the novel's tendency at once to diffuse its social criticism and to draw attention to its own self-censorship" (144), Collins's use of Rosanna's hidden letter can instead be seen as a subtle yet politicized critique of the *cultural submersion* of the "subjugated knowledges" (Foucault, *"Society"* 7) of the marginalized and a demonstration of the difficult process of reconstructing such knowledge. The novel here not so much "papers over the traces of its own exposé" of different types of domination, as Heller argues (143), but in fact reenacts the social process of ordering knowledge with a view to exposing it.

Rosanna is introduced early on in Betteredge's narrative, as a relatively new arrival in the household, retrieved by the lady of the house from a London reformatory that "intended to save forlorn women from drifting back into bad ways, after they had got released from prison" (Collins, *Moonstone* 54)—a gesture paralleling that of Mrs. Evans in Robinson's *Memoirs of Jane Cameron*. Such practice was not uncommon, especially among people with an activist conscience such as anti–Contagious Diseases Acts campaigner Josephine Butler, who employed as servant an infanticide who had served a sentence at Newgate (Mitchell 41). But with the action set in 1848, we can imagine Rosanna as one of the women who would have found refuge in Dickens's "Home for Homeless Women," opened in 1847, which Collins must have been aware of.

Elisabeth Gruner has illustrated the way *The Moonstone* drew on real-life sources, such as the infamous murder at Road Hill House in 1860, and we can easily assume that Dickens's home and other reformatories provided similar inspiration for the author.[22] Collins had met Dickens in 1851, when the latter was still involved with the management of "Urania Cottage." Collins also knew the institution's sponsor, Angela Burdett-Coutts, personally, dining with her on several occasions in 1853 and 1854, including a dinner at Dickens's holiday residence in Boulogne.[23] In 1853, the year when Dickens published in *Household Words* his euphemistically titled article "Home for Homeless Women" on the reformatory, the two authors spent significant periods of time together, in France, Italy, and Switzerland, and Collins was already a contributor to Dickens's magazine.[24] It is therefore likely that Collins read the piece.

The inmates of Urania Cottage were made up of a diversity of women, from poor needlewomen of good character to violent girls from ill-conducted workhouses, young women of the streets, "disorderly" women released from prisons, thieves, domestic servants who had been seduced, and women who had attempted suicide (Dickens, "Home" 129). Rosanna comes to metonymically represent many of these women—she is a former thief and prisoner; a servant who falls in love with a gentleman and commits suicide; a potential needlewoman in her friend Lucy's unrealized scheme to go and work together in London (Collins, *Moonstone* 227). As Jenny Hartley has argued in *Charles Dickens and the House of Fallen Women*, Dickens used the stories and voices of the women he encountered through Urania Cottage for his plots; in Rosanna Spearman, we can imagine Collins doing the same by association.

Although Collins, similar to his mentor, ridicules grand philanthropic schemes as humbug, through his representations of the delusional Miss Clack and the hypocritical Godfrey Ablewhite, the novel does not overtly challenge Lady Verinder's practical philanthropy in offering Rosanna a second chance. Yet the narrative is far from an idealized celebration of convict reformation. It explores how, on the one hand, former prisoners can become trusted servants, while on the other hand, their old lives in criminal circles easily come to haunt them. When Rosanna becomes a suspect in the case of the moonstone's disappearance, Collins lends credence to ex-convicts' ability to mend their ways by having even Sergeant Cuff suggest, "Our experience of the Reformatory women is, that when tried in service—and when kindly and judiciously treated—they prove themselves in the majority of cases to be honestly penitent, and honestly worthy of the pains taken with them" (210). Cuff's moral endorsement of former prisoners is balanced against the detective's suspicion that Rosanna may have acted as a go-between, owing to existing "relations" with men "in the money-lending line" stemming from her days as a thief in London (210). Collins implies that for ex-offenders, it is difficult to reclaim a clean reputation. Rosanna's sympathizer Betteredge is acutely conscious of such social stigma when he refuses to disclose her background to Superintendent Seegrave, who is investigating the case, and then also to Blake, in response to the gentleman's query about Rosanna's odd behavior: "I could not bring myself to tell him the girl's story, even then. It would have been almost as good as telling him that she was the thief" (128). Despite the house steward's efforts to shelter Rosanna, the plot's development subtly hints that reformation in itself may be a futile and insufficient form of personal and social regeneration, both through overt critiques of the social system by Betteredge and Limping Lucy *and* the fact that, despite Rosanna's reclamation, she fails to find a happy place in life.

With Rosanna's tale, Collins anticipates his later goal in *The Fallen Leaves* (1879), a book which, in the words of one character, tells the stories of women like Miss Mellicent, "people who have drawn blanks in the lottery of life—the people who have toiled hard after happiness, and have gathered nothing but disappointment and sorrow; the friendless and the lonely, the wounded and the lost" (29). Filling the seemingly neutral space of the "lottery of life" with a politicized critique, though, *The Moonstone* extends its project toward an interrogation of structural inequalities in the law that will always see the socially disadvantaged pay more dearly for their mistakes. As Betteredge comments on Rosanna's former life, "Rosanna Spearman had been a thief, and not being of the sort that get up Companies in the City, and rob from thousands, instead of only robbing from one, the law laid hold of her, and the prison and the reformatory followed the lead of the law" (Collins, *Moonstone* 54). The text here voices a critique of the invisibility of white-collar crime and the silent collusion between big business and the law, which simultaneously keeps the poor trapped in a vicious circle of crime and punishment.

"Can You Sleep"? | Thwarted Female Convict Reformation and the Complicity of Gentlemen

Reformation itself, rather than the character of reformatory women, carries negative connotations in *The Moonstone*; Betteredge informs the reader that

Rosanna's fellow servants resent her most for her "silent tongue and her solitary ways" (55), arguably virtues learned under reformatory discipline. In her life story addressed to Blake, Rosanna reveals,

> My life was not hard to bear, while I was a thief. It was only when they taught me at the reformatory to feel my own degradation, and to try for better things, that the days grew long and weary. Thoughts of the future forced themselves on me now. I felt the dreadful reproach that honest people—even the kindest of honest people—were to me in themselves. A heart-breaking sensation of loneliness kept with me, go where I might, and do what I might, and see what persons I might. It was my duty, I know, to try and get on with my fellow-servants in my new place. Somehow, I couldn't make friends with them. They looked (or I thought they looked) as if they suspected what I had been. I don't regret, far from it, having been roused to make the effort to be a reformed woman—but, indeed, it was a weary life. You had come across it like a beam of sunshine at first—and then you too failed me. I was mad enough to love you; and I couldn't even attract your notice. There was great misery—there really was great misery in that. (363–64)

Rosanna identifies being made "to feel [her] own degradation" at the reformatory as the trigger for her descent into isolation and misery, *not* her criminal career. With her misshapen shoulder (56), Rosanna symbolically bears the marks of her institutional past on her body, which has *de*formed as much as *re*formed her. Having internalized the reformatory regime's rhetoric of moral corruption, Rosanna confesses to Betteredge that she continues to be haunted by the "stain" on her character (57) and wonders whether "the life here is too quiet and too good for such a woman" as she is (58). Her comment echoes a statement by Captain George Laval Chesterton, an acquaintance of Dickens and governor of Coldbath Fields House of Correction, which provided many of the candidates for Urania Cottage, suggesting that some potential contenders came up with excuses, "shrink[ing] from the irksomeness of quiet domesticity," preferring their old life on the streets (qtd. in P. Collins 98). Rosanna's statement is also reminiscent of Robinson's prison narratives (as discussed in chapter 2), which suggest that reformed prisoners like Jane Cameron feel compelled to escape from their lives as servants because they may find it too "still and quiet" (Robinson, *Memoirs* 2:169). Although this rejection of domesticity thus becomes a trope that risks stereotyping such women to some extent, the authors succeed in providing a literary platform for the difficulties that former prisoners experienced in adapting to gendered expectations.

It could be argued that Collins subsequently displaces Rosanna's critique of the limits of the reformatory (and larger social) system onto her unsuccessful romance with Blake, which is presented as the primary reason for her suicide; however, the novel in fact employs the servant's misplaced infatuation as a vehicle for problematizing how gentlemen are—knowingly or not—implicated in the fates of women like Rosanna, be it simply through these men's inability to take "any notice" of such women (Collins, *Moonstone* 363). The word "notice" is mentioned repeatedly in Rosanna's letter and echoed a little later in Blake's own narrative (374). By emphasizing Blake's fundamental failure to *see* this servant, her feelings and predicament, Collins symbolically forces the reader to look at women like Rosanna and makes her story, as well as Blake's complicity in her death, visible.

Although Rosanna's own letter absolves Blake of responsibility, placing all the blame on herself ("I don't blame *you*, sir. It's my fault—all my fault"; 362), her only friend, Limping Lucy—a strong woman with "a will of her own" (350), who, as Mukherjee notes, displays the same kind of "subaltern defiance" (172) as her namesake Lucy Audley in Mary Elizabeth Braddon's *Lady Audley's Secret* (1862)—pronounces Blake as Rosanna's "murderer" in front of Betteredge (Collins, *Moonstone* 226). Taking Rosanna's unhappy attachment to a gentleman and its consequences as emblematic of the injustice of class relations, Lucy declares, "Where's this gentleman that I mustn't speak of, except with respect? Ha, Mr Betteredge, the day is not far off when the poor will rise against the rich. I pray Heaven they may begin with *him*. I pray Heaven they may begin with *him*" (227). Alongside this vision of class struggle, Lucy places her own homosocial, working-class utopia against Rosanna's unhappy attachment to a wealthy gentleman, rejecting male patronage and imagining herself in the role of sororal provider for her friend:

> I loved her. . . . She had a miserable life, Mr Betteredge—vile people had ill-treated her and led her wrong—and it hadn't spoiled her sweet temper. She was an angel. She might have been happy with me. I had a plan for our going to London together like sisters, and living by our needles. That man came here, and spoilt it all. He bewitched her. Don't tell me he didn't mean it, and didn't know it. . . . I had saved up a little money. I had settled things with father and mother. I meant to take her away from the mortification she was suffering here. We should have had a little lodging in London, and lived together like sisters. (227)

Repeatedly stressing sisterhood, Lucy here and elsewhere acts as a more confident double or alter ego for Rosanna, offering an alternative, less submissive response to the gentleman's conduct and acting on Rosanna's behalf, eventually leading Blake down the path to the Shivering Sands in her friend's footsteps (353). Collins evokes parallels between the two working-class women on a number of occasions—both are marked as different through physical disability;[25] both are described as ghostlike in Blake's accounts. Rosanna surprises Blake at the billiard table as she unexpectedly appears next to him "like a ghost," anxious to speak (178). After Rosanna's suicide, as the gentleman enters the Yollands' cottage to obtain from Lucy the dead woman's letter, he perceives Lucy this way: "the apparition at the open door, with a letter in its hand, beckoning me out!" (352). When Blake reaches the beach by himself to search for Rosanna's box, he is shaken by fear of "some spirit of terror" underneath the Sand and the possibility of encountering the servant's ghost: "In this position, my face was within a few feet of the surface of the quicksand. The sight of it so near me, still disturbed at intervals by its hideous shivering fit, shook my nerves for the moment. A horrible fancy that the dead woman might appear on the scene of her suicide, to assist my search—an unutterable dread of seeing her rise through the heavy surface of the sand, and point to the place—forced itself into my mind, and turned me cold in the warm sunlight" (357). Similar to other artists in the 1860s who deployed gothic ghost images to alert their audiences to wealthy women's complicity in the deaths of needlewomen, Collins uses the language of the supernatural to symbolize Blake's inability to accept the "real" existence of women like Rosanna and his submerged, unacknowledged share in Rosanna's death, which comes to haunt him.[26] Blake's desperate effort to sever existing ties with Rosanna is reinforced in his refusal to finish reading her confessional letter—a task he assigns to the deceased's fellow servant and paternal sympathizer Betteredge. Whereas Anthea Trodd argues that this gesture of "reject[ing] the servant narratives" allows Collins to reaffirm Blake's "fitness as hero[]" (85), this incident, together with the use of gothic imagery, can instead be read as the author's vehicle for problematizing wealthy men's attempts to absolve themselves of any connection with the fates of lower-class women.

Owing to the "dialogical" structure of the narrative as a whole—a series of witness statements, which often challenge one another, and the absence of an overarching authoritative narrative voice—opposing responses to Blake's share in Rosanna's fate are presented alongside one another, leaving the reader at liberty to assess their validity.[27] Betteredge, indeed, imagines the reader in the role of "a Judge on the bench" (Collins, *Moonstone* 233). When Lucy finally confronts Blake after Rosanna's death—"Can you sleep? . . . When you see a poor girl in service, do you feel no remorse?" (353)—the gentleman dismisses as insanity Lucy's outrage in response to his negative reply: "The one interpretation that I could put on her conduct has, no doubt, been anticipated by everybody. I could only suppose that she was mad" (353). Blake's overly anxious rejection of Lucy's anger challenges readers to consider whether they share this supposedly "inevitable conclusion" (354). Just as Braddon forces her readers to consider whether Lucy Audley's desire to better herself and to do away with her first husband is a rational, rather than irrational, response to this husband's abandonment of her, Collins provokes his audience into debating whether Limping Lucy's language is not so much madness as an impassioned, yet *reasoned*, reflection on Blake's apparent lack of consideration for her friend and, by implication, other female servants, disabled women, or former prisoners.[28]

Collins's depiction of Rosanna and Blake—who stand as representatives for their respective class—draws on other codes that allow the author to interrogate class relations and questions of guilt and responsibility. Rosanna traces her career in thieving to her family history, offering a concise causal chain of events as explanation to Blake: "I was put in the prison, because I was a thief. I was a thief, because my mother went on the streets when I was quite a little girl. My mother went on the streets, because the gentleman who was my father deserted her" (362). Identifying her gentleman father as the origin of moral corruption and the mother's and daughter's descent into crime, Rosanna concludes, "There is no need to tell such a common story as this, at any length. It is told quite often enough in the newspapers" (362). This reference to media reportage—a gesture familiar across the genre of sensation fiction—allows Collins to evoke proximity to the reader's own historical moment and underscores the authenticity of Rosanna's story as that of an everywoman who was failed by her family and society alike, with her gentleman father's irresponsibility as the ultimate cause of her damaged life.

As Mukherjee has noted, Collins's novel establishes analogies between different groups of the marginalized—the Indians, Rosanna, and Jennings—and suggests that the "roots" of their supposed deviance "lie in the common oppressive presence of the British genteel class" (185). But by deploying codes of illicit sexuality throughout the novel, Collins also subtly promotes a gendered critique of class relations and the social production of female criminality. He insinuates particularly evocative links between the responsibility of Rosanna's father for the Spearman women's criminal careers and Blake's implication in Rosanna's fate, which comes to stand in for other relationships between gentlemen and women who are not their wives. Betteredge speculates on Blake's involvement with "some unmentionable woman" in continental Europe (Collins, *Moonstone* 48), hinting at an illegitimate sexual union paralleling the one that resulted in Rosanna's birth. Betteredge's account of Blake's father as a man who had "had the misfortune to be next heir to a Dukedom, and not to be able to prove it" (46) equally evokes a coded theme of illegitimacy attached to the young man. The fraudulent gentleman Godfrey Ablewhite, too, is revealed to have led a secret life, "with a villa in the suburbs which was not taken in his own name, and with a lady in a villa, who was not taken in his own name, either" (506). Blake reads "French novels" (455)—representative of sexual irregularity—while his illicit nightly excursion into Rachel's boudoir, resulting in the loss of her "Diamond" and a stain on his nightgown, in itself serves as a cryptic erotic reference, with a secret sexual encounter between Rachel and Blake also being Rosanna's initial interpretation of the soiled garment (366).

By falling in love with a gentleman, Rosanna tragically reenacts aspects of her own mother's life; the "pleasure" (374) she experiences wearing Blake's nightgown underlines the transgressive nature of her cross-class desire. Although Blake never suspects "the girl's fancy for him," Sergeant Cuff cynically suspects that "he would have found it out fast enough if she had been nice-looking" (151). Blake's lack of interest in the servant, then, is portrayed as incidental, a result of her unattractiveness, rather than of his superior morals. Combined with the symbolic use of drowning in the Shivering Sands as Rosanna's choice of death—a trope typically associated with sexually fallen women—Collins's novel demarcates Blake as implied, if not actual, perpetrator, who shares his class of men's responsibility in this woman's "crime" of suicide, a death that comes to signify the sacrifices that working-class women in general make for men like Blake.[29] That the relationships between gentlemen and working-class women might have been at the forefront of Collins's mind at this moment is particularly plausible considering his own long-term commitment to Martha Rudd, his mother's housemaid, in the wake of his mother's death, events which coincided with the production of *The Moonstone*.[30]

Finally, the anthropomorphic representation of the quicksand, Rosanna's grave, functions as a metaphor for the servant class's, and former prisoners', futile attempts at social ascent, as Rosanna suggests: "It looks as if it had hundreds of suffocating people under it—all struggling to get to the surface, and all sinking lower and lower in the dreadful deeps!" (58). Betteredge's own image of the sand similarly suggests its association with the agonized facial features of Rosanna and other servant girls: "The broad brown face of it heaved slowly, and then dimpled and quivered all over" (58).[31] As a dismayed Betteredge notes, the fact that Rosanna, "a young woman of five-and-twenty" (58), elects this "lonesome and . . . horrid retreat" (56) as her "favourite walk" (56) and "grave" (58) once more evokes the limitations of a reformatory system that does not go hand in hand with larger social transformations and fails to offer a viable future to former prisoners like Rosanna.

Collins, through his representation of Rosanna and her story, turns a socially disadvantaged woman, a marginal character in the Verinder household, and a seemingly peripheral figure in the novel into a key player, just as Eliot made Hetty's confession the kernel of her novel. As an anonymous reviewer of *The Moonstone* suggested in the *Times*, Rosanna is a character "upon which Mr. Collins has perhaps bestowed peculiar pains" ("Moonstone"). It is Rosanna's voice that discloses the first mystery pertaining to the diamond's disappearance to the reader. According to Jenny Bourne Taylor, alongside other marginal texts such as the Indian frame narrative, Rosanna's letter "become[s] central by *remaining* peripheral" (180). By implying that "the more embedded and qualified a testimony, the stronger its significance becomes," the novelist subtly provokes a "reversal of narrative authority" (180). Collins provides a clue to this hidden agenda of his in another peripheral text, his preface to the first edition of *The Moonstone*, in which he writes, "In some of my former novels, the object proposed has been to trace the influence of circumstances upon character. In the present story I have reversed the process. The attempt made, here, is to trace the influence of character on circumstances. The conduct pursued, under a sudden emergency, by a young girl, supplies the foundation on which I have built this book" (27). It would be easy enough to read the author's reference to the "young girl" who provides motive and "foundation" for his novel as being to Rachel Verinder. But could we not imagine that Collins might be speaking about Rosanna Spearman here? With this preface, the author issues an implicit warning to readers that the "circumstances" of a prior conviction for theft must not prejudice them against a servant's "character." Rosanna's character is, instead, shown to be one of immense loyalty, as she is eager to shelter the gentleman culprit from harm. It is as if Collins, by leaving his reference to "a young girl" ambiguous, challenges his readers once more to avoid falling into Blake's trap of failing to "notice" her (363).

Conclusion

Despite Limping Lucy's evocation of an impending revolution—aligning her with the upheavals sweeping across Europe in 1848 (the year when the narrative's actions are set)—the social order is reestablished at the end of *The Moonstone*. Eclipsing the now-deceased Rosanna's illicit desire for Blake and jealousy toward Rachel, the wealthy young couple are ultimately united in marriage. Akin to Eliot's exploration of the impossibility of Hetty and Arthur's cross-class union in *Adam Bede*, *The Moonstone* as a whole realistically suggests that, although Rosanna may have seen Blake as "a prince in a fairy-story" (Collins, *Moonstone* 362), no fairy-tale ending is possible for women like her—yet. It was thirteen years later before fellow writer Robinson conceived of a happy ending for the reformed prisoner Daisy March, with one significant difference, however—unlike Rosanna (and Hetty), Daisy chooses wisely by becoming engaged to an earnest, hardworking farmer, rather than reaching beyond her station.[32]

Similar to *Adam Bede*, the ideological limitations of the closure of *The Moonstone*'s ending are arguably undercut by Collins's critical interrogations elsewhere in the text. Nayder's advice, drawing on Paul Cantor's work on nineteenth-century authors, is useful here, as it warns against an over-emphasis on "what writers fail to achieve rather than what they manage to accomplish" (214). The happy ending for Rachel and Franklin is haunted by unsettling undercurrents that point to the implication of the wealthy in Rosanna's demise, most forcefully echoed in Limping Lucy's statements, just as *Adam Bede*'s ending is overshadowed by the account of Hetty's fate.

Regardless of Eliot's reluctance to present her novel as an overtly feminist treatise on fallen women, the ultimate containment of Dinah's ambitions as a preacher in marriage, and the use of literary convention to seal Hetty's death, the text's project is protofeminist in several ways; through Dinah's successful prison ministry, Eliot provides an early record of women's achievements in the tradition of prison visiting, while affirming working-class women's solidarity in the prison scene. Conversely, by creating a narrative space for Hetty's story, the novelist invites her readers to sympathize with, and critically assess, the offender's motivations for the infanticide, partially driven by fear of her community's contempt. The novel thus also hints at society's unacknowledged collective share in women's crimes. Similarly, Collins implicitly problematizes gentlemen's roles in the history of female criminality, while—through the Lucy-Rosanna-Betteredge triad—celebrating laboring-class cohesion. The search for Rosanna's confessional letter, which is hidden in the quicksand, functions metaphorically, as it signals the difficulties in retrieving former convicts' voices. Like Robinson's prison tales, Eliot's and Collins's narratives ensure that such women's stories continue to be commemorated in their country's collective memory.

CHAPTER 4

"A Clamorous Multitude and a Silent Prisoner"

Women's Rights, Spiritualism, and Public
Speech in Susan Willis Fletcher's *Twelve
Months in an English Prison*

While mid-Victorian novelists such as George Eliot and Wilkie Collins
used embedded narratives of female offenders to explore these women's
subjectivities and the social conditions surrounding their crimes and punishment, middle-class women who had come into conflict with the law
began to formulate their own life narratives in the final third of the century.
As this chapter and the following one will illustrate, these texts, through
their distinctive exploration of gender, class, and otherness, marked an implicit contrast to male-authored middle-class convict memoirs at the time
and anticipated some of the concerns of suffragette prisoners who began to
express more self-consciously feminist critiques a few years later.

Susan Willis Fletcher, an American spiritualist convicted of gaining possession of property through false pretenses, was imprisoned for one year,
following her trial at the Old Bailey in London in April 1881, which became
a cause célèbre. The case excited the English press: the *Times* printed regular, detailed transcripts throughout the trial; other newspapers such as the
Pall Mall Gazette included shorter accounts; and spiritualist journals and
smaller, local papers such as the London-based *County Gentleman: Sporting
Gazette and Agricultural Journal* and the *Owl* of Birmingham reported on it.[1]
The trial also divided the spiritualist community in America and Britain.[2]

Although Fletcher's postrelease narrative *Twelve Months in an English
Prison* (1884), by its title, categorizes itself as a prison autobiography, it
takes an eclectic approach, focusing on the legal proceedings and her life
story as a whole, while also constructing an exculpatory narrative for spiritualism. The sections concerned with her actual incarceration are relatively

short, with large parts of her autobiography dealing with the supposed existence of otherworldly phenomena. A reading of this text only makes sense within the broader context of mid- to late nineteenth-century spiritualism, since the author's conviction for fraud and her profession as a spiritualist are inextricably linked. I argue that it is in fact the socially progressive environment of early spiritualism, which had long provided a platform for female agency, that inspired this ex-prisoner to claim the right to tell her side of the story to the public.

According to Sidonie Smith, the woman autobiographer, always writing from the margins of her culture, "greets, identifies with, rebels against, cannibalizes, and ultimately transforms public forms of selfhood" (175). Fletcher grapples in her autobiography with the "public forms of selfhood" assigned to her as a female spiritualist and convicted prisoner. *Twelve Months* illustrates how the generic and social spaces of spiritualist autobiography, female prison autobiography, and feminism, which are usually considered in isolation from one another, created a new joint platform for women's public speech that anticipated the agenda of Edwardian suffragettes.

Susan Fletcher; her husband, John William Fletcher; and their friend Francis Morton, a fellow American and legal counselor, were accused of fraud and conspiracy to lure their English client and companion, Juliet Anne Theodora Heurtley Hart-Davies, into parting with her jewelry and other property, with the help of messages purporting to come from Hart-Davies's dead mother. Hart-Davies initiated legal action while traveling with the Fletchers in the United States. Encouragement came from mesmeric healer Dr. James McGeary (alias "Dr. Mack"), who convinced Hart-Davies that she had been defrauded.[3] The Fletchers were initially confronted with charges of larceny in Boston; Susan spent a night in jail, before reaching a settlement in court. When the couple learned about similar accusations in England, Susan decided to travel and face charges, leaving her husband behind, allegedly on account of his ill health. She was arrested upon arrival of the steamer and brought before Magistrate Flowers at Bow Street Police Court in London on 3 December 1880. After several hearings, the case was moved to the Central Criminal Court, the Old Bailey, where Judge Hawkins presided over the trial, which lasted one week, concluding with Fletcher's conviction on 12 April 1881. Fletcher's advocates applied for a summons against Hart-Davies on account of perjury after the spiritualist's conviction, but the application was eventually rejected.[4]

Following Fletcher's release in March 1882, *Twelve Months* was published in Boston, New York, and London two years later.[5] Its parent publishing house was Boston-based Lee and Shepard, well known for its populist titles targeted at a mass market of "average" readers in New England (Kilgour v). The company's miscellaneous fiction and nonfiction catalogue in the early 1880s included titles on women's rights and, between 1884 and 1886, also demonstrated an increasing interest in spiritualism and socialism.[6] Accordinging to Raymond Kilgour, the publishers were happy to support controversial topics, radical social and political causes, with a marked "desire for public service" rather than simply financial profit (v, 205). Yet *Twelve Months*, with its combination of prison memoir and defense of spiritualism, was a "salable novelty" (Kilgour 217), which, as Bridget Bennett notes, also drew on other formal conventions, including moral fable, domestic drama, and spiritualist autobiography, although the book "reads initially like a relatively stylised account of a conversion narrative (in this case, of a conversion to a belief in spiritualism)" (3–4).

The book received brief mentions in a number of English journals targeted at an educated readership, although it appears to have been relatively unknown beyond spiritualist circles. A brief survey of books on prison life in the *Academy* in 1897 labeled Fletcher's text "a curious volume" which "few seem to know" even thirteen years after its publication (R.).[7] Longer contemporaneous responses in both England and the United States suggest that the autobiography was not particularly well received. The Boston-based *Literary World* dedicated a leading review to *Twelve Months*, calling it "a disreputable book" and wondering why a "reputable" publisher such as Lee and Shepard had agreed to print it, although the reviewer admitted that the chapters dealing with prison life had "some interest" ("Mrs. Fletcher's Story"). With evident disgust at the "public repetition of [the court case] in detail" and the "unsavoury story" hidden behind an "innocently sounding title," the periodical dismissed Fletcher's text as a thinly disguised attempt "to obtain a revision of sentence" and "of feeding the common appetite for literature of the police gazette order." Referencing the New York–based *National Police Gazette*, the *Literary World* thus associated Fletcher's autobiography with a popular, mostly working-class, readership trained to crave sensationalist crime reporting by a tabloid which often featured socially marginal figures in conflict with authority, including strong, confident women.[8]

In a bitterly sarcastic multipage review in an 1888 edition of London's *Time*, Graham Everitt saw *Twelve Months* as emblematic of an American lack of sophistication and "the trash which is permitted to issue from American presses" (88), calling the autobiography "a wild, ungrammatical, rhapsodical book" (77) that had to be dismissed as a "preposterous farrago of nonsense" (88). Everitt took the publication as an occasion for pursuing his vendetta against American spiritualism, framing his reading with a juxtaposition of English common sense against American credulity and the "moral monstrosities" (76) promoted by religious sects. In spite of Fletcher's use of recognizable stylistic conventions, her themes and approach, as Bennett points out, "go[] wholly against the notion of conventional middle-class female autobiography" (3), which may have been another reason why readers such as Everitt were troubled by it. Aside from spiritualist phenomena, Fletcher's book contained many elements that would have been familiar to readers of mid-Victorian sensation novels, including sexual jealousy and intrigue, fraud, and wrongful incarceration.

Although Everitt focused on the book's spiritualist rhetoric, Fletcher's narrative is also pitched as a contribution to debates around prison and law reform; chapter 44 is titled "A Plea for Prison-Reform"; the appendix contains material on the question of "What Prisons Are, and What They Might Be." The short preface by the publishers stresses this aspect, presenting the text—no doubt for commercial as much as for humanitarian reasons—as a contribution to the contemporaneous debates around "outcast London" and efforts for "the restoration of fallen women," many of whom were imprisoned alongside Fletcher (iii–iv). The *Pall Mall Gazette*, under W. T. Stead's editorship, had taken up the theme of Andrew Mearns's *The Bitter Cry of Outcast London: An Inquiry into the Condition of the Abject Poor* (1883), running a series of articles in October 1883, the year before Fletcher's text appeared. *Twelve Months'* publishing context and the publishers' reference to "outcast London" immediately locate Fletcher within a wider framework of Anglo-American liberal reformism. As this chapter will illustrate, the book contributes to emerging feminist critiques of the criminal justice system, as well as the media.

"Woman's Wrongs" | Early Life and Initiation into Spiritualism

Fletcher was born in the manufacturing town of Lowell, Massachusetts, into a family of "religious people" (Baptists). Anxious to establish a reputable pedigree from the start, she describes her father, Alvah H. Webster, as "one of the numerous New-England family of Websters, which has produced a famous lawyer and statesman and a great lexicographer" (Fletcher 3). That her father was not a professional himself is only hinted at in her comment that he went to California around 1850 to try and make a fortune in the gold fields. The writer's efforts to claim a respectable upbringing did little for contemporaneous reviewers such as Everitt, though, who insinuated that Fletcher came from an "uneducated class of women" (78). Fletcher's association with spiritualism already began in the month of her birth, in March 1848, when the Rochester rappings in upstate New York marked the formal beginning of American spiritualism.[9] The same year also saw the inauguration of the American women's rights movement with the Seneca Falls convention, only a few miles from Rochester. Spatially and conceptually, these two movements were closely linked from the start, and although not all women's rights campaigners identified as spiritualists, most spiritualists promoted women's rights (Braude 3, 129).[10] Conversely, prominent feminists such as Susan B. Anthony and Elizabeth Cady Stanton, who were not spiritualists, stressed the political affinities between the two causes. Their *History of Woman Suffrage*, written in the 1880s, praised spiritualism's support of women's suffrage and its promotion of women as public speakers (R. Moore 84; Braude 2). The linkage between the two movements was further cemented in the public imagination by nineteenth-century novels such as Nathaniel Hawthorne's *The Blithedale Romance* (1852) and Henry James's *The Bostonians* (1886), published on both sides of the Atlantic. *Blithedale Romance*, set in a cooperative community in New England modeled after the real-life Brook Farm and often regarded as an intertext for James's later novel, features the young Priscilla, who performs as a "Veiled Lady," and women's rights advocate Zenobia, who may have been based on feminist writer Margaret Fuller.[11] James's character Verena Tarrant, a medium, is described as "a high-class speaker" (48) who delivers trance speeches on women's rights.

Research on spiritualism has demonstrated that the movement was home to a broad spectrum of viewpoints, even if it generally aligned itself with progressive causes such as women's rights, abolitionism, Fourierism, and prison and health reform (R. Moore 70–71, 117; Braude 7). Although spiritualism offered women many opportunities for empowerment and involvement in the public sphere, its relationship with nineteenth-century gender ideology was at times ambivalent. R. Laurence Moore has shown that many "female mediums did not reject the Victorian concept of womanhood in its entirety" and were in fact "extremely reluctant to accept personal responsibility for [their] vocational voice" (106), which they attributed to spirit controls that forced these actions onto them. Women's spiritualism and mediumship simultaneously built on and subverted traditional gender stereotypes by celebrating women's supposed passivity as a virtue that made them particularly susceptible to spirit messages (Braude 161; A. Owen). In spite of this insistence on the medium's feminine passivity, mediumship began to be associated with female insubordination in the form of sexual immorality, infidelity, divorce, and remarriage (R. Moore 117).[12] Spiritualism's advocacy of "free love" meant that many people regarded the movement as a threat to the family and social structure, despite the fact that for most of its supporters, "free love" signified not promiscuity but simply consensual sex as an antithesis to coercive sexual relations within the supposedly respectable institution of marriage (Braude 128–29).

Spiritualism's impact as a progressive social force declined in the 1870s, accompanied by new medical theories on both sides of the Atlantic that regarded mediumship as pathological and that established links between a supposedly defective female physique, spiritualism, and rebellion against traditional gender roles.[13] In this climate, mediumship in the 1870s and 1880s "ceased to be a source of power for women" (Braude 176) and increasingly emphasized passive roles in which, rather than giving public speeches, mediums were blindfolded or gagged and offered magic performances with materializations of flowers or white doves, often under the supervision of male business associates. In this context, Fletcher's publication can also be interpreted as an attempt to (re)claim an alternative form of public speech after other channels within her profession of spiritualism had closed for her—Fletcher too worked as a flower medium in the early 1870s (*Twelve Months* 33)—because of both her notoriety and a larger trend within spiritualism that increasingly eroded opportunities for women's public speaking.

Fletcher's personal and professional history represents all the developments just described. By her own account, she discovered a vocation to "preach" early on and nurtured it, encouraged by her grandfather. Even as a young girl, she felt a longing for public recognition: "When about seven years old, walking alone in the fields one day, I climbed upon a rock for my pulpit, and began to preach; and it seemed to me that when I looked up into the trees I saw them full of hands applauding me" (*Twelve Months* 5). Her craving for public speaking, and this example of an early performance, strikingly contrast with the silence imposed on her during her trial and imprisonment and give an indication of why this highly articulate woman was keen to publish the story of her life, conviction, and imprisonment in a tome amounting to, with appendices, just under five hundred pages.

Fletcher pursued her talent and became known as a medium in Lawrence, Massachusetts, where the family had moved; from about the age of twelve, she hosted séances at home. Having gained notoriety at such a young age, she describes her early sense of being a social outcast, who was stared at in the streets and "pointed at as a witch" (15). The trope of witchcraft—with particularly troubling and evocative connotations in Fletcher's birth state, Massachusetts, home of the Salem witch trials—recurs throughout her story, since one of the initial charges against her (later dismissed by the judge) was the pretense of witchcraft and sorcery. Even after the witchcraft charge was formally abandoned, Fletcher attributes her final condemnation to "the old anti-witchcraft feeling" (162), employing the witch label tactically to place her own conviction into a wider social history and to stress her status as a wrongly persecuted woman. The series of references associating Fletcher with the figure of the witch includes an early episode when her local minister warned the young girl, who had claimed to have seen the spirits of two "beautiful ladies" in her Baptist church, to relinquish this "witchery" (11). Being confronted with Fletcher's personality and imagination, members of the public and male authority figures represented by church and prosecution evidently drew on the image of the witch, traditionally seen as a "strong, independently-minded" woman who posed a threat to the social order because of her rejection of feminine conduct and her use of "the power of words" (Larner 84, 87). Late nineteenth-century commentators continued to evoke the witchcraft trope; Dr. F. C. Hake in 1889 called hypnotism "the old witchcraft restored, renovated, and adapted" (qtd. in Pearsall 17), and Henry James in *The Bostonians* (1886) has one character compare a meeting of mediums and radicals to "a rendezvous of witches on the Brocken" (3).

This persisting language of witchcraft illustrates how older models of explaining female deviance from gendered norms of behavior continued to coexist with new discourses, such as medicine, which located such conduct in supposedly physical disorders. The fact that the judge in Fletcher's trial dismissed the initial charge of witchcraft as "bad," while refraining from overt endorsements of medicalized models during his summing up, suggests not only that the older paradigm was increasingly superseded but also that late nineteenth-century court trials were a space of contestation between different models of knowledge production—religion and the secular domains of medicine and law.[14] Fletcher is careful in her autobiography to both instrumentalize and reject the image of the witch, retaining its symbolic value to signal misunderstood femininity, while tempering any suspicion of undue female powers with familiar spiritualist tropes of feminine passivity. For instance, she insists that, as a teenager, she developed into a "writing as well as a trance medium" by being "controlled to write unconsciously, without [her] own volition" (15). At times, Fletcher, be it inadvertently or tongue-in-cheek, uses iconography that continues to associate her with witchery, writing about a black cat that came to her cell at the Boston jail, sharing her dinner and bed (120).

Fletcher's career is a fascinating example of how nineteenth-century women's lives were caught between the traditional constraints of womanhood and aspirations for new public roles. Still under the influence of her parents during her teenage years, Fletcher was married, at age fourteen, to her father's business assistant William M. Willis, who also happened to be the son of her father's medium. Her autobiography offers only a coded glimpse of the effects of such an early union: "Of marriage and all that belongs to it, no child was ever in more profound ignorance" (16). This arranged marriage provokes speculation of whether mother-in-law and parents might have seen profitable business opportunities in the match, given that the girl had already demonstrated a gift for drawing in the crowds to her séances. Although Fletcher reports that her spirit visions ceased at the beginning of her marriage, she developed into a public medium at the age of fifteen and began to deliver trance lectures, speaking "with great eloquence and power" on the question of "Woman's Rights" in a state of unconsciousness (19). Describing her reaction to the content of her speeches after hearing about it from an admirer, Fletcher writes,

> I was deeply disgusted; because I did not believe in woman's rights, nor care of woman's wrongs, and I did not wish to speak in public. I said it was all the work of the Devil, and passionately declared that I would have no more to do with it.
>
> I busied myself with my domestic and maternal duties, and in my eighteenth year gave birth to my second child. (19)

This public renunciation of feminism, followed by a professed devotion to conventional feminine duties of domesticity, dating back to the early 1860s but apparently endorsed by the author in 1884, is oddly incongruous with spiritualism's close connection with women's rights discourse and the positions expressed by the writer elsewhere in the text. Fletcher's public disavowal almost certainly serves as a tactical device, disassociating her from her movement's reputation for scandalous sexual politics at the time of publication, when the progressive agendas of spiritualism had already lost some of their impact and spiritualists were faced with considerable cultural opposition. Fletcher's refutation simultaneously strengthened the image of respectable femininity that she strove to construct for herself throughout the narrative, in stark contrast to the damaging publicity she had received during the trial.

Unlike the antifeminist rhetoric in the preceding passage, the autobiography as a whole offers evidence that the spiritualist made several unconventional choices, rather than focusing on "domestic and maternal duties," although she repeatedly delivers justifications that make her actions seem either inevitable or traditional. After the death of her second child, when Fletcher is eighteen years old, she succumbs to what she describes as the requests of a female spirit to give up her resistance to spiritualist work. This renewed turn to spiritualism is followed by a divorce from her husband, who had become an alcoholic. Fletcher's language is again coded here but suggests that she might have been the victim of physical and/or sexual abuse: "I suffered from wrongs I do not wish to dwell upon, and had an experience which made me sympathize with every woman who suffers" (23–24). The author's choice of words revises her previous renunciation of an interest in "woman's rights, nor . . . wrongs" and replaces it with a declaration of female solidarity that implicitly aligns her with the feminist cause and with the titles of treatises such as fellow American Gail Hamilton's *Woman's Wrongs* (1868), a reflection on free will and marriage in response to the Reverend John Todd's conservative *Woman's Rights* (1867).[15]

After Fletcher gained "legal emancipation," she gave "inspirational addresses" across New England for several years, before meeting her future husband, John William Fletcher, also a native of Massachusetts, a medium and trance speaker, and four years her junior (24).[16] Fletcher dissolves her engagement to another man after John William's Native American spirit guide "Winona" predicts she will marry a spiritualist instead, and her fiancé asks her to give up public speaking and to "take [her] proper place in society" after their marriage (26). Defying gender conventions, Susan and John William Fletcher embarked on a relationship that also served as a professional partnership, like the marriages of other American progressives such as Thomas Low and Mary Sargeant Gove Nichols, who became the Fletchers' friends in London later on.[17]

Spiritualist Partnership, "Free Love," and Relocation to England

If we believe the portrayal of the Fletchers' relationship by Susan Elizabeth Gay, an English friend and advocate of the couple, Susan was the stronger of the two, with the sickly John William relying on his wife's support and guidance (Gay, *John William Fletcher* 11–12). The Fletchers attended US-spiritualist camp meetings at Silver Lake and Lake Pleasant, where they both earned money by offering séances; in the early 1870s, they moved to Boston, where they became associated with the spiritualist paper the *Banner of Light* (Fletcher 29, 32). The *Banner* was a journal with a history of advocacy for women's rights and in 1873 even issued a suffrage petition for readers to cut out and send to legislators (Braude 79, 196). Susan's autobiography also suggests that she was acquainted with other well-known figures in spiritualist circles, including the test medium Maggie Folsom; Helena Blavatsky, one of the founders of the Theosophical Society; and Mary Baker Thayer, the "celebrated flower medium" (Fletcher 33, 36, 38).

Information on the exact dates and circumstances of the Fletchers' move to London is contradictory, but they both appear to have settled there by the summer of 1877, taking up residence in Bloomsbury (Fletcher 53).[18] American spiritualists, and the Fletchers more specifically, already had a reputation in British circles long before their arrival in the capital. John William's biographer Gay speaks of an antipathy toward American mediums, who were seen by some British spiritualists to "have ruined the cause" in England (*John William Fletcher* 39). She complains that William Harrison, the editor of the English paper the *Spiritualist*, was against the Fletchers from the start (40–41). Anti-spiritualist publications such as psychiatrist L. S. Forbes Winslow's *Spiritualistic Madness* (1876) blamed Americans for the spread of spiritualism in the first place. John Burns, editor of the influential *Medium*, later *Medium and Daybreak*, gave the Fletchers a particularly cold welcome because of the association of American spiritualists with sexual license, although he was willing to pass on some contacts to them (Barrow 131). Fletcher accuses Burns in her autobiography of "slanders" because he called her "'the champion of Mrs. Woodhull' and of 'Free Love'" (97).[19] Gay's account suggests, however, that Susan indeed actively promoted free love and thereby provoked a substantial amount of criticism in Britain, although the biographer insists that this was a "much-misunderstood doctrine" which did not involve "freedom of license, but of liberty" and "simply means harmonious instead of inharmonious marriage" (*John William Fletcher* 20).

The Fletchers' move coincided with a difficult phase for spiritualists, who increasingly found themselves faced with accusations of fraud after high-profile court cases against mediums such as Daniel Dunglas Home in 1868 and Henry Slade in 1876.[20] Defying all difficulties, the Fletchers set up their spiritualist practice, with Susan confining herself to private séances with "intimate friends" (Fletcher 56). She anxiously distanced herself from the suspicion of professional mediumship by insisting, "Only once had I spoken in public,—at the celebration of the Anniversary of Spiritualism at the Cavendish Rooms, April 2, 1879" (56). John William gave both private séances and public lectures, ranging from religion and spiritualism to the emancipation of slaves in the US South to prison reform and women's rights, including an attack on conventional marriage as an objectionable "commercial arrangement" (Gay, *John William Fletcher* 266).[21]

Even if Susan's writing is careful not to promote causes such as women's rights explicitly, all this contextual evidence suggests that the Fletchers embraced, were known in, and were linked in the public mind with progressive circles and attitudes. One of their most vocal supporters was the American doctor Thomas Low Nichols, renowned for his advocacy of unconventional ideas. Nichols served as Susan's bail and character witness during her trial and, after the conclusion of the case, circulated his *Memorial to the Home Secretary in Behalf of Mrs. Susan Willis Fletcher*, challenging the guilty verdict and providing a long list of accompanying documents as further evidence (Susan herself complained that Home Secretary William Harcourt—branded by *Punch* as the "Never-at-home-Secretary"— did not even read these testimonies; Fletcher 398).[22] Five years after the Fletcher case, some of Nichols's work rose to new and questionable fame, when during the Adelaide Bartlett murder trial in 1886, Bartlett and her deceased husband were revealed to have owned a copy of his *Esoteric Anthropology*, which dealt with birth control. Cementing already-existing linkages in the Victorian imagination between the transgression of gender or sexual norms and female lawbreaking—what twentieth-century feminist criminologists came to call double deviance—the presiding judge branded this kind of literature a corrupting influence on women.[23]

In campaigning on behalf of Fletcher, Nichols was perhaps partially driven by his own experience of four months' imprisonment for libel as a young editor in upstate New York in 1839, an experience he had described in his *Journal in Jail* (1840).[24] In turn, Fletcher dedicated her autobiography to Thomas and his wife, Mary Sargeant Gove Nichols, alongside her own husband and son. The Nicholses were a generation older than the Fletchers and had lived in England since the beginning of the Civil War.[25] The Nicholses' early friends in England included reformers William and Mary Howitt and Charles Dickens, and they were well established in literary circles (Silver-Isenstadt 236). It seems likely that the Nicholses introduced the Fletchers to some of their acquaintances. The older couple had built an eclectic reputation as medical practitioners and prolific writers on women's history, marriage, religion, health, and dress reform.[26] In mid-1850s America, Thomas Nichols had lectured on the "free love" doctrine within spiritualism.[27] Although the Nicholses had formally forsaken spiritualist and Fourierist ideals in favor of a conversion to Catholicism, they remained committed to social reform, including women's rights, found consolation in spirit visits from their deceased daughter years after they had formally changed their faith, and continued to participate in séances, including one with Susan Fletcher after her release (Silver-Isenstadt 238; Gay, *Spiritualistic Sanity* 18–19; Fletcher 413, 415).

Aside from the death of a child, Mary and Susan shared the experience of an unhappy and abusive first marriage (Mary had written on women's sexual health in this context). The intimate bonds between the Fletchers and the Nicholses are underlined by the fact that Mary regarded Susan, who was only two years older than her own, deceased daughter, as her "heart-child" (Mary Nichols to the Secretary of State, in Nichols, *Memorial* 43); Susan called Mary "Mama" (Susan Fletcher to Mary Nichols, in Nichols, *Memorial* 42).[28] Susan stayed with the Nicholses after being released in March 1882, and it is likely that she wrote her autobiography at that time, possibly with the Nicholses' assistance, which would explain some of the overlap between *Twelve Months* and Thomas Nichols's *Memorial to the Home Secretary*.[29]

Another fervent supporter of Fletcher and character witness was John William's biographer Susan Gay. In the late 1870s, she had contributed two titles on women's role in society and later became a prominent author on feminist issues in theosophical journals (Dixon 157–59). Gay wrote *Spiritualist Sanity* (1879) in response to *Spiritualistic Madness* (1876) by psychiatrist

L. Forbes Winslow; Winslow's book had linked spiritualism with mental illness. Winslow was famous for his role in the Georgina Weldon affair in 1878; he had unsuccessfully attempted to confine the singer-reformer to a lunatic asylum, upon the instigation of her husband. Weldon's interest in spiritualism was used as a reason for her alleged madness, but the woman retaliated by making the story of her narrow escape known across a spectrum of discursive sites, from newspapers via medical journals to music halls, drawing on the educated public's knowledge of melodramatic plots of wrongful confinement in sensation fiction (Walkowitz, *City* 171–72). The Fletchers must have been personally acquainted with Weldon, not only because of the latter's interest in spiritualism but also because John William spoke at Weldon's weekly concerts at Langham Hall and at her Institution for Orphans at Tavistock House (Fletcher 54, 61). Alex Owen notes that Weldon defended John William "in times of trouble" (161).

Susan is likely to have taken inspiration for publishing her own life story from Weldon and explicitly establishes a connection between the two women by remarking that she spent the first night after her conviction in the same Newgate prison cell previously occupied by the singer (Fletcher 319).[30] As Judith Walkowitz has shown in detail, Weldon—like other acquaintances of Fletcher—was associated with radicalism, including dress reform, vegetarianism, and the occult, and had successfully played law and medicine, still firmly in the hands of men, against each other. Praised for her eloquence at the trials, having rejected legal counsel, Weldon became known as the "Portia of the Law Courts" (Walkowitz, *City* 184), conducting several successful lawsuits between 1883 and 1888. She appeared before the same legal authorities as Fletcher—Mr. Flowers at Bow Street Police Court and Judge Hawkins, who had been responsible for Fletcher's case at the Old Bailey (Bennett, Introduction 9).[31] At the time of the publication of Fletcher's autobiography, Weldon had already sued her husband, satirically, for restoration of conjugal rights in 1882, under the brand-new Married Women's Property Act, and had begun proceedings against those who had tried to confine her to a mental institution (Walkowitz, *City* 183).

Weldon, by representing herself in court, did what Fletcher could only dream of, but the singer's presence as a cultural icon and personal acquaintance serves as a significant backdrop for the American's effort to make her voice heard and to challenge public and legal perceptions of herself and spiritualism as a movement. Like Weldon, Fletcher did not take a deliberately "theorized approach to 'female consciousness and identity'" (Walkowitz,

City 188) and extended, rather than rejected, "the boundaries of 'separate spheres'" (180). Although Fletcher did not present *Twelve Months* as an explicitly feminist treatise on women in the context of spiritualism, the media, and the criminal justice system, her text belongs to this broader cultural context of individual activism and collective, progressive reformism that had begun to challenge women's subordinate role in all these arenas. Using gender discourse tactically, Fletcher variously presents herself as the helpless victim of social and judicial conspiracy or the heroic outcast and martyr with philanthropic ideals who willingly sacrifices herself for the movement of spiritualism.

"Punning and Leering" | Fletcher's Critique of the Law Courts

Bennett, the editor of the 2003 edition of Fletcher's *Twelve Months*, contrasts the "liveliness" of the early sections of the book about spiritualism with the remainder of the text, complaining about the tediousness of "the minutiae of the court case" and the lengthy newspaper extracts in the later parts of the volume (5). Yet there is a point to Fletcher's seemingly "obsessive" (Bennett 5) account of the trial details and the way they were reported; these sections are in fact central to understanding the intervention that Fletcher was trying to make with her autobiography. The spiritualist's central complaint against her trial proceedings is that she was not able to give evidence herself, a silencing she found exacerbated by widely negative coverage in the media and her inability to respond to these accusations. The autobiography substitutes for formal evidence in court and constitutes her reply to what she saw as misrepresentations in the press. The act of writing therefore presents a challenge to the institutions of the law and the media.

Fletcher's account emphasizes her lack of input in the Old Bailey trial, which only allowed her to speak four words: "NOT GUILTY, MY LORD!" (190). The transcript of the proceedings, running over twenty pages, is indeed largely a record of the testimony given by Fletcher's opponent, Hart-Davies, who was examined and cross-examined as a witness by the prosecution and the defense (Trial of Susan Willis Fletcher, Old Bailey Proceedings). Fletcher and her supporters argued that the trial was unfair in that it chiefly relied on Hart-Davies's account, which, they claimed, was biased and false. In the trial records, Hart-Davies comes across as an articulate and sharp woman who was not afraid to counter the defense's searching questions with snide remarks. The solicitor Henry James Francis, who appeared as a witness, described Hart-Davies as "very shrewd and sensible" (Trial of Susan Willis Fletcher). It must have stung the rhetorically skilled Fletcher to sit in silence, listening to the lengthy speeches of such a capable opponent, while being prevented from contributing herself. While Fletcher was sent to prison and effectively silenced, Hart-Davies seized the opportunity to further publicize her views shortly after the trial, writing a letter to the editor of the *Times* and refuting allegations that her relationship with John William Fletcher had been one of "unbridled, if not criminal, passion" (Hart-Davies).

Fletcher's autobiography promises to disclose her side of the events leading to her conviction, beginning with a trope common to convict literature, an appeal to, in Judith Scheffler's words, a "presumably more enlightened and just posterity" (Introduction 1):

> All this time *my own story* of the matters connected with my accusation, trial, and imprisonment, *has not been told*. Condemned without a hearing, undefended at my trial, my witnesses uncalled, and, by the criminal procedure then in force, not allowed to tell my own story to the jury, I now, in the first hours of my freedom, after undergoing the full sentence of the law, desire to tell the whole story of my life to all whose love of truth and justice may make them willing to read it. (Fletcher 2, original emphasis)

The fact that she was, as she bemoans repeatedly, "condemned unheard" due to the legal evidence procedure practiced at the time is used as the major justification behind her writing.

Legal evidence reform for criminal trials in nineteenth-century England had shifted verbal agency from the defendant to his or her counsel. After the Prisoners' Counsel Act in 1836, courts trying felonies were usually unable to hear a defense counsel and the defendant at the same time, with very few exceptions.[32] Fletcher complains against this legal convention, noting that "there was no law for it. It was only the convenience of the judges" (185). Having dismissed conventional legal procedure as a matter of "convenience" for paid officials, rather than justice, she sarcastically concludes, "The judges, a year after my conviction, mercifully decided that thenceforth every accused person might exercise the right to tell his own story, even if he had counsel, if dissatisfied with the manner in which his story had been told. Of course this was always the *right* of a prisoner, only the judges had not recognized it, or had trampled it under their feet" (185–86). Beginning in the 1880s, changing legal evidence conventions were ultimately formalized with the Criminal Evidence Act of 1898, when defendants were officially given the option of complementing the formal defense by counsel with evidence as a witness (Schramm, "Is Literature More Ethical than Law?" 429–30, 435; Cowen and Carter 205–18; Cairns 118–19). Such developments came too late for Fletcher's benefit, but she expresses satisfaction that in the future, "prisoners are to be heard" (244). Her discussion here can be seen as an active intervention into the debates preceding the passing of the Criminal Evidence Act.[33]

Before these changes toward the end of the nineteenth century, counsel had to follow rules that prevented them from telling the prisoner's story unless evidence could be provided (Schramm, "Is Literature More Ethical than Law?" 430). This posed a dilemma for indicted spiritualists, who could not offer "hard" proof of the existence of spirit phenomena that was likely to convince the court. Fletcher's defense barrister in fact relinquished his right to call witnesses who would testify to the reality of spiritualism, upon the advice of the judge, who only wanted character witnesses. Fletcher herself regarded this as a "fatal" error arising from the fact that the barrister did not believe in spiritualism himself (Fletcher 222). Her objection to legal procedure was echoed decades later by Charles Kingston in *Judges and the Judged* (1926), one of the very few books mentioning the Fletcher case, in which he regrets that the judge did not allow witnesses such as Alfred Russel Wallace, who had claimed to have found scientific proof for spiritualist phenomena and was willing to testify on the woman's behalf (Kingston, *Judges* 223).

The original change toward more power for legal counsel was in theory designed to help defendants make a more effective case. It was correctly assumed that most prisoners lacked the rhetorical ability to successfully compete against trained professionals, but some defendants who were confident in their use of public speech, such as Fletcher, saw this as a form of unfair disempowerment. Christine Krueger has shown how Victorian women writers Charlotte Elizabeth Tonna, Elizabeth Gaskell, and George Eliot problematized the containment of women's voices in the nineteenth-century legal sphere and wider public realm ("Witnessing Women"). Fletcher's autobiographical account makes a similar intervention, substituting her published autobiographical narrative for the public speech denied her during the trial. Her writing systematically enacts at various points what, from her perspective, should have been an interrogation in court, with opportunities to respond to a series of questions. Her dramatization of such an imagined question-and-answer session emphasizes her act of speaking by repeated use of the word "say": "'But the letters read in court?—what have you to say to them?' . . . 'I have to say that . . .'" (313).

Legal evidence procedures were not the only point of contention for Fletcher, who also criticizes the fact that her case was sent to the Old Bailey in the first place, with implications for testimony: "Had it been a civil suit, I could have been put into the witness-box, and it would have been the oath of one woman against the oath of another. The jury would have heard the story of each, and been able to judge which was the true statement of the case. As I was accused of a crime, no such justice could be allowed to me" (184). Comparing her situation to the case against Daniel Dunglas Home, she notes that although "exactly similar" to hers, his was only a civil suit and Home was not "prosecuted as a criminal, was never a day in prison, and was condemned to no penalty but the restoration of the property" (148). The spiritualist insinuates that since her case was taken up shortly after the introduction of a public prosecutor in England, it was sent to the Central Criminal Court for political reasons and that the government, bolstered by sensationalist reporting in the press, wished to make an example of her, as a potential deterrent to other spiritualists (149–50). Fletcher believed herself at a clear disadvantage in view of a government that, regardless of all expenditure, chose to invest enormous resources into the case "to crush out the heresy of Spiritualism" (188). Conjuring evocative imagery, she depicts the long parchment roll with the indictment, drawn up by "well-paid solicitors of the treasury," as "an immense boa-constrictor" whose unrolling makes "a great impression on the jury, as well as upon the spectators" (174). By stressing the cost of the parchment and the trial to the taxpayer, she uses another strategy to avert attention from the many charges against her and to win readers over to her side. Her metaphors, familiar from popular fiction and contemporaneous news coverage, alternately cast her as a gothic-style damsel in distress, with the forty yards of parchment as "a monster ready to strangle [her] in its coils" (190), and a heroic resistance fighter, who, like the Egyptian "Arabi Pacha" (also known as Ahmed Orabi), struggles against oppression by the British government (188). Ironically, by comparing herself to the Egyptian colonel, she implicitly and perhaps unconsciously marks herself as "other" in a way that connects her with Orientalist stereotypes, including sexual decadence. But the American's metaphor also evokes a discourse against British imperialism, which sets her writing apart from other, English, late nineteenth-century prison autobiographies that, as Frank Lauterbach has argued, typically create a juxtaposition of respectable middle-class prisoner and racial other and participate in the construction of a national "imagined community" in Benedict Anderson's sense (Lauterbach 134). Fletcher, instead, underscores her outsider status as a foreign female, who repeatedly aligns herself with racial others such as Arabs or Native Americans (in the form of spirit guides).[34]

The spiritualist combines her critique of the legal proceedings with a number of personal attacks on legal professionals, such as "the bigoted, partial, and prejudiced Mr. Flowers" (138), who had already sentenced the medium Henry Slade to three months' imprisonment, and Judge Hawkins, who, she claims, bore an "*animus*" against her (224). Aside from her awareness of the damaging effects of legal precedents and an antispiritualist climate, she extends personal criticisms to her own defense lawyer, who, in her view, completely failed to make a good case: "had I gone into the prisoner's dock utterly undefended, or if I had made my own defence, I should not have been in any worse position" (189). Later she concludes, "It may be that no English counsel or barrister could have done more. What I could, and I now see should, have done, was to avail myself of the only opportunity I could have, at that time, to tell my own story, and put my declaration from the prisoner's dock against the oath of Mrs. Hart-Davies in the witness-box" (236). The spiritualist's retrospective attempt to appropriate legal authority extends to her comments on Judge Hawkins also. Criticizing the judge for failing to note that she had traveled to England out of free will, to face the charges against her, Fletcher imagines a role reversal, fancying herself in the judge's position: "Had I been on the bench in gown and wig, and he in the prisoner's dock, I should certainly have mentioned it" (245). The woman's written defense in the form of her autobiography "before a higher court and a larger public" is thus contrasted to official legal procedure, questioning the legitimacy of the court and presenting itself as a more valid method of truth finding (189). Similar to nineteenth-century novelists such as Dickens and Eliot—as outlined by Schramm—Fletcher contrasts the supposedly authentic account of her own innocence with flawed legal representation, criticizing lawyers as mercenary, unethical, and opportunistic: "they expect to be well paid, and are engaged on one side unless they can receive more on the other" (188).[35] Her complaint that only costly barristers were allowed to speak at the Old Bailey, on behalf of the defendant, represents legal evidence reform as a ploy that gave legal professionals both discursive power *and* financial gain, at the expense of defendants who were robbed of "the comforting advantage of telling [their] own story" (189).

Apart from a more general critique of the legal system, Fletcher draws attention to its gendered dimensions, interrogating how gender identity impacts on the law as well as the conduct of the exclusively male legal professionals. Other nineteenth-century prisoners complained of gender prejudice in the criminal justice system; the Frenchwoman Louise Michel (1830–1905), a militant activist during the 1871 Paris Commune, writes in her memoirs, authored during her imprisonment from 1883 to 1886, in the same decade when Fletcher was undergoing her punishment, that "women are not judged the same way men are" (139). Similarly, Fletcher attacks the English male professionals' sexism and obscene language by protesting against "the punning and leering between comfortable, well-fed officials, while the liberty and honor of an unoffending woman were at stake" (203). Sexual innuendos were used throughout the trial by both sides to damage the other party, often drawing on the sexual undercurrents that were known to exist in spiritualist circles. As Owen has shown, physical contact was part of spiritualist healing practice and of séances, where participants would join arms or hands. With reference to the Fletchers, Owen suggests that for "the selected few," their séances might indeed "have provided opportunities which went beyond a little spirit pinching" (219).

Fletcher reprints large parts of the trial records, not always commenting on them, but to the reader, it is evident that during Hart-Davies's cross-examination by the defense lawyer, Addison Q.C., the court audience and legal representatives were greatly entertained by the sexual connotations in the witness's account of a trance session with John William Fletcher: "My hand was in his all the time; and he told me not to take my hand away, as it might bring on serious consequences, and affect his system seriously. [A roar of laughter.] He shivered so much, that I had to hold on tightly to keep hold of his hand. MR. ADDISON.—Then, you 'shivered' together? [Laughter.]" (205–6). Addison further pressed the witness by asking more explicitly if other meetings with the man had involved any "cuddling" or "hard" kissing (213).

The court also debated the "trinity" of love, wisdom, and truth between the Fletchers and Hart-Davies, allegedly requested by one of Susan's spirit messages and sexually coded by the legal representatives as a ménage à trois (234). The prosecutor presented the defendant as "a woman who was conniving at, if not planning, her husband's adultery,—a woman engaging in a most revolting intrigue" (225). To discredit Susan further, the prosecution used a photograph of her wearing Hart-Davies's jewels and a low-cut dress that Hart-Davies described as "most indecent" ("Central Criminal Court, April 7"). Fletcher, distancing herself from the sexualization of her character and its suggested link to her supposed criminality, dismisses the photograph as an inappropriate form of evidence that "had nothing to do with [her] guilt or innocence in any way whatever" and had solely been intended as "a private keepsake for [her] husband, not intended to be shown, [and that it was a dress] not more scandalous than may be seen at dinners, balls, the opera, and the Queen's drawing-rooms" (315).

During the trial, the defense counsel retaliated against the prosecution's attempts to morally disgrace the defendant not only by insinuating that Hart-Davies had been infatuated with John William but also by presenting her as an adulteress and divorcée who was, furthermore, mentally unstable and "subject to hysteria" ("Central Criminal Court, April 11"), a condition also alluded to by Fletcher herself (67, 78). That the legal professionals drew on discourses circulating at the time, connecting spiritualism with mental illness, is evident in puns on "medium" and "medicine" ("Central Criminal Court, April 7"). Fletcher responds to the men's medicalized and sexualized language through ambivalent rhetorical maneuvering, using such discourses tactically to further discredit Hart-Davies while displaying moments of female solidarity and outrage at how both women are treated in court, caught between the banter of the male judge and barristers (203). Similar to her previous strategies of disavowal in the context of women's rights discourse, Fletcher explicitly distances herself from the air of sexual scandal by apologizing to the reader for having to discuss such delicate details while simultaneously supplying compromising evidence about Hart-Davies, who, she suggests, suffered from a kind of sexual "mania" (103). Such information is necessary, according to Fletcher, to "give the reader a clear understanding of [her] story" (94). Describing the moment when she found out about Hart-Davies's alleged adultery, which had supposedly led to the latter's divorce from her first husband, Fletcher portrays herself as the forbearing friend of a fallen sister, underlining the need for forgiveness and female solidarity while rejecting a sexual double standard: "Nor can I understand why women should be more unforgiving to each other than they are to men" (91). Thus, the spiritualist doubly reinforces her own credibility and respectability while damaging Hart-Davies's reputation in the eyes of the reader. Such tactics, however, did little to dissuade contemporaneous readers such as Everitt from labeling Fletcher a representative of "a class of women happily unknown in this country, who are brought up under conditions which are detrimental to the natural development of a healthily constituted mind" (88). Although Everitt did not regard the spiritualist as "mad," he presented her as the mentally disturbed victim of an unwholesome environment and clearly coded her as somebody outside the respectable middle classes.

Fletcher's representation of her encounter with Hart-Davies suggests that both shared the experiences of divorce, remarriage, and possibly physical abuse. The spiritualist's expression of female empathy, based on this common history, however, is counterbalanced by her insinuations that Hart-Davies invented stories of male maltreatment because of her mental condition, a charge which implicitly aligns Fletcher's account with theories of the male medical establishment to validate her own credibility (61, 66–67, 78, 91). Hart-Davies's alleged story that her current husband was "plotting to put [her] into a lunatic-asylum" (79) evokes the generic conventions of sensation fiction and Georgina Weldon's real-life case. For the reader, it is next to impossible to disentangle fiction from historical truth at this point and to judge whether it was Fletcher or indeed Hart-Davies who drew on such well-known stories to exploit them for her own narrative of female victimization. Commenting on the outcome of the trial, the *Saturday Review*, although displaying no sympathy for Hart-Davies, sided with the supposed victim's side of the story, suggesting that the Fletchers' story "might almost have been written without knowledge of the actual facts by an intelligent novelist" ("Spirits in Prison"). On the basis of the available historical records, though, there is no doubt that both Fletcher *and* her opponent were adept at using language effectively to construct convincing plots of sexual intrigue and wrongful condemnation, like the best of sensation writers.

"In the Pillory" | Trial Reportage and Media Representation

In the chapter "In the Pillory," Fletcher complements her critiques of the criminal justice procedures with an attack on what she sees as biased and sensational trial reports in the press. The *Times*, overall, presented relatively neutral accounts of the trial proceedings, reprinting statements made by the legal officials and testimonies given during the cross-examinations without much commentary. Yet there is some evidence that the paper promoted prejudice against Fletcher and mediums to some extent, for instance, by calling the American "a 'medium' of considerable notoriety in all kinds of society" even before the start of the trial ("Charge against a Spiritualist," 4 Dec. 1880). Fletcher undertakes a systematic analysis by quoting passages from newspapers such as the *Times*, interspersing these with her own comments to correct, in her view, the false accusations and to present her own position: " 'The prisoner was removed from the dock; and three ladies, each holding a bouquet, two of which were white, emblematic of purity, tried to get at her as she was removed to the cells.' As if I were a cripple unable to walk, or some wild beast requiring as much force as poor Jumbo to remove me!" (145). The spiritualist evidently takes issue with the objectifying representation in the passage; claiming agency, she covertly alludes to, and rejects, her identification with stereotypical representations of female prisoners as "wild beasts," tropes that became prominent in the mid-Victorian period and that were even employed by writers who were otherwise sympathetic to the situation of women convicts, such as Frederick William Robinson.[36]

Further attacking the practices of journalists, Fletcher draws attention to the circulation of conflicting stories around the alleged crime and criminal, presenting her case as a prototype: "Evidently it did not occur to the writers for the press that there was any other side than the one which had been presented to the jury. In my case, which was a type of many more, there was a clamorous multitude and a silent prisoner" (267). Her act of speaking out through her autobiography therefore becomes, symbolically, an act of speaking for all the muted prisoners misrepresented in court and the media. Fletcher includes American papers reporting on her initial arrest in her critiques and makes their sensational coverage responsible for the significant amount of bail set for her, before correcting the press statements once more: "I was accused of swindling a beautiful young English girl of sixteen out of an immense fortune. It may be well to state here that Mrs. Davies was at least thirty-eight years old" (123).

To Fletcher's chagrin, large parts of the spiritualist press in Britain and America did not do much to support her or were overtly hostile. She notes how the *Medium and Daybreak* was "consistently silent" or sided with her enemy Dr. Mack, who had teamed up with Hart-Davies, while insinuating that the *Spiritualist* supported her accuser "with peculiar malignity" because the paper's editor allegedly had a romantic interest in the woman (171). The *Light* took a neutral position but also printed letters from the Fletchers' supporters.[37] The American found herself denounced by the *Chicago Spiritualist Journal*, while other organs such as the *Banner of Light* (Boston), *Mind and Matter* (Philadelphia), and *Miller's Psychometric Journal* (New York) stood by her (Fletcher 172). The *Banner* printed a letter from her supporter Thomas Nichols, setting her prosecution into a wider context of cases against spiritualists in England, such as those of Home and Slade, for the benefit of American readers.[38]

As Fletcher points out, the London-based mainstream papers from the *Times* and the *Daily Telegraph* to the *Standard* endorsed the guilty verdict. The *Saturday Review* was equally pleased but regarded the sentence as "very moderate" ("Spirits in Prison"). According to the ex-prisoner, negative coverage was largely due to the judge's "malignant" (238) and partial summing up, which, she felt, set a bad example for the press. Nichols and some papers agreed with her assessment of the unnecessary "torrent of invective" (182) from the judge, who had accused her of having entered into a "filthy league" (241) with her husband to beguile and defraud Hart-Davies. Nichols complained in his letter to the editor of the *Light* about a lack of "chivalry" in the courtroom, which had given the legal professionals license to verbally abuse Fletcher as the "silent and helpless victim, who sat there bound and gagged, and who could neither answer nor resist" (14 Apr. 1881, in Fletcher 251). Deliberately or unwittingly ironic, Nichols's spiritualist imagery here, conjuring the idea of the female medium tied and locked in a cupboard, implies that legal procedure is no better than spiritualist ritual. He also partially anticipates arguments of twentieth-century feminist criminologists, who challenged the so-called chivalry thesis—the idea that women are treated more leniently in the criminal justice system— although most present-day feminists would reject Nichols's implicit call for male paternalism.[39]

Fletcher happily picks up on Nichols's language of "chivalry" and female victimization when criticizing the damaging accounts of her case in the press: "When a woman is once locked up in prison, it is quite safe, and I presume it is considered manly and honorable, to libel her, and 'say all manner of evil against her, falsely.' Whether it is considered manly and honorable, and worthy of the character of English gentlemen, to strike, or kick, or cover with torrents of abuse and lies, an utterly unprotected, imprisoned woman, I have no means of knowing. I think, however, that it is not usual, even in the case of criminals who are unquestionably guilty" (261). Mobilizing metaphors of physical and verbal abuse to validate her arguments, Fletcher attempts to drum up support by proponents of English humanitarianism against what she presents as uncivilized treatment. Drawing on the rhetoric of paternalism, she casts herself in the role of a helpless female victim at the mercy of unworthy and dishonorable Englishmen, while subtly distinguishing herself from "criminals who are unquestionably guilty."

The *Law Times* and *Western Morning News* shared this concern over the judge's loaded language. Shortly after the trial, the *Law Times* wrote, "The long lecture delivered by Mr. Justice Hawkins to Mrs. Fletcher, when passing sentence in what is known as the Spiritualist case, may have a salutary effect upon public morality: we, however, are disposed to doubt it, and we heartily deprecate discourses of this nature" (16 Apr. 1881: 415, in Fletcher 247). Demonstrating gender awareness, the paper further complained about the "jocularity" during the trial and the judge's admonishments in excess of formal punishment that had a potentially damaging effect on the female prisoner's reputation: "To be scolded and discoursed upon by the judge may in some cases be a severe addition to the statutory punishment; and where the prisoner is a woman the severity of this additional punishment may be very great." Fletcher uses such statements as evidence to support her own position. She also quotes from the *Western Morning News*, which similarly noted the judge's cynicism during the trial, and his evident pleasure in *"double entendre"* (Fletcher 248).[40]

Trial reports of the sexual intrigues in the case and highly charged banter at the proceedings doubtlessly cemented negative ideas about the Fletchers' circles and spiritualism in general in the minds of an already suspicious public. Following the verdict, the *Standard* apparently wrote, "No man who respects himself would allow his wife or his daughters to attend professional *séances*, or to habitually associate with professional mediums" (Fletcher 260).[41] In a particularly biting evaluation of the trial, the *Saturday Review* complained about the "nauseous language, the indecent photographs, the sordid cupidity of the mediums," depicting John William Fletcher as "a vicious and vulgar Yankee adventurer" and his wife as "a greedy harpy and possible *entremetteuse*" ("Spirits in Prison").

Yet Susan also had proponents who publicly defended her reputation against such intimations. Mary Boole, the pioneering female mathematician and a character witness at the trial, sent a letter to the editor of the *Times*, correcting misrepresentations of the spiritualist as a former "shampooer at a Turkish bath," which had further compromised Fletcher's image by associating her with Orientalist stereotypes of sexual licentiousness (to a greater extent than her own comparison to Arabi Pacha mentioned earlier).[42] As reported in the *Pall Mall Gazette*, the judge had taken up Boole's language in his summing up, noting that little was known about the accused except that she "had been a rubber at a Turkish bath" ("Alleged Spiritualist Fraud"). Boole explained in her letter to the editor that she had only used the phrase at the trial as an alternative word for "healing medium," being unfamiliar with spiritualist terminology. She insisted that Fletcher was "one of the best and sweetest" women she had ever known (Boole). Boole further underlined her support by writing in reply to Mary Gove Nichols's campaign on behalf of Fletcher, despite her own "strong prejudice against all spiritualistic mediums." The mathematician confirmed her belief in the prisoner's "quixotic generosity and imprudent confidence in strangers," again implying that Fletcher, rather than Hart-Davies, was the victim in this case (Boole to Mary Gove Nichols, 3 Aug. 1881, qtd. in Nichols, *Memorial* 44).

With historical hindsight, it is impossible to establish Fletcher's guilt or innocence, although there are aspects justifying either version. The spiritualist may well have been the target, rather than the instigator, of a conspiracy, duped by professional enemies and her alleged victim, Hart-Davies, who may have harbored hopes of financial compensation similar to that awarded the wealthy Mrs. Lyon following the trial against medium Daniel Dunglas Home. If that was the case, Fletcher's decision to cross the Atlantic with the sole purpose of facing her accusers and obtaining "a triumphant acquittal" (Nichols, *Memorial* 11) was simply a tragic miscalculation. As Thomas Nichols argued, the judge had omitted mitigating factors that could have convinced the jury of the defendant's innocence, including the spiritualist's determination to confront the charges in England in the first place (*Memorial* 18). In 1926, Charles Kingston wrote that, at the very least, "the defence of the American woman must now be given more credence than it gained at her trial in 1881" (*Judges* 225). On the other hand, there are questions about the reliability of Fletcher's own version, which occasionally tends to exaggerate evidence in her favor or to omit proof that could work against her. She writes that the jury took three hours, rather than the one and a half hours reported elsewhere, to reach a verdict, thus magnifying the torture inflicted on her and insinuating that the jury's decision might not have been reached straightforwardly (Fletcher 182).[43] Similarly, she conveniently neglects to mention the testimony given at Bow Street Police Court by James Maddocks, a house decorator, who claimed to have faked spirit manifestations with the Fletchers, once even in collaboration with one of the Cook sisters, probably the professional and controversial medium Florence Cook.[44] By carefully selecting the tone and content of the autobiography, Fletcher put considerable effort into constructing an image of respectability that was further enhanced by her reflections on prison reform.

"A New People to Me" | Fellow Prisoners and the Respectability of Female Prison Philanthropy

To validate the usefulness of *Twelve Months* and preempt charges of self-interest, both writer and publishers framed the book as a contribution to larger debates around social and penal reform. Fletcher describes experiences of three different prisons—in Boston, Newgate, and Tothill Fields in London, the latter being the institution where she spent most of her sentence. Underlining her respectability, all these accounts emphasize the "consideration" offered by her warders and the special treatment she received to "protect [her] from contact with other prisoners" (320). Gay's account of Susan in the biography of John William Fletcher, published just one year before *Twelve Months*, underscores the convict's own efforts to reclaim respectability. Reporting a prison visit, Gay describes the spiritualist in prison dress as "a woman more honoured than a queen in her robe of purple" who "wore the insignia which earth has given to her noblest and best" (*John William Fletcher* 296). Fletcher's own account of the warm and tearful welcome she claims to have received from many friends and her seventeen-year-old son upon release supplements such dignified imagery (Fletcher 407–8).

Fletcher, affirming her outsider status in prison, describes herself as a "spectator of things," observing the penal routine "much as if I had been sitting in a theatre, and seeing a play enacted on the stage" (319). Commenting on the yard exercise with her fellow prisoners, she again sets herself apart by casting herself in the role of the viewer, rather than participant, similar to later suffragette prisoners such as Katie Gliddon.[45] Fletcher writes, "It was a curious sight to see this regiment of women, from eighty-five years old to twelve, all dressed alike, but looking so different,—a regiment composed almost entirely of drunkards, prostitutes, thieves" (325-26). However, this distancing strategy is complemented by her account of a developing interest in the other prisoners' fate during her imprisonment, suggesting a moment of cross-class solidarity. She writes of her personal transformation, "When I entered the prison, I was absorbed in my own sorrows and wrongs. I was very selfish, and had no time or space for the greater griefs and greater wrongs of so many others; but, when I began to look about me, I found a new world, and soon came to think of others as well as myself. My fellow-prisoners were a new people to me, forming an entire new world, of which I had hitherto had no idea" (350). Fletcher also uses her autobiography to present the stories of some of these fellow convicts, questioning their treatment at the hands of society and the criminal justice system. Most explicitly, she attacks the official story about one such prisoner, a sixty-year-old woman who dies in prison. According to the physician's verdict, the woman's death is due to old age, but Fletcher disagrees and insists, "We who had watched her knew that she had died from the exhaustion of grief, cold, and an insufficient and inappropriate diet" (388). The American's autobiography here criticizes the way imprisonment is organized in England by attacking the living conditions in women's prisons, *and* she attempts to unmask how official narratives try to conceal what Fletcher presents as "the truth" of convict experience.

Fletcher supplements standard philanthropic concerns over the conditions in prison with overt attacks on the social structures that bring women to the institution in the first place, returning to an interest in women's rights, the sexual double standard, and health reform, all of which were characteristic of spiritualist agendas, as outlined in more detail earlier. Fletcher's call for "the conditions of health,—plenty of light, pure air, pure water, pure, healthy food" (404)—in prisons fuses broader nineteenth-century anxieties over sanitation with her own progressive circles' interest in health regimes. The Nicholses were known advocates of the "water cure."[46] John William Fletcher's Native American spirit guide "Winona" promoted "the purification" of the body by bathing, a "simple, pure diet," and abstinence from "hurtful indulgences" (Fletcher 40). Such ascetic ideals find further expression in Susan's discussion of her fellow prisoners' alcohol consumption, which she makes responsible for the incarceration of the vast majority of them. She attacks the government's role in "tempt[ing] these poor women to drink" in order to collect a big share of the sellers' profit in tax revenue (323–24). Stressing men's roles in the criminalization of women—alcohol is sold to women by "respectable men licensed by government" (323–24)—Fletcher goes on to identify sexual double standards that result in unequal treatment of men and women. She tells the story of "poor Mabel Wilberforce, who had been convicted of perjury, and sentenced to nine months' imprisonment, for doing about what is considered as the proper and honorable thing for men who are co-respondents in divorce-suits" (335).[47] Close in tone to French socialist Flora Tristan's attacks on a social system that reproduces, rather than eradicates, criminality, Fletcher presents female prisoners as the products of class and patriarchal structures—"victims of social conditions and institutions, victims of what men do, and neglect to do" (405–6).[48] She comments on one working-class woman with children to feed who was sentenced for failing to redeem a garment she had pledged because her husband had spent all their money on drink (387–88). Fletcher demands a reformed prison that could serve as a "womanly . . . model sanitarium for body and for soul" (405). Rather than evoking the gender-specific regimes of reformers such as Elizabeth Fry, though, Fletcher, perhaps inspired by her own history of abuse, paints the image of an all-female utopian space where sympathetic women help other women recover from male mistreatment or neglect. Her male ally Thomas Nichols, who had a longstanding interest in women's rights (and married a woman formerly abused by another husband), complemented the spiritualist's reform campaign through a series of articles in his journal, *Herald of Health*, in 1882, calling for more female physicians in women's prisons and for "another Howard, and another Mrs. Fry" (qtd. in Fletcher 464).[49]

In the plea Fletcher made for social and prison reform, she implicitly built on the work of reformers such as Fry and Mary Carpenter, as well as the more radical language of Tristan, but she also anticipated some of the suffragette prisoners' demands for active civic and legislative involvement in the country's social organization, representing women as more suited than men to help their fallen sisters.[50] Like many of the suffragettes, Fletcher reached for a language of solidarity with the "unfortunate" (323) while reinforcing a categorical difference between the wrongfully incarcerated reformer-activist and the common prisoner to stress her own respectability. Whereas the suffragettes vocally demanded the right to political participation in no uncertain terms, Fletcher coquets with women's involvement in the administration of the state while apologizing, tongue-in-cheek, for "diverging into politics, with which women have no business—except to suffer whatever masculine legislation may inflict" (326–27). At the same time, she ventures into a careful appeal that could be read as a covert call for women's suffrage: "Surely men who can vote and legislate might do something better than that for their victims. If they really cannot, then let us women try. We could not do worse" (411).

Conclusion

On the basis of Fletcher's supporter Gay's account, which describes Fletcher as a true reformer "so truly belonging to the future that she could hardly hope to be recognised as one of the rarest women of our time" (*John William Fletcher* 287), the spiritualist would indeed seem to be the suffragettes' spiritual antecedent. It is certainly striking how many pioneering women gathered around the convicted spiritualist—from women's health activist Mary Gove Nichols to mathematician Mary Boole—and that Fletcher herself repeatedly used strong, unconventional women, such as Georgina Weldon or Helena Blavatsky, as a reference point. Gay paints a picture of the American as a highly independent and principled woman, "one of the very few who really own their own souls, and bow to neither man nor woman" (288) and—in language anticipating the suffragettes' construction of their leaders as savior-like—one who became a Christ-like martyr, "innocent and heroic" (285), by willingly sacrificing herself for her movement.[51] Like the suffragettes, Fletcher drew legitimacy for her comments on prison reform from her own experience of incarceration, while building on her spiritualist networks' women's rights agendas.

There is only scant information on what happened to Susan Fletcher after her imprisonment. She left England, together with her son, in May 1882 and arrived in New York later that month (Fletcher 417–18; "Criminal Calendar"). Her husband is known to have offered his services as a palmist on the East Coast at the beginning of the twentieth century.[52] Given that he had been charged alongside his wife, it is unlikely that either of them returned to England after her release—he would have faced arrest. John William died, as he had lived, under suspicious circumstances, during a police raid in 1913, possibly after swallowing poison when the officers arrived to arrest him.[53] Newspapers reported the mysterious disappearance of his brain from the body and hinted at contestations of his will but did not mention Susan.[54] For all we can guess, this was a woman who lived at the edge of middle-class respectability. Few sources exist outside of newspaper trial reports and some supporters' accounts that could offer an insight into her life and work before or after conviction. With the writing of her autobiography, she at least seized some control over how she wished these to be represented.

CHAPTER 5

Adultery, Gender, and the Nation

The Florence Maybrick Case
and *Mrs. Maybrick's Own Story*

This crime will darken England, and dethrone
Justice.—On one side, human, prone to err,
Twelve men, and men, moreover, judging her
For one sin mainly—sin confessed and known.
But on the other side, as hourly shown,
The soul of England, greater than her laws:
The voice that bids the ermined Hangman pause:
The nation's sob, that deepens to a groan.

Carry out the sentence? What dishonour then
Shall rest for ever on the hands that slew,
Though England cried, "This woman's cause is mine!"
Reverse it? From the hearts of living men
Honour, and time's vast tribute nobly due
To those who held the helm in 'eighty-nine.

> George Barlow, "On the Impending
> Execution of Florence Maybrick"[1]

Debates around the highly publicized murder case of Florence Maybrick in 1889, only a few years after fellow American Susan Willis Fletcher's trial, extended some of the concerns about unfair treatment raised by spiritualist Fletcher's supporters into a more explicit critique against a sexual double standard within the English criminal justice system. Whereas Fletcher and her proponents had seen her primarily as a victim of an antispiritualist climate—while also complaining against media misrepresentation and the sexualized banter at the trial—Maybrick's supporters (male and female) argued that the defendant had been the victim of sexual bias in the male judge and jury, because of Florence's alleged adultery before the suspected murder of her husband. As summarized by Helen Densmore, an American doctor living in London at the time of the trial who, together with her husband, Emmet, offered shelter to Maybrick after the latter had returned to America, "this unfortunate woman was in reality put on trial for adultery instead of murder, and upon testimony that would never have been received in a divorce court" (*Maybrick Case* 25).[2] Attacking a flawed English justice system, pro-Maybrick commentators also established explicit connections between gender and the nation. Released after fifteen years in prison, Maybrick joined public debates around her case by publishing her autobiography, *Mrs. Maybrick's Own Story: My Fifteen Lost Years* (1905). With this publication, Maybrick, similar to Fletcher (discussed in the preceding chapter), inaugurated a distinctly female, modern tradition of prison autobiography, calling for reform of the legal and prison systems and engaging with the media's role in representing criminal cases. Like Fletcher, middle-class Maybrick evoked cross-class solidarity through her tales from prison, thus anticipating some of the concerns expressed in suffragette prison writings only a few years later. Furthermore, Maybrick's story demonstrates how a former prisoner was able to turn herself into an expert commentator, using memoir and newspaper publications for financial benefit and as a platform for disseminating her views, despite an ambivalent relationship with the press and the public.

"As Romantic and as Sad as That of Any Heroine of Fiction" | The Life and Trial of Florence Maybrick

Florence Elizabeth Chandler from Alabama had married forty-two-year-old English cotton merchant James Maybrick at the age of eighteen. The Maybricks had two children and led a fashionable life in a well-to-do area of Liverpool, England, before their marriage started disintegrating.[3] Behind a façade of respectability, James's business and the Maybricks' marriage were faltering; he was habitually taking drugs (arsenic and strychnine) and allegedly keeping a parallel family consisting of a former mistress and several children. In late April 1889, Florence went to London, telling her husband that her aunt was having an operation but instead checking into a London hotel and meeting her husband's business partner, Brierley. What really happened remains a matter of contestation; the prosecution argued that Florence was having a clandestine affair with the man and that they were staying at the hotel as a married couple, seemingly evidenced by a letter from Florence to her alleged paramour intercepted by a servant after the lady of the house had returned home. This incident was aggravated by reports of a quarrel between the Maybricks, following a visit to the Grand National, where Florence had walked with Brierley against her husband's wishes. In the ensuing fight, James gave his wife a black eye, but the couple eventually made up following negotiations of their family doctor. Shortly after these events, James, who had been concerned about his health for a while, was taken ill and died soon afterward. His brothers, alerted by a servant about the secret letter to Florence's apparent lover, suspected their sister-in-law of poisoning James with arsenic and had her arrested.

At the high-profile Liverpool trial in August 1889, Florence was found guilty of murder and sentenced to death, before shortly afterward Queen Victoria, upon the advice of her home secretary, Henry Matthews, reluctantly commuted this sentence to penal servitude for life, because of reasonable doubt that arsenic poisoning had caused the death. Victoria regretted "that so wicked a woman should escape by a mere legal quibble!" (Victoria to Sir Henry Ponsonby, in Buckle 527). While the queen recognized that "the *law* is not a moral profession" (528), she demanded that the sentence "must never be further commuted" (528). Maybrick served fifteen years and, despite repeated attempts to secure her liberation, was not set free until 1904, returning shortly thereafter to the United States. By her own account, her release was due to her "unbroken record of good conduct" (*Own Story* 212), rather than outside petitioning, although the *New York Times* claimed, rather confidently, that "the decision to release Mrs. Maybrick was entirely due to efforts on this side of the Atlantic" ("Mrs. Maybrick to Be Freed").

The trial received tremendous publicity at the time, with large audiences benefiting from new opportunities of active participation in such events through letters to the editor in newspaper columns.[4] Aside from medical and legal inconsistencies, it was the delicate details of adultery at the heart of the case that titillated the public and inspired heated responses by the defendant's followers. The large publicity can certainly in part be explained by the fact that the case had all the ingredients familiar from sensational murder mysteries in fiction and melodrama. "For seven days," Charles Kingston wrote in 1923, "a crowded court listened to a sordid story of intrigues, poison, and death" (*Famous Judges* 44). At the basis of this trial was, as Edward Abbott Parry suggested in 1924, "the eternal triangle of modern West End drama" (92). Arsenic poisoning in a domestic setting had also featured in popular detective narratives by well-known sensation writers, such as Wilkie Collins's *The Law and the Lady* (1875). Maybrick's judge himself was apparently influenced by striking parallels to the world of fiction, for one contemporaneous pamphlet, drawing on the *Liverpool Daily Post*, complained about his musings on sensation novels during the trial, which to the writer seemed "rather incongruous when followed immediately by the Judge's elucidation of the prisoner's motive" (F.J.L. 23). Even after the trial, the public's imagination remained captured by Maybrick's story, which the *New York Times* in 1895, six years into the woman's prison sentence, called "as romantic and as sad as that of any heroine of fiction" ("Six Years a Prisoner"). Indeed, as George Robb has noted, with themes of betrayal and the tragic consequences of a young American's marriage to an Englishman, "Florence Maybrick's story reads like the plot of a Henry James or Edith Wharton novel" (57).

The case not only appeared to draw its characters and plot elements from the world of the imagination, but it in turn inspired the publication of popular ballads, literary and dramatic adaptations, and scores of hefty legal and medical treatises. It also became a cultural reference point in "high" art, with James Joyce having Molly Bloom muse on the alleged murderer in *Ulysses* (1922).[5] Madame Tussaud's memorialized the alleged murderess in the Chamber of Horrors dedicated to notorious killers, only to move the wax figure elsewhere after Maybrick's reprieve (Boswell and Thompson 146).[6] The controversial case was used as an argument against the death penalty as late as the 1960s, and it continues to stimulate the imagination of writers to the present day.[7]

The contemporaneous press and public opinion were split over the question of guilt, but by the time the verdict was imminent, the vast majority expected an acquittal because of conflicting medical evidence. The judge, Sir James Fitzjames Stephen—Virginia Woolf's uncle and a leading authority on criminal law—was attacked by an angry crowd when he was leaving the court after the trial had ended.[8] What made the unexpected verdict controversial was that it was unclear whether James Maybrick, whom the defense revealed to be in the habit of regularly taking arsenic, had actually died of poisoning. Furthermore, there was no proof that his wife had administered the substance to him, although she had been soaking flypapers to extract arsenic around the time of his death, allegedly for cosmetic purposes.

Unlike Susan Willis Fletcher, Florence Maybrick had made a statement in court in her own defense, which was arguably an ill-advised move, because her comments about flypapers and confession of "the fearful wrong" she had done to her husband were used as incriminating evidence against her (qtd. in Irving 229). Despite such apparent clues, many commentators blamed the judge for the outcome, maintaining that his summing-up, which lasted two days, had been biased and "*monstrously unfair,*" for he had played down that there was significant doubt over the cause of death and Florence's alleged attempt to administer arsenic to her husband with an intention to murder him (Brief of Messrs. Lumley and Lumley, qtd. in Maybrick, *Own Story* 307). Judge Stephen suggested to the jury that the woman's adultery constituted a clear motive for murder, and this argument of an apparent "motive" took over in the absence of conclusive evidence.

Stephen noted in his summing-up that Maybrick's counsel, Sir Charles Russell, had spoken effectively about the inequality in the world's judgment on the conduct of men and of women but insisted that it was not his business as a judge to "speak as a moralist" (qtd. in Christie 138).[9] Nevertheless, Stephen went on to talk about Maybrick's alleged adultery, insinuating that Brierley was not the only man she had met in London and concluding that "it is easy enough to conceive how a horrible woman in so terrible a position might be assailed by some fearful and terrible temptation" (qtd. in Christie 141). The judge reminded the jury, "She, while her husband lived and, according to her own account, while his life was trembling in the balance—even at that awful moment there arose in her heart and flowed from her pen various terms of endearment to the man with whom she had behaved so disgracefully. That was an awful thing to think of and a thing you will have to consider in asking yourselves whether she is guilty or not guilty" (qtd. in Christie 141). Florence's advocates used different strategies to respond to her alleged adultery—central to the judge's summing-up—all with the purpose of vindicating her. The American feminist Mary Abigail Dodge, who wrote under the pseudonym Gail Hamilton, corresponded about the case with eminent individuals such as English philosopher Herbert Spencer, founded the International Maybrick Society in 1891, and lobbied on the prisoner's behalf in high places.[10] Hamilton suggested that the unhappy wife had sought Brierley's help in her intention to press for a divorce and that adultery was possible but "not proven" (Hamilton to Home Secretary H. H. Asquith, in Densmore, *Maybrick Case* 91).[11] The case united female activists such as Hamilton and male commentators, from the poet George Barlow and the psychiatrist L. Forbes Winslow to the liberal journalist and purity campaigner W. T. Stead, known for his campaigning on behalf of prostitutes.[12] Stead, provocatively and ironically titling his article in the *Review of Reviews* "Ought Mrs. Maybrick to Be Tortured to Death?," sharply contrasted the "debauchery" of Maybrick's husband before his death with the woman's alleged single sexual faux pas that, considering the absence of conclusive evidence about the murder, was widely seen as the reason for her condemnation by judge and jury (392). The journalist here echoed concerns about a sexual double standard in the context of the Contagious Diseases Acts—a double standard that Josephine Butler, one of the leading figures trying to repeal the acts, also found in the Maybrick case when she complained in the *Liverpool Review* in 1889 "that such strong expressions should be reiterated *ad nauseam* when dealing with a woman, while they are not made use of at all in the case of men" (qtd. in Robb 67).

Like Butler, Stead noted that there had been no discussion of James's promiscuity at the trial and that the dead man therefore falsely appeared as a husband wronged at the hands of an unscrupulous wife. Drawing on medicalized language, Stead exculpated Florence's potential sexual offense by suggesting that she might have been "almost out of her senses with excitement and hysteria" (392) in view of the strained relations with her husband at the time. In an interesting gender reversal, the journalist blames Florence for withholding information on her *husband's* sexual conduct, making the "fatal chivalry of the loving heart of a deeply injured woman . . . responsible for the hideous miscarriage of justice" (392). Through this rhetorical move, Stead implicitly condemned the deceased husband (and male prosecutors, judge, and jury) for a *lack of* male chivalry while underlining Florence's selflessness as a way of reinstating her feminine virtue. Like Thomas Low Nichols in Susan Willis Fletcher's case a few years earlier, Stead, through this role reversal, implicitly debunked the "chivalry" thesis that was later criticized explicitly by late twentieth-century feminist criminologists, although, unlike recent feminists, he victimized Maybrick and saw male paternalism as the law court's true duty.[13]

Convinced that the judge was "much prejudiced against wives suspected of misbehaviour," Stead complained that Stephen "raged like a violent counsel for the prosecution, leaving no stone unturned to excite prejudice against the unfortunate woman in the dock" (393). With resonances of similar protests against Judge Flowers's summing-up in Susan Willis Fletcher's trial, the barrister MacDougall equally reprimanded Stephen for his use of highly charged language in his address to the jury on the subject of Florence's letter to Brierley: "I am going to put it to my readers whether they intend to allow any judge any such license of language, and of laceration of any woman when conducting criminal trials under the shelter of the privilege of immunity granted to judges to say whatever they please when sitting in a judicial capacity?" (545). Following the trial, it emerged that Judge Stephen was suffering from a degenerative mental condition, which may have clouded his judgment—Stead spoke of "senile malevolence on the Bench" (392). The judge was forced to resign in 1891, aged only sixty-two, and died in a private asylum three years later (Christie 145).[14] On the basis of contemporaneous responses by Maybrick's supporters, it makes sense to assume that the judge's vicious and confused treatment of the female defendant may have been a combination of an already existing sexist attitude and the onset of dementia.

In MacDougall's detailed and polemical analysis of the case, the barrister worked on the assumption that Florence may have had an affair, although he contended that actual evidence of adultery was thin, being based on the testimony of a hotel waiter, rather than a chambermaid (18). He insisted that "it was Brierley, not Mrs. Maybrick, who should have been lacerated by Mr. Justice Stephen" (524), constructing Florence as the victim of a "consummate scoundrel" (532) who allegedly took unfair advantage of a woman's unhappiness after she had found out about her husband's untruthfulness. In an attempt to discredit the deceased husband, the barrister furthermore wrote passionately against the injustice of James's use of physical violence as a reply to his wife's disobedience: "Well! I dare say there are plenty of wives who do not always choose to be ordered about in this sort of way by their husbands when taken out for a holiday, but I do not think there are many husbands who would resent a disobedience of this kind by giving their wives a thrashing and a black eye for it!" (147). MacDougall here implicitly condones wifely insubordination and condemns male domestic violence as an inappropriate response. Florence's defenders evidently walked a thin line between painting the prisoner as an independently minded woman with sexual desires beyond her marriage and, conversely, an innocent victim of unfortunate circumstance and male abuse in need of (proper male) protection.

Following the guilty verdict, women wrote letters to the editors of newspapers, vehemently complaining about what they saw as a structural disadvantage in the courtroom. One wrote, "Of course the jurors decided for their sex. Doubtless each one was a husband and became bitter on the dishonouring wife" (qtd. in Christie 148). Another agreed that an all-male jury had created an unfair bias: "I feel certain that no jury would on such evidence have convicted a man for the murder of his wife, and I venture to doubt whether a jury of six men and six women would have agreed in this case" (qtd. in Christie 148). The Maybrick verdict thus became a fresh catalyst for broader arguments about gender parity in the criminal justice system, inciting women to demand, as Mary Hartman notes, not just "a place in the courtroom" but "seats on the jury" (252).[15] Late nineteenth-century women's ad hoc concerns about legal bias in one specific murder case are underscored by recent statistical evidence suggesting that in nineteenth-century England, women accused of killing male relatives were treated more harshly than were men.[16] Furthermore, theoretical treatises by Victorian criminologists such as William Douglas Morrison argued that women were more likely to kill by poisoning than were men. Legal and criminological views thus mutually reinforced each other, creating adverse conditions for women who had come under suspicion.

In 1895, women who were already engaged in feminist organizing intensified the stalling efforts to release Maybrick by founding the Woman's International Maybrick Association, which regarded the prisoner as a martyr and whose members included prominent American abolitionists and women's suffrage activists such as Elizabeth Cady Stanton and Julia Ward Howe ("Six Years a Prisoner"). Female Maybrick advocates read papers on the subject at a meeting of the American Woman's Suffrage League in New York in 1896 ("Maybrick Case Discussed"). Despite such exertions, and plenty of supportive medical and legal evidence that the defendant had not received fair treatment at the trial, appeal was impossible since a court of criminal appeal did not exist in England until 1907. According to Maybrick's own account, five thousand petitions with almost half a million signatures were sent to the Home Office in the days immediately following her trial, and the proceedings inspired legal publications arguing for a court of criminal appeal (*Own Story* 226).[17] Campaigns on both sides of the Atlantic, arguing for Maybrick's release, spanned the entire period of her imprisonment; her case was repeatedly debated in the House of Commons, although wider public interest faltered initially after the successful commutation of the death sentence.[18]

"Murder of Mrs. Maybrick by the British Government" | Criminal Justice, Gender, and the Nation[19]

Not least because of Maybrick's status as an American immigrant by marriage, campaigners for her release coded their interventions along national terms that scrutinized the English criminal justice system. Barrister Mac-Dougall regarded the bias in the judge's rhetoric as a "question of national importance" (545). With repeated official attempts of intervention on the woman's behalf under several American administrations, the case also took on political significance in the relationship between two nations; in Densmore's words, it became "an interesting study of international comity and policy" ("English Dreyfus Case" 602). After Queen Victoria's death in 1901, the Washington-based, British correspondent from America A. Maurice Low suggested that King Edward, in appreciation of the sympathy offered by the American nation on his mother's death, "cannot do better than cut through the red tape of the Home Office and issue a pardon to Mrs. Florence Maybrick," which would be received "as an indication that when America asks a favour—and it has never asked the release of Mrs. Maybrick as a right but always as an evidence of friendly consideration—a deaf ear will not be turned to its pleading" (83). An impressive list of American dignitaries lobbied for Maybrick's release, including the vice president of the United States, Levi P. Morton; several cabinet members; the Speaker of the House of Representatives; and the attorney general (Maybrick, *Own Story* 247). Writing to the American minister to the Court of St. James, Robert Lincoln, Secretary of State James Blaine expressed his urgent "desire to help an American woman in distress," despite his belief that she had formally lost her American citizenship by her English marriage (qtd. in Maybrick, *Own Story* 249). Reversing the English stereotype of American vulgarity, Blaine wrote that his countrywoman "may have been influenced by the foolish ambition of too many American girls for a foreign marriage, and have descended from her own rank to that of her husband's family, which seems to have been somewhat vulgar," but he excused this mistake on account of her young age (qtd. in Maybrick, *Own Story* 249).

Feminist Hamilton echoed this sentiment, fearful that this pure, young American girl might have been corrupted by her marriage "into a coarse, cruel and vicious family" (Hamilton to Lady Henry Somerset, 10 Nov. 1892, in Densmore, *Maybrick Case* 102–3). Further joining discourses of gender and the nation, Hamilton pleaded with English honor when she wrote a letter to the new home secretary, H. H. Asquith, published in the *New York Tribune*. She challenged Asquith, who had rejected appeals for a release with the argument that he could not undo his predecessor's decision, asserting that the system of "public trial makes it not only the inalienable right but the sacred duty of all citizens to watch the courts of justice, to protect against all wrong-doing, and to enforce the rights of even the weakest—of the woman and of the stranger within the gates" (3 Oct. 1892, in Densmore, *Maybrick Case* 93). Elsewhere, Hamilton speaks of the "murder of Mrs. Maybrick by the British Government," a "murder committed by one of the most powerful organizations in the world upon one of the weakest—an innocent and helpless young mother of infant children." The feminist depicts the refusal to free Maybrick not only as an attack on this individual woman but as an affront by a barbaric old-world regime against the democratic American nation: "It is wilful and continuous tyranny torturing an unresisting woman, and attended by a senseless, vulgar and brutal insolence towards a friendly republican nation pleading for its own citizens" (Hamilton to Lady Henry Somerset, 10 Nov. 1892, in Densmore, *Maybrick Case* 102).[20]

In a particularly fierce letter to Prime Minister William Gladstone, Hamilton reaffirmed the notion of British barbarism—and her own nation's post–Civil War state of enlightenment—by associating the European country's penal practices with slavery: "Mrs. Maybrick is an enslaved woman. The great power of England seals her to eternal silence before it slanders her" (4 Jan. 1893, in Densmore, *Maybrick Case* 136). Like many nineteenth-century feminists, Hamilton established a parallel between womanhood and slavery, seemingly oblivious to the irony in this analogy, given that Maybrick's southern family had gained parts of its wealth before the Civil War through slaves (Graham and Emmas 13). Hamilton was so outraged by the English nation's refusal to grant a pardon to her fellow American that she wrote in a private document that she "hate[s] the English so that [she] would not take [her] Yankee blueberries [for breakfast] because it left, or would leave, a taste of English jam in [her] mouth!" (27 July 1893, in Hamilton, *Life in Letters* 2:1045). Densmore, more temperate in tone than Hamilton, covertly draws on a feminist anti*sati* discourse: "If Miss Dodge's arraignment may seem to the friends of Mr. Gladstone unnecessarily bitter and impassioned, I must ask them to consider how they would view it if a sister or daughter innocent of any crime was thus *immolated*; if such sister or daughter was in penal servitude, subject to all the horrors of surroundings bad enough for a hardened criminal, and revolting and unbearable to a sensitive nature innocent of crime" (*Maybrick Case* 140–41, emphasis added). While the language of immolation allows Densmore to covertly appeal to the English for their sense of enlightenment, her contrast of middle-class sensitivity and innocence with the "hardened criminal" reaffirms Maybrick's respectability.

By contrast, writing on "woman and crime" in 1912, Hargrave L. Adam expressed satisfaction that the English authorities had not bowed to "the flood of violent invective which poured over here from the United States, especially issuing from the female scribes and champions of Mrs Maybrick's 'cause'" (87). But rebukes by American women were actually complemented by attacks on the English criminal justice system by male commentators in the United Kingdom. Noticeably, Irish nationalists such as T. P. Connor and Michael Davitt pushed for Maybrick's release in the years following the defeat of the Home Rule Bill.[21] The conservative paper the *Graphic* had already explained the split in public opinion during the trial through the Irish question, with Maybrick's defense counsel, Sir Russell, on the side of Home Rule and Judge Stephen, a "staunch Tory," on the other (Robb 63). The paper made the "Liverpool mob" responsible for the agitation following the verdict—Liverpool, of course, had a large Irish population (qtd. in T. Christie 149). Scottish commentators seized the opportunity to highlight differences in the English and Scottish justice systems. An article in the *Scottish Leader*, a ministerial organ, distanced itself from legal procedure south of the border, calling for a pardon and asking provocatively, "What can the public think, except this, that John Bull has got his back up, and would rather let an innocent woman die in jail than acknowledge that his law and his courts can make a mistake? This is not an admirable condition of mind, nor does it prevail in Scotland" (qtd. in Densmore, *Maybrick Case* 147). Equally unimpressed, Englishman W. T. Stead wrote that "a sorrier exhibition of all that is worst in the blundering, wrong-headed illogical side of John Bull has seldom or never given occasion for his enemies to exult and his friends to wince" (392), and he feared that the Home Office was bound to become "the laughing-stock of the world" (394). Male commentators' defenses of Maybrick in Britain therefore complicate Judith Knelman's argument that the American press was pro-Maybrick and the English, male-led newspapers were deferential to the state in this matter ("From Yellow Journalism" 281).

Mrs. Maybrick's Own Story (1905)

Like Susan Willis Fletcher, Florence Maybrick entered the public debate around her conviction and incarceration, publishing her autobiography shortly after her release from prison. The book received several brief mentions in British periodicals targeted at an educated readership, such as the *Athenaeum* and the *Saturday Review*.[22] While the *Review of Reviews* regarded it as fit for "the general public rather than the specialist" ("Review's Bookshop"), the New York–based *Critic* recommended *Mrs. Maybrick's Own Story* only to readers with an interest in prison life, rather than a broader audience, presumably because of the absence of racy details about Maybrick's alleged adultery that the wider public might have hoped for (qtd. in T. Christie 236).

Critical treatments of the Maybrick trial, including more recent and otherwise thorough scholarly accounts such as those by George Robb and Mary Hartman, have tended to mention the woman's autobiography merely in passing, neglecting it as a significant primary source for studying the case and (self-)representations of female prisoners more generally.[23] Despite Trevor Christie's (somewhat unfair) complaint in his popular 1968 study of the Maybrick case that the autobiography was "so badly written, so mawkishly phrased, so poorly organized" (236), the book, published both in Britain and the United States, had enjoyed enough popularity to warrant a second printing in 1909 by philanthropist and journalist Arthur Pearson (Voelker 481). Charles Boswell and Lewis Thompson, in their otherwise sensationalized account of the Maybrick case for Fawcett's Gold Medal Books—the back cover calls Maybrick "that American Hussy, the lovely, lonely girl"—maintained that "the book does not stand in the front ranks of prison literature" but recognized that the ex-prisoner's "strictures against prevailing penal practices transcended preoccupation with merely her own plight and revealed a quick sympathy for everyone in the same unhappy condition" (161). It is not least Maybrick's identification with the concerns of other convicts that distinguishes her approach as noteworthy.

In all likelihood, Maybrick's supporters Helen and Emmet Densmore, both experienced authors who took Maybrick in after release, contributed to the project of the autobiography.[24] While Christie explains what he sees as the poor quality of the volume through the absence of "a 'ghost' writer" and "little direction from her editors" (235), the book contains sections whose mixed tone suggests that her friends might have supported her in the writing process. Maybrick's text engages with medical discourse and literary conventions of the time, with which the Densmores would have been familiar. Maybrick also covertly addresses critical dismissal by remarking that prisoners, having found themselves discouraged from self-expression for so long, are typically excluded from access to "literary composition" (*Own Story* 14) and hence opportunities for positive critical appraisal. Assessing the autobiography through aesthetic standards of literary value would miss the rhetorical, thematic, and social significance of Maybrick's text—one of the first extensive autobiographies by a former female prisoner available to us.

Whereas fellow American Fletcher's *Twelve Months in an English Prison* (1884) functioned as both a prison autobiography and a personal history of spiritualism, thus appealing to multiple audiences, Maybrick's sober account concentrates on a detailed description of prison life and its problems, not least because of her significantly longer term of imprisonment, during which she served time in Liverpool's Walton Jail (later made famous by Lady Constance Lytton's imprisonment as a suffragette), Woking Convict Prison, and Aylesbury. Defying readers' expectations of scandalous details, Maybrick only makes brief and vague reference to the controversial question of her alleged adultery and desire to separate from her husband, dismissing the alleged "motive" this way: "[It] was surely no incentive to murder, as inasmuch if I wanted to be free there was sufficient evidence in my possession (in the nature of infidelity and cruelty) to secure a divorce" (*Own Story* 368). Similar to Fletcher, Maybrick goes through and dismisses alleged evidence against her. Alongside a more extensive, factual account of prison routine and regulations, the psychological effects of incarceration, and her coping mechanisms, she also offers an insight into other prisoners' stories and recommendations for prison reform.

Maybrick justifies her musings on prison reform by the fact that she speaks from "a large, intimate personal experience" and thus complements treatises written by outsiders, which "must of necessity be to a certain extent superficial" (206–7). Her autobiography is divided into two parts; the first part, with a foreword, provides a summary, in over two hundred pages, of her family background, the events before the court case, the actual trial, and the period of imprisonment. The second part largely consists of an "analysis of the Maybrick case," reprinting documents from the campaign for her release, such as a dossier with new evidence compiled by the convict's legal advisers during her incarceration. The presentation of this material, which would already have been known to those who had been following the release efforts, is interspersed with short assessments by Maybrick herself to contrast her enforced silence during imprisonment. Even the title and subtitle of her publication—*Mrs. Maybrick's Own Story: My Fifteen Lost Years*—capture the movement from silenced object to speaking subject.

In contrast to spiritualist Fletcher, though, Maybrick depicts herself as a reluctant author who was forced by "well-meaning friends" and publishers ("these dread taskmasters"; 13) to present her side of the story to the world. Part of this posturing could be read as a strategic disavowal with the image of respectable femininity in mind, not dissimilar from Fletcher's efforts to distance herself from the active pursuit of public speaking, although Maybrick also convincingly suggests that writing about her lengthy incarceration brought back painful memories. She dispels any potential readers' romanticized notions of solitary confinement at Woking as "an elysium that one should voluntarily desire to hark back to, . . . nor is penal servitude in Aylesbury an Arcadian dream" (10). Rather than presenting the writing of her story as a liberating experience, Maybrick likens the process to another phase of captivity.

Maybrick's foreword is particularly interesting for its explicit commentary on, and attempt to resist, prescribed forms of self-analysis and representation. Noting her lack of experience, because "the art of writing" was "distinctly discouraged" in prison, Maybrick describes the advice she was given for her autobiographical project: "I was told to look at myself objectively; then to pry into myself subjectively; then to regard both in their relation to the outside world—to describe how this, that, or the other affected me; in short, as one of them, more deep in science than others, expressed it, 'We want as much as possible of the psychology of your prison life'" (14). Friends and publishers (no doubt with the ulterior motive of marketability in mind) encouraged Maybrick to think of the process of life writing as a psychological case study, presented from both a subjective and an objective viewpoint. The former prisoner is horrified "that it was [her] soul they wanted [her] to lay bare" and "vehemently protested that that belonged to

[her] God, and [she] had no right to expose it for daws to peck at" (14). She is only persuaded by arguments that "possibly the humanities might be furthered a bit if the story of a woman . . . be given in fullest heart detail to a sympathetic world" and finally submits to the request in the hope "that somewhat of good may come of it" (15). Maybrick's pious coyness here may well serve to affirm a sense of feminine propriety, but it also exposes the former prisoner's discomfort with the demands to "lay bare" her soul for the scrutiny of publishers and the wider public, here represented metaphorically through the eerie image of the pecking daws, evoking connotations of thievery or, even more disturbingly, vultures feeding on carrion.

Maybrick's reservation alerts us to the fact that the project of prison autobiography is an ambivalent one, which offers former convicts a rare opportunity to tell their own story but also mirrors the disciplinary institution's preoccupation with producing rehabilitated convict souls, theorized in detail by Michel Foucault, who warns that "the soul" is "the effect and instrument of a political anatomy," rather than simply a site of freedom (*Discipline* 30). However, Maybrick's prison autobiography resists any clear disciplinary patterns and the formal conventions of associated forms of life writing, such as conversion narratives, since hers is not a case study of conversion and rehabilitation. Rather, she insists on her innocence throughout and includes critiques of the penal system. Like Fletcher, Maybrick occasionally calls on discourses used elsewhere to classify and constrain female prisoners, such as "hysteria," but she usually does this with a tactical purpose, thus offering a personal account at the blurry juncture of (self-)discipline and resistance, within a larger context of publication defined by pecuniary interests (of self and publishers) and audience expectations.

Similar to Fletcher, and echoing supporters such as Helen Densmore, who spoke of a plot against Maybrick comparable to the French Dreyfus Affair, Maybrick presents herself as the victim of a conspiracy between "unscrupulous enemies" (379)—female servants, male relatives, police officers, and doctors.[25] Maybrick's descriptions call to mind the spiritualist Fletcher's metaphors of domestic violence, when the alleged killer presents herself as "a weak, defenceless woman" who was "struck at" and condemned "unheard" (49)—a language also employed by Densmore, who, in *The Maybrick Case*, portrays the alleged poisoner as "a lone woman, powerless in a net" (27) and deprived of the patriarchal support of chivalrous male relatives (30). Maybrick, in her account of the events leading up to her arrest, stresses her own passivity and hints at diminished responsibility by recounting repeated fits of unconsciousness. She emphasizes her position as a woman at the mercy of different groups of men. Her ill treatment at the hands of one of her brothers-in-law—who, in a scene figuratively coded as rape, enters her chamber when she is lying in bed, holds her "arms tightly gripped," and shakes her "violently" (23–24)—is mirrored by the subsequent intrusion into her bedroom of "a crowd of men" who arrest her (26) under the silent complicity of the male doctor (25).

Recalling the literary trope of female incarceration in gothic and sensation fiction, Maybrick's text casts her as a prisoner in her own house, where the patriarchal regime of the family home is depicted as even more oppressive than actual imprisonment: "I was denied in my own house, even before the inquest, the privacy accorded to a convicted prisoner" (27). The similarity between family home and legal/penal institution is underscored by her description of "formal proceedings taking place in [her] bedroom" to finalize arrangements for her remand, in the presence of a number of male professionals (31). Although devoid of explicit analogies, the autobiography, like Fletcher's *Twelve Months*, is reminiscent of formulas from sensation fiction and real-life cases such as Georgina Weldon's narrow escape from enforced confinement in a lunatic asylum, such as when Maybrick recalls her shudder at the sight of "the tall, gloomy building" of Walton Jail (33) and warns of female victimization through wrongful incarceration by men usually regarded as beacons of public welfare: "it seemed to me a frightful danger to personal safety if the police, on the mere gossip of servants, and where a doctor had been unable to assign the cause of death, could go into a home and take an inmate into custody in the way I have shown" (41–42).[26]

Maybrick extends her complaints against the treatment received at her home to a sustained critique of the official procedures of the man-made English criminal justice system, in which women "are guarded and controlled by women, but men make the rules which regulate every movement of their forlorn lives" (121–22). The American protests against regulations about petitioning procedures, so that convicts are excluded from all communication and information, with no opportunity to challenge misrepresentations of character (146–47). She echoes her supporters' attacks on individual judges ("a prisoner's fate may depend upon the incompetent construction of one man, and there is no appeal"; 149) and the operation of the Home Office, placing her own case in the context of a list of people who had been unjustly convicted, including Eliza Fenning, who featured prominently in early nineteenth-century broadsides.[27] The language used by Maybrick and supporters such as

Helen Densmore, castigating the prisoner's exposure to the policemen's "rough hands and sacrilegious touch" (Densmore, *Maybrick Case* 28), mirrors that employed by the earlier street literature, which had juxtaposed Fenning's innocence and purity with "the executioner's vile hands" ("Heroes of the Guillotine" 6), suggesting the longevity of gender-specific tropes and a continuity of thematic concerns across different genres of writing about women in the English criminal justice system.

Like many middle-class prison autobiographies, including Fletcher's, Maybrick's text displays some efforts to present the "delicately nurtured" prisoner as an extraordinary, rather than ordinary, convict, in contrast to common offenders (88), and criticizes the lack of sufficient separation between prisoners of the "Star Class," such as herself, and the "habitual criminals" (90–91). Yet such distancing tactics are counteracted by attempts to express commonalities and feelings of solidarity with her fellow convicts, despite clear differences in social background: "I believe I had the sympathy and respect of all my fellow prisoners, and when I left Aylesbury, my feelings were those of mingled relief and regret. I could not but feel attached to those with whom I had lived and suffered and worked for so many weary years. I knew, perhaps, more of the life history of these poor women, their inner thoughts and feelings, than any one else in the prison. In suffering, in sympathy, in pity, we were all akin" (207). Arguably, similar to Fletcher, Maybrick uses the sympathy and respect expressed by fellow prisoners (or prison staff) as a way of establishing her own respectability, which suggests a feeling of superiority on her part. Furthermore, through her reformist approach, which points out faults in the penal system, Maybrick aligns herself with the tradition of middle-class prison reform *and* a literary tradition of attacks on the penal system by authors such as Dickens, whom she mentions explicitly (208). The fact that she presents herself as a figure of authority within the prison, a person who is trusted by fellow prisoners and supported by officials such as the chaplain, underlines her status as a moral woman on the right side of the law who in some ways stands above other convicts (173, 175). But Maybrick also makes it clear that she identified with other prisoners ("we were all akin") and that her fellow inmates' respect was something she had to *earn* through interaction with them: "At first the difference that marked me from so many of my fellow prisoners aroused in them something like a feeling of resentment; but when they came to know me this soon wore off" (187). Moments of cross-class solidarity are evoked elsewhere, when she reports on the sympathy offered her by working-class women—her former greengrocer and a policeman's daughter who watched her at the courthouse—which contrasts with the lack of empathy from her "well-dressed" female peers during the trial (38, 42, 43).

Maybrick's account as a whole stresses shared feeling and experience, rather than difference from other convicts, underscored by her repeated use of the collective pronoun "we" ("We are here to be punished. . . . We tramp back to our work"; 72). The American even notes that during her solitary confinement at Woking Convict Prison, she was not able to "enjoy the privilege of working in company with [her] prison companions" (69), coding her inability to associate with other convicts in negative terms. Maybrick shares this sense of identification and collective suffering with Oscar Wilde's almost contemporaneous "Ballad of Reading Gaol" (1898), dedicated to a fellow prisoner who was executed, in which he wrote, for instance,

> We sewed the sacks, we broke the stones,
> We turned the dusty drill:
> We banged the tins, and bawled the hymns,
> And sweated on the mill:
> But in the heart of every man
> Terror was lying still. (11)[28]

But this type of paracommunal language also distinguishes Maybrick from other (male) middle-class authors of prison autobiography to some extent—as Frank Lauterbach has noted, the author of *Twenty-Five Years in Seventeen Prisons: The Life-Story of an Ex-Convict, With His Impressions of Our Prison System* (1903), "No. 7," primarily presents himself as an observer, rather than a participant, in the prison routine, a strategy also occasionally evident in Fletcher's writing.

Like Fletcher's work, though, Maybrick's writing is characterized by a tension in that it seeks both to transcend class-based distinctions—through its invocation of a community of convict women who are all "alike" (68)—*and* to bolster them by references to middle-class respectability. Maybrick's language of companionship and similarity is further offset by her attacks on a system that erodes all sense of desirable "individuality," turning convicts into "human automat[a]" (66). The American compares prisoners to both machines and animals but underlines her own desire to resist "the almost universal tendency among prisoners to mere animality" (189) by anxiously insisting on her own respectable manners of appearance and conduct (188). At the same time, her ambivalent status within the penal regime is reinforced by the concession that she, too, willingly submitted "to the level of the mere animal state"—a position shared with her fellow prisoners—by dulling her senses in order to survive mentally (104).

In spite of enforced uniformity, Maybrick received some preferential treatment in prison due to her class background. While she was given lighter work in the prison library, restoring old books and preparing material for other prisoners, she shows herself aware of the situation of the less privileged. When she notes the positive effects of a temporary relief from the "vacuity of the solitary system" through reading, she mentions the fact that such a respite is not available to the illiterate prisoners (84). Here, Maybrick anticipates some of the more fully formulated concerns with class distinctions in the prison system in suffragette texts, such as Lady Constance Lytton's *Prisons and Prisoners* (1914).

A particular tension noteworthy in Maybrick's autobiography is the occasional use of language inflected by a scientific vocabulary that had gained increasing currency by the beginning of the twentieth century. Whereas Fletcher's *Twelve Months* had hinted at the material causes of crime, Maybrick's account attributes criminality to "physical and mental degeneration" (171). This technical and scientific tone jars with Maybrick's language in other passages; we may speculate if the voice of medical doctor Helen Densmore is at work here. Elsewhere, however, Maybrick's text implicitly counters scientific language and social labeling attempts by calling for empathy with the sufferings and humanity of what other commentators at the time saw as a hopeless class of habitual offenders.[29] Maybrick insists, for example, that "many of these women have their tender, spiritual moments" (96) and asks, "Why should a woman be considered less loving, less capable of suffering, because she is branded with the name of 'convict'?" (176).

Maybrick, like Fletcher before her, supplements her complaints against the criminal justice system with criticisms of the media and their role during her trial and after her release. She assigns primary responsibility for the judge's and public's bias even before the beginning of the actual trial "to the sensational reports in the press" (45, 51). Her advocate, MacDougall, had already offered a more detailed attack on these reports in his section "Trial by Newspaper," in which he contrasted the press's duty to "vigilantly watch and criticize the administration of justice in our Courts" with unfair sensationalism at the expense of the defendant (153). Maybrick condemns media reports on alleged incidents during her imprisonment (involving bad conduct and self-harming) as "pure fabrications" (108). We might also question whether a (supportive) *New York Times* article published in 1900, titled "Mrs. Maybrick Talks," is truthful, since it is unlikely that a journalist could have had access to the prisoner's verbatim statement (unless it was secretly passed on by her counsel).

In Maybrick's autobiography, the ex-convict describes being pursued by an information-hungry "ubiquitous reporter" even beyond release—during her visit to her mother's in France and after her arrival in New York—as a new form of captivity (11, 12). Indeed, the *New York Times* reported that the mother's French home had been besieged by London reporters, requiring police intervention ("Mrs. Maybrick's Trip Put Off"). Yet Maybrick speaks of the "ubiquitous reporter" almost with fondness, oxymoronically designating him her "genial enemy" (11). Overall, reportage on her case, especially in the United States, was not always sensationalized; the press played a crucial role in publicizing discontent with the verdict and efforts for the prisoner's release. The *New York Times*, for example, published a constant trickle of generally supportive articles over the period of Maybrick's imprisonment. Maybrick, then, must have realized that the print media could be used for her own purposes; her relationship with the press clearly changed again when she actively began to pursue such aims.

Early twentieth-century American newspapers displayed a keen desire to offer a space for Maybrick's own views, surely owing in part to the expected boost for sales figures through such supposedly firsthand accounts, rather than purely humanitarian considerations. Although it is difficult to disentangle, from historical hindsight, whether citations or indeed entire articles attributed to her are authentic or at least partially written by professional journalists—as difficult, in fact, as disentangling which parts of her autobiography might have been penned by the Densmores—these journalistic contributions offer a fascinating and unusual public platform for the exploration of a former prisoner's perspective.

Like "One Dug Up from the Grave" | From Convict to Expert Journalist and Speaker

After being released, Maybrick initially led the life of a public persona. Whereas the spiritualist Fletcher's existence before imprisonment had been marked by public appearances, especially in her younger years, her prison sentence finally forced her into obscurity, except for her publication of *Twelve Months*. For Maybrick, however, incarceration and her status as a media celebrity opened up opportunities for a public role and public speaking that she would not have been able to enjoy before. In a postrelease interview with the *Daily Chronicle* in August 1904, also excerpted in the *New York Times*, Maybrick seized the opportunity to reassert her innocence and thank her supporters ("Mrs. Maybrick Would Forgive and Forget"). Following the publication of *Mrs. Maybrick's Own Story*, the author embarked on a tour, visiting several American prisons, including "The Tombs" (a Manhattan jail where she encountered the actress Nan Patterson, who, like Maybrick, had been charged with murder but insisted on her innocence) and Auburn and Sing Sing prisons in New York State.[30] Maybrick wrote a series of articles for the *World*, offering her impressions on these prisons.[31] The *New-York Tribune Sunday Magazine* was also quick to capitalize on the famous convict's reemergence, printing an article that purported to be written by Maybrick, which contrasted the highly topical, ongoing Nan Patterson trial with the English court case (see figure 5.1).

The former prisoner's account of the Patterson trial is validated by her own "bitter experience," as well as alleged firsthand observation facilitated by "a friend at court" who provided her with "a retired yet favourable nook from which to observe the proceedings" (Maybrick, "Criminal Court Procedure"). Maybrick offers a detailed comparison of proceedings in both countries, from the organization of the court to the roles of counsel, jury, judge, defendant, and defendant's family. For instance, she deplores the fact that she had been given a "'common' jury" on "the verge of illiteracy," whereas in the Patterson trial, newspapers reported that the accused was able to approve jury members before the defense accepted them. Maybrick also mocks the English court's insistence on surrounding her with a towering officer in uniform ("the tallest policeman on the force") and a female warder, "lest the terrible creature so hedged about fling herself contumaciously over the railing upon the periwigged heads beneath, and peradventure lay violent hands on their august persons." Regardless of whether we may suspect the helping hand of a professional journalist behind such elaborate language, Maybrick emerges empowered in the role of one of those lady spectators who had witnessed her own court appearance. She picks up the language of her former supporters, contrasting the "uplifting surroundings" of an American court with the "travesty of justice" she had endured, concluding with the impression that her trial had "happened not in enlightened, Christian England, but in some remote region still under the influence of the dark ages."

CRIMINAL COURT PROCEDURE
in England and America
By FLORENCE E. MAYBRICK

Nan Patterson's Trial in New-York City Contrasted With Her Own Trial

From the Mural Paintings.

Criminal Courts Building, New-York.

It often has been said to me since my return to America that a travesty of justice, such as marked my case in England, would be utterly impossible under a form of law in any part of this country, and the opinion also has found frequent expression in the public press. In view of the fifteen years of bitter experience which a judicial misdirection forced me to undergo, I trust it will not seem altogether strange that I should have felt a desire to witness some part of a trial in my native land, provided it could be arranged without attracting public notice, under circumstances where the person accused of a capital offense should be a woman, and the evidence, as in my case, wholly circumstantial.

When, therefore, a recent trial of extraordinary public interest presented to a marked degree the salient features desired, and a friend at court not only placed his protection at my service, but also the advantage of a retired yet favorable nook from which to observe the proceedings, I felt that an opportunity so exceptional might not be lightly passed over. And accordingly, under the guidance of one well versed in the ways of American courts, I was enabled to possess myself not only of material for a comparison of judicial procedures, but also to note how, in what is happily again my country, a person accused of a crime is not only considerately safeguarded by both the community and the law against which one is suspected of being an offender, but that by the treatment accorded her on every side it is made clear that it is not in theory only, but in practice as well, that she is held here inviolably to be innocent until beyond any reasonable doubt proved guilty.

From what I had been told, I naturally expected to see marked differences in both procedure and treatment from English ways. Yet hopeful as I was of witnessing a state of things far better than fell to my experience, I hardly conceived it possible that between two countries so alike in blood, speech and religion as England and America a contrast so great could exist. And while it was with feelings of pride in my countrymen and thanksgiving from a full heart that I observed the altogether humane way in which the unfortunate are here treated, on the other hand it was nearly impossible amid such uplifting surroundings to rid myself of the feeling that through some juggle of time all that I had so needlessly and cruelly undergone, both during the weary months of preliminary detention and the heart-crushing days of my protracted trial, happened not in enlightened, Christian England, but in some remote region still under the influence of the dark ages.

During the months preceding my trial, while detained in Walton jail, excepting the short hour devoted to physical exercise and a half-hour of chapel service, to all intents and purposes I was in solitary confinement. By way of contrast, I find that here in New-York the female prisoners in the "Tombs" (a well-lighted building adjoining the court) awaiting trial during the entire day have the freedom of a commodious corridor or hall, with such community life as each, under the circumstances, may make for herself.

In England, for some inscrutable reason, the jails and the places where the assizes are held are almost invariably long distances apart, especially in the larger cities, and the daily transport of prisoners from jail to court and back again in every respect is an outrage on the humanities; while here in New-York the person accused of a crime (and mayhap innocent) passes quietly in charge of a "plain clothes" deputy-

sheriff from one place to the other, thus involving neither hardship nor public notice.

The torture I was forced to undergo in going to and from court almost passes belief. At Walton jail I was packed into a closed van—somewhat smaller, perhaps, but in appearances not unlike the furniture vans one sees on the streets—and for three hours each day, going and returning, more than once within its narrow limits was forced into fellowship with the lewd and

vicious—with beings foul in person as well as speech—who perchance also were on their way to trial or penal punishment. I never recall this experience without an overwhelming sense of wrong, of unutterable repulsion, of indignant protest, because it seems to me now even more than it did then a wholly gratuitous form of torture. What such an infliction was to a sensitive and delicate woman in my position, as a preparation for the ordeal of trial in court, may be left to the reader's imagination. In the last days, because of a threatened collapse, on the recommendation of the prison medical officer I was allowed a carriage, and against this concession to the humanities there was an almost universal outcry in the public press.

As I entered the spacious court-room where the trial of the young woman was proceeding, I could hardly trust my eyes. It was fairly flooded with light, and all its belongings seemed in cheerfulest keeping. One could not imagine easily an English court-room a place for the display of decorative art, yet here the walls in softest colors pictorially typified justice in such various ideal forms as only the fancy of poet and painter might portray.

On the other hand, anything more soul-crushing than the impression that an average English court-room, with its somber fittings, its solemn ceremonials, its black gowns and antiquated wigs, makes upon anyone so unfortunate as to be arraigned at its bar it is difficult to conceive. In England everything possible has been done to magnify the position of the judge, and at the same time to degrade and reduce to utter ignominy the unfortunate wretch in the dock. Whatever the intention or theory of the setting up of legal machinery in England may be, it is certain that in practice (at least as far as my observation and experience stand in proof) strict justice has little part in it, the only apparent object and aim of it all being conviction—for it is a stigma on the police if a person once brought into court for trial by any chance slip through their meshes.

Accordingly, arrangements are so ordered that a conviction if possible follows solemn rules; for aside from the supposed disgrace that attaches to failure, it frequently means also a loss of fees and rewards to nearly all concerned in the prosecution.

To properly impress the community with the awesomeness of the task before him, the justice before opening the assizes solemnly proceeds in state, in an official carriage, to a special divine service. How this as a mode of preparation on the judicial side, contrasts with the prisoner's, by way of her unspeakable van journey, hardly need be pointed out. And, to being the accused wretch still further into a fit and proper state of mind to appear in the presence of the personified majesty of the law, on arrival at the court she is detained for a good part of an hour in the gloomiest of subterranean cells, flanked by ever-silent guardians.

And when finally the fanfare of trumpets makes proclamation that the arbiter of life and death in all the panoply of his exalted office has taken his seat, the prisoner, after threading various dark passages, ascends to the upper region by a long stone stairway, suddenly to find herself in what is technically called the "dock"—an elevated and inclosed platform, situated nearly in the center of the court-room. From this inenviable vantage she now literally looks down upon everybody, except the judge, who occupies an equally high place facing the prisoner, while the "benches" of counsel (and such they are) and the bar of the circuits, as well as members of the press, occupy the floor space between these two instrumen-

Florence Elizabeth Maybrick

From Her Most Recent Photograph

Echoing Gail Hamilton's furious attack on old-world barbarism, Maybrick similarly constructs America as a progressive, enlightened nation where the "unfortunate" are treated in an "altogether humane way" ("Criminal Court Procedure"). This journalistic critique of the English criminal justice system complements Maybrick's complaints in her autobiography, in which, despite her admiration for her defense counsel, Lord Russell, she speaks in no uncertain terms of her dissatisfaction with her adopted country's legal system, concluding, "It looks as if justice in England were growing of late more than ordinarily blind" (*Own Story* 154). Contrasting the English government with the English *people*, the American writes, "The supineness of Parliament in not establishing a court of criminal appeal fastens a dark blot upon the judicature of England, and is inconsistent with the innate love of justice and fair play of its people" (89). Through her lengthy discussion of the case of the Norwegian Adolf Beck, in the words of one commentator "an innocent and inoffensive foreigner" who was convicted twice for crimes committed by somebody else, she further emphasizes nationality as a contributing factor and lends credence to her own account of American innocence unjustly condemned (159).[32]

In the "Criminal Court Procedure" article, Maybrick, by declaring "pride in [her] countrymen," arguably mobilizes a nationalist rhetoric to firmly reposition herself from former pariah to patriotic citizen who deserves her hard-won place in the bosom of her nation. Through an analysis of English court architecture and protocol, which she reads as a reflection of social hierarchies, she affirms the democratic values promoted in the US Constitution as opposed to the autocratic power enjoyed by the English judge, who represents "the personified majesty of the law." Ironically, the accompanying illustration of "Mrs. Maybrick on Trial," reprinted from the *London Graphic*, undercuts this argument by emphasizing the female defendant's imperious presence in the center foreground, while the judge appears diminutive in the background (see figure 5.2). Maybrick's celebration of America's supposed egalitarianism is further undermined by her dismissive comments about the constitution of her "'common' jury" elsewhere, comments which betray her classist attitudes.

Throughout the article, similar to the autobiography, Maybrick walks a fine line between asserting female independence—not least by speaking out in public—and promoting the necessity for paternalistic support for falsely accused women, for example, by highlighting the role of Patterson's "aged father" during the trial: "her white-haired, natural protector was ever by

Counsel for Prosecution | Judge | Counsel for Defense | Witness | Jury

Male Warder | Bar of Northern Circuit | Prisoner | Spectators | Female Warder

Mrs. Maybrick on Trial—From a Drawing in "The London Graphic"

FIGURE 5.2 Florence Maybrick on trial, from a drawing in the *London Graphic*, reprinted in the *New-York Tribune Sunday Magazine*, 22 Jan. 1905

her side to cheer and support her." Reflecting on the selection of the jury, she concedes that not all women may be able to choose "in their own interest" but also insists that women's "intuitions" can and should be brought to bear. Close in tone to the spiritualist Fletcher's call for a female defendant's right of active involvement, Maybrick concludes that regardless of women's qualifications for making informed legal choices, a sense of ownership in the process is key: "there surely is something satisfying in the mere thought that you have not been dragged to your doom." With this in mind, she recalls occasions during her trial when she "felt a strong impulse to direct [her] counsel's attention to testimony which apparently to him at the time seemed unimportant, but later proved to have a weighty bearing against [her]." Complaining against what she presents as the English court system's convention to facilitate communication between counsel and defendant in writing only, she praises the American model, which permitted Patterson, "surrounded by friends and counsel," to construct a more effective defense.[33] Maybrick's article ends by juxtaposing "the innate love of justice of the English people" with the outmoded procedures endorsed by the country's "Government." Echoing her prior acknowledgment of English people's belief in "fair play" (*Own Story* 89), she aligns herself with both the English public and the "hapless" prisoners of England, calling for the implementation of a court of appeal and thus presenting herself as an advocate of judicial as well as wider social reform.

Later that year, the *New-York Tribune Sunday Magazine* published another piece under Maybrick's name, titled "My Year of Freedom"; the article offered a moving account of the difficult process of adjusting from a life in solitary confinement to "the volume and sound and the perpetual movement" of "normal life," which had left the former prisoner "fairly dazed and stunned" at first. Cut off from the world for fifteen years, Maybrick struggles to reconstruct the puzzle of social, political, and scientific developments in the intervening years—including changes in fashion—finding herself "in a mental state bordering on chaos." Maybrick's piece functions not only as an early psychogram of postrelease experiences—modern in its recognition that the "automatic obedience" required under prison regimes makes it difficult for prisoners to "take a responsible place" in the world when their sentences come to a close—but also as a meditation on the process of a woman's reacculturation to the customs of her native, but now unfamiliar, country.

Changes in gender relations are only one of the challenges faced by Maybrick, who, still used to nineteenth-century chivalry, discovers that in the new century, "the distinction of sex has almost ceased to exist." Confronted with "young women college graduates," she is full of admiration for these young women, whom she finds to be "as charmingly simple and devoid of self-consciousness as one could wish," despite some people's accusations of "man-like demeanor." The illustration framing her article, showing a woman at her writing desk with the iconic symbol of an empty birdcage and multiple birds about to fly into open space, evokes Maybrick's liberation from prison as much as a larger social process of female empowerment, both of which she is embracing only tentatively herself (see figure 5.3). These newspaper publications about a former prisoner thus take on a dual function, becoming allegorical representations of women's social emancipation in the wider sense.

Aside from Maybrick's journalistic writing, and despite her earlier denials of plans to appear onstage or on the lecture platform, Maybrick also began to give talks on prison reform, without doubt at least partially motivated by the need to provide for herself and her mother after the expensive legal battles.[34] The ex-prisoner embarked on a lecture tour around the United States after being signed up by the Slayton Lyceum Bureau of Chicago (T. Christie 238).[35] Such instances of public speech in oral or print format markedly contrast with the ex-convict's critiques of the debilitating effects of the silent system—the weakening of prisoners' memory and overall linguistic proficiency because of limited word use—in her autobiography (*Own Story* 80). However, although Maybrick seized the opportunity and

FIGURE 5.3 Florence Maybrick's "My Year of Freedom" in the *New-York Tribune Sunday Magazine*, 19 Nov. 1905, illustrated by J. L. S. Williams

the right to speak after a prolonged period of enforced silence, her public performances can only partially be understood as liberating. At best, they were an ambivalent enterprise, for, driven by financial need, they were not entirely voluntary. Even if they entitled Maybrick to express her views to large audiences, they also allowed others, such as her manager, to make a profit by displaying her as a public spectacle. After a short but intense period of fame, Maybrick concluded her life in relative seclusion, opting for anonymity as "Mrs. Chandler" (her maiden name). She died in her modest cottage in Connecticut, aged seventy-nine, in 1941.[36]

Conclusion

Maybrick's case offers insight into opportunities for former prisoners to make their voices heard at the beginning of the twentieth century. The multiple public platforms available to the American were certainly unusual—a combination of her middle-class background, her already-existing celebrity status across the nation following high-profile campaigning on her behalf, and mass-market media that were increasingly accessible to women as authors and consumers.

Mrs. Maybrick's Own Story is also noteworthy for its identification with other convicts, which challenges readings of middle-class prison autobiographies as texts that solely delimit separate social identities and simply mirror the rhetorical strategies of reformist or official writings.[37] While Maybrick, like Susan Willis Fletcher before her, participated to some extent in what Lauterbach sees as the construction of a middle-class group identity, the two women also disrupted such a coherent sense of social identity in a number of ways, precisely *because* of their gender and national identity. There is no doubt that *Mrs. Maybrick's Own Story* and Fletcher's *Twelve Months* are middle-class texts, published in book format for a middle-class audience, but their representational strategies, Maybrick's in particular, challenge stereotypical depictions of female convicts in other sources and purely middle-class concerns by evoking moments of cross-class solidarity and by drawing attention to the prison experiences of nonelite women.

Maybrick thus implicitly gestured toward a model of female intersubjectivity, anticipating some of the more self-consciously political cross-class and feminist articulations to be found in the prison writings of British suffragettes only a few years later, discussed in the following chapter. While the American, like the spiritualist Fletcher, shied away from explicitly feminist arguments, she seized opportunities for public speaking—in print and on the lecture platform—to offer her views on the treatment of women at the hands of the criminal justice system. No matter how ambivalent these opportunities proved to be, Maybrick's and Fletcher's efforts, and the debates around them, must be seen as emblems of increasingly pressing cultural concerns over the legal and social subordination of women and attempts to rectify it by public debate. Most importantly, regardless of questions of guilt or innocence, *Twelve Months*, *Mrs. Maybrick's Own Story*, and Maybrick's journalism are evidence of a recognition that female (ex-)prisoners deserve the right to actively participate in such discussions.

CHAPTER 6

Gender and Citizenship in Edwardian Writings from Prison

Katie Gliddon and the Suffragettes
at Holloway

Only this age that loudly boasts Reform,
hath set its seal of vengeance 'gainst the mind,
decreeing nought in prison shall be writ,
save on cold slate, and swiftly washed away.
　　　Sylvia Pankhurst, "Writ on Cold Slate"

Debates around the treatment of women, as well as gender and class inequities in the legal and penal systems, reached a new level in the context of the women's suffrage campaign in Edwardian Britain, especially during the militant struggle for the vote, which saw many activists incarcerated for disturbances at political meetings or willful damage against property.[1] Imprisonment and suffragettes' responses to it took on an important symbolic meaning in this context: they metonymically signified the constraints imposed on women in patriarchal society and women's resistance to such confinement. However, as this chapter will demonstrate, beyond prison's symbolic value, the suffragettes' firsthand experiences of imprisonment and encounters with nonsuffrage prisoners inspired social critiques targeted at the material conditions in women's jails and ordinary women's living conditions in the larger sense.

If incarceration was a punishment for militant suffrage activism and an attempt to silence the suffragettes' political demands, the writings of suffragette prisoners functioned as deliberate efforts to counter these sanctions. As Jason Haslam suggests, such "prison narratives . . . undermine the effects of the silencing that imprisonment imposed" (Introduction 26).

Using Daisy Dorothea Solomon's memoir *My Prison Experiences* (1913) as an example, Haslam argues that many suffrage prison narratives "invert the penological theory that drives the institution. Whereas the prison is supposed to transform the prisoner through isolation and silence, for the suffrage prisoner it removes isolation, and strengthens her (collective) voice" (28). Suffragettes thus responded to the tight control of the criminal justice system through making their experiences visible and audible by, in Barbara Green's words, "bringing life-writing to the service of feminist activism" (84).

The suffragettes' prison narratives share some characteristics with those written by Susan Willis Fletcher and Florence Maybrick (discussed in the previous two chapters), for instance, an implicit or explicit critique of man-made laws and a more general desire, expressed by many authors writing from prison, "to inscribe themselves as fully human in the midst of a system designed to dehumanize them and to render them anonymous and passive" (Smith and Watson 277). However, while I have argued that Fletcher's and Maybrick's texts, too, can be read as accounts that aim to make visible and alleviate the conditions for other, "ordinary" convicts, and thus have a broader agenda than vindicating the individual author, the suffragettes, who saw themselves as political prisoners, located their prison writings more clearly as part of a broader feminist agenda and struggle. Their accounts thus become a "collective enterprise," similar to more contemporary women's narratives of political imprisonment (Harlow, "From a Women's Prison" 506).[2]

This chapter examines in detail some of the writing produced by incarcerated suffragettes during the concerted window-breaking campaign of spring 1912. Although I draw on suffragette writings from other years and some retrospective accounts of prison experiences in autobiographies to provide a wider context, my main focus here is on texts secretly penned inside the penal institution, including the material produced by one specific suffragette, the middle-class artist Katie Gliddon, during her imprisonment at Holloway in March and April 1912.[3] Gliddon kept a secret prison diary inside her copy of *The Poetical Works of Percy Bysshe Shelley*, and her diary is likely to be one of the most extensive records of life in Holloway actually compiled within the prison that is known today. This chapter places Gliddon's diary in a wider context of the women's suffrage campaign and the role of reading and writing for imprisoned suffragettes. Contextualizing Gliddon's text allows us to complicate our understanding of women's relationships in prisons, between political prisoners, "ordinary" convicts, and officers. Gliddon, alongside other, more well-known campaigners such as Sylvia Pankhurst, creates platforms for the voices of "common" prisoners, designed to change public perceptions of these women, but she also facilitates new cross-class relations by evoking a uniquely transgressive gaze between women in prison. Although Gliddon documents the material conditions experienced by *all* incarcerated women at the time to some extent, her view is necessarily constrained by her middle-class perspective. I share Julia Swindells's concern with how representation is at work in autobiographical texts "to see whose voices, whose story, whose history emerges" ("Liberating the Subject?" 30). My analysis is therefore attentive to how Gliddon and other suffragettes shape "common" prisoners' stories for posterity.

This chapter is informed by efforts in feminist autobiographical studies to reclaim women's letters and diaries as rich genres worthy of serious consideration that invoke "issues of historical, social, and self-construction" and offer "an important record of historical place and time" (Bunkers and Huff 1, 5).[4] For pioneering researchers such as Suzanne L. Bunkers, reading such texts facilitates new perspectives on social history through the "intensive re-examination of the lives of unknown women" ("Reading and Interpreting" 15).[5] Early critics such as Mary Jane Moffat and Charlotte Painter conceptualized women's diaries produced between the early nineteenth and the mid-twentieth century as a form particularly conducive to women, since the genre was "private" and "restricted" like these women's lives (5). Such interpretations take on a new significance in the tightly regulated architecture of the solitary prison cell, which imposes an even heavier restriction on women's lives, while forcing the inmate into a space that is both hyperprivatized and always public, with random access for prison officials that cannot be controlled by the prisoner. If, as Harriet Blodgett has argued, "the very nature of the diary as a personal record counters the limiting and devaluing of the female self entailed by accommodation to a male-dominated culture" (97), the clandestine journals and letters composed by imprisoned suffragettes doubly challenge the degradations imposed by patriarchal social structures, including the treatment of women in the institution of the prison and the legal apparatus.[6]

Context | The Suffrage Campaign and Imprisonment in Edwardian Britain

Over one thousand female campaigners were sent to prison between 1905 and 1914, most of them to Holloway Prison in London, which had exclusively housed women since 1902.[7] From the moment of the first convictions, the suffragettes' imprisonment resulted in public critiques of prison conditions, such as insufficient clothing, food, hygiene, or heating—critiques which led to some material improvements over the next few years, the appointment of the first female inspector of prisons, Mary Gordon, in 1908, and a renewed interest in prison reform.[8] Following the Prison Act of 1898, all prisoners were sentenced to one of three divisions, with the first division reserved for political prisoners, the second for "respectable" characters, and the third for "ordinary" prisoners, which was the category applied most frequently (Crawford, "Prison" 569). In the early years of the campaign, suffrage prisoners were granted first-division status, but this decision was reversed. The Liberal Secretary of State Herbert Gladstone washed his hands of any responsibility in the matter and insisted in 1908 that decisions over first-division status were at the discretion of magistrates, and "their view is that the persistence of such offences renders it undesirable to adopt that course any longer" ("Home Office Memo"). Although the leaders of the Women's Social and Political Union (WSPU), Emmeline Pankhurst and Emmeline Pethick-Lawrence, successfully negotiated special conditions for suffragette prisoners—for instance, the right to talk during exercise—the political establishment's unwillingness to formally grant suffragettes political-prisoner status remained a point of contention for many years, resulting in the first hunger strikes in 1909, followed by numerous episodes of forcible feeding (Crawford, "Prison" 570–71).

Firsthand accounts of and attacks on forcible feeding in prisons were printed in the WSPU's weekly newspaper, *Votes for Women*.[9] Critics of the violent procedure, including some doctors such as W. Hugh Fenton, branded it as a "beastly" and "dangerous" form of torture (qtd. in "Doctors as Torturers"). Some commentators likened the invasiveness of forcible feeding to rape.[10] In the most highly publicized case of forcible feeding, Lady Constance Lytton, who had been born into a prominent family—her father was the Viceroy of India between 1876 and 1880 and son of the novelist Edward Bulwer-Lytton—disguised herself as a working-class woman, "Jane Warton," to prove that such activists were treated less circumspectly during imprisonment. Having escaped forcible feeding and enjoyed certain privileges on a previous occasion because of her heart condition and "influential friends" (Lytton [1914 ed.] 109), Lytton/Warton was forced to undergo the procedure at Walton Gaol, Liverpool, after a cursory medical examination. Lytton's act of cross-dressing and subsequent description of her experiences in her autobiographical account *Prisons and Prisoners* (1914) highlighted class differences that not only impacted on prison treatment but also plagued the suffrage movement itself—a topic that I discuss in more detail later.

Forms of sentencing and prison treatment of suffragettes were not only dependent on class privilege; they were generally inconsistent and subject to the whims of individual magistrates and politicians in changing governments.[11] In 1910, Home Secretary Winston Churchill had introduced Rule 243a, which awarded certain privileges to second-division prisoners, for example, visits and letters once a fortnight, the wearing of one's own clothes rather than uniforms, group exercise twice daily, first-division food (in the form of food parcels from outside), books, and the ability to do one's own work rather than prison labor.[12] Churchill's rule was a careful compromise that granted special treatment while avoiding reclassifying suffragettes as political prisoners. However, under the new home secretary, Reginald McKenna, women sentenced to hard labor—including many of those convicted of window breaking in March 1912—were in theory not meant to benefit from such privileges, at least not until mid-April 1912, when McKenna extended the rule, in slightly modified form, to all suffragettes who had displayed good behavior.[13] In practice, suffragettes benefited from privileges even before they were officially granted them, with prison treatment depending on the institution and individual officers.[14]

In *Crime and Criminals, 1876–1910*, the former governor and medical officer of Holloway Prison, R. F. Quinton, sourly complained, "I am not disclosing any prison secrets in stating that the Suffragettes were not dealt with according to the rules at all, that they were shifted in whole batches from the divisions in which they had been placed by magistrates, and that they had, in whatever division they found themselves, privileges and indulgences to which they had no title" (193–94). The Prison Commission itself (later to become the Prison Department of the Home Office) recognized this problem of inconsistency, noting that the actions of individual magistrates aggravated the situation at Holloway in the spring of 1912, because some suffragettes who had participated in the concerted window-breaking campaign in early March were given summary convictions with hard labor, while others were tried at Sessions for more violent offenses but ended up without a hard-labor sentence.[15]

The militant struggle for the vote, which had grown increasingly violent to include bombings and arson attacks on empty buildings, reached a new phase with the introduction of the Prisoner's Temporary Discharge for Ill-Health Bill (the so-called Cat and Mouse Act) in 1913. It allowed for the temporary release of prisoners on hunger strike who had become too weak, circumventing the need for forcible feeding. Shortly afterward, the militant suffrage campaign came to an end when the First World War broke out in 1914; the government awarded amnesty to suffragettes in prison at the time, and the WSPU declared an armistice during wartime. In February 1918, nine months before the end of the war, the Representation of the People Bill enfranchised women over the age of thirty who met certain property qualifications—a political victory that is sometimes seen as a reward for women's contributions to the war effort rather than the result of long-term feminist campaigning.[16]

Writing about Imprisonment | The Suffragettes' Fight over (Self-)Representation

Despite the abrupt halt to the militant campaign and the sense that it had had little direct impact on women's formal citizenship status, the militant activities constituted a significant intervention into the representation of women in the broadest sense—political representation, on the one hand, but also public and private perceptions of women's abilities, skills, and aspirations, on the other hand. As Mary Jean Corbett has argued, feminists in the late-Victorian and early Edwardian periods "demanded a transformation of law and legislation as well as male views," and "questions of representation and self-representation" were at the heart of all suffragette activity (152, 154). The suffragettes' attempts to stage, write down, and publicize their experiences served as a conscious, active effort in self-representation. They also functioned as a collective act of resistance against the regime responsible for their incarceration, because they made visible conditions in the criminal justice system that were usually exempt from internal scrutiny and offered critiques of wider legal and social structures. Some of the suffragettes' accounts explicitly complain against the criminal justice system and its employees, while others concentrate on the women's own feelings in view of a day-to-day struggle to cope with incarceration. These mundane aspects of prison experience were important too, because, as Glenda Norquay suggests, "the imagery and incidents of daily life become the means of representing the wider legal, social and ideological constraints women faced" (172).

While some suffragettes found ways to write surreptitiously during their period(s) of imprisonment, others commented on their prison experiences from hindsight, in autobiographies and memoirs, written after a lapse of time.[17] The texts produced by suffragettes in prison are particularly fascinating documents, however, because they are evidence of the tactics that such women developed in the face of strict institutional control, which included the policing of all acts of communication. These tactics comprised illicit writing activities on scraps of paper, on toilet paper, or in books; writing in a foreign language; and smuggling such accounts out of jail. Diaries and letters by imprisoned suffragettes, like those written under less adverse conditions, are characterized by an "immediacy," resulting from the writers' "lack of foreknowledge about outcomes of the plot of [their lives]" (Smith and Watson 266). In contrast to carefully edited autobiographical accounts produced from hindsight, these texts are, in Bunkers's words, "a commentary on a life as it *was* lived, on life as *process*, not *product*" ("Reading and Interpreting" 15). Yet, as Rebecca Hogan reminds us, diaries, too, are constructed; "shaping and selection" inevitably play a role in journal and letter writing ("Engendered Autobiographies" 104).

While the suffragettes' prison experiences in Edwardian Britain have received some critical attention, the texts and artifacts produced by incarcerated women have undergone little close analysis, not least because of problems with accessibility.[18] Typically, more detailed textual readings have focused on well-known figures such as Constance Lytton, whose activities and autobiography, *Prisons and Prisoners: Some Personal Experiences by Constance Lytton and "Jane Warton, Spinster"* (1914), have caught the interest of researchers in different academic disciplines.[19] Lytton's account, as well as the memoirs of the militant movement's most famous personas, Emmeline Pankhurst, leader of the WSPU, and her daughters Christabel and Sylvia, which also contain discussions of imprisonment, are widely available and have been reissued in modern editions.[20]

In this context, the artist Gliddon's prison diary offers a new vantage point from which to study the experience of imprisonment in Holloway in the spring of 1912, not least because it was written during confinement, rather than postrelease.[21] This document, like all diaries, is necessarily subjective and limited in viewpoint. Swindells warns us not to read diaries as simply "mimetic" ("Liberating the Subject?" 29), and other scholarship has reconceptualized such texts from a supposedly "transparent site of diurnal recording" to documents that need to be "theorized as a complex practice of life writing" (Smith and Watson 267). However, some scholars, such as Corbett, insist that we must not overemphasize textuality, that the autobiographical and the historical are in fact "compatible," and that the autobiographical, while personal and partial, is also "more local, grounded, and specific with respect to the events recorded" than is a supposedly objective history written after the fact (178). This comment is particularly pertinent when considering experiences of incarceration, which were so rarely recorded by prisoners themselves.

Reading and Writing at Holloway

In November 1911, the WSPU resumed militancy following the government's decision to replace the Conciliation Bill, which would have given the vote to some women, with a proposal to introduce universal male suffrage instead. On 5 March 1912, Gliddon was among nineteen women sentenced to two months with hard labor, after being arrested for window breaking at a post office in London's West End.[22] The hard-labor sentence must have come as a shock, since Gliddon had expected to "come off very easily" and "get about 5 days."[23] She spent most of March and April at Holloway Prison in London, recording her thoughts by secretly writing in the margins of the last two hundred or so pages of her copy of *The Poetical Works of Percy Bysshe Shelley*; she also drew pictures of Holloway (see figure 6.1).

The journal contains fairly long daily entries for most days until 3 April, when Gliddon's records become much shorter, but they are complemented by more detailed accounts on loose sheets from that day onward.[24] Gliddon wanted her account to be published under the title "Letters from Holloway," leaving instructions for the title page inside her prison diary (Silver iii).[25] It is unclear why this plan did not come to fruition, but I have speculated elsewhere that her decision not to join in the hunger strike might have impeded her publication plans ("Bless the Gods"). Her personal papers also contain an extensive draft autobiographical account—a revised version of her prison diary, which is presumably the text she was preparing for publication. Included alongside this account are critical comments by

FIGURE 6.1 Katie Gliddon's drawing of her prison cell at Holloway. Reproduced by permission from The Women's Library @ LSE

an unknown reader.[26] The significant amount of labor that Gliddon invested in the writing of her journal and the later revisions suggest the importance these narratives had for her personally and the potential she saw in making her record available to a wider audience.

Given that the painter envisioned publication, her original diary is, in Lynn Z. Bloom's words, both a private account *and* a "public document[], intended for an external readership" (23), by a writer with, as William H. Gass puts it, an "eye on history" (49). If truly private diaries are texts that are, as Bloom suggests, coded and therefore require extratextual information for the reader to be able to fully understand them, whereas public journals are clearly written for a public audience, Gliddon's diary contains features of both. On the one hand, the private nature of the diary is enhanced by problems with legibility; it is here that reading the original journal together with the author's draft autobiographical account and other contextual material can provide a more complete picture.[27] On the other hand, the journal deals with themes that were targeted at a wider readership, possibly with a view to educating this audience, for example, regarding the imprisonment of prostitutes. The twenty-first-century reader especially, though, needs some contextual knowledge of the suffrage campaign, the penal system, and the characters mentioned (such as politicians or other suffragettes) in order to make full sense of Gliddon's account.

Reading Practices at Holloway

Reading and writing were immensely important activities for incarcerated suffragettes, but they were also highly regimented. Like all prisoners, Gliddon was allowed some reading. Typically, inmates at Holloway were given a Bible, a prayer and hymn book, a book on "fresh air and cleanliness," and a tract called "The Narrow Way." They also had access to a prison library.[28] Gliddon mentions obtaining books from the matron, including the Belgian Maurice Maeterlinck's *Wisdom and Destiny*, a philosophical essay on human happiness and justice, which she had presumably ordered from the library (*Prison Diary* 51). Prisoners under Rule 243a were entitled to "books at own expense, not bearing on current events, and unobjectionable" ("Statement"), but the hard-labor sentence meant that Gliddon was not granted the right to have her own books. She deplores that the *Golden Treasury* had been sent to her but that she was not allowed to have it (*Prison Diary* 35).[29] She also asked her mother for a copy of *Middlemarch*, but it is unlikely that she obtained it.[30] Yet there was room for negotiation on a local level, since another suffragette with hard labor, Dr. Louisa Garrett Anderson, apparently "insisted upon keeping her books" (Gliddon, *Prison Diary* 19) and got away with it, possibly because of her status as a doctor.[31] By contrast, three years earlier, in 1909, a tutor's official petition, asking for permission to send books to his imprisoned pupil so that she could study for Cambridge, was declined, but the petitioner was advised that he could donate the books to the prison library instead. One comment in the minutes on the relevant Home Office file states cynically that "a lady who runs the risk of imprisonment has presumably calculated that her action is of more importance to her than her prospects of getting into Cambridge" (Ransome).

Aside from such practical educational purposes, reading for suffragettes, whether in prison or in the outside world, became a tool for expressing their feminist agenda and, in Kate Flint's words, "one means of joining with other women" (248). The importance of reading had already been depicted in the "New Woman" fiction of the fin de siècle and in some suffrage novels (Flint 312).[32] The WSPU's newspaper *Votes for Women*, especially its coeditor until 1912, Emmeline Pethick-Lawrence, promoted reading (Flint 236). Books therefore took on a particular significance for incarcerated suffragettes, because they helped establish a sense of community and, of course, because they provided relief from boredom as well as providing intellectual nourishment and inspiration. As Maroula Joannou notes, "Books that were perceived to oppose the double standard, to offer a critique of patriarchal values, or to contain a feminist vision of the future . . . were taken into the women's prisons and read there by suffragettes" (105). Constance Lytton reports in her autobiography of reading Charlotte Perkins Gilman's *The Man-Made World* (1911) during her stay in Holloway in November 1911 and recalls a storytelling Sunday evening by the fire in the same prison two years earlier, when Emmeline Pethick-Lawrence recited Olive Schreiner's feminist allegory "Three Dreams in a Desert" (Lytton [1914 ed.] 333, 156). Gliddon writes of discussions with a fellow suffragette on "narrative poetry and on Browning" (*Prison Diary* 2, 9 Apr. 1912, 3–4). Such oral traditions are further evidence of the significance of stories for mutual support and inspiration, as well as of the resourcefulness of suffragettes in the absence of actual reading material.[33]

Gliddon sarcastically comments on the reading material provided by the prison, especially "The Narrow Way": "I think I as a prisoner of the Liberal Government I know quite enough about the narrow way without opening that book! I think it rather an insult to have given it to me" (*Prison Diary* 11). But she also suggests how official literature could be used subversively. For instance, when the chaplain gives her Macaulay's *History of England*, she ends up reading about the Celtic rebellion (*Prison Diary* 17). Similarly, she points out the illogicality of denying her access to the *Golden Treasury* while letting her read the "Percy Religious" with a ballad of Adam Bell, Clym of the Clough, and William of Cloudesley, "three bold archers who one fine day slew three hundred men and more in Carleile town" (*Prison Diary* 35). Gliddon draws attention to the irony of having a suffragette immerse herself in the popular myths of these famous, violent outlaws: "This is indeed thrilling reading kindly provided by a fatherly Government for my instruction. It is so absurd that we should not be able to have our own books" (35). Her response to official policies on prison reading illustrates how prisoners either resisted prescribed material altogether or used available literature for purposes other than those intended by the regime's agenda of reformation.[34]

Despite such regulations, Gliddon's prison diary offers evidence that suffragettes were able to access reading material through fellow women, either secretly or with the tacit support of prison officers. She mentions reading Giuseppe Mazzini (1805–1872)—the philosopher of the Italian Risorgimento and supporter of popular uprisings who had also been imprisoned for his political ideals—lent by another prisoner.[35] Her comments clearly indicate how such material helped frame the suffragettes' understanding of their own political actions:

> He spoke of "the progress of all through all under the leading of the best and wisest" as being upon the "beautiful ensign of democracy." We are part of the uprising of democracy of which Maltzini [*sic*] speaks, a part that has been overlooked, but we are calling loudly for justice now and nothing will stop our cry. How many more long days must women spend in captivity? They are willing to spend their lives in prison if necessary. Will the blindness of a nation demand that sacrifice? Or will it at last realise that we wish not to conquer but to serve? (*Prison Diary* 46)[36]

Other suffragettes such as Emmeline Pethick-Lawrence and Katherine Price Hughes, who was active with her husband in the Working Girls' Club, a part of the West London Mission, had been inspired by Mazzini's "Young Italy." Pethick-Lawrence's autobiography, *My Part in a Changing World* (1938), describes how Price Hughes had seen the Italian's ideals of liberation and solidarity as a model for "young women of the leisured classes" in England (72).[37] An edition of Mazzini's memoir and essays had received positive commentary in the *Englishwoman's Review* in 1875, which guaranteed exposure among the journal's middle- and upper-class audience ("Review of *Joseph Mazzini*").[38]

Holloway prisoners, then, were able to swap reading, even if doing so was against official policy. Opportunities for association at chapel or exercise offered possibilities for exchanging material or notes.[39] Gliddon describes how she observed her leader, Emmeline Pankhurst, who was at Holloway at the same time, inquiring after everybody's reading requirements: "Mrs. Pankhurst was walking about on the balcony above us and she asked the suffragettes on the top balcony whether they had any novels to read as she had just had a lot sent in" (*Prison Diary* 32). Pankhurst was also allowed to receive the *Times*, the *Standard*, and the *Daily News*, and Gliddon notes, "All news we get comes in that way" (47). The artist longed for "a daily paper" with topical news from the outside world, but she especially craved updates on developments in the movement through the WSPU's publication: "O I do want my 'Votes for Women' so badly. I wish I knew what is happening to us" (2).[40] Yet her entries also suggest that she was not always in the mood for reading or lacked the "energy" to do so, feeling "faint" from being kept indoors and having trouble eating (9).

The Shelley volume was clearly a significant part of Gliddon's daily prison routine. As she explained in an interview in 1965, she had smuggled the book into prison, together with pencils sewn into the collar of her coat.[41] Combined with singing and a sense of community with the other suffragettes, Shelley provided Gliddon moral support during adversity. Describing her evening activities on 6 March, Gliddon writes, "Read Shelley. Pigeons came and ate crumbs of mine on my windowsill. Someone, possibly [G McOver?] walked down the corridor singing 'O rest in the Lord.' It was a nice incident and I loved the singer for her courage. Those things make me feel the togetherness of it all. We are looking after one another in here. Yelled from window. Sang to myself, 'March of the Women' and Marsaillaise. Read Shelley aloud and went to bed about 8pm. Slept all night" (*Prison Diary* 2). The artist's use of the Romantic poet and rebel's work is highly symbolic. In her own notes, she explicitly engages with the poetry, transposing its revolutionary message to her own social context—the struggle for women's suffrage. Thus, Gliddon copies lines from Shelley's "Fragment:

To a Friend Released from Prison, 1817" on her front page and dedicates them to her leader Emmeline Pankhurst:

—let the tyrant keep
His chains and tears, yea, let him weep
With rage to see them freshly risen,
Like strength from slumber, from the prison,
In which he vainly hoped the soul to bind
Which on the chains must prey that fetter humankind![42]

The suffragette here appropriates the male poet's bondage imagery, suggesting that imprisonment will only strengthen the feminist cause, with ultimate benefit for all of humanity.

As Deborah Tyler-Bennett, drawing on Flint's *The Woman Reader*, remarks in her study of poetry in the suffrage movement, poetry—and Shelley in particular—played an important role for young female readers, since it offered a valve for "violent emotion" that continued to maintain "a subversive appeal" for adult women (120). Shelley was popular reading among suffrage activists, militant and nonmilitant alike. Charlotte Despard and Mabel Collins's suffrage novel *Outlawed* (1908) depicted its protagonist as a keen supporter of liberty, expressed through her passion for Shelley (and Mazzini).[43] A Christmas card for 1910 designed by the Artists' Suffrage League quoted from Shelley's *Prometheus Unbound* ("And women, too, frank, beautiful, and kind . . .").[44] The pacifist Helena Swanwick wrote in her autobiography, *I Have Been Young* (1935), that it was writers such as Shelley—and John Stuart Mill—who provided feminist inspiration (81). Gliddon's use of this particular author in prison therefore situates her within a broader feminist reading tradition.

"Bless the Gods for My Pencils and Paper" | Secret Writing Practices[45]

Reading, then, was one occupation that helped incarcerated suffragettes maintain a sense of collectivity and political purpose, but Gliddon's illicit acts of writing and drawing suggest that these active ways of *producing* something, of leaving a mark and testimony, were also crucial, if not more important. Green notes with reference to suffragettes Helen Gordon and Kitty Marion that the "project of writing" during incarceration functioned "as both something to live for and an enlivening practice denied the prisoner" (99). Records of one's thoughts on the slate or the prison wall were erased the following day, something also deplored by Sylvia Pankhurst in her poem "Writ on Cold Slate," secretly penned during her imprisonment for sedition in 1920–21.[46] Rule 243a did "not include the use of writing materials," but suffragettes and their supporters, in their insistence on gaining full political prisoner status, repeatedly petitioned the Home Office to obtain pen and paper (Letter to the Home Office). Catherine Douglas Smith requested in vain "to be allowed the use of pencil and paper or note book": "in order that those studies which I am able to make here—being allowed French German and History books—may be furthered"; she also wished to use the notebook to write down her ideas, which she had there "ample opportunity to think out" (Petition). Frederick Pethick-Lawrence asked Member of Parliament T. B. Silcock to plead with the secretary of state on behalf of his imprisoned wife, who "feels particularly the deprivation of pencil and paper." This request was also refused, with the reasoning that his wife was "not a political prisoner. It was decided that the privilege asked for led to abuses and should not be granted to suffragettes. Mrs Lawrence has incited others to insubordination" (F. Pethick-Lawrence).

Allowing (political) prisoners access to writing material was perceived as a potential danger to the penal and wider social system. As Barbara Harlow notes in her study of political imprisonment, drawing on Foucault's *Discipline and Punish*, the penal apparatus appropriates the "power of writing" with the aim of documenting and objectifying the prisoner. Political internees, "many of whom are detained as a result of their literary and cultural activity, present already a serious threat to the authorities' control over this 'power of writing'; their narratives of incarceration and all forms of written and oral communication among them while inside the prison, contest that other control" (*Resistance Literature* 125). By keeping a secret diary, Gliddon and other suffragettes managed to escape the official censure of writing material and expression of thought on paper. Some, such as Daisy Dorothea Solomon, managed to illegally obtain pencil and paper but, when they were found out, were punished with two days' solitary confinement (Solomon 5).

Although pen and paper were prohibited, suffragettes under Rule 243a were granted a fortnightly letter. Prison officials provided preprinted paper, which only allowed for the most basic information to be conveyed. Regulations about communications between prisoners and their family and friends

FIGURE 6.2

Portrait of Leonora
Tyson. Reproduced by
permission. © Museum
of London

were printed on the front page of the blue paper, with the first regulation
stating, "The permission to write and receive Letters is given to prisoners
for the purpose of enabling them to keep a connection with their respectable friends and not that they may be kept informed of public events" (Tyson, *Prison Letters* 2003.46/4). Women such as Leonora Tyson, the honorary
WSPU branch secretary in Lambeth and Streatham who was imprisoned
with hard labor for window smashing, managed to circumvent such regulations (see figure 6.2).[47] Rather than accepting the authorities' attempt to in-
fantilize the prisoner, instructing her to "behave well" like a stern parent
would a child, Tyson wrote *over* the preprinted prison paper in black ink,
in a much more detailed fashion than the official format stipulates, defying
calls for particular kinds of conduct by the prison regime and, by extension,
those men in the government and legal system who had convicted and incarcerated her. Tyson's act of writing refuses to adopt the official subjectivity imagined for the prisoner, the voice of the "I" prefabricated on prison

paper (see figure 6.3; Tyson, *Prison Letters* 2003.46/4).[48] Gliddon appropriated the official paper in a similar way, crossing out the line "If I behave well . . ." and writing instructions as to the kinds of things she wanted to be sent (bath towels, a pillow case, a linen bag for her clothes).[49] Interestingly, she also notes in the letter that the wardresses are "charming"—possibly a strategy to stay on the officers' good side, given that all official letters were

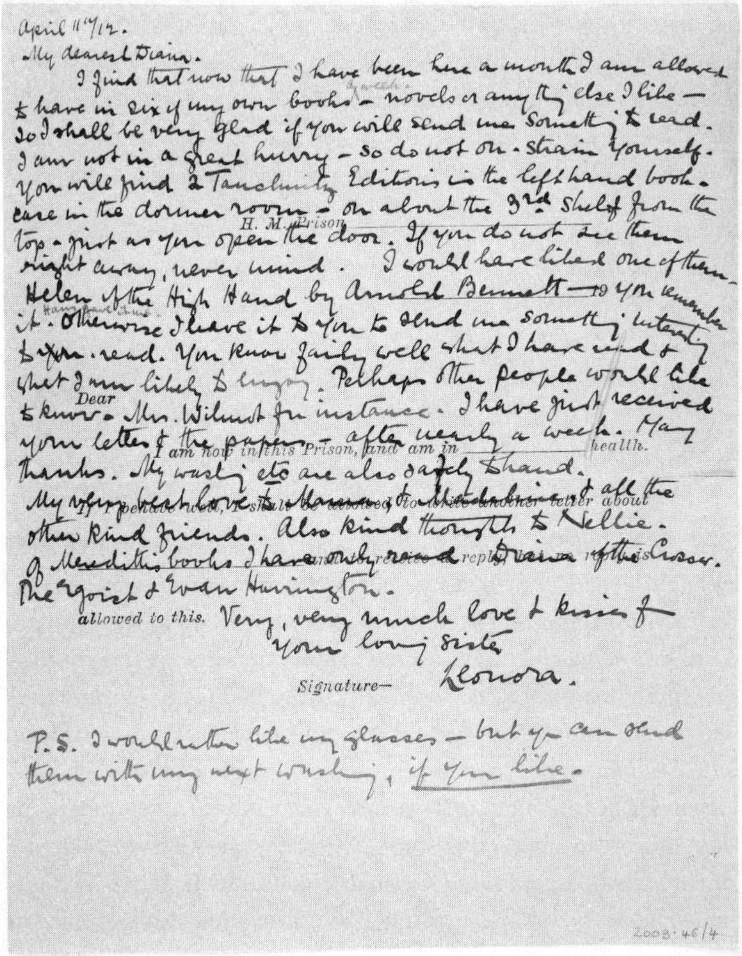

FIGURE 6.3 Prison letter by Leonora Tyson (1912). Reproduced by permission.
© Museum of London

inspected prior to posting, although she repeated this assessment in her diary, which she did not expect to be read by staff.

Suffragettes defied prison rules not simply by appropriating official prison letters for their purposes; they also found ways of secretly writing letters. Both Gliddon and Tyson wrote them on a regular basis and smuggled them out with their laundry baskets (suffragettes were allowed their own clothes), which suggests either that such baskets were not always inspected thoroughly or that wardresses acted as collaborators. Tyson produced stacks of letters while in prison, including some written on toilet paper. Being bilingual—her father was of German descent—Tyson switched between English and German in many of these writings.[50] After being awarded Rule 243a privileges in mid-April, which included use of one's own books, she hid letters in the book spine and was anxious to find out whether her family had received them. Writing to her mother and sister, she explains at the end,

> Hoffentlich habt Ihr meinen letzten Brief mit meiner Waesche erhalten. Sagt es mir ob ja od. nein weil so viel drin stand. Man kann Briefe ganz ausgezeichnet hinten in Buechern verstecken. Zwischen [?] Deckel und dem Buch hinten—da ist doch gewoehnlich bei ordentlich gebundenen Buechern ein kleiner hohler Raum? Es muss natuerlich nur ein kleines, duennes B. sein. One of the wardresses fainted in Chapel yesterday, 3 ord. prisoners and lots of suffs. amongst them Mrs. Casey. Perhaps they will do something about the ventilation soon now. Best love and many kisses to you all. Leonora.[51]

It is noticeable that Tyson only uses German in the passage dealing with the smuggling of letters, which suggests that her bilingualism here serves as a strategy for protection. If the letter was found, prison officials would have been unlikely to be able to decipher the German sentences. Kitty Marion, another bilingual suffragette originally from Germany, explicitly commented on using this strategy in her unpublished autobiography. She modified the German saying "und bist du nicht willig, dann brauch' ich Gewalt" (and if you are not willing, I will use force) in an official letter from prison to secretly convey an impending hunger strike: "'und isst du nicht willig, etc.' . . . which Lilla, speaking German would understand as not 'eating' willingly instead of not 'Being' willing" (219). Women writing from prison, such as Marion, Gliddon, and Tyson, then, were proactive in changing the behavioral scripts supplied by the authorities, actions that symbolically also functioned as an effort to challenge the wider life narratives that society dictated to women at the time.

Despite such disobedience, fear of discovery is a recurring theme in these clandestine documents. Gliddon, in a secret note to her sister Gladys, warns of the need to self-censor: "There are a lot of things I do not say in these letters that are smuggled out. Because ten [?]—not mine—of them have been found by the authorities. So it is safer not to say things as you never know your luck."[52] Awareness of an audience—both an intended and an unintended audience—inevitably influences the imprisoned writer of letters or the diarist, as Hogan notes with reference to the Soviet Jew Edward Kuznetsov, who was imprisoned in the USSR in the early 1970s following a failed attempt at escape ("Diarists" 9). Kuznetsov concedes in his own prison diary, "anyone's behaviour tends to be somewhat unnatural, if they even *suspect* someone is looking over their shoulder" (15). This possibility of discovery, like the limited availability of paper, surely also shaped the suffragettes' approach to their secret letters and diaries. Gliddon explicitly records anxiety in her journal: "If anyone discovers this book and pencil I shall die of sorrow. It is my only chance of getting through these days at all. It is funny that there should be so much to say when nothing is happening at all" (*Prison Diary* 7). By writing extensively, Gliddon defied such fears and the potential consequences of discovery. Aside from the occasional reference to the need for caution, there is little sense of how much the worries over being discovered might have formed and transformed her prison writings. The impossibility of determining any potential omissions, and how they may change our readings, is another reminder that we need to treat the evidence provided in prison diaries as partial and selective.

Cross-Class Relations in Women's Prisons

While prisoners such as Gliddon were fearful of discovery, there are clear indications that relations between suffragette prisoners and officers at Holloway were not always marked by tension and that official policy was often circumvented at the local level. Several accounts suggest that relations with female staff were sometimes amicable, given the circumstances. Although Alyson Brown is certainly right in saying that relationships between suffragettes and women officers were challenging at times, especially during episodes of hunger strikes and forcible feeding, there is enough evidence in suffragettes' prison writings to balance her claim that there existed "an almost impassable wedge between them" (631). Class tensions were one factor that made it difficult to entirely overcome the structural barriers between suffragettes, many of whom came from middle- or upper-class families, and female officers, typically from modest backgrounds.[53] Although Brown claims that "possible class differences were less prominent and blurred—hidden behind the staff/prisoner status divide" (632)—it is precisely those class differences that contributed to occasional tensions between suffragettes and female prison staff.

Class indeed became a determining factor not only in the suffragettes' relationship with women officers but also in their contact with, and representation of, "ordinary" convicts. Although the suffragettes were not free from class prejudice, their writings are characterized by attempts to bring about social and institutional changes with a positive impact on *all* women, including "ordinary" convicts and prison officers. In particular, Gliddon's prison writings open up spaces for "ordinary" prisoners' voices and a new intersubjectivity between women, based on an erotics of the gaze.

Suffragette prisoners recognized the difficulties faced by female (and male) staff. Although Constance Lytton's *Prisons and Prisoners* complains about some officials who speak to convicts in a mechanistic, rather than an individualized and humane, way, she also sees how the system takes its toll on prisoners and staff alike, noting that the chaplain looks "ill" and that the matron seems "very tired" and wondering "whether any part of her work gave her satisfaction" ([1914 ed.] 98). Hunger strikes and forcible feeding constituted a particular trial for both imprisoned suffragettes and the officers in charge of them. Yet, even then, prisoners wrote favorably of female staff. In a letter to the editor of a local newspaper after being released in August 1912, Elsie Duval describes her experience of being held down by four or five wardresses while being fed through a nasal tube by two doctors. Although she had to endure "this excruciatingly painful and degrading process nine times" and still carried "finger marks and bruises," she insists, "In regard to the wardresses, I must say in justice to them, that they carry out their odious task with as much humanity as is possible under the circumstances." Since Duval added this comment as a postscript, it is given a prominent visual position in her letter and suggests that she wanted to publicly emphasize female solidarity rather than to portray the wardresses as callous executioners of an inhumane, patriarchal system.

Gliddon equally noted during the first month of her imprisonment that the matron was "a nice intelligent woman" and that the wardresses on her ward were "charming" and "make things as easy for [the prisoners] as possible" (*Prison Diary* 6, 27). A year later, Harriet Roberta Kerr expressed something akin to gratitude toward, and solidarity with, the female prison workers, as she wrote in a secret letter in 1913: "Baths also I am cut off during hunger strike, but the wardresses are really great dears and bring me the best equivalent they have. . . . They would also bring me books if they dared, but someone would discover it and tell on them and I should hate to get any of them into trouble." Lytton's autobiography even describes moments of emotional comfort and physical support between prisoner and officer. She recalls a conversation with the night wardress, who had consoled the crying suffragette, as "one of the sunlit flower patches of [her] time in Holloway" ([1914 ed.] 112). Describing a scene bordering on an erotic encounter, Lytton writes of how the officer, who was suffering from a cough, allowed the suffragette to "return her kindness" and "open her dress" in order to rub ointment on her chest, which could easily have resulted in the wardress's dismissal. Although Lytton "would gladly have talked to her all night about prisoners, the working conditions of wardresses, her own life," subsequent adherence to the regulations prevented this deeper exchange (111–12). Such incidents suggest that suffragettes and officers at least momentarily overcame social and institutional divides.

Despite such moments, differences in class background hindered potential alliances between suffrage prisoners and female staff. Gliddon complained about a wardress who interrupted a fellow suffragette's dance, performed for the amusement of her colleagues, commenting, "It is the sense of class hatred that comes out so often in the uneducated woman which gives her pleasure in this exercising of power over any member of the cultured classes who may come into her power" (*Prison Diary* 35–36). Rather than reading the wardress's effort to stop the dance as an act of official duty, Gliddon interprets it as a gesture of personal and social revenge, driven by both ignorance and anger at class difference. The painter's writing here also implies that the aesthetic appreciation of art is exclusive to "the cultured classes," an elitist gesture which reinforces the separation between women of different class backgrounds as much as the wardress's act of aborting the dance does.

Like female prison officers, working-class women and "ordinary" prisoners feature in suffragette prison writing. Several critics have discussed the suffragettes' ambivalent relationship with working-class women—inside and outside the prison.[54] Kabi Hartman speaks of "the complex amalgamation of idealisation, romanticisation and manipulation for propaganda purposes of the symbol of the working-class woman that marked WSPU thinking" (40–41). Haslam asserts that the suffragettes' use of "the figure of the common prisoner in their narratives serves to cast those people within often silent and non-agential positions, replicating the denial of women's voices and opinions in the larger public sphere" (Introduction 31). Some texts challenge these readings to some extent, however. Most emphatically, the socialist Sylvia Pankhurst used her status and resources to publish accounts of "ordinary" convict voices in her poems.[55] Her prison poetry must be read in conjunction with her earlier efforts to make visible the living and working conditions of women in prison in a series of sketches published in the *Pall Mall Magazine* in 1907, accompanying her article "What It Feels Like to Be in Prison" (see figure 6.4).[56] In this article, which calls for prison reform, Pankhurst chooses second-person narration for parts of her descriptions of prison life, inviting her readers directly to empathize with the position of "ordinary" prisoners—women who "are broken down by poverty, sorrow, and over-work" (557): "Imagine that you are one of these prisoners. . . . You find yourself at last in a small whitewashed cell" (554–56).

The poem "The Cleaners" dedicates five stanzas to the first-person perspective of nonsuffrage prisoners who, like servants, were in charge of doing chores, such as tidying the suffragettes' cells, and were therefore called the "cleaners." These stanzas portray how the cleaners, with "weary limbs" (line 2), are chased from task to task and imagine how a cleaner herself would have represented her onerous daily routine: "and two long corridors must also scrub / before the great ones come, swift marching through; / and as I scrub they call me 'Cleaner! Here!'" (lines 4–6). It is possible to read the phrase "the great ones" as a coded reference to, and critique of, suffragettes, as much as to prison officers or visiting officials. Pankhurst's account of the ordinary prisoner's perspective contrasts with other poems such as Kate Evans's "The Cleaners of Holloway," which, although sympathetic to the "cleaners," is written in the third person while glossing over potential resentment and alienation when it describes the working women as "cheerful," "kind," and "willing" (lines 10, 12). Although Pankhurst's verses are not the actual writing of a "cleaner"—who, in that regard, remains "non-agential" in Haslam's sense—her text nevertheless conveys the laborers' agency by offering a rare glimpse into an otherwise hidden viewpoint.[57]

In Gliddon's prison diary, too, "ordinary" prisoners feature as both "non-agential" objects and speaking subjects, however limited their speech may be. As in Pankhurst's poem, Gliddon demonstrates awareness of these women's labor and, unlike the verses, explicitly notes the extra effort that

Ready for Supper

Scrubbing the Bed

Dinner

The Bread Basket

Sketches at Holloway.

FIGURE 6.4 Sketches of prisoners at Holloway, after drawings by Sylvia Pankhurst.
From *Pall Mall Magazine* 39.169 (May 1907), p. 555. Reproduced with permission from an
image produced by ProQuest LLC for its online product, *British Periodicals, 1681–1920.*
www.proquest.com

suffragettes cause these women, wishing that "Asquith and the cabinet ministers had to do all the hard work [the suffragists'] entertainment means, instead of the women officials here and the ordinary prisoners" (*Prison Diary* 3).[58] After a loosening of regulations, Gliddon talks in private with one of the "cleaners." She discovers that the woman had been on remand for one month: "[The woman] was told if she liked to put on prison clothes she could do work. This she was glad to do as being shut up all day alone is such a terrible thing we can hardly bear it" (46). Gliddon's writing initially reproduces the other woman's comments in third person, offering some insight into her point of view, before eventually slipping into a first-person-plural perspective in the second half of the sentence. The diary here does not so much silence the remand prisoner as shift into a collective voice that suggests identification. Simultaneously, rather than erasing difference, Gliddon indicates that she is fully aware of gaps in understanding and the dissimilarity between her own imprisonment and that of others. Having defined solitary confinement as almost unbearable, she concludes, "What it must be to a woman who is not a suffragette I cannot imagine" (46). The diary thus conveys a sense of other voices and solidarity with "ordinary" prisoners while recognizing difference.[59]

Gliddon also offers a platform for other voices when she writes about prostitution. The fact that she dedicated parts of her journal to such a theme stresses the public-private nature of her diary, in Bloom's sense, since prostitution speaks both to her immediate encounters in prison and to a wider social issue of concern to an external audience. In her awareness of the sex trade and trafficking in young girls, Gliddon was certainly partially influenced by her social circle. She was friends with two daughters of the Reverend Benjamin Waugh, who was the founder of the National Society for the Prevention of Cruelty against Children (NSPCC) and supported the editor of the liberal *Pall Mall Gazette*, W. T. Stead, in his fight against "white slavery."[60] Gliddon explicitly refers to Stead, who had been in Holloway Prison following his investigation for "The Maiden Tribute of Modern Babylon" (1885), an exposé of child prostitution.[61] Furthermore, contextual evidence suggests that she read George Bernard Shaw, a favorite writer with the suffragettes who shared their sympathetic interest in prostitutes and whose play *Mrs Warren's Profession* (1898) fell afoul of the censors for its explicit treatment of prostitution and its refusal to condemn and punish the play's "fallen woman," Mrs. Warren, for her actions.[62] Her interest in social problems such as prostitution and sweated labor would have been further stimulated by suffragette publications and speeches on these themes at her WSPU branch meetings.[63]

The views on the sex trade of WSPU members such as Gliddon support June Purvis's claim that the WSPU as an organization was "feminist socialist in orientation" ("Prison Experiences" 107), but they also reveal ambivalent attitudes toward women of the lower social strata. On the one hand, the artist's diary offers clear evidence of an interest in the reform of social predicaments such as prostitution, predominantly affecting poor women.[64] Sex workers are given the status of martyrlike figures and become the raison d'être of the movement and of imprisonment, in that they symbolized women's oppression at its extreme.

In this context, the suffragettes' stays in prison functioned as an extension of visits to spaces previously closed to middle-class women, such as working-class homes or urban streets rife with poverty, where from the late nineteenth century on, well-to-do women were increasingly active in the role of social investigators.[65] The parallels between visits to destitute adults and children, sweatshops, and prisons are made explicit in suffragette Annie Biggs's statement. Drawing connections between a struggle for wider social justice and imprisonment for women's suffrage, Biggs summed up her motivations for activism in the following way: "We have seen the homeless homes / We have seen the little children—*Poor little things!* / We ourselves have no homes— / We have been into the sweating dens. / And—We have been into *Prison*" (6, original emphasis). Similarly, Gliddon's entry for 24 March identifies solidarity with women workers and prostitutes as one of the motivations behind her political crusade and a social reality that makes life in prison bearable for relatively privileged women such as her:

> For years when our women have gone to prison it has always made me depressed and angry to think of them there. My own imprisonment has been made easy for me by Helen Saunders' remark last November when I was troubled about the suffragettes in Holloway. She told me not to worry about the women who were unhappy for one or two months. The sweated workers and the little white slaves were wretched all their lives. And the imprisoned suffragettes were always conscious of the good cause for which they were working. We must go into dark places ourselves if we are to carry the light there. (*Prison Diary* 37–38)

The language here taps into religious imagery frequently used in suffrage propaganda such as *Votes for Women*. As Kabi Hartman notes, the paper's editor, Emmeline Pethick-Lawrence, cast suffragettes in the role of "soldiers of light," and "suffragette prison writings exploit the biblical dichotomy of light versus darkness, employing light as a metaphor for the spirit of Christ and truth" (41).[66] Similar images of philanthropic militancy had already been used for female foreign missionaries, who were portrayed as "soldiers of Christ" (Rowbotham). Gliddon's account combines religious vocabulary of light versus darkness with references to the importance of female friendship and tutelage for the suffragettes' personal development, since it is clearly her friend Saunders's comment that contributed to a transformation in her attitude and perhaps even her willingness to get involved in militant activity in the first place.

Inevitably, in such instances, prostitutes in their role as emblems of a larger social problem are objectified and silenced—they become a *cause*—but Gliddon's other entries suggest that her abstract mission statements gain a new dimension when she is confronted with concrete encounters in prison. On 30 March, after attending chapel, where Gliddon was looking at the "ordinary" prisoners, she reminds herself that some of them are prostitutes (*Prison Diary* 42). References to "girls of the streets" (43) occur at various points in her diary; for example, Gliddon witnesses conversations between two such women from her cell: "They are in the cells below. I was up at my window watching the clouds when they started to talk. One girl's name was Lily and the other's name was Doll. . . . They talked as is the way of all prisoners in the form of question and answer and sometimes it was like the form of the psalms" (45). Although we do not know what exactly the conversation between these women consisted of, Gliddon draws attention to its existence and offers an insight into the day-to-day experience of incarceration for "ordinary" prisoners, including prostitutes, and the strategies such women developed in order to maintain contact with each other and to stay sane, despite solitary confinement. For the writer herself, being confined alongside these women evidently opened up a new world to which she had previously not had access. Through her simile "like the form of the psalms" in the passage just quoted, she compares "the sound of the Doll and Lill" (45) to religious verse—a particularly transgressive gesture considering that the women are prostitutes. Through this equation, Gliddon extends religious language, usually reserved for suffrage prisoners, to other women in prison.[67]

Gliddon goes further in her attempt to give voice to "ordinary" prisoners by reporting some of the dialogue between a young prostitute and her friend:

In the cell underneath me now is a young girl, a prostitute off the London streets. She is frightened of the night, poor little thing. She is knocking on her wall to her companion. When they were talking earlier, her refrain was "I wish it was morning." Now she has just called out of her window feverishly, "Violet, how are you?" The other one has answered. O how cruel it is to lock that frightened little creature in a cell. It is agony to us sometimes to look at the door and to know we cannot open it although we have the knowledge that it is for the sake of women like that little frightened one below that we are here. Few women would come to prison for political power if it were not as a social power by means of which society will be cleansed. Hundreds of women would come to prison if they could hear that frightened knocking like a bird caught in a net. But you have to come to prison to hear it. (48)

The painter's sympathy with one especially frightened prisoner, who becomes symbol and motivation for the suffrage campaign, suggests that prison here functions as a space that enables this insight across social boundaries. Just as Lytton insisted on becoming Jane Warton in order to get "first-hand experiences" (Lytton [1914 ed.] 42) that would enable her not only to understand but also to *represent* working women's viewpoints, Gliddon suggests that one must have personal encounters with women in prison to fully understand the need for social and political change.

The campaign against prostitution and trafficking in women and children was an important aspect in the women's suffrage campaign. As Susan Kingsley Kent has shown, the fight for women's votes was not simply about political representation, but it aimed to "redefine and recreate, by political means, the sexual culture of Britain" (3). Gliddon's diary entry confirms this argument by suggesting that women who were willing to risk imprisonment did so in the assumption that "political power" would mean "social power," which, in turn, would change relationships between the sexes and specifically result in an end to the sex trade. The image of the girl as a "bird caught in a net" operates on a double level, suggesting that prison only acts as an extension of society for young women who are already trapped in prostitution; the metaphor also implies that this "bird" must be liberated by others, namely, female activists and reformers. Gliddon explains how years of unsuccessful voluntary efforts finally convinced female activists to fight for full citizenship, even if it meant imprisonment, in order to facilitate fuller civic involvement for women, on behalf of other, forgotten, members of their sex "who are cursed by the lust of men" (*Prison Diary* 48). She contrasts "an endless procession of women and girls" who are doomed to return to prison again and again with the relative innocence of the terrified young prisoner in the cell below her, while acknowledging that even recidivists "have all been like that little frightened one below, first offenders, once" (48).

Although the passage displays empathy and solidarity with the young streetwalker, and with prostitutes in general, Gliddon's victimization of these women—reinforced by the repetition of the diminutive "little" with reference to the prostitute—allows her to imagine female reformers as their saviors who "bring light to those who sit in darkness" (48). Her language draws not only on religious imagery but also on colonial discourses that had been appropriated by reformers to depict social relations on a more local level. In *The Criminal Prisons of London and Scenes of Prison Life* (1862), journalists Henry Mayhew and John Binny had already established an explicit analogy between the criminal underworld of London and Africa, implying that both needed civilizing (4). In 1890, the founder of the Salvation Army, William Booth, framed reformist writings about his home country, *In Darkest England and the Way Out*, with a discussion of the explorer Henry Morton Stanley's account *In Darkest Africa*, published the same year. Gliddon's rhetoric indicates that suffrage activists were not always able or willing to distance themselves from discourses that reinscribed otherness and social inequalities, even as they were fighting to overcome others.

The artist's notion that society must be "cleansed" from social ills such as sex work similarly draws on problematic imagery in Victorian and Edwardian campaigns against prostitution that often remained caught in a double-sided discourse. According to Judith Walkowitz's influential study on prostitution in Victorian Britain, "Pollution became the governing metaphor for the perils of social intercourse" between prostitutes as members of the social underworld and the rest of society (*Prostitution* 4). This image maintained its power during the battle against the Contagious Diseases Acts and the social purity movements in the wake of the successful repeal of the acts. At worst, the rhetoric of pollution and social purity stigmatized women who had engaged in prostitution as infectious outcasts and continued to "demarcate pure women from the impure" (70). The effects of such an ideology are evident in an incident that took place in Holloway, simultaneous with Gliddon's incarceration, when the suffragette Mary Nesbitt successfully demanded a transfer to another cell because she would not tolerate staying in a room that had been inhabited by a prostitute (Purvis, "Prison Experiences" 110).

There is no evidence suggesting that Gliddon similarly pursued physical distance from such fellow inmates. Rather, she expresses outrage that imprisonment should be regarded as an appropriate form of punishment for such social pariahs at all. Comparing herself to three prostitutes whom she encountered in prison, she recognizes the injustice of social inequities: "Disease and early death are the only things in front of those 3 girls yet we shall live, so I suppose, quiet lives for many years. It is so unfair that their lives should be so miserable and short and ours so happy and full of the joy of life" (*Prison Diary* 48). Yet, by drawing on the metaphor of pollution, Gliddon's account remains constrained by the term's ambivalence and, at least rhetorically, does not vehemently refute the damaging distinction between pure and impure women that some advocates of prostitutes had sought to overcome.[68] The writer's choice of the adverb "feverishly" to describe the young streetwalker's calling further associates the girl with disease and excessive passion.

Despite such limitations, Gliddon demonstrates some awareness of difference, even if she is less self-reflexive in her approach than were other suffragettes such as Lytton, who explicitly acknowledged the need to distinguish between having "respect and whole-hearted sympathy" for women from lower-class backgrounds and the right to "represent them" ([1914 ed.] 42).[69] Nevertheless, Gliddon's diary also gestures toward creating a site for a new ideal of community and what Corbett has called "intersubjectivity," which "can potentially allow for both identification and conflict, both connection and difference" (162). If Lytton strove to establish connections through cross-dressing and literally embodying a working-class woman, Gliddon's writing creates such spaces by giving voice to "ordinary" prisoners and by implicitly suggesting the potential of an intersubjective erotics of the gaze between women in prison.

Between Women | Female Prisoners and the Politics of the Gaze

Expanding and revising earlier critiques of the gaze, such as Laura Mulvey's influential "Visual Pleasure and Narrative Cinema" (1975), more recent work in feminist film and visual culture theory has turned attention from women as objects of the gaze to women as actively gazing subjects. Writing on relationships between women in the last third of the nineteenth century—the period preceding the historical moment under scrutiny here and the cultural context into which women such as Gliddon were born—Sharon Marcus argues that "Victorian commodity culture incited an erotic appetite for femininity in women, framed spectacular images of women for a female gaze," and "encouraged women and girls to desire, scrutinize, and handle simulacra of alluring femininity" (112).[70] With more specific reference to a prison context, critics such as Green have alluded to, rather than fully explored, the possibility of eroticism between women in prison and within the Edwardian suffrage movement, which "allowed women to put themselves on display for other women" (56–57). Most assertively, queer readings of the historically later women-in-prison film—a genre that capitalizes precisely on such possibilities of erotic attachments, in more or less explicit terms—suggest that this film genre is "predicated on the possibility that women observe other women" (Mayne 117), often with sexualized undertones which are complicated through race, and, I would add here, class. The women-in-prison film creates, in Judith Mayne's words, "dramas of surveillance and visibility" (117), by engaging with women's role as both object of the gaze *and* gazing subject.[71]

Despite significant dissimilarities between the women-in-prison film, a popular genre from the 1950s, and a 1912 diary—from obvious differences in form to the fact that many of the films traditionally have an implied male audience—Gliddon's text sets a similar stage for such spectacles of visibility by casting herself as an active, gazing subject in a prison context. A preoccupation with female bodies—prisoners of all classes *and* wardresses—and admiration of their physical beauty is noticeable throughout the diary and distinguishes it from other prison writings. The writer finds "the joy of seeing beautiful women in this desert place . . . so comforting" (*Prison Diary* 18) and notes the welcome contrast between the "brilliant coloured hair" of "a lovely auburn haired suffragette" and "this colourless dwelling place" (28). She records that Emmeline Pethick-Lawrence looks "so handsome" (27) and observes corporal detail in other women, for instance, her cleaner's "striking blue eyes and black eyebrows" and her "nicely pointed fingers" (46) or the shape of the auburn-haired suffragette's "throat and chin" (28).

Gliddon's interest in female beauty could merely be interpreted as an artist's penchant for aesthetic appreciation—an artist who, after all, had attended life-drawing classes with female models during her studies at the progressive Slade School of Art.[72] But her observations also open up interpretations that, more transgressively, acknowledge the possibility of romantic feeling or even erotic desire between women, across boundaries of class and institutional role. The strong romantic or erotic attachments in women's prisons, between matrons and prisoners and among inmates (the so-called palling-in or palling up), were already publicly recognized decades before Gliddon entered Holloway, for instance, in Frederick William Robinson's 1860s narratives on female prisoners, which insisted that "women do fall in love with each other in prisons" (*Memoirs of Jane Cameron* 2:93), as discussed in chapter 2. The legal historian Lucia Zedner notes that the "tampering" with female convicts was a theme in nineteenth-century sources on women's imprisonment, even though the line between "emotional and sexual intimacy" is often hard to establish from historical hindsight (161–62). The spiritualist Susan Willis Fletcher, incarcerated for fraud at London's Tothill Fields Prison, in her 1884 prison autobiography quotes what appears to be a love letter from her former warder, who, addressing her as "my dear darling baby," describes feeling "miserable and unhappy" after Fletcher's release (409). The spiritualist only appears to use this evidence of devotion to underline the notion that prison staff regarded her as special and worthy of attention, brushing over this confession with little commentary, other than the remark that this officer was dismissed soon after. This letter nonetheless offers a tantalizing glimpse of the emotions that women in nineteenth-century prisons might have felt for one another, even across the barriers of institutional roles.

In Gliddon's writings, compiled nearly three decades after Fletcher's, the middle-class woman's active gaze functions as a potentially powerful enabler of cross-class connections, in which "ordinary" women and matrons become the target of affection and closeness, rather than a marker of distance, even if this does not necessarily guarantee an egalitarian relationship. The diary here hints at a potentially "radical" energy that works to "dissolve unequal power dyads," which Jenni Millbank has identified in more recent textual representations of lesbian desire in prison (155). It is difficult to make a conclusive statement about the exact nature of Gliddon's comments and her gaze; while I am not suggesting here that this suffragette was necessarily a lesbian who harbored romantic or erotic desires for other (imprisoned) women, we need to acknowledge such desire as a historical possibility, rather than an interpretive anachronism.[73]

Admiration and fetishization of women's bodies and body parts go hand in hand in Gliddon's account, and they are not restricted to "ordinary" prisoners, although their objectification through her gaze is more problematic in that it symbolically reinscribes these women's particular lack of agency. However, in Gliddon's case, objectifications are counteracted by attempts to give insight into these women's thoughts and feelings, as in the case of the remand prisoner cleaning the suffragette's cell, discussed earlier. Analyzing middle- and upper-class suffragettes' complex strategies of disavowal and identification during encounters with working women and "the crowd" in the context of street activism, Green has identified two coexisting perspectives adopted by suffragettes: "the gaze of the *flâneur* and that of the social investigator" (33). According to Green, "suffragettes were canny theorists of the problems of spectatorship that complicated their attempts to envision collectivity" (33). Gliddon's acts of gazing at other women in prison may be less self-aware, but they, too, exemplify how suffragettes endeavored to go beyond conventional representations of common people, for instance, through representations of encounters with "ordinary" prisoners during chapel service—a topos in many suffragette prison accounts. In *My Prison Life and Why I Am a Suffragette*, Biggs veers between, on the one hand, describing such convicts as "human weeds" and longing, with the zeal of the reformer, "to be able to plant them in fresh soil" (13) and, on the other hand, the insight that, at closer inspection, "the great majority" of these women's faces did not seem "vicious" or warrant classification as unwanted wildflowers (17). Such revisions indicate how relatively close contact with "ordinary" prisoners enabled suffragettes to review their own (and wider social) misperceptions of these women.

Gliddon describes her impressions after looking at the "ordinary prisoners" during chapel service, comparing the experience to "looking at paintings in Bruges and there was one woman with her hair brushed severely back and a white cap on top of it who looked exactly like a figure from a Memling painting" (*Prison Diary* 31). She goes on to depict one particular prisoner in terms of an artist's model: "One woman, very tidy looking, sat just in front. She looked rather nice. The colour of her bodice was the same colour as her face. One can imagine a painter choosing that particular dress so that he might work out the difference of the colours of the face and the bodice. She looked a most law abiding person" (31). Gliddon here slips into the role of a male painter—indicated in her use of the pronoun "he"—in order to study the prisoner's physique and clothing. Beyond a linguistic convention, this symbolic gender-crossing could also be seen as a protective code for what might otherwise seem like an improper move by a woman, who, in her language, clearly goes beyond the kind of social reformist agenda evident in Biggs's account.

While Gliddon's portrayal remains marked by a tension—she clearly positions herself as the viewer in relation to the "crowd" of ordinary prisoners at chapel, implying a degree of objectification of these women—her descriptions are characterized by admiration, even desire, rather than disgust. They contrast with writings of other suffragettes such as Tyson, who depicts the atmosphere in the chapel as "very close, owing partly to the mass of humanity clothed in prison dress—grotesque in its ugliness" ("Day in Holloway" sheet 2). Where Tyson, potentially attending the exact same service, only perceived "ugliness" and an indistinguishable "mass of humanity," Gliddon noticed the beauty of individual prisoners.

Gliddon's account is reminiscent of some mid-nineteenth-century representations of female convicts, especially Mayhew and Binny's *The Criminal Prisons of London and Scenes of Prison Life*. On a visit to the chapel at Brixton Prison, Mayhew took similar pleasure in the female prisoners' appearance, describing the space "filled with the convict-congregation, habited in their dark claret gowns and clean white caps" as one of the prettiest and most touching sights in the world (Mayhew and Binny 186).[74] For Mayhew, these women provided a sublime spectacle, becoming the objects of his gaze. Symbolically, then, Gliddon revises the socially dominant account of the male prison investigator from the viewpoint of a woman, herself object of disciplinary surveillance. While she subjects those women, who are already exposed to the institution's surveillance, to her own middle-class gaze, she simultaneously gestures toward transgressive connections with other, "ordinary," prisoners in spite of the system's insistence on separation.

Conclusion | Hunger Strikes, Martyrdom, and Narrating Imprisonment

Gliddon's account is a compelling instance of how middle-class suffragettes, in their relationship with "ordinary" women, were caught between the objectifying gestures of the flâneur and the social reformer, harking back to the nineteenth century, and a new, more democratic impulse that sought to establish connections between women across social boundaries such as class. Both Lytton and Gliddon used the prison as a platform to forge such new bonds—the former through her act of cross-class dressing and performing a chest rub on the wardress, the latter by cross-gendering and inscribing a transgressive, protolesbian erotics of the gaze.

Although Gliddon was willing to risk imprisonment for her suffrage activism, she did not fit in with a tendency in the WSPU to represent suffragettes as "martyr-saviour[s]" and prison as a site for "near-death and new birth" (K. Hartman 41). As she only notes explicitly in her draft autobiographical account, she was one of twelve suffragettes in Holloway's E wing who closely observed, but did not participate, in the hunger strike and forcible feeding (*Draft* 179). Her diary entry on 16 April 1912 hints that she saw herself as isolated, perhaps regretfully so: "Hunger strike started. . . . I am extraordinarily near a very great thing yet quite outside it" (*Prison Diary* 51). Similarly, a day later, she confesses, "It is ghastly to be such a coward. I am so glad that there are others who are in the same boat" (*Prison Diary* 2 sheet 1). Writing retrospectively, in her draft autobiographical account, Gliddon adds a seemingly exculpatory sentence insisting that "most of the women who did not hungerstrike were bound by promises to their friends outside not to do so" (*Draft* 179, sec. VIII, 16 Apr. 1912).

Given the importance of heroic tales of self-sacrifice to the suffragettes' image, carefully constructed through accounts of hunger and forcible feeding, Gliddon's peculiar position as a convicted suffragette who refused to join in this ultimate collective action could, at least partially, explain her absence from other suffragettes' and researchers' accounts so far and her inability to publish her autobiographical narrative. Her own extensive collection of newspaper clippings is telling in that regard, because it includes a large number of articles focusing on the hunger strike, forcible feeding, and the controversies around the "Cat and Mouse Act" from 1912 onward. If many militant suffragettes successfully spun a collective identity through the experience and testimonies of hunger striking and forcible feeding, the writings of prisoners such as Gliddon instead point to a different form of intersubjectivity.[75] The cross-class connections that emerge in Gliddon's texts derive from the different voices that are given a platform in her account—however limited this platform may be—enabled by an erotics of the gaze between political prisoner, "ordinary" inmates, and female officers.

That even a relatively privileged prisoner such as Gliddon, who courageously managed to overcome institutional hurdles to read and write surreptitiously during her incarceration, was unable to publish her writings is a further reminder of the pressures on (former) offenders to make their voices heard and of the dangers of generalizing about prison experiences. Gliddon's personal papers offer inspiration for, and place an obligation on, feminist researchers to look beyond readily available narratives of imprisonment—in this case political internment during the women's suffrage campaign—to uncover a diversity of perspectives on the penal experience.

CHAPTER 7

Postscript: Rewriting Women's Prison History in Historical Fiction

Margaret Atwood's *Alias Grace* and Sarah Waters's *Affinity*

The contemporary novelists Margaret Atwood and Sarah Waters have taken up the call to move beyond readily available forms of representing women offenders and their imprisonment. Attentive to the difficulties of recovering historical voices of the socially marginalized, these writers use the genre of historical fiction to imagine more diverse perspectives on women's experiences in the nineteenth-century penal system and to problematize the process of mediation.[1] The British author Waters, confronted with the voicelessness of female prisoners in the nineteenth century, whose experiences, she notes, were typically "mediated" by "male commentators," resorts to her "imagination" to envision these women's stories and "the paths that women might have taken to end up in prison" (Interview 124). Similarly, the Canadian Atwood, faced with "hints and outright gaps" in historical records, "felt free to invent" when writing *Alias Grace* (Author's afterword 542). These contemporary novelists' projects, then, build on and extend the agenda of mid-Victorian author Frederick William Robinson, who, under the guise of A Prison Matron, endeavored to turn male lawmakers' representations of female imprisonment in "dry volumes of facts and figures" into women's stories of "flesh and blood" (*Female Life* 1:40).[2] Atwood and Waters creatively resurrect the buried viewpoints of female prisoners yet are careful to resist essentializing such women's voices. Through thematic content and narrative structure, they complicate narratives of women's historical experiences of social discrimination and imprisonment; by examining the intersections of gender, class, sexuality, and in Atwood's case, ethnicity, they interrogate the process of writing history and fiction.[3] Atwood's novel, with its complex structure, cautions its readers to distrust simplistic or one-sided stories about female prisoners and to be aware of the vested interests of all agents involved, while insisting on the need to include an extensive version of the incarcerated woman's own perspective into the picture.[4] Waters adds new layers to the critical exploration of prison historiography by challenging female middle-class viewpoints in representing women's prison experience and by moving lesbian desire in prisons center stage.[5] Both novels open up spaces for resistance, either where the female prisoner returns the disciplinary male gaze, as in *Alias Grace*, or where, as in *Affinity*, the novelist appropriates the theme of panopticism for an exploration of the complex scopic, social, and erotic relationships between women in prison.[6]

"Shut Up inside That Doll of Myself" | Tales of Incarceration in *Alias Grace*

Atwood's *Alias Grace* (1996) reconstructs the story of (and stories around) the immigrant maid and alleged "murderess" Grace Marks in mid-nineteenth-century Canada. At age sixteen, Grace was accused, together with her fellow servant and alleged lover, James McDermott, of murdering her employer, Thomas Kinnear, and the housekeeper, Nancy Montgomery, who was also Kinnear's mistress.[7] McDermott was hanged a few months after the murders in November 1843, but his codefendant had her death sentence commuted, because of her gender and young age. She spent nearly thirty years at Kingston Penitentiary, with an intermittent stay at Toronto's Lunatic Asylum, before being pardoned in her midforties in 1872. After being released, Grace went to New York State, where she may have married, but historical records of her circumstances at this point cease to exist (Atwood, Author's afterword 539).

Atwood's retelling of the historical figure Grace's life takes the form of a patchwork of narratives.[8] Alongside historical documents, Atwood draws on a vast array of generic conventions, including the ghost story and gothic and detective fiction, to illustrate the truth claims of competing discourses of knowledge—including medicine, law, literature, the media, spiritualism, and religion—that all produced conflicting stories around Grace's identity and supposed innocence or guilt. The novel's structure and changing narrative perspectives reaffirm the notion that Grace's offender identity is constructed at the intersection of multiple discursive sites, rather than fixed, and continues to be elusive for both contemporaneous commentators and present-day researchers. In the end, Atwood suggests, "the true character of the historical Grace Marks remains an enigma" (Author's afterword 539). As Marie-Thérèse Blanc suggests, the novel "resembles an adversary trial" (105) which juxtaposes competing accounts and implicates the reader as "a contemporary judge" (108), similar to nineteenth-century sensation novels such as Wilkie Collins's *The Moonstone*.[9] Importantly, Atwood carves out significant narrative space for Grace's own perspective on her life and imprisonment, which the novel then submits to the same critical scrutiny as other competing voices, although Grace's self-representation arguably paints her as an intriguing, dignified figure, who increasingly enjoys the reader's sympathy over other characters.

The process of knowledge production and significance of storytelling in the act of offender (self-)representation is exemplified most compellingly in the central relationship between Grace and Simon, the young doctor who regularly visits her during her confinement to test his new theories of the unconscious in the hope that he may "find the right key" to Grace's "locked box" (Atwood, *Alias Grace* 153) of a mind (she claims to have no recollection of the actual murders).[10] Atwood skillfully interweaves the prisoner's and the doctor's story to expose inequalities of class and gender in the prison system and beyond. As Grace's story unfolds, a picture emerges of recurring themes of sexual harassment and potential abuse by employers and fellow servants *before* the murders and by doctors, prison officers, wardens, and chaplains *during* imprisonment, plus a highly ambiguous dream that might signal child sexual abuse.[11] In highlighting the constant threat of abuse, Atwood draws attention to experiences shared by many women offenders, as recognized in today's penal debates.

However, Atwood refuses to oversimplify class and gender discrimination or to present women such as Grace as a silent, helpless victim of social circumstance. Rather, she plots to tentatively offer a more affirmative history, eschewing the weighty evidence of actually existing structural inequalities to imagine a "contest of wills" between prisoner and doctor (*Alias Grace* 374), which ultimately ends with Grace having the upper hand and securing her pardon (although not, as she assumes, with Simon's help) and the doctor's own mental demise, culminating in partial memory loss following a head injury in the US Civil War. Beyond the ironic twist of having the prisoner's mad doctor go crazy himself, the slow reversal between doctor and convict extends to Simon's fantasies of murdering his landlady and her husband, suggesting that criminal potential is not intrinsic to the servant class but may equally be lurking under the façade of respectable professionalism (476).

While Atwood's novel underlines the importance of providing space for the convict's own perspective, the narrative also problematizes the challenges involved in listening to the prisoner's voice—the account may not be complete or truthful—and the high stakes for the convict in exposing her narrative to external scrutiny. Grace is wary of the written word in particular, based on her trial experience: "In the courtroom, every word that came out of my mouth was as if burnt into the paper they were writing it on, and once I said a thing I knew I could never get the words back; only they were the wrong words, because whatever I said would be twisted around, even if it was the plain truth in the first place" (79). Grace explains how her own voice became caught up in conflicting demands from different social agents, so much so that she finally lost sense of what that voice may be, resulting in double incarceration: "I was shut up inside that doll of myself, and my true voice could not get out" (342). Atwood thus draws attention to naïve assumptions about the recovery of female prisoners' voices, suggesting that these voices are not merely shaped by the women's own motivations but also subject to influences in a complex discursive field, which forms part of a larger pattern of social power relations.[12]

The novel as a whole, with its conflicting perspectives, including Grace's own, offers a sustained critique of culturally dominant forms of representing incarcerated women like Grace in literature, science, reform discourse, and the media by having her respond to a range of labels attached to her. She recognizes that she is variously seen as a "model prisoner" (5), a "romantic figure" (27), a "case" (36), a "wild beast" and "monster" (36), an "actress," and a "liar" (81). Grace's self-conscious performances and enactment of facial expressions may seem to corroborate accusations of acting, but the novel presents such behavior at least partially as a response to others' expectations, rather than simply the result of deceptive intent (29, 43, 261). After receiving news of her pardon from the warden's daughter, Grace cries, because she recognizes that the other woman "felt some tears were in order" (512) and that her new situation, as a potential "object of pity rather than horror and fear, . . . calls for a different arrangement of the face" (513). Similarly, after release, Grace, now married to her old and guilt-ridden friend Jamie Walsh, whose testimony had partially been responsible for her conviction, performs forgiveness for him and tells exaggerated tales of her sufferings, even though they are painful to her, because he finds them erotically stimulating (530–32). To some extent, Atwood suggests, an ex-prisoner like Grace will always remain trapped in the stories of her life.

Alongside contemporaneous social labeling attempts, sensational media reportage, and the competition of traditionally masculine knowledge discourses such as medicine, religion, and law, Atwood analyses and revises her own perception and misperception of Grace, problematizing the role of the contemporary woman writer of historical fiction together with that of her nineteenth-century predecessor, the author Susanna Moodie. *Alias Grace* can be understood both as a rewriting of and a critical commentary on Moodie's account of Grace in *Life in the Clearings versus the Bush* (1853) and a revision of Atwood's own CBC television play *The Servant Girl* (1974), exclusively based on Moodie's text (Atwood, Acknowledgements 545). By making explicit her own influences as a writer and the gradual process of disassociating herself from literary ancestors such as Moodie, Atwood also implicitly addresses the genesis and ethical responsibilities of the present-day professional woman writer and feminist researcher.

Atwood's printing of excerpts from Moodie's text in her patchwork of perspectives not only challenges nineteenth-century representations of female convicts—and her own reception of them—but also critically engages with the tradition of prison visiting by philanthropic ladies. Moodie visited Grace both at the Provincial Penitentiary in Kingston and the Lunatic Asylum in Toronto, where Grace had been transferred—both institutions which, as Atwood points out, "were visited like zoos" (Author's afterword 538). Moodie's *Life in the Clearings*, itself influenced by the literary conventions of its time, depicts "the celebrated murderess Grace Marks" (215) in melodramatic and phrenological terms but also implicitly hints at the prisoner's resistance to her objectification at the pleasure of such lady visitors. At the penitentiary, Grace turned her head, so that Moodie "could not get a glimpse of her face" (232); at the lunatic asylum, she fled "shrieking" when she realized she was being watched. Atwood develops this subtext of resistance by having the prisoner retaliate against Moodie's physiognomy-based descriptions through Grace's dry comment that the lady visitor "looked like a beetle. . . . Round and fat and dressed in black, and a quick and scuttling sort of walk; and black, shiny eyes too" (*Alias Grace* 416–17). Contrary to Roxanne Rimstead's argument that *Alias Grace* promotes "a universalizing feminism" (62) and obscures "class tensions among women" (59), the novel in fact examines such tensions by problematizing Moodie's representations of Grace, as well as the relationship between Grace, the governor's wife, and her lady friends elsewhere in the novel.[13]

Prison Philanthropy, Class, and "Palling Up" | Queering Women's Prison History in *Affinity*

The politics of female prison philanthropy and prisoners' responses to it are also examined in Sarah Waters's *Affinity* (1999). Waters complements *Alias Grace*'s attempt to imagine convict agency and resistance but specifically highlights a lesbian perspective on women's prison history by constructing her narrative around the relationship between three women: a lady visitor, an imprisoned spiritualist, and the prisoner's lesbian lover, who also acts as servant to the lady visitor's family. The novel draws on themes of literal and metaphorical imprisonment that were typical of the genres of gothic and sensation fiction, but it also capitalizes on historical records of sexual undercurrents in spiritualism and women's prisons. Waters evokes the "laying on of hands" in spiritualist circles (*Affinity* 145) and the romantic or erotic connotations of the "palling up" (67) of prisoners documented in nineteenth-century texts such as Frederick William Robinson's tales—one of Waters's likely sources; one of Robinson's tales insisted that "women do fall in love with each other in prisons" (*Memoirs of Jane Cameron* 2:93).[14] With a plot that sees the lady visitor outwitted by the object of her charity and the latter's companion, *Affinity* stages, in Foucault's terms, an "insurrection" of the "subjugated" secret "knowledges" of prisoner and servant, to critically reflect on nineteenth-century gender, class, and sexual relations (Foucault, *"Society"* 7).

Affinity presents the events surrounding the visits of Margaret Prior, the unmarried daughter of a late scholar, who is mentally fragile after her father's death, to Millbank Prison in London between September 1874 and January 1875.[15] Whereas Atwood highlights the relationship between prisoner and doctor to challenge the role of male professionals in constructing knowledge about women in prison, Waters focuses on the encounters and ensuing "friendship" between the visitor and the imprisoned spirit medium Selina Dawes, incarcerated for fraud and assault. As documented in more detail in the introduction, in England, prison visiting became a popular occupation, primarily for upper-middle-class women, after 1816, when the Quaker Elizabeth Fry launched her systematic prison work at Newgate

Prison in London. Waters has Margaret read Fry's pioneering writings on female prisoners, as well as Henry Mayhew and John Binny's *The Criminal Prisons of London and Scenes of Prison Life* (*Affinity* 57). The novelist reimagines the Quaker's model of prison visiting and Mayhew's investigative, journalistic gaze on female convicts by portraying a relationship between Margaret and Selina that increasingly becomes erotically charged, while teasing out the class-based ambivalences underlying the project of prison visiting.

The relationship between lady visitor and prisoner, even though perceived in terms of female friendship, is an asymmetrical one that is regulated by strict institutional codes, as illustrated by the rules laid out in Fry's *Observations on the Visiting, Superintendence, and Government of Female Prisoners* (1827). In the view of Millbank officials such as the governor, Mr. Shillitoe, and the principal matron, Miss Haxby, who stand for socially dominant ideas in the mid-nineteenth century, the prisoners' hearts equal those of children or "savages" that require shaping by a refined but sympathetic lady (Waters, *Affinity* 12). Margaret, who says that she "had come to Millbank to make friends of all the women" (44), is warned that her interest in individual women must not become too strong or "specific," though, to avoid conceit in the prisoners (214). Waters challenges the humanitarian rhetoric of nineteenth-century prison visiting by suggesting that the agenda of visitors like Margaret, who were caught between social and familial demands for feminine domesticity—Margaret's mother reminds her, "You must take up your proper duties in the house. Your place is here, your place is here" (252)—and their own desire for bourgeois public-sphere activity, although well meaning, was not necessarily an innocently selfless one.

Similar to Grace in *Alias Grace*, who unmasks Simon's hidden "desires" (46) in his visits to her, Selina identifies what she suspects to be Margaret's secret purpose: "You have come to Millbank, to look on women more wretched than yourself, in the hope that it will make you well again" (Waters, *Affinity* 47). As in *Alias Grace*, such recognition marks the beginning of a gradual power reversal, which casts Selina in the role of Margaret's therapist, ultimately culminating in the mental collapse (and, in all probability, suicide) of the visitor and the liberation of the prisoner. Yet Waters, like Atwood, is careful not to dismiss philanthropic activity too easily, emphasizing the project's ambivalences and the ambiguous social status of those who were engaged in it; Margaret's position as a lady visitor is, in Mark Wormald's phrase, characterized as one of "*marginalized* privilege"

(194, my emphasis), just like Simon in *Alias Grace*, who, as a young man of limited means and peer support, finds himself on the periphery of his profession.

The beginning of the novel highlights Margaret's structurally more powerful position, with family connections to the world of the law—Shillitoe and Selina's prosecutor have been guests at Margaret's family home (Waters, *Affinity* 7, 97–98). As Margaret begins her visits at Millbank, she is in control, having voyeuristic access to Selina in her prison cell: "I put my fingers to the inspection slit, and then my eyes. And then I gazed at the girl in the cell beyond" (26). Similar to Grace in Atwood's novel, however, Selina contests prison decorum and social hierarchies by returning Margaret's "gaze" (43), which the lady finds "unsettling" (64). The prisoner's hold over Margaret is mirrored in the lady's growing identification with feeling incarcerated. She increasingly associates the scenes at home with routines of prison life, comparing her mother, whose oppressive gaze she feels on herself all the time, to the matrons, while also finding herself the subject of actual matrons' "reports," which are typically reserved for prisoners (213).[16] The power/knowledge that Selina acquires over Margaret, with the covert assistance of her lover, Ruth, who has taken up a position in Margaret's household, helps her establish a full picture of the lady's life style and mental state, which lays the foundations for Selina's escape. Ruth possesses the secret knowledge of a servant—like Dora in *Alias Grace*, who shares details about Simon's domestic habits with Grace, or Rosanna in *The Moonstone*, who is the first to discover the gentleman Franklin Blake's role in the disappearance of the diamond.[17] Ruth has access to Margaret's room and diary, overhears conversations about her prison visits to Selina, and witnesses Margaret unraveling emotionally (101–2, 253–54). By contrast, Selina remains a blank for Margaret, as she cannot find any "trace of the life" that she thinks Selina "must have led" (239).

Through the secret knowledge that Selina and Ruth gain, they capitalize on Margaret's feeling of entrapment in the heteronormative environment of her middle-class family and her longing for a companion to replace her intimate friend Helen, who chose Margaret's brother over her. In order for Selina to convince the visitor of her escape plan, she employs the queer codes of spiritualism to evoke a lesbian utopia beyond mainstream society's "laws" (273), facilitated by the free union—or "affinity"—of souls (210) and realized in Margaret and Selina's imagined self-imposed exile in Italy. Through the novel's twist, which has Selina and Ruth flee with provisions designed for the escape of the prisoner and *Margaret*, Waters exposes the limits of female philanthropy and suggests that the imagined queer utopia cannot transcend social class distinctions, thereby also implicitly revising uncritically universalist traditions of lesbian writing.[18] Whereas critics such as Jeannette King have focused on "an identity between vulnerable women" such as Selina and Margaret in the novel's "parallel narratives" about them (92), *Affinity* arguably alerts its readers to the importance of *difference* within the realm of imprisonment and lesbian experience, for example, by having Margaret disassociate her own feelings for Selina, rather snootily, from the "gross" and "commonplace" infatuations of Millbank "pals" Jane Jarvis and Emma White (268).[19]

Affinity challenges the dominance of middle-class values through not only the novel's content but also its structure. The reader follows the entire Millbank plot through Margaret's eyes, through her first-person diary entries, although these are juxtaposed with shorter entries from Selina's diary before her imprisonment, providing hints as to the events leading to her conviction. Waters signals the importance of Selina's perspective by framing the narrative as a whole with records from the spiritualist's diary. The much-shorter entries from Selina's diary allude to the existence of the submerged and untold stories of women of humble origin, like Selina and Ruth, who have to work for a living but whose voices remain largely unrecorded. As the dramatic plot unfolds, though, the narrative works a ruse on the reader, who is increasingly drawn into Margaret's middle-class perspective, even if this viewpoint is gradually presented as unreliable (due to the woman's mental instability). It is precisely this perspective that makes it difficult for the reader to see the truth before Margaret does. Her habit of calling the household's new servant by her last name, "Vigers"—just as the matrons call the female prisoners by their last name, a gesture criticized by Selina— makes it hard for readers to see that this servant is identical with Selina's companion "Ruth," a crucial clue that would help explain the source of spirit gifts sent to Margaret's room.[20]

The flashback ending of the novel, which witnesses Selina and Ruth's initial plans for their escape to southern Europe, ultimately dislodges the authority of the narrative's dominant middle-class perspective by concluding with one of Selina's diary entries and by giving the last words of the tale to the servant. Foreshadowing the fraud scheme targeted at Miss Silvester and potentially further plots in Continental Europe aimed at "pale English ladies" (352), like Margaret, who seek warm climes in the hope of recovery, the final scene shows Ruth carving out a plan for herself and Selina to escape from a life of servitude to the English middle class.

While the surprise turns of the plot—familiar from the conventions of Victorian sensation fiction—constitute a powerful evocation of female lower-class solidarity, which can be read as a politically subversive gesture on Waters's part, this gesture is not unproblematic. Although the novel's plot challenges nineteenth-century paradigms of female prison visiting, Ruth and Selina's escape reconfirms the stereotype of the "lower orders" as untrustworthy and criminal.[21] It corroborates Miss Haxby's early warning to Margaret not to tell prisoners anything of "the world beyond the prison walls," because they will "hold the knowledge against you, and use it to make all manner of mischief" (Waters, *Affinity* 16). The ending of the novel is also foreshadowed earlier on in the comments of Arthur Barclay, Margaret's future brother-in-law, comments that validate the hegemonic view of spiritualists as frauds: "They are an evil crew, the lot of them. . . . A lot of clever conjurers. And they make a very handsome living, preying on fools" (98). But as in *Alias Grace*, some doubt remains over whether the prisoner Selina is indeed a perpetrator or perhaps the victim of Ruth's schemes or both.[22] Like Atwood, who refuses to resolve the question of Grace's guilt, Waters ultimately leaves open the riddle of how to interpret Selina's identity and alleged crime and her relationship with Ruth. Both novelists decline to assign a straightforward identity to the prisoner, challenging their readers to question overly facile explanations of female criminality while emphasizing the need to *reread* and *reinterpret* women's prison history.

Conclusion

Despite Atwood's and Waters's emphasis on perspective and the complexity of representation, the two authors also remind us that such narratives, and the women at the heart of those stories, are grounded in material realities, which words can illuminate but not transcend or revoke, thus carefully negotiating the "battle between . . . textuality and experience" that feminist writers often find themselves embroiled in (Anderson 134). Both writers ask their readers to consider the material conditions that typically lead to women's incarceration—in the nineteenth century as much as today. The Canadian's novel is haunted by experiences of sexual threat and abuse, poverty and drudgery, ultimately resulting in Grace's criminalization, while the "criminal" acts by Waters's characters Selina and Ruth are committed by two women at the edge of society who long to break free from a life of servitude "passed in the homes of strangers" (*Affinity* 136). The conclusions of both novels are only cautiously optimistic for the two prisoners, however. Grace resigns herself to married life, which finally allows her to be mistress of her own home but also requires the satisfaction of her husband's sexual fantasies. By leaving open the question of whether the "heaviness" (*Alias Grace* 533) in Grace's stomach is a fetus or a tumor, Atwood further withholds an unambiguously happy ending for the ex-prisoner and resists the generic conventions of romance fiction. Similarly, *Affinity*'s resolution hints that Selina, regardless of her escape to Italy, may not be entirely free but will, as Kohlke argues, remain trapped in "her former existence as fetishized spectacle" subject to the "gaze" of wealthy ladies ("Into History" 162). In the conclusions of both novels, then, the writers caution against simplistic notions of liberation—from incarceration as much as from wider social constraints. Rather, Atwood and Waters interrogate how the subjectivities of (former) prisoners are situated within complex power relations, as well as possibilities for individual agency and resistance.

If both Waters and Atwood reflect on their own role as female writers and feminist researchers, their novels also place such demands on their readers. The tricks on the implied (female) reader in Waters's novel, highlighting class-based blind spots, constitute a metacritical gesture that establishes an implicit analogy between Margaret's pleasure in the prison experience and the female reader's own unquestioned gratification in consuming "women's history"—and the appropriation of marginalized lives for pleasure, in particular—through fiction. Atwood and Waters challenge their readers into questioning their preconceptions about Simon's supposed respectability or Margaret's altruistic motifs in their encounters with female prisoners. Rather than highlighting the prisoner's own voice (or, rather, voices), as Atwood does, Waters's focus on Margaret's limited understanding in conjunction with only cryptic excerpts from Selina's diary underlines the gaps in this perspective, drawing the reader's attention to the stakes in ignoring the prisoner's—and the servant's—viewpoint.

CODA

Contemporary novelists Margaret Atwood and Sarah Waters, in their creative writing and research methods, implicitly take up feminist criminologists' call for self-reflexivity in approaches to women's imprisonment.[1] As this book has illustrated, such awareness can already be found in nineteenth- and early twentieth-century (self-)representations of female prisoners, from Frederick William Robinson's mid-Victorian use of metacommentary in his Prison Matron's reflections on appropriate forms of documenting female prison experiences, via Susan Willis Fletcher's and Florence Maybrick's first-person accounts of their encounters with "common" convicts, to the Edwardian suffragettes' negotiation of class privilege and intersubjectivity during incarceration. The variety of texts investigated in this study all contributed to the construction of new public platforms for culturally submerged convict viewpoints, while also affording their audiences with opportunities for examining the identities of nonimprisoned women.

The textual spaces identified here suggest the formation of a more or less explicitly articulated (proto)feminist consciousness which takes women's imprisonment as a starting point for debating social inequalities or, in the case of the suffragettes, as its culmination. As my detailed readings have indicated, this awareness was far from uniform and not without contradiction. Joan Wallach Scott's observations on the "paradoxical" nature of feminist agency are useful here; the history of feminism, like the sociocultural moments it emerges from, is "an effect of ambiguities, inconsistencies, contradictions within particular epistemologies" (*Only Paradoxes* 16). Women such as spiritualist and ex-prisoner Fletcher, for instance, explicitly rejected a women's rights discourse while covertly aligning themselves with such a language elsewhere to denounce women's victimization at the hands of men and patriarchal social structures.

Over the course of this recovery project, I have attempted to model a feminist textual practice that is attentive to such ambiguities, complexity, and diversity in (ex-)prisoners' voices, as well as their contexts and the gendered and classed dynamics of mediation. During this process, the book has focused on texts that authorize female perspectives, including the viewpoints of female convicts but also those of other (nonelite) women, such as prison employees. Moreover, I have considered not only how writers imagined discursive agency for (convict) women but also how they problematized the conditions under which such agency can or cannot be seized—for instance, George Eliot's interrogation of the infanticide Hetty Sorrel's inability to speak in court, as opposed to her confession facilitated by informal female prison ministry. The book has drawn attention to new models of female intersubjectivity and collectivity—within and beyond class boundaries— imagined by writers to help articulate marginalized women's experiences, from the execution broadsides' encouragement of nonelite, female audience identification to privileged suffragettes' examinations of cross-class prison communities. I have also traced textual explorations of gender-specific forms of oppression, for example, Fletcher's and Maybrick's complaints against a sexist bias in the criminal justice system.

The methods outlined in this book can serve as models for approaching female prisoners' voices—and women's perspectives more generally—in other historical and contemporary contexts to inform the appreciation and commemoration of otherwise hidden forms of knowledge. In this particular study, these methods have highlighted the distinctive epistemological vantage point that imprisoned women inhabit, with a view to increasing our understanding of gender and class relations in general and individual and collective responsibilities in the context of women's offending behavior more specifically.[2] The book as a whole, then, has aspired to provide a template for intersectional textual analysis which keeps sight of the particular and the collective, an analysis which uncovers impulses to promote material change for *all* (imprisoned) women while remaining attentive to individual differences between women and their experiences.

Historical novelists such as Atwood and Waters challenge us to consider the links between historical and contemporary settings. Atwood's *Alias Grace*, as the postscript indicated, problematizes the notion that telling one's story was necessarily a desirable strategy for female prisoners in the nineteenth century. The character of Grace Marks, who remains a "locked box" (153) for the doctor Jordan, illustrates reasons why imprisoned women, if they were given the opportunity at all, may have wanted to withhold their stories, lest they be appropriated within the structures of authority that already enfolded them. In the contemporary context, the voices of the incarcerated are easily claimed for agendas of "rehabilitation," which presuppose a normative subjectivity that offenders should pursue, without necessarily questioning larger issues in social organization that are typically at the root of lawbreaking.[3]

It is for this reason that some radical proponents of the prison abolition movement reject prison writing programs or the category of "prison writing," for they see them as complicit with, rather than resisting, the penal system. In an article on US women's writing workshops in prison and jail, Tobi Jacobi takes a more pragmatic view, arguing that literacy education and creative writing activities in penal institutions, with related opportunities for publication, can work tactically to empower incarcerated women and to inform local communities with the long-term goal of "a decarcerated social structure" (52). In Britain, charities such as Women in Prison, cofounded in 1983 by ex-prisoner Chris Tchaikovsky, provide platforms for diverse prisoner perspectives—Women in Prison's quarterly magazine, distributed for free to women's prisons in England, showcases creative work by prisoners, for example. The charity also offers practical support to women during their imprisonment and after their release, as well as lobbying for a shift from punitive sentencing to addressing the root causes of offending behavior in women, many of whom have been subject to physical abuse and have histories of mental illness and substance abuse.[4] Another charity, the Prisoners' Education Trust, established in 1989, promotes a variety of learning opportunities in prison and provides channels for learners to have a voice during the process.[5]

New technologies have facilitated multifarious ways of bringing female prisoners' voices and experiences to public attention, from Jane Evelyn Atwood's photojournalism *Too Much Time: Women in Prison* (2000) and Nick Broomfield's documentary *Aileen: The Life and Death of a Serial Killer* (2003) to BBC Scotland's *Girls behind Bars* (2008). As Broomfield's earlier documentary *Aileen Wuornos: The Selling of a Serial Killer* (1993) showcases, though, female offenders deemed to be sensational enough can easily fall prey to attempts by those around them to profit from their life stories. But the ethical implications of mediating such women's experiences are always problematic, even in the case of supposedly well-meaning and sympathetic filmmakers such as Broomfield, who, according to Tanya Horeck, ends up as a "Columbo-like" character urging Wuornos, convicted to death for killing several men, to disclose more details about her damaged life (143). Audience responses to such representations, too, in the nineteenth-century context as much as today, can be conflicting, including new awareness or reaffirming viewers'/readers' preconceptions about female offenders.

The various sources analyzed in this study signal that such tensions equally existed in historically earlier periods. We might like to conceptualize Robinson's prison tales as a forerunner of television series such as *Bad Girls* (1999–2006), *Orange Is the New Black* (2013–), or other films in the women-in-prison genre, veering between sensationalism and titillation, on the one hand, and a serious, sympathetic exploration of the lives of women in prison, on the other hand. The task still ahead of us is twofold, then. First, we must listen to prisoners' voices, available through a range of creative avenues, historical and contemporary, while remaining conscious of how the reification of such women's experiences can be made to fit opportune political narratives or exploited for commercial gain and of our own role in this process (this book, too, inevitably appropriates prisoners' stories even as it seeks to increase their visibility). Second, beyond an interrogation of the effects of (self-)representation, we need to support those who work to bring to the fore, and to alleviate, material social inequalities that lead to the incarceration of women in the first place, with "a decarcerated social structure" firmly in mind.

While it would be presumptuous to suggest that an academic monograph can make a material difference in this context, this book has offered some strategies for thinking about female prisoners' voices in a wider social matrix. In the spirit of Michel Foucault's genealogical method, which brings together scholarship and "local memories . . . to constitute a historical knowledge of struggles and to make use of that knowledge in contemporary tactics" (*"Society"* 8), this book has sought to complement practical initiatives to help raise awareness around women's imprisonment, on the basis of the recognition that many of the issues tackled in the historical material under scrutiny here resonate in the present moment. My work continues to be inspired by, and hopes to help inform, scholar-activists and practitioners who use institutional leverage and resources to create opportunities for prisoners.[6] Although I am conscious that (former) prisoners themselves may not be among the most likely readers of this book, it is my sincere wish that those who do come across it will find that it does justice to their concerns in some shape or form—at the very least in its insistence on prisoners' right to be heard.

NOTES

Introduction

1. For other recent examples of studies on the life narratives or voices of the socially disadvantaged or "humble," see Atkinson; Fernandez.

2. The Howard League for Penal Reform's "Submission to the Justice Select Committee's Inquiry on Women Offenders" in September 2012 noted an increase of 24 percent in the number of women in English prisons between 2000 and 2012 (3).

3. *Who Lie in Gaol*, taking its title from a line in Oscar Wilde's "Ballad of Reading Gaol" (1898), was published in the United States as *Women in Prison*. Scheffler's anthology *Wall Tappings* offers a useful biographical introduction alongside an excerpt (92–96).

4. Caine's "Feminist Biography and Feminist History" similarly stresses "an awareness of the complexity and diversity of Victorian and Edwardian feminism, of the impossibility of reducing it to a set of particular demands and campaigns" (258–59).

5. See for instance Blagg and Wilson, who in a 1912 tract published in the Fabian Women's Group Series explicitly called for "an official share in judicial procedure and in the administration of the penal system," including a women's auxiliary to the police force, female judges, magistrates, and jurors (27). Logan offers a detailed historical account of how women professionals began to enter the criminal justice system from 1920 onward.

6. Although Nash is critical of what she sees as the concept's "unexplored paradoxes," she offers a useful overview of feminist debates on intersectionality (4). As Nash notes, black women often feature as "prototypical intersectional subjects" in feminist theory (4). While I do not wish to diminish the importance of racial, ethnic, and national differences, my analysis mostly focuses on the intersections of gender and *class*, because race and ethnicity resonate less strongly in the historical texts under discussion here. I will examine questions of ethnicity and nationality alongside class and gender where they occur. By addressing the identities of different kinds of female prisoners, from nonelite to relatively privileged women—and their interaction—I hope to help extend intersectionality's reach as a critical paradigm which previously tended to omit "an examination of identities that are imagined as either wholly or even partially privileged" (Nash 10).

7. Now-classic studies of prison writing include Davies; and Franklin, *Prison Literature in America*. For more recent examples of scholarship on prisoner self-

expression and life writing, from both a historical and contemporary perspective, see Broadhead; Burke; Ek; Gready; Haslam, *Fitting Sentences*; Haslam and Wright; J. James; Kaiser; D. Q. Miller; Nellis; Rolston; Rymhs; Schur; Tarter and Bell; Whalen; and the special journal issues *Prison Writing / Writing Prison in Canada* (Rimstead and Rymhs); *Reading and Writing in Prison* (Schwan); *Prison Writings in Early Modern England* (Sherman and Sheils). A special issue of *Texas Studies in Literature and Language* titled *Cultures of Detention* (Barrish) contains some articles dealing with the reading and writing practices of (former) prisoners, as does the *PMLA*'s issue 123.3, which also features a roundtable titled "Prisons, Activism, and the Academy." Frost and the collection by Frost and Maxwell-Stewart explore convict experience in colonial Australia. There has also been a proliferation of anthologies of prisoners' writings. See for instance Bould; Chevigny; Franklin, *Prison Writings*; Gaucher; Mapanje. For editions dealing with female prisoners in particular, see Johnson; Lamb et al.; Padel and Stevenson; Scheffler; Walford; Wyner. Jane Evelyn Atwood's photojournalism in *Too Much Time* combines pictures of incarcerated women with testimony, while Lawston and Lucas's collection brings the written and visual work of imprisoned women in conversation with scholars, artists, activists, and educators. Illustrating a wider cultural interest in and recognition of the value of prisoners' viewpoints in the current British context, the *Guardian* publishes regular contributions from former prisoners such as Erwin James and Caspar Walsh. The Prisoners' Education Trust's website features a section on the "learner voice" with prisoners' views on opportunities for learning in prison: http://www.prisonerseducation.org.uk/index.php?id=104.

8. On issues relating to self-reflexivity with regard to women, crime, and criminology, see the preface to Worrall's *Offending Women* by series editors Cain and Smart. Worrall's book uses interviews with female lawbreakers to problematize the notion of expert knowledge on women's criminality. For overviews of the debate around prisoner life writing in criminology, see Dearey et al.; and Morgan. Criminology has also witnessed a recent interest in prisoner life stories in the context of prison ethnography. See Crewe and the rest of Drake and Earle's special issue *Prison Ethnography* of the journal *Criminal Justice Matters*.

9. On prison literacy in the nineteenth century, see Crone; Zedner 142–43.

10. I do not wish to rehearse the well-known debate over the concept of *experience* and the challenges around its recovery in the wake of poststructuralist ideas about the discursive constitution of the subject. For a starting point, see the critical discussion between Scott, "Evidence of Experience"; and Downs.

11. On the significance of "the counter-discourse of prisoners" in Foucault's vision, see also his "Intellectuals and Power" (209).

12. For examples of post-Foucauldian readings emphasizing the constraining mechanisms of nineteenth-century discourses and literary genres, see D. A. Miller's

influential study *The Novel and the Police*. Leps uses Foucault to investigate discursive knowledge production about offenders in nineteenth-century criminology, journalism, and crime literature. R. Thomas's work on the relationship between nineteenth-century detective fiction and early forensic science draws on Foucault's concept of disciplinary power (although Thomas acknowledges that "detective literature both reinforces and resists the disciplinary regime it represents"; 14). For a critique of "the absence of prisoners from the history of the prison," see also Goldsmith's work on prison life in nineteenth-century Massachusetts, although he relies solely on official prison records (110).

13. For a good overview of debates over Foucault's involvement with GIP, see Hoffman, who argues that Foucault's prison activism and concern with prisoner resistance crucially inspired *Discipline and Punish*. Schwan and Shapiro make a similar point in the introduction to *How to Read Foucault's "Discipline and Punish."*

14. Feminist critiques and appropriations of Foucault's work provided much inspiration in the early phases of this research project. See, for instance, Diamond and Quinby; Fraser; Hekman; Howe; McNay; McWhorter; Ramazanoglu; Sawicki. McLaren, who looks at possible affinities between Foucault's conception of the self and feminism, provides an excellent, extensive overview of the various ways in which Foucault has been adopted, criticized, or rejected by feminist scholars. For a feminist discussion of Foucault in relation to crime more particularly, see sociologist Smart's *Law, Crime and Sexuality*, which draws on and expands Foucault to analyze law as a gendered "discourse" (72). Worrall's methodology in *Offending Women* makes use of Foucault's concepts of power, knowledge, and discourse in relation to the construction of female deviance.

15. For a similar project concerned with the narrative representations of offenders' interiority in the Victorian novel, see Rodensky.

16. The chaplain of Chester Castle Gaol, H. S. Joseph collected convict autobiographies and letters from former prisoners in *Memoirs of Convicted Prisoners* (1853). Walter Clay's biography of his father, *The Prison Chaplain: A Memoir of the Reverend John Clay* (1855), contained excerpts from the chaplain's notes of conversations with inmates. John Field, chaplain of Reading Gaol and a strong proponent of the separate system of imprisonment, used prisoners' statements extracted from testimonies given to the Inspectors of Prisons to confirm the advantages of his preferred model of incarceration (*Prison Discipline* 32–39). See also Ellen O'Neill's *Extraordinary Confessions of a Female Pickpocket* (1850), the alleged testimony of a young Irishwoman awaiting transportation at Preston House of Correction. According to the frame narrative, O'Neill's tale is the result of her examination by a writer of the *Daily News*, "conducted in the presence of the Rev. John Clay, chaplain of the gaol, who had the evidence copied out under his own inspection, and who can vouch for its entire accuracy" (3).

17. For the early modern context, see Chess; Clark; Stavreva; Wiltenburg; and R. Martin's anthology *Women and Murder in Early Modern News Pamphlets and Broadside Ballads*.

18. The Ordinary's Accounts were "biographies of condemned convicts written by the chaplain of Newgate Prison" (Hitchcock and Shoemaker xx).

19. On female self-representation in the eighteenth-century legal context, see also Doody.

20. For a more detailed discussion of these changes, see Allen 3; Beattie 356–76; Cairns 3–6; Langbein 266–73; Manchester 168–69; May 176–201.

21. See Cairns 3; Langbein 272; Manchester 169.

22. See Bentley 108–10.

23. See chapter 4.

24. Pettitt offers a useful, short exploration of some of the problems with such an approach (75–76).

25. Early Methodist women working in prisons include Hannah Ball and Sarah Peters. See chapter 3 for a more detailed discussion of Methodism and female prison ministry. See also the prison work of the evangelical dressmaker Sarah Martin at Great Yarmouth Borough Gaol, comprehensively analyzed by Rogers.

26. For a brief historical overview of some of these changes, see Heidensohn 64. Robert Peel's Gaol Act of 1823 ordered the strict separation between female and male prisoners; required that a matron reside in every prison with female prisoners; required that men visiting the female wards be accompanied by female officers at all times; and required that female prisoners be attended by female officers only (4 Geo. 4 c. 64 s. 10). See also 5 Geo. 4 c. 85 s. 10, demanding the classification of female prisoners into at least three classes; and 2 & 3 Vict. c. 56 s. 6, establishing that the keys to the cells of female wards be kept in the custody of the matron and different locks be used for male and female parts of prisons. These changes were not always implemented consistently, though, as noted across a number of Inspectors' Reports. Zedner emphasizes the gaps between theory and practice existing in many local and convict prisons (see especially her chapters 4 and 5).

27. See for instance the 1857 report for Millbank Prison in *RDCP for 1857*, PP 1857–58 (2423) xxix, 49 [531]); and Zedner 120.

28. On Fry's early philanthropic and organizational activities, see Summers, "Elizabeth Fry" 84. See also the British Society's *Sketch of the Origin and Results of Ladies' Prison Associations*.

29. On Fry's national and international influence, see Logan 9–10. Van Drenth and de Haan offer a detailed account of Fry's influence on Dutch prison reform. Fry was born into a wealthy family of bankers, the Gurneys of Norwich, and later married Joseph Fry, a tea merchant. Her younger brother Samuel also became a famous banker and philanthropist (J. Rose 50). Her brother Joseph John Gurney, at the head of the Quakers' evangelical branch (also termed *Gurneyism*), was in-

volved in abolitionism and prison reform, as illustrated by his *Notes on a Visit* (1819); her brothers-in-law Samuel Hoare and Sir Thomas Fowell Buxton were active members of the Society for the Improvement of Prison Discipline (Summers, "Elizabeth Fry" 85). Hoare was also a Surrey magistrate (McConville 304).

30. See J. Rose 70. On the moral significance of convict clothing in Fry's reform efforts, see Ash (especially her introduction and chapter 1).

31. Fry's fervent opposition to capital punishment had caused a rift with Lord Sidmouth and the government in 1818. See the commentary on the case in Fry, *Memoir* 1:298; 1:309–10.

32. McConville offers an account of these changes in prison administration, including the 1840s as "a decade of rapid expansion and consolidation in central government's prison interests" (215).

33. See J. Rose 187.

34. On women's philanthropy and struggles between male professionals and female philanthropists in the mid-nineteenth century more generally, see Elliott (especially chapter 4).

35. See also Carpenter's *Six Months in India* (1868) and her speech "An Account of Visits to Gaols in India" in front of the Social Science Association in 1866. For a more detailed discussion of Carpenter's work, including these writings, see Schwan, "Dreadful beyond Description."

36. Wrench published *Visits to Female Prisoners at Home and Abroad* in 1852. Zedner offers a brief discussion of her work (145, 171). See also Grundy for a brief overview of Elizabeth Heyrick's philanthropic activities in the early nineteenth century—she was a former Methodist who became a Quaker and prison visitor. Onslow offers a critical discussion of how a number of nineteenth-century female activists and reformers used journalism to stake a claim in debates around (women's) criminality, simultaneously promoting employment opportunities for women in the social sector.

37. Critics disagree as to Tristan's ideological position. Dijkstra sees her as a forerunner of Marx and Engels, while Cross and Gray regard her as an inconsistent socialist. For a discussion of some of the inconsistencies in Tristan's thinking, see also Livingston. Nord offers an analysis of Tristan's encounter with one particular female prisoner. Grogan examines Tristan's attraction to various nineteenth-century pseudosciences, such as physiognomy and phrenology.

38. Tristan's travel account was published in England, in French, but the Owenist journal the *New Moral World* was the only printed organ to mention it (Hawkes xxiv). Hence, its circulation and impact would have been fairly minimal.

39. In a 1996 article, Pat Carlen and Chris Tchaikovsky, a former prisoner, spelled out the necessity for any analysis of female incarceration to "query the relationships between classes, racisms, genders and imprisonment," concluding that "prison populations composed of disproportionate numbers of poverty-stricken

and/or black people are *illegitimate*" (213). See also Smart, *Women, Crime and Criminology.*

40. The Quaker's name appears in suffrage novels such as Constance Elizabeth Maud's *No Surrender* (1911) alongside a list of other female role models. Fry also featured in inspirational speeches by suffragettes, one of which likened her to the suffragettes' leader Emmeline Pankhurst (*Papers of Katie Gliddon*, 7KGG/4/3 Croydon WSPU Press Cuttings 1910, 9). The Women's Library in London holds the design for a suffrage campaign banner with Elizabeth Fry's name and the door of a prison cell, which indicates how suffrage activists used the success of pioneering female reformers to legitimize their own claims for enfranchisement (The Women's Library @ LSE, ref. no. 2ASL/11/24/2). Fry's legacy is now officially enshrined in Britain's collective memory, as she appears on the Bank of England's five-pound note, reading to the female prisoners at Newgate (although this image is supposed to be replaced with former prime minister Winston Churchill beginning in 2016—somewhat ironically, considering Churchill's ambivalent role as home secretary during the suffragettes' imprisonment; see chapter 6).

41. Forsythe's entry on Gordon in the *Oxford Dictionary of National Biography* gives a useful overview of her background and professional activities.

42. The sketches originally appeared in *Blackwood's Magazine* between November 1888 and August 1889. For a brief overview of Skene's life and work, see Sanders.

Chapter 1: "Shame, You Are Not Going to Hang Me!"

1. This was one of the first hangings away from public scrutiny, after the abolition of public executions in 1868. It was also reported in newspapers (see "Execution of a Woman at Lincoln" in the *Bradford Observer*). Broadsides and chapbooks are listed in a separate section in Works Cited, in alphabetical order according to their title.

2. On nineteenth-century estimates of sales figures, see Mayhew 1:284; Charles Smith 258. For scholarly reflections on these estimates, see Altick 46; and Hepburn 74–75.

3. The context of the production, distribution, cost, and readership of execution broadsides has been extensively documented elsewhere. For more details about the origins and history of street literature, including gallows literature, see the following nineteenth-century accounts: Hindley, *Curiosities* and *History of the Catnach Press*; Mayhew, "Of the Street Sellers of Stationery, Literature, and the Fine Arts," *London Labour* 1:213–323. For critical treatments, see Collison; Shepard, *History*. Gatrell's study of executions in England is also a valuable resource.

4. On Catnach, see Mayhew 1:220; and Hindley, *History of the Catnach Press*. Catnach was succeeded by his niece, Mrs. Anne Ryle, the only woman in a leading role in the broadside industry, who initially went into partnership with Catnach's employee James Paul (Shepard, *Broadside Ballad* 82–83; and Mayhew 1:220).

5. For a detailed discussion of the different forms of (murder) broadsides, see O'Brien, *Crime in Verse* 23–24 and her chapter 1.

6. On the use of woodcuts, see Mayhew 1:234; and Rickards 138, 314. Many execution broadsides are littered with spelling mistakes and misprints, to the point that occasionally several versions of the offender's name are given in the same text. In quotations in the text, I have corrected obvious typographical errors to facilitate legibility, without indicating the changes.

7. A report in the *Morning Chronicle* corroborates that Browning could "read and write very well" ("Confession of Martha Browning").

8. For more detailed discussions of the Browning case, see Knelman, *Twisting* 215–17; and Kingston, *Judges and the Judged* 66–72. The case was widely reported in the press, including several pieces in the *Times* in December 1845 ("Central Criminal Court, Wednesday, Dec. 17," "Westminster Murder," "STOCKHOLM, Dec. 9," and a Letter to the Editor by I.C.C.). The Chartist organ *Northern Star* used the execution of Browning and another convict as an opportunity for attacking capital punishment, sarcastically commenting, "A great moral lesson has been preached to the multitude—the preachers a dead, law-slaughtered man and woman, Martha Browning and Samuel Quennell—suffocated carcases!—have been hung to a beam to illustrate the sacredness of human life" ("'Moral Lesson' of the Gallows").

9. The terms *broadside* and *broadsheet* are often used interchangeably, simply meaning "a large printed sheet of paper." Specialists tend to use *broadside* for a single-sided sheet and *broadsheet* for material on which both sides are printed (Rickards 64). I choose the term *broadside* since the material used here is generally printed on a single-sided sheet of paper, unless indicated otherwise.

10. On the remuneration of the writers, see Mayhew 1:220; 3:197. Mayhew's work suggests that broadsides printed in the Seven Dials area were authored by a small group of street poets (3:196). On the life of the only known Seven Dials poet, John Morgan, see Hindley, *History of the Catnach Press* xi–xxx.

11. Jackson gives the example of an 1865 broadside falsely recording the execution of the convicted child-murderer Mrs. Winsor, although the prisoner had actually had her sentence commuted to penal servitude for life ("Trial" 13–14).

12. A comment by one of Mayhew's informants suggests that the well-to-do also read broadsides hawked in the streets but sent employees to purchase them (1:223). On the broadsides' readership in the metropolis and the provinces, see also Gatrell 168–75.

13. On the emergence of "the Sorrowful Lamentation sheet," see also Mayhew 1:283.

14. For a more detailed discussion of these legal changes, including the 1836 Prisoners' Counsel Act, see the introduction. On the Prisoners' Counsel Act in the context of street literature, see also O'Brien, *Crime in Verse* 79.

15. The phrase is Elkins's (264).

16. See also Michael Denning's readings of nineteenth-century American dime novels "as a contested terrain, a field of cultural conflict" (3).

17. See Thackeray; and Dickens, "Letters to the Editor of *The Times*" and "Finishing Schoolmaster."

18. Two satirical interventions into the debate include "The March of Knowledge: or Just Come from Seeing 'Jack Sheppard'" in *Penny Satirist* (1839) and "Useful Sunday Literature for the Masses" in *Punch* (1849), both rpt. in King and Plunkett 38–39, 346–47. In the same volume, see also Fanny Mayne's "The Literature of the Working Classes" from *Englishwoman's Magazine, and Christian Mother's Miscellany* (1850; 40–43). For a more detailed discussion of the "moral panic" around cheap literature, especially the so-called penny dreadfuls, see Sutter.

19. For examples of such views, see Carpenter, *Juvenile Delinquents* 84–85, 110, and *Our Convicts* 2:209.

20. Similar arguments have been made for women and street ballads in the early modern period. See Stavreva; Clark.

21. Frederick George Manning and Marie (or Maria) Manning, a former maid to the daughter of the Duchess of Sutherland, were executed in 1849 for murdering Marie's (alleged) lover Patrick O'Connor. Dickens famously attended the execution and, in two letters to the editor of the *Times*, subsequently complained about the corrupting effects of such public spectacles. He also addressed the Mannings' death in his *Household Words* article "Lying Awake" (1852). For a brief discussion of Dickens's response, see Schwan, "Crime."

22. For a transcript, see Trial of Mary Ann Hunt, Old Bailey Proceedings.

23. The wide newspaper coverage of Hunt's case ranged from the *Times* and other London-based papers such as the *Standard* and the *Morning Post* to northern publications, such as the *Glasgow Herald* and the *Bradford & Wakefield Observer*. Mary Howitt used *Howitt's Journal*, coedited with her husband, William, to advertise her petition to the queen, seeking a commutation of the death sentence. On the commutation of Hunt's sentence, see "The Convicts Annette Meyers and Mary Ann Hunt" in the *Standard*. For background information on legal procedures to establish whether a convict was pregnant, see Bentley 90–91.

24. Like many other broadsides, this text is not dated, but the fact that it was printed by Catnach suggests that it is from the first half of the nineteenth century (the estimated date given in the John Johnson Collection is the 1820s). I was unable to trace any reports of this event in contemporaneous newspapers, which suggests that the case presented in the verses may be fake.

25. See also chapter 5 on *Mrs. Maybrick's Own Story: My Fifteen Lost Years* (1905), which contains an explicit reference to Fenning.

26. For a discussion of the evidence in this case, see Sibly. For a transcript of the trial, see Trial of Eliza Fenning, Old Bailey Proceedings.

27. See Watkins and Hone. For a more detailed discussion of the Fenning case and on Hone's response to it, see Gatrell 356–67; and Ledger 39–41.

28. Page numbers refer to the pamphlet inserted at the back of Hindley's *Curiosities of Street Literature*, which reprints this text.

29. On the historical evidence, see Gatrell 369. Knelman also offers a brief discussion of the man's possible guilt (*Twisting* 187). For more explicit and general critiques of the law's class bias in a broadside ballad, although not in relation to a female convict, see, for example, "The Rich and the Poor, or the Gentleman & the Bricklayer," a ballad comparing two murder cases in which the gentleman is certified insane and escapes the death penalty while the poor murderer is hanged.

30. The *Times* printed a detailed appeal for mercy to the judge, signed by the jury. See "Abolition of Capital Punishment."

31. On the commutation of sentence, see "Convicts Annette Meyers and Mary Ann Hunt" in the *Standard*. For an advertisement of her wax figure, see the sheet promoting an exhibition in Dewsbury, Yorkshire ("Last Moments of Anne Boleyn"). For an early-twentieth-century discussion of Meyers's case, including a somewhat contrived account of her life history (as the allegedly illegitimate daughter of a baronet), see Kingston, *Judges and the Judged* 56–64.

32. See also Krueger's article "Literary Defenses and Medical Prosecutions," which briefly discusses how the ballad tradition helped form a cultural consensus to shelter infanticides from prosecution and punishment. Krueger's examples are taken from canonical authors such as William Wordsworth and Elizabeth Barrett-Browning, however.

33. See also the broadside "Dreadful Occurrence!"

34. See "Assize Intelligence" in the *Morning Chronicle*. On the wider history, including medical contexts for infanticide, in the nineteenth century, see Arnot; Jackson, *Infanticide*; McDonagh, *Child Murder*; L. Rose.

35. For an example of a newspaper report on Colley, see "Dreadful Murder of Three Children by Their Mother" in the *Standard*. For a detailed analysis of representations of infanticides in the English and Australian press, see Goc, who considers "the duality of press discourse," arguing that such discourse "objectified and judged" these women while also making them "visible" (173).

36. The ballad referred to by Vicinus in this context is "The Esher Tragedy: Six Children Murdered by Their Mother." See Hindley, *Curiosities* 199.

37. For a detailed discussion of Baker's trial, see "Assize Intelligence" in the *Examiner*. Baker was recommended to mercy and subsequently obtained a reprieve,

with a view to having her sentence commuted to transportation for life. See "Condemned Convicts in the Provinces" in the *Standard*.

38. My argument here does not revolve around an assumed representativeness of such examples. Attempts to employ empirical methods for a critical evaluation of the broadsides' content are problematic, as we cannot establish from historical hindsight how representative the texts now available in archives might be. The mere fact that articulations dealing with women's motivations existed in *some* broadsides suggests that this was a concern for nineteenth-century writers and audiences.

39. For examples of newspaper reports, see "Child Murder at Measham" in the *Leeds Mercury* and "Female Crime" in the *Lancaster Gazette*.

40. Broadside stories were often copied by other publishers or reprinted, sometimes many years later, in a slightly different version, with changed names and sometimes a different type of crime. Rickards notes that "pirating" of material was common, both inside London and throughout the country (37). This is most certainly the case for "An Account of the Execution of Mary Hardcastle" and the "Awful Confession of Jane Thompson," which contain identical lines. Practically the same text as in the Hardcastle broadside, word by word, can be found on a sheet dated some five years earlier, under the title "An Account of the Execution of Margaret Harvey." The only changes pertain to the name of the prisoner, the date of execution, and the prisoner's hometown and age. This gives a strong indication of the inauthenticity of gallows literature. It could also suggest that real crime cases were often quite similar in nature and were responded to in broadsides in the form of certain stock narratives.

Chapter 2: The Lives of Which "There Are No Records Kept"

An earlier version of this chapter appeared as "From 'Dry Volumes of Facts and Figures' to Stories of 'Flesh and Blood': The Prison Narratives of Frederick William Robinson," in *Stones of Law, Bricks of Shame: Narrating Imprisonment in the Victorian Age*, ed. Jan Alber and Frank Lauterbach, 191–212. © University of Toronto Press 2009. Reprinted by permission of the publisher.

1. For some examples of how Robinson has been used, see Dobash, Dobash, and Gutteridge (who attribute *Female Life* to a "Francis" Robinson); McConville; Oxley; A. Smith; Wiener; Zedner. Radzinowicz and Hood acknowledge the fictionality of *Female Life*, although they, quite rightly, insist that it is also a rare "realistic" account of women's imprisonment (*History* 524n. 28). More recently, Fludernik has briefly noted literary motifs in *Memoirs of Jane Cameron*, which, she suggests, "raise[] the suspicion of fictionality" (165), but she does not associate the text with Robinson's name.

2. See Schwan, "Frederick William Robinson."

3. For an overview of women's contributions to the criminal justice system,

see Logan. On the recent preoccupation with offender perspectives, see the introduction.

4. Robinson authored over fifty works of popular fiction. For a more detailed discussion of Robinson's life and work, see Schwan, "From 'Dry Volumes of Facts and Figures'" and "Frederick William Robinson."

5. Robinson's novels of "low life" include *Owen: A Waif* (1862) and *Mattie: A Stray* (1864). Margaret Oliphant reviewed *Owen* for *Blackwood's Magazine* alongside Dickens's *Great Expectations*. See Schwan, "Frederick William Robinson" for an analysis of these novels, especially *Owen*.

6. See Carpenter's reference to the "Prison Matron's narrative," presumably *Female Life in Prison*, which, according to Carpenter, presents a "true picture" of "the unfortunate women" in jail (*Our Convicts* 1:32). She also quotes from *Memoirs of Jane Cameron* and a review of the book by the *Spectator* (*Our Convicts* 1:39–42, 2:230–38). Ironically, as a letter to the editor in response to the *Athenaeum*'s obituary points out, Halkett and Laing's *Dictionary of Anonymous and Pseudonymous Literature* had erroneously attributed *Female Life* and *Memoirs of Jane Cameron* to Mary Carpenter (A. Gordon). The 1926 edition of the *Dictionary* notes this mistake in its entry on "Female Life in Prison," and correctly gives credit to Robinson (Halkett and Laing 278).

7. On the use of female pseudonyms by male fiction writers in the 1860s and 1870s more generally, see Tuchman with Fortin.

8. The image was the well-known painting *Mrs Fry Reading to the Prisoners in Newgate in the Year 1816* by Jerry Barrett (see figure 0.1). All my references to *Female Life* are taken from the 1862 edition published by Hurst and Blackett.

9. Occasional references in the narratives suggest that the implied reader (perhaps a mirror image of the disguised male author) might have been male. Describing a scheme to defraud gentlemen, Robinson's Prison Matron remarks, "There is scarcely a reader of this book, perhaps, who has not been watched and followed in his time, a marked man, to be pounced upon at the first opportunity" (*Memoirs of Jane Cameron* 1:297).

10. See Jacobs on rates and readerships of nineteenth-century circulating libraries. He notes that data on customers are sparse but speculates "that although women and relatively lower-class readers patronized circulating libraries disproportionately (given their lower literacy rates), both groups were numerical minorities among the patrons of circulating libraries, especially of large metropolitan ones" (6). This does not mean, of course, that books formally borrowed by wealthy male patrons were not also consumed by other members of the household. On the profile of the *English Woman's Journal*, see Dredge; Rendall.

11. For example, a classified ad in the *Times* on 31 December 1863 presented the newly published *Memoirs of Jane Cameron*, citing press reviews from the *Examiner* and *Athenaeum* ("Now Ready").

12. Watts-Dunton notes that Dante Gabriel Rossetti read Robinson's work (813). It is not clear whether this applies to the prison narratives, too.

13. For further reviews, see the *Times* ("Female Life in Prison"); *Chambers's Journal* ("Female Felons"); the *Reformatory and Refuge Journal* ("Jane Cameron"); *Meliora* ("Petting and Fretting"); the *Dublin Review* ("Female Life in Prison"), which discusses all three prison tales; and the US periodical *Littell's Living Age* ("Female Life in Prison," reprinted from the *Christian Remembrancer*).

14. On decentralizing tendencies and heteroglossia in popular fictional genres more generally, see Bakhtin 273.

15. The Prison Act of 1865 recommended hard labor as a deterrence.

16. For a discussion of some of these sources, see Schwan, "From 'Dry Volumes of Facts and Figures.'"

17. For some more details on the case, see Knelman, *Twisting* 128–30; and R. Smith 154–55. Both appear to misspell the name "Somner." I use the original nineteenth-century spellings in Robinson and newspapers.

18. On Robinson's influences and place in a wider literary tradition of "low life," see Schwan, "Frederick William Robinson."

19. Most of the speakers in Field's account are male by implication. Only one explicitly refers to evidence given by a female convict. Regardless of whether these testimonies are "authentic," their value is compromised by the environment in which they were given; the position of the questioners (in this case Inspectors of Prisons) may well have influenced the prisoners' answers. See Grass's more detailed discussion of the use of prisoners' statements by prison chaplains John Field, H. S. Joseph, and John Clay (15–36).

20. See also my discussion of Robinson's depiction of Owen's mother—a fallen woman—in *Owen*, which affords the reader with a similar opportunity to enter the woman's thought process (Schwan, "Frederick William Robinson").

21. Carpenter's *Our Convicts* associates female offenders with that which is non-British, non-Christian, and uncivilized (e.g., 2:208). See also M. E. Owen's 1866 article "Criminal Women" in the *Cornhill Magazine* (153).

22. Zedner briefly refers to cases of "tampering" with prisoners by female attendants (161–62). For a contemporary attempt to recover a hidden lesbian history in the penal sphere, see Waters's historical novel *Affinity* (1999), which explores the theme of desire between a lady visitor and a female prisoner at Millbank in the 1870s (for a more detailed discussion, see the postscript).

23. McConville discusses the financial situation of prison employees in the nineteenth century. He cites an annual salary of £250, supplemented by one-twenty-fourth of the profits from the women convicts, for the matron at Millbank. However, he points out that the position "declined in importance and remuneration," and by 1835, the annual salary had decreased to £180, with a further £100 paid to an assistant matron (148n. 49). Using the salaries paid at the Northampton house of

correction as a "fairly typical range of salaries" (290), he notes that a matron's annual income was—at £35—significantly smaller than that of all other employees, including the lower-rank turnkeys and the night watchman, who were paid £52 (291). See also his table of the salaries of governors and keepers of 178 jails and houses of correction for 1840 (291). On the discrepancies between male and female salaries in the prison service, see Forsythe, "Women Prisoners" 537. Mary Gordon, the first female inspector of prisons between 1908 and 1921, noted inequities in salary, compared to her male colleagues (Cheney 124).

24. For examples of feminist writings in this context, see Bodichon; and Parkes, "What Can Educated Women Do?" (which draws on writings by Anna Jameson). See also "It Is a Common Practice" in the *Times*.

25. While Zedner suggests that female prison officers came from lower-class backgrounds (122), Robinson offers a more complex account, presenting the majority of matrons as "well-educated," with most of them having "some sad story to tell of early orphanage, or improvident speculations that brought a family from affluence to beggary—of widowed mothers or sick sisters to support—a few of husbands who died early and left them in the world with little children to work for in some way or fashion" (*Female Life* 1:31). Robinson implies a similar background for his two matrons in his later story "Daisy March, the Prison Flower," as they end up in the prison service because their father had carelessly "speculated in . . . bubble companies" (442).

26. The University of Buckingham's *Dickens Journals Online* site attributes this anonymous review ("Gone to Jail") to Eliza Lynn Linton, who was a regular contributor to Dickens's journals. See http://www.djo.org.uk/ (accessed 28 Apr. 2014).

27. On this debate, see Ellis's "The Distressed Needlewomen, and Cheap Prison Labour" in the *Westminster Review*. The article discusses the objects of the Distressed Needlewomen's Society.

28. Tristan visited several London prisons in 1839, including Newgate. See the introduction for a more detailed discussion.

29. Waters's historical novel *Affinity* (1999), potentially inspired by Robinson's prison tales, similarly suggests an analogy between the living conditions of servants and of people in prison (see the postscript).

30. Robinson had already offered a similarly happy prospect for a reformed prisoner in *Poor Humanity* (1868)—the story of George Carr, a convict returned from transportation, and his daughter Nella, imprisoned a second time after breaking out of a reformatory. Robinson draws both characters as repentant, ending this novel with the vision of a blissful future, foreshadowing Nella's life as wife and mother.

31. "Daisy March" was number 4 of volume 1 of the *Crystal Stories* (available at the British Library). Each number contained a complete story. The title pages of issues often only advertise the stories with reference to "By the author of . . ."

rather than specifying the author's name, although authors' names, including Robinson's, do appear on advertisements for other issues in the stories. Robinson is listed as the author of "The Woman Who Saved Him" (vol. 1, no. 1, of the *Crystal Stories*), which went into multiple editions.

32. For a more detailed discussion of the panic around "penny dreadfuls," see Sutter.

33. For a brief account of the *British Workwoman*'s profile, see Beetham.

34. For a brief overview of the magazine's aims and its readership, see Trahey. Collins and Dickens's coauthored mystery "No Thoroughfare" appeared in December 1867. Braddon's "To the Bitter End" was serialized between March 1872 and January 1873. The original spelling of the magazine's title was "Bazar," which changed to "Bazaar" in the twentieth century. Digitized versions of the nineteenth-century issues of the magazine are available from the Albert R. Mann Library, Home Economics Archive: Research, Tradition and History (HEARTH), Cornell University, http://hearth.library.cornell.edu/h/hearth/browse/title/4732809 .html (accessed 9 Aug. 2012).

35. Sponsored by Burdett-Coutts, Dickens managed Urania Cottage, located in London's Shepherd's Bush, which opened in 1847. The home's purpose was to reform women who had gone astray, through practical training in feminine duties (such as household chores), and to facilitate their emigration to the colonies (although some of them ended up in employment in Britain—including one who temporarily worked for the Dickens family, as noted by Hartley, *Charles Dickens* 96). Dickens's acquaintances Augustus Tracey and George Laval Chesterton, governors at Westminster House of Correction in Tothill Fields and Coldbath Fields House of Correction, respectively, provided candidates for Urania Cottage. Dickens comments on Urania Cottage's regime in his *Household Words* article "Home for Homeless Women." For a detailed history and analysis of Dickens's involvement with the institution, see Bodenheimer 135–42; P. Collins's chapter "The Home for Homeless Women" in *Dickens and Crime*; and, most extensively, Hartley's *Charles Dickens and the House of Fallen Women*.

36. For a more detailed discussion of this argument about execution broadsides, see chapter 1.

37. Sarah Featherstone was sentenced to death at the Chester assizes for the murder of her child in 1854, but her punishment was subsequently commuted to transportation for life (see report in the *Times*: "THE CROPS.—VIENNA"). In contrast to Robinson's suggestion, it is generally assumed that Eliot's inspiration for Hetty was Mary Voce, a condemned infanticide accompanied to the scaffold by Eliot's Methodist aunt, although McDonagh has argued that the child-murder theme suggested itself to Eliot through a range of sources, including literary ones ("Child-Murder Narratives"). It may well be that debates around Featherstone's case contributed to Eliot's thinking about representations of infanticide, although

McDonagh warns against overemphasizing the immediate context of child-murder debates in the 1850s instead of other historical discourses available to the novelist. For a more detailed discussion of Eliot, see chapter 3.

Chapter 3: The Limits of Female Reformation

1. Eliot's suggestion that Hetty tried to return to England after serving her sentence is not entirely realistic. As Oxley notes, most convict women were unlikely to return home, because costs for the voyage were "prohibitive" and authorities did not offer to repatriate them after the sentence had expired (55).

2. For a reading that privileges Adam's sympathy, see B. Martin, whose formalist analysis reads Hetty's story merely as a plot device and Hetty as a "transforming agent" (762) to enhance the reader's understanding of the principal character, Adam.

3. For an extensive argument about class-based limitations at work in Eliot's mantra of "the extension of our sympathies" ("Natural History of German Life" 270), see Dentith. A number of critics have taken issue with Eliot's treatment of Hetty. Raymond Williams writes that the novelist "abandons [Hetty] in a moral action more decisive than Hetty's own confused and desperate leaving of her child" (173), and more recently, Hertz notes that the character is "dismissed from [the novel] not once but twice" and then "killed off, it would seem gratuitously, in the Epilogue" (96). McDonagh reads Eliot's gesture of expelling Hetty metaphorically, in the context of a larger project of nation-making, in which the infanticide's banishment becomes a cleansing act that reinforces Britain's aspiration to become a country of "child-loving civilisation and enlightenment rationality" (*Child Murder* 128).

4. For accounts of these events surrounding Voce's execution, see the relevant excerpt from Zechariah Taft's transcript of Elizabeth Evans's journal in Chilcote, *Her Own Story* 175–76; Eliot, *Journals* 296; McDonagh, *Child Murder* 133, 136; Mottram 191–96, 199–202.

5. See also John Wesley's sermon 98, "On Visiting the Sick," in *The Works of the Rev. John Wesley* 125–26.

6. On Peters's story, see E. Brown 73; Chilcote, *John Wesley* 95–96; Wesley, "Some Account of Sarah Peters."

7. This quotation is from a letter to Sara Sophia Hennell, dated 7 Oct. 1859. Eliot's partner, George Henry Lewes, also wrote several letters on her behalf, denying that the novel's characters are portraits of real people and that Eliot had had access to her aunt's journals and notes of sermons. Despite such efforts, a later publication by one of Eliot's relatives, William Mottram, still conflated Elizabeth Evans with Dinah Morris.

8. Dinah's occupation is noted in *Adam Bede* 22, 108. On Evans's employment, see McDonagh, *Child Murder* 135.

9. On the role of class in the internal split within Methodism following Wesley's death and its impact on the restrictions imposed on women, see Lloyd 46–48. Another example of a working-class woman involved in charitable work was Sarah Martin (1791–1843), a dressmaker who visited prisoners in Great Yarmouth. For a detailed analysis of Martin's prison work, see Rogers.

10. See McDonagh's article "Child-Murder Narratives." Mitchell suggests a number of other potential intertexts.

11. For a reproduction of the frontispiece and a short discussion, see Meisel 290–91.

12. Rather than considering Hetty's silence as a consequence of fear and the gendered constellation of the courtroom, Berger reads it "as a capitulation to Adam's view of responsibility" (314).

13. *Report from the Select Committee on Secondary Punishments*, PP 1831–32 (547) vii, 127 [685].

14. See chapter 2 for a detailed discussion of "Daisy March."

15. On love and romance in relation to Dinah's Methodist vocation, see Clapp-Itnyre. Krueger problematizes Dinah's choice of Adam, "who quietly affirms patriarchal control and removes her to the domestic sphere," over Seth, "who would defy male authority in order to guarantee Dinah's right to preach"—the route chosen by Eliot's aunt and uncle (*Reader's Repentance* 262).

16. For an overview of this struggle for influence, see the section "Gendering the Prison Reform Debate" in the introduction.

17. The first edition of the novel was published in three volumes by Blackwood in 1859, after the editor had decided against serial publication. Eliot, in her *Journals*, copied the letter she had received from a poor man, asking her for a copy of *Adam Bede* because he was unable to afford her "inimitable books." Dismissing cheap literature targeted at his class as "trash," he claimed, "Many of my working brethren feel as I do" (299).

18. For a brief explanation of Dickens's involvement with this institution, see chapter 2, note 35.

19. For a general discussion of representations of women's criminality in Collins's fiction, see Mangham. Pal-Lapinski explores the figure of the female poisoner in *Armadale* and *The Legacy of Cain*.

20. In contrast to Nayder and Mukherjee, Roy considers Collins's agenda as reaffirming, rather than challenging, the colonialist project. Mukherjee locates his own interpretation "at a deliberately irresolute distance from the resolutely conclusive readings of Nayder and Roy" (179).

21. On representations of servants as potential "household spies" in Victorian fiction, including sensation novels such as *The Moonstone*, see Trodd's chapter 3 in *Domestic Crime in the Victorian Novel*.

22. Summerscale offers a semifictionalized, highly readable, and well-researched account of the Road Hill murder—which made sixteen-year-old Constance Kent a suspect in the death of her young half brother Saville—including some references to *The Moonstone*.

23. See Wilkie Collins to Mrs. Harriet Collins, 1 Sept. 1853, 16 Oct. 1853, and early June 1854, in Collins, *Letters* 1:96, 1:98, 1:120.

24. On Collins's travels with Dickens, see Law and Maunder xi.

25. On the role of disability in Collins's writing and other sensation fiction, see Holmes and Mossman, who argue that *The Moonstone* critically explores not only "classist" but also "ablist" attitudes through Blake's responses to Rosanna (499). See also Mossman.

26. For the use of similar gothic imagery in critiques of the condition of needle-women, see John Tenniel's cartoon "The Haunted Lady, or 'The Ghost' in the Looking-Glass" in *Punch* (1863), rpt. in Anne McClintock's *Imperial Leather* (97) and in Lynn M. Alexander's *Needlewomen in Victorian Art and Literature* (169).

27. See Nayder's observations on the dialogical nature of the narrative, based on Mikhail Bakhtin's work.

28. Other sensation plots subtly undermine the social and medical construction of female madness through male figures of authority. Braddon's *Lady Audley's Secret*, for instance, interrogates Robert Audley's power to declare Lucy Audley insane by raising doubts over his own mental stability. Lucy Audley repeatedly accuses Robert of monomania, and the bachelor himself expresses fears that he suffers from "nervous fancies" (254).

29. For a discussion of shifting attitudes toward self-murder and the question of whether it constitutes a crime, see Gates.

30. Ackroyd bases this information on a "very well-informed obituary" which referred to Rudd as one of Harriet Collins's servants (127). He speculates that Wilkie Collins "may have seduced her while she was in his mother's employment, or he may have taken the opportunity of Harriet's death to bring her to London" (128). Rudd and Collins had three children together, and Collins provided for them in his will.

31. For a close reading of the symbolism of the Shivering Sand, see also Heller 149–51.

32. For a detailed discussion of Robinson's "Daisy March," see chapter 2.

Chapter 4: "A Clamorous Multitude and a Silent Prisoner"

1. See the reports in the *Times* on 4 and 22 Dec. 1880; 8, 22, 24, and 29 Jan. 1881; 28 Feb. 1881; 8, 9, 12, 13, 14, 18, and 23 Apr. 1881; 6, 20, 23, and 24 May 1881 (the last four dealing with Fletcher's opponent Juliet Hart-Davies); *Pall Mall Gazette* on 5–9, 11–12 Apr. 1881; "Man about Town" in the *County Gentleman*; "Chance Lost" in *Owl*.

2. See A. Owen 259n84; and coverage around the time of the trial in spiritualist papers such as the *Light* (London), the *Spiritualist* (London), and *Banner of Light* (Boston).

3. The spelling of these names varies from source to source, with the variants "MacGeary" and "McGeary," "Dr. Mac" or "Dr. Mack."

4. See reports in the *Times* on 23 Apr., 6 May, 20 May, 23 and 24 May 1881; Fletcher, *Twelve Months* 401–2. Page references here and elsewhere are to the original pagination of the 1884 edition reprinted in the facsimile Routledge edition, edited and introduced by Bridget Bennett.

5. Susan Willis Fletcher, *Twelve Months in an English Prison* (Boston: Lee and Shepard; New York: Dillingham; London: Trübner, 1884).

6. See Kilgour 205, 217.

7. For other brief mentions see "Acknowledgments" in *Academy*; "Literary Gossip" and "On Our Library Table" in *Athenaeum*.

8. The *Gazette* repeatedly featured articles and illustrations on female murderers, boxers, and cross-dressers. On the paper's readership, see introduction to "Image from the *National Police Gazette*, 1879," in Link and Link 129.

9. On this historical context, see Braude.

10. On the connections between the women's-rights movement and spiritualism in Victorian Britain, see Basham; Oppenheim; A. Owen.

11. Margaret Fuller (1810–1850) was author of the influential *Woman in the Nineteenth Century* (1845) and well connected in American Transcendentalist circles.

12. For a discussion of how spiritualism as a movement influenced "new conceptions of feminine sexuality and marriage," see Tromp 78.

13. For an overview of such medical theories, see Braude 157–60; McGarry 121–53; A. Owen 38; Walkowitz, *City* 294n3.

14. In this context, see McGarry's critical analysis of Foucault's "secularization narrative" in his lectures at the Collège de France, exploring cultural shifts in perceptions of the female mystic's body, from witch to the possessed to the hysteric (McGarry 133).

15. Gail Hamilton was the pseudonym used by Mary A. Dodge.

16. For biographical details on John William Fletcher, see Gay's hagiography *John William Fletcher, Clairvoyant*.

17. On Mary Gove and Thomas Low Nichols, see Silver-Isenstadt.

18. Fletcher's and Gay's account contradict each other on the exact dates of travel and whether Susan or John William went ahead to Europe.

19. Victoria Woodhull was a sensational medium and was elected president of the national association of spiritualists in America. She was associated with radical causes, including free love, and her extreme views made her unpopular even in

her own circles. See Braude 129, 162; R. Moore 71, 84. Woodhull was briefly imprisoned on an obscenity charge in 1872 (Shaplen 162–63).

20. On Home and Slade, see Shepard, *Encyclopedia of Occultism* 1:433–36 and 1:838–40, respectively; Doyle 105–18, 157–67.

21. On the themes of John William's lectures, see Gay, *John William Fletcher* 152–73. There is also a brief account of one of John William's Sunday lectures at Steinway Hall and a description of a private séance with him in the actor and writer Florence Marryat's *There Is No Death* 107, 172–81. See also Member of Parliament Percy Wyndham's article on John William in the *Spiritualist*, titled "Clairvoyance."

22. Fletcher slightly misquotes the original article in *Punch*, which refers to Harcourt as the "Seldom-at-Home Secretary" ("Seldom-at-Home Secretary").

23. On the Bartlett trial, see Altick 247–49. For a discussion of how double standards of morality impacted the treatment of women at the hands of the law in the twentieth-century context, see Smart, *Women, Crime and Criminology*. For a concise summary of these debates in recent feminist criminology, see Marchbank and Letherby's section "Crime and Deviance" in *Introduction to Gender* 292–94.

24. For a brief discussion of the libel case, see Silver-Isenstadt 118.

25. For a dual biography of the Nicholses, see Silver-Isenstadt.

26. On Mary Gove Nichols's work, see Keetley; Myerson.

27. See his related publication *Free Love: A Doctrine of Spiritualism*.

28. Mary Nichols's letter was addressed to the secretary of state, William Harcourt, dated 13 June 1881; Susan Fletcher's letter is undated, but Thomas Nichols claims that it was written shortly before she received her sentence, that is, in early April 1881.

29. Fletcher notes that she had written her book shortly after discharge, while still in England: "every morning, from six o'clock to nine . . . while fresh in my memory" (408).

30. Weldon was incarcerated at Newgate for libel in 1880 and again at Holloway in 1885. She became interested in prison and judicial reform and wore a prison uniform while speaking about these, like W. T. Stead (Walkowitz, *City* 186).

31. As Walkowitz points out, though, Flowers and Hawkins were sympathetic to Weldon, which suggests that they were not necessarily antispiritualist or antiwomen in principle (*City* 180, 184).

32. See Schramm, "Is Literature More Ethical than Law?" 429. For a more detailed discussion of these changes in legal evidence procedure, see the introduction and the following legal histories: Allen; Beattie 356–76; Cairns 3–6; Langbein 266–73; Manchester 168–69; May 176–201.

33. For an overview of these particular debates, see Allen 144–80.

34. On Native American guides, see McGarry's chapter "Indian Guides: Haunted Subjects and the Politics of Vanishing" in *Ghosts of Futures Past*. Fletcher's

reference to Egypt may not be coincidental for personal reasons. Her husband traveled in the Middle East, including Egypt, before settling in London, in 1876 or 1877 (Fletcher 52). See also Gay, *John William Fletcher* 22–25.

35. On Dickens and Eliot in this context, see Schramm, "Is Literature More Ethical than Law?" 431.

36. Frederick William Robinson's *Female Life in Prison*, published under the anonym of "A Prison Matron," contained a whole catalogue of jungle creatures to refer to female convicts, including lionesses, tigresses, hyenas, panthers, and elephants. See chapter 2.

37. See J. G. Meugens, "The Case of Mrs. Fletcher," letter to the editor of *Light*, 11 June 1881, rpt. in Nichols, *Memorial* 41–42.

38. See the appendix to Fletcher's *Twelve Months* 432–36.

39. The chivalry thesis goes back to Otto Pollack's *The Criminality of Women* (1961). For a critical discussion, see Smart, *Women, Crime and Criminology* 46–53; Heidensohn with Silvestri. A concise summary of these debates can be found in Marchbank and Letherby's section "Crime and Deviance" in *Introduction to Gender* 292–94. For a more detailed discussion of how male politicians in the Victorian period deployed the language of chivalry, see Griffin 185–86. For the use of "chivalry" by male supporters of the Edwardian suffrage campaigns, see A. John 89, 93–94, 105–7; and Holton, "Manliness and Militancy" 112–14.

40. Fletcher does not provide a date for this newspaper article. I have been unable to verify the quotation.

41. Fletcher does not offer details of this article. I have been unable to verify it.

42. On Boole's life and work as a mathematician, see "Boole, Mary (Everest)," in Ogilvie and Harvey 158–59.

43. The *Times*'s report "Central Criminal Court, 12 April" on 13 April 1881 and Nichols's *Memorial to the Home Secretary* (16) both record one and a half hours.

44. Maddocks's testimony is included in "Charge against a Spiritualist," 29 Jan. 1881. On Florence Cook, see Doyle 130–41; on the Cook sisters, see also Marryat 139–52.

45. On Katie Gliddon's imprisonment and representation of other prisoners, see chapter 6 and Schwan, "Bless the Gods."

46. On the Nicholses' involvement in, and publications on, hydropathy, see Cayleff 111–14.

47. Unlike Fletcher, Wilberforce made her own defense at her trial in October 1881. See Trial of Mabel Wilberforce, Old Bailey Proceedings.

48. Tristan had visited several London prisons in 1839, including Newgate, where Fletcher was later incarcerated. In her *London Journal*, the Frenchwoman made "systems based on privilege" and "large scale poverty" (96) responsible for crime in general and gendered prejudice against women for female crime in partic-

ular (for instance, prejudice toward unwed mothers). She also identified "the indissolubility of the marriage tie" (97) as a cause of crime. See my more detailed discussion of Tristan in the introduction.

49. These *Herald of Health* articles, reprinted in Fletcher 460–70, were commented on in the House of Commons, when Member of Parliament Broadhurst asked Secretary of State William Harcourt whether he had made inquiries into Nichols's claims that conditions for women prisoners at Tothill Fields were poor. Harcourt replied that reports by the institution's officials suggested that these accusations "were not well founded" (House of Commons Hansard, 2 May 1882, Parliamentary debates).

50. For a brief overview of the reformist efforts and writings about prisons by Fry, Carpenter, and Tristan, see the introduction. On the suffragettes, see chapter 6.

51. On the suffragettes' rhetoric of martyrdom, see K. Hartman.

52. See "Fletcher, John William" in Shepard, *Encyclopedia of Occultism* 338.

53. On the alleged suicide, see "Palmist Takes Poison." Shepard claims that John Fletcher died from heart failure during the raid ("Fletcher, John William" in *Encyclopedia of Occultism* 338).

54. On the disappearance of Fletcher's brain, see "Stolen Brain Foils Spirits" in Nebraska's *Dakota County Herald* and *North Platte*.

Chapter 5: Adultery, Gender, and the Nation

1. Dated 13 August 1889, this sonnet first appeared in the *New York Times* around the time of Maybrick's impending execution. It is included in Barlow's *The Poetical Works of George Barlow* 10:198.

2. On the Emmets and Maybrick, see Ryan with Havers 247–48.

3. For a more detailed biographical account, see M. Hartman ch. 6.

4. On this wider context of publication, see Erber and Robb 6.

5. On Joyce's relationship with the Maybrick case, see Voelker. For the most comprehensive contemporaneous accounts of the trial, see MacDougall; Irving. For legal accounts, see Densmore, *Maybrick Case*; Grinnell. On the medical evidence more specifically, see Tidy. For a list of popular adaptations from the late nineteenth to the mid-twentieth century, see T. Christie. The melodrama *The Poisoner*, based on the case, was performed at the Sadler's Wells theater soon after the trial (T. Christie 153). The one-penny edition *Florence Maybrick: A Thrilling Romance* is only loosely based on real events and turns the case into a melodramatic plot full of intrigue and jealousy, casting Florence as "an angel of purity and goodness" (16). The *Full Account of the Life and Trial of Mrs. Maybrick: Interesting Details of Her Earlier Life* is one in a series of titles that mixed famous crime cases,

from Sweeney Todd to the Maria Marten murder at the Red Barn, with entertaining material on conjuring, ventriloquism, or advice on "how to become a detective." The account of Maybrick's case documents events in a more or less factual manner, combined with sensationalized passages, with the overall aim of allowing the reader to slip into the role of the detective. Contemporaneous writers of detective fiction used female murder cases such as Maybrick's as the basis of their stories, for instance, Emmuska Orczy's Lady Molly of Scotland Yard series, featuring one of the early female detectives in literature (Kestner, "Emmuska Orczy" 51). (Kestner gives an incorrect date for the Maybrick trial, though.) According to Mike Holgate's *Agatha Christie's True Crime Inspirations*, the plot of *Evil under the Sun* (1941) was based on Maybrick's story (110–12), underlining the significance of the trial for the genre of crime and detective fiction. Gabrielle Margaret Vere Long's *Airing in a Closed Carriage* (1943), published under her pseudonym Joseph Shearing, aims to offer a new interpretation of the case by adapting legal transcripts and other historical material for a novel—a project not dissimilar from that of contemporary women writers of historical fiction. Critics have suggested that Maybrick also inspired nineteenth- and early twentieth-century adaptations that were particularly feminist in spirit. Elizabeth Carolyn Miller argues that L. T. Meade's fiction played on the resonance of women and poison in the popular imagination at the time to reclaim misogynistic representations of female poisoners "for feminist purposes" (97). Similarly, according to Anthea Trodd, the Maybrick trial occurs as a subplot in Rebecca West's *The Fountain Overflows* (1957), with the figure of the judge represented as a misogynist (24). More recently, Julian Symons's *The Blackheath Poisonings* (1978) contained elements of the Maybrick story. On the use of Maybrick in the BBC's radio adaptations of famous trials in the 1950s, see Shale. The most comprehensive twentieth-century treatments of the case and its representations in the nineteenth-century press from a scholarly perspective can be found in M. Hartman; Knelman, *Twisting* and "From Yellow Journalism"; and Robb. Knelman's discussion of Maybrick in "Why Can't a Woman Be More Like a Man?" places the case in a wider social and legal context, comparing attitudes toward husband murder and wife murder.

6. According to Morland (who also reprints an illustration of the wax model), fifty thousand visitors viewed Maybrick's figure during the two weeks between her conviction and the reprieve (174).

7. On the legal debate, see Hammelmann 218. To this day, researchers do not agree on whether Maybrick was guilty. While Katherine Watson does not doubt the woman's innocence (55), John Emsley is convinced of her guilt (192–93). Maybrick's family has risen to new notoriety over the past two decades, after researchers tried to link the infamous Jack the Ripper murders to her husband, James. Related discussions in popular histories or online forums are endless. For a starting point, see S. Harrison; Cameron; Graham and Emmas; C. Jones.

8. Stephen was author of, among other works, *A Digest of the Criminal Law: Crimes and Punishment* (1877) and *A History of the Criminal Law in England* (1883).

9. For a transcript of Sir Russell's closing speech for the defense, see Irving 234.

10. On Dodge's involvement with the Maybrick Society, see M. Hartman 253.

11. This letter, dated 3 October 1892, was also published in the *New York Tribune*. On Hamilton's activities in the matter, see also her letters of 3 Mar. 1891 (unaddressed), to Cardinal Gibbons 1892, and to "Charlotte," 20 May 1892, in Hamilton, *Gail Hamilton's Life in Letters* 2:1018, 2:1029–30, 2:1032.

12. On Stead's complex role within, and reception by, the women's movement at the time, see Delap and DiCenzo. Aside from this chapter's epigraph, quoting "On the Impending Execution of Florence Maybrick," which first appeared in the *New York Times* around the time of the impending execution, Barlow also penned the sonnet "The First Stone," dated 24 August 1889, shortly after Maybrick's reprieve. Both poems were published in his *Poetical Works* 10:198–99. As his later sonnet "Woman Suffrage" (11:340) suggests, Barlow was by no means a feminist; rather, his support for Maybrick was arguably driven by conventional ideals of chivalry. Similarly, Forbes Winslow—a problematic figure from a feminist point of view owing to his involvement in the Georgina Weldon affair—recalled the furor around Maybrick's trial, describing with a strong dose of self-aggrandizement his "gigantic efforts made on her behalf," including agitation in the press and public meetings to bring about a change in verdict (*Recollections* 162).

13. For a brief explanation of the chivalry thesis and relevant scholarly sources, see note 39 in chapter 4.

14. For a general discussion of Judge Stephen's conduct during the trial, see also Parry 98–104. More recently, M. L. Friedland has wondered whether Stephen's professed occasional opium consumption might account for his "lapse of concentration" in the Maybrick trial (327n171). For an attempt to salvage the judge's reputation, see Kingston, *Famous Judges* 45–47.

15. In 1880, Elizabeth C. Wolstenholme Elmy had already called for a revision of the Criminal Code, which she attacked as "an exclusively male legislature" (16). She noted that women "have never in the case of a criminal trial the protection of a jury of their peers—they are prosecuted or defended by men, tried by men, judged by men" (16). Despard and Collins's suffrage novel *Outlawed* (1908) also problematizes the court as a masculine space (132, 135).

16. See Conley 107, 111–12.

17. For a publication specifically dealing with the absence of a court of criminal appeal, see Levy's *The Necessity for Criminal Appeal*, reviewed in the *Harvard Law Review* by J.H.B. Jr.

18. For a chronological overview of release efforts in the early years of Maybrick's imprisonment, see the pamphlet *Efforts and Reasons for the Release of Florence E. Maybrick: 1889 to 1893*.

19. Gail Hamilton (Mary Abigail Dodge) to Lady Henry Somerset, 10 Nov. 1892, in Densmore, *Maybrick Case* 102. Hamilton's letter was also published in the *New York World* on 13 Nov. 1892, as noted by Densmore (*Maybrick Case* 95).

20. Densmore herself used a similar contrast between republicanism and absolutism, associating English law with a divine rule (and a monarchy) that must not be questioned (*Maybrick Case* 9).

21. See the following articles in the *New York Times*: "Balfour on Conference," "Commons and Mrs. Maybrick," "Michael Davitt on Dreyfus."

22. See "This Week's Books" in the *Saturday Review*; "New Books Received" in *Academy and Literature*; "List of New Books" in *Athenaeum*.

23. Knelman, too, refers to *Mrs. Maybrick's Own Story* in passing rather than dedicating a more detailed analysis to the text, even though the title of her chapter is "The Feminine Perspective" (*Twisting* 235).

24. Ryan argues that "Helen Densmore worked closely with Florence Maybrick on the book" (248), although the source of this claim is unspecified.

25. See Densmore, "English Dreyfus Case."

26. On Weldon, see Walkowitz, *City*.

27. For a more detailed discussion of Fenning, see chapter 1.

28. O'Brien offers a more detailed reading of "The Ballad of Reading Gaol" (*Crime* 104–8). She argues that Wilde's poem "suggest[s] a strategic identification with the public poetics of the 'criminal' classes" (104).

29. On late-Victorian concepts of the "habitual" female offender, see Zedner.

30. See "Mrs. Maybrick at the Tombs"; "Mrs. Maybrick Visits Tombs"; "Mrs. Maybrick at Sing Sing."

31. See the advertisement "100 Pages Out To-morrow."

32. For a more detailed discussion of how national and ethnic identity became factors in media representations of criminal cases at the time, see Conley ch. 2.

33. The trial transcript in Irving contradicts this version, for it notes how Maybrick and her defense counsel, Sir Charles Russell, consulted during "a short whispered conversation" about whether the defendant still wanted to go ahead with her own statement (Irving 227). What Maybrick does not mention here either is that her counsel had also made a deliberate decision to keep her family—in particular, her mother, the Baroness von Roques, who had married a Prussian aristocrat—at a distance during the trial, because of rumors that the Baroness had poisoned her first two husbands (M. Hartman 250).

34. See "Mrs. Maybrick's Denial"; "Mrs. Maybrick Condemns the Sing Sing Prison."

35. On Maybrick's performances, see also her manager's account (Wagner).

36. For more details on this phase of Maybrick's life, see M. Hartman; Robb.

37. For such a reading, based on late-Victorian middle-class prison autobiography by men, see Lauterbach.

Chapter 6: Gender and Citizenship in Edwardian Writings from Prison

An earlier version of parts of this chapter appeared in "'Bless the Gods for My Pencils and Paper': Katie Gliddon's Prison Diary, Percy Bysshe Shelley and the Suffragettes at Holloway," *Women's History Review* 22.1 (2013): 148–167. Reprinted by permission of the publisher. www.tandfonline.com. See Schwan, "Bless the Gods."

1. I use *militant* here to refer to illegal activities such as stone throwing and window breaking and follow common practice by using *suffragette* to discuss women involved in, and incarcerated during, this struggle, while bearing in mind that these terms have been subject to critical interrogation. Several scholars have noted that the distinction between *militant* and *constitutional* suffrage activists was not always as clear-cut as originally assumed. See Holton, *Feminism and Democracy*. On the history of the suffragettes, see Eustance, Ryan, and Ugolini; B. Harrison, "The Act of Militancy, Violence and the Suffragettes, 1904–1914" in *Peacable Kingdom*; Holton, *Suffrage Days*; Joannou and Purvis; Kean; Liddington; Mayhall, *Militant Suffrage Movement*; Purvis, "Deeds, Not Words"; Purvis and Holton; Raeburn; van Wingerden.

2. Harlow analyses third-world women's prison narratives. See also her study *Barred*.

3. For a more detailed account of Gliddon's life and involvement with the suffrage campaign, see Schwan, "Bless the Gods."

4. On the analysis of diaries, see also Culley; Hogan, "Diarists on Diaries" and "Engendered Autobiographies"; Huff, "Reading as Re-vision"; Langford and West; Lejeune. On diaries in the context of the suffrage movement, see Hannam. On letters, see Bray; Huff, "Women's Letters"; L. Stanley.

5. See also Bunkers, "Diaries."

6. For terminology, I am following scholars such as Bunkers and Lejeune, who use the terms *diary* and *journal* interchangeably, although some critics make a distinction between the two, regarding the diary as more "intimate" and the journal as "a chronicle of public record" (Smith and Watson 272–73). As this chapter demonstrates, secret prison diaries such as Gliddon's cannot easily be classified as either "intimate" or "public record" but function in both ways.

7. Purvis, "Prison Experiences" 103; Crawford, "Prison" 567.

8. On these reform efforts, see Crawford, "Prison" 568–69; Blagg and Wilson. On the first female inspector, see Cheney. Several accounts by suffragettes like to stress the improvement of prison conditions thanks to the activists' presence and quote "ordinary" prisoners to that effect. See, for example, Solomon 7. Ethel

Smyth's letter to the editor of the *Times* (19 Apr. 1912) decries the poor conditions that suffragette leaders such as Emmeline Pankhurst and other prisoners were exposed to. (This letter was also reprinted in *Votes for Women* 94 (1912): 3. *Suffragette Collection Leaflets* SC13. 50.82/534. Museum of London).

9. See, for example, "Fed by Force." Helen Gordon also gives an extensive account of forcible feeding in *The Prisoner*. Both of these are reprinted in Mulvey-Roberts and Mizuta.

10. On the rape analogy, see Purvis, "Prison Experiences" 122–23. For scholarly criticism on accounts of forcible feeding, see Howlett.

11. For a detailed discussion of the treatment of suffrage prisoners from the Home Office's point of view, see Crawford, "Police."

12. For a comparison between the privileges of prisoners in first division, second division, and under Rule 243a, see the table in the "Prison Commission's Papers" with instructions for governors. The same set of papers also contains a note on the announcement by the secretary of state on 10 June 1912 that three prisoners (Emmeline Pankhurst and the Pethick-Lawrences) were to be transferred from Rule 243a treatment to first-division status.

13. Radzinowicz and Hood, "Status of Political Prisoner" 1473–74; Crawford, "Prison" 572.

14. Although under a hard-labor sentence and therefore not entitled to special privileges granted under Rule 243a initially, Katie Gliddon received luxury items from home early in her sentence in March 1912, including fruit and bedding. She alludes to the complicity of prison staff in this matter (*Prison Diary* 10, 17). Page references to this text are usually to the transcript (*Prison Diary*). As the transcribed version is not always accurate, the original, handwritten diary should be read alongside it (*Prison Diary 1* and *Prison Diary 2*).

15. See document dated 14 March 1912, PCOM8/228/15, National Archives, London. The hard-labor sentence was, as Gliddon notes in her diary, only "symbolical" (*Prison Diary* 8). For the suffragettes, it usually involved some needlework.

16. For a chronology of events, see van Wingerden xviii–xix.

17. Examples of prison accounts include Biggs; Lilley; Kenney; Richardson; Marion.

18. For the most comprehensive overviews of the suffragettes' imprisonment, see Purvis, "Prison Experiences"; and Crawford, "Prison." See also van Wingerden (89–95). Green discusses prison autobiographies and diaries at some length, especially in the context of the suffragettes' hunger strike. Norquay's anthology *Voices and Votes* makes available some excerpts from prison writings, with little critical commentary.

19. On Lytton, see Corbett 150–79; Green (especially ch. 1); Myall; Jorgensen-Earp; S. Thomas; Haslam, Introduction and "Being Jane Warton" in *Fitting Sentences* 137–62; Mulvey-Roberts; Tilghman.

20. See E. Pankhurst; E. S. Pankhurst; C. Pankhurst. There are two new editions of Constance Lytton's *Prisons and Prisoners*, published in 1988 and 2008.

21. The concept of *experience* and whether and how it is possible to access thoughts and emotions through historical evidence has been a matter of debate among historians and feminist scholars over recent decades. For a starting point, see the conversation between Scott, "Evidence of Experience"; and Downs. Despite an awareness of strategies of representation and textuality, I concur with Purvis's helpful summary that "a suffragette's experience of prison life, as evident in the various texts documenting that experience, was not a mere abstraction or a 'discursive' reality; to claim that it was would be to deny that woman a subjectivity from which to speak. Although any one text . . . is not that suffragette's experience but a representation of it, it was a lived experience even if mediated through her material, social and interpersonal context—as well as the discourses of the day" ("Prison Experiences" 127). On related issues of methodology, see also Purvis, "Doing Feminist Women's History."

22. According to a document from the Police Commission, Holloway received 129 suffragette prisoners on 5 March 1912, of whom 87 were remanded, 17 committed for trial, and 25 sentenced. Of the 25, 19 were sentenced to hard labor and 6 to simple imprisonment ("Treatment of Suffragette Prisoners since March 1st 1912").

23. Transcript of letter originally written on a newspaper wrapper in Marylebone Police Station (*Papers of Katie Gliddon*, Correspondence, 7KGG/2/1, p. 5). It may well be that Gliddon played down her imminent sentence for fear of distressing her family. In another letter to her sister Gladys, she writes that she has "not told Mother about the hard labour because it would frighten her" (*Papers of Katie Gliddon*, Correspondence, 7KGG/2/1, pp. 14–15).

24. Gliddon, *Prison Diary 2*. The sheets were probably sent in secretly with Gliddon's washing, since she comments in an unofficial letter to her mother, "Mrs Pankhurst got the Matron to let us have our baskets—hence decent notepaper" (*Papers of Katie Gliddon*, Correspondence, 7KGG/2/1, p. 25).

25. The transcript of Gliddon's diary contains an introduction by her great niece Elaine Silver, née Gliddon, written in January 2007. According to a note in the original volume (*Prison Diary 1*, p. 872), Gliddon intended publication by "the Women's Press" (the Woman's Press, as it was correctly called). The original prison diary was given to the Women's Library in London (now The Women's Library @ LSE) in May 2008, by Katie's nephew Michael Gliddon. Another nephew, Gerald Gliddon, donated drawings in the same year; he had already given other personal papers to the library in April 1986.

26. It is beyond the scope of this chapter to offer a comparison between the original diary and the revisions for Gliddon's draft autobiographical account and a discussion of the role of the critical commentary on these records by another

reader. More research in this context could offer fascinating insights into the process of translating the immediacy of a prison diary entry into an (unpublished) autobiographical narrative. Stanley and Dampier's concept of the "simulacrum diary"—a life narrative that takes multiple forms—could be instructive here. Gliddon's work could play an important role in helping to establish the usefulness of this critical term—a challenge given that, as Smith and Watson note, "relatively few texts have multiple forms and circumstances of production" (267).

27. Since the transcribed version of Gliddon's prison diary is not always entirely accurate, I shall silently correct small errors and indicate more substantial corrections where necessary.

28. Purvis, "Prison Experiences" 108–9; Crawford, "Prison" 568. See also Hartley, "Reading," on debates around appropriate reading materials in Victorian prisons.

29. This is a reference to the *Golden Treasury of English Verse*, a popular anthology of poetry compiled by Francis Turner Palgrave, first published in 1861.

30. See transcript of postcard to her mother just before going to Holloway (*Papers of Katie Gliddon*, Correspondence, 7KGG/2/1, p. 7).

31. The transcript reads, incorrectly in my view, "Dr L Grant Anders." The context of the passage with several other references to "Dr Garrett Anderson" and Gliddon's own transcript of the day's entry in her draft autobiographical account suggest that she can only mean Elizabeth Garrett Anderson's daughter Louisa. See the original, handwritten diary (*Prison Diary 1*, p. 831); and *Draft Autobiographical Account 3* (*Papers of Katie Gliddon*, 7KGG/1/6).

32. On the importance of reading and libraries in the formation of the women's and suffrage movements more generally, see also Crawford, "Libraries."

33. Other titles consumed by imprisoned suffragettes included John Stuart Mill's *On Liberty* and *On the Subjection of Women*, a book about Joan of Arc, novels by George Eliot, Kropotkin's *Memoirs of a Revolutionist*, Charles Dickens's prison novels, and William Morris's utopian *News from Nowhere* (Crawford, "Libraries" 348–49).

34. For a historically earlier period, Rogers shows how prisoners in early Victorian jails were able to use limited opportunities for reading in subversive ways. Sweeney argues similarly for contemporary African American women's reading practices in prison.

35. This might have been a "Miss Collier," who was also reading the life of Mazzini at Holloway, most likely the biography edited by Emilie Ashurst Venturi, which contained essays by Mazzini (Crawford, "Libraries" 349).

36. Gliddon here repeatedly spells the name "Maltzini." Contextual evidence suggests that she means Giuseppe Mazzini, since other suffragettes were reading him, and she herself references Mazzini in some of her other papers. The transcript of the diary refers to the "Italian feminist Mozzoni," but this is not what the

original suggests. On Mazzini and the suffragettes, see Mayhall, "Rhetorics of Slavery."

37. See also Flint 237 for a discussion of this.

38. See also Flint 237.

39. See Solomon's account of exchanging a pencil and paper (4–5).

40. The suffragettes' newspaper did indeed reach Holloway, but there is no evidence that Gliddon gained access to it. According to Alice Ker's report, "Votes came in once, cut into strips, wrapped in oiled paper, in the stuffing of a roast chicken" (qtd. in Crawford, "Libraries" 348–49). Leonora Tyson writes of women who, during exercise, "read, surreptitiously, the last number of V.F.W. that has penetrated the prison walls, no one knows how!" ("Day in Holloway" sheet 2).

41. Undated newspaper clipping in the *Papers of Katie Gliddon*; year specified in the Women's Library @ LSE's guidance notes.

42. Shelley's "Fragment" was probably written for his friend, the radical writer and editor Leigh Hunt, who was imprisoned for attacking the Prince Regent (Bradley 35).

43. For a brief discussion of *Outlawed*, see Flint 313.

44. Crawford, "Artists' Suffrage League" 17. The original passage is in *Prometheus Unbound*, III.iv, l. 153 (Shelley 268).

45. Quotation from Gliddon, *Prison Diary* 32.

46. On Pankhurst's political imprisonment on this occasion, see B. Winslow 132–33.

47. On Tyson's biographical background, see Crawford, "Tyson Family"; A. Ward.

48. Arguably, pre-printed prison paper may have had benefits for illiterate prisoners who might otherwise not have been able to communicate with the outside world at all.

49. Letter without addressee, signed "Katherine Gray," (Gliddon's pseudonym), 18 Mar. 1912, *Papers of Katie Gliddon*, MS 7KGG/2/1-9.

50. Tyson's father, Gustav Wolff, was a doctor of music. His family might have changed its name to the Anglo-sounding Tyson in the anti-German climate following the Franco-Prussian War of 1870 (A. Ward 6).

51. Tyson to Mrs. and Miss Tyson, 22 Apr. 1912, *Prison Letters*. In English, the lines read, "Hopefully you have received my last letter with my laundry. Tell me if yes or no because there was so much in it. One can hide letters very well at the back of books. If it's a well-bound volume, isn't there a little hollow space between [?] cover and the back of the book? Of course it has to be a small, thin b." (my trans.).

52. 24 Mar. 1912, in Notebook "Letters from Holloway," *Papers of Katie Gliddon*, Correspondence, TS 7KGG/2/1, p. 28. The *Papers of Katie Gliddon* do not contain any original letters.

53. On the salaries of nineteenth-century prison matrons, see McConville 290–91. Forsythe discusses discrepancies in pay for male and female prison staff ("Women Prisoners" 537). For a more detailed discussion of the class background and working conditions of female officers in the nineteenth century, see chapter 2.

54. The WSPU's attitudes toward women who did not come from bourgeois or upper-class backgrounds have been the subject of debate among feminist scholars. Critical assessments range from dismissing the WSPU "as a bourgeois movement" to claims that the WSPU actually sought to alleviate social inequities and problems such as sweated labor and sexual slavery (Purvis, "Prison Experiences" 105). For an overview of critiques of a middle-class bias from within the suffrage movement, see Corbett 169–73.

55. Early in 1914, Sylvia Pankhurst founded the East London Federation of Suffragettes (ELFS) —later called the Workers' Suffrage Federation and the Workers' Socialist Federation—growing out of the WSPU's East London Federation, after disagreements over strategy with her mother and sister Christabel. Working women were the base of the ELFS; in March 1914, Pankhurst launched the *Women's Dreadnought*, a paper for working-class women (later to become the *Workers' Dreadnought*; Crawford, "East London Federation").

56. "Sketches at Holloway," illustrations for the *Pall Mall Magazine*, after drawings made at Holloway by Sylvia Pankhurst, redrawn by an engraver. For a contextual discussion of these drawings, see R. Pankhurst 63–74.

57. Corbett has argued similarly with reference to Lytton's disguise as working-class suffragette Jane Warton. Not losing sight of the fact that Lytton's act constitutes an appropriation of the working-class voice, Corbett contends that it is precisely the assumption of this perspective by a more privileged subject such as Lytton that guarantees it will be heard (169). For readings of other poems in Pankhurst's *Writ on Cold Slate* and Keats's poetry as an intertext, see Tyler-Bennett.

58. Herbert Henry Asquith was the Liberal prime minister at the time.

59. On the importance of "difference" in the suffrage movement, see Purvis, "Prison Experiences" and "Doing Feminist Women's History" 185.

60. See L.G., "The Child's Champion," review of Rosa Waugh's *The Life of Benjamin Waugh* (1912), unknown newspaper, 18 Dec. 1912, *Papers of Katie Gliddon*, 7KGG/4/5. On Benjamin Waugh, see also Behlmer.

61. See Gliddon, *Prison Diary 2*, entry for Monday, 22 Apr. 1912, 7KGG/1/2, p. 2. Gliddon expresses regret over the drowning of Stead on board the *Titanic*, an event she only finds out about during her family's prison visit.

62. Gliddon cites an aphorism from the Irishman's "Maxims for Revolutionists": "Prison is as irrevocable as death" (*Prison Diary 1*). The typed transcript quotes the Shaw line as "Time is as immutable as death" (*Prison Diary*). "Maxims for Revolutionists" was published with Shaw's play *Man and Superman* (1901–3),

which also dealt with the role of women in society. The original line reads "Imprisonment is as irrevocable as death" (Shaw, *Man and Superman* 221). Shaw publicly supported suffragettes, for instance, in a speech made at an event protesting the "Cat and Mouse Act" (E. Pethick-Lawrence 296). See also Shaw's "Unmentionable Case." For brief comments on Shaw's relationship to the suffrage campaign, see A. John. On the ambivalence of Shaw's feminism, see Peters; Powell.

63. See "Women's War," clipping from unknown newspaper, 5 Nov. 1910, Croydon WSPU Press Cuttings 1910, *Papers of Katie Gliddon*, 7KGG/4/3, p. 19; and related newspaper cuttings on Croydon branch meetings from 1911 in 7KGG/4/4.

64. The first female inspector of prisons, Dr. Mary Gordon, who sympathized with the suffragettes' cause, noted that of all the prostitutes in jails, "the great majority were very poor and ignorant, and came from the labouring classes" (84).

65. On women as investigators in nineteenth-century urban spaces, see Nord 207–36.

66. For more religious language in Gliddon, see also passages in which she compares prison to "Bethlehem" and her leader, Emmeline Pankhurst, to "a Pope" (*Prison Diary* 7, 13).

67. For a detailed discussion of religious language in suffrage texts, see K. Hartman.

68. On attempts to challenge the distinction between pure and impure women in prostitution debates, see Kent 73.

69. It should be noted that the difference in form might also account for some of these variations: Lytton's published autobiography offered an opportunity for a carefully considered, polished, and edited account, whereas Gliddon's diary did not. For a discussion of Lytton's *Prisons and Prisoners* as a text "with a high degree of consciousness" about differences in "standpoint," see Corbett 167.

70. Marcus concentrates on such "female homoeroticism as an element of Victorian women's heterosexuality," rather than as homosexuality or a "rebellion" against heterosexuality (283–84n2).

71. As Zalcock notes, the women-in-prison film has precursors in 1920s Hollywood, but the award-winning *Caged* (1950) is typically seen as the prototype, with a multitude of similar titles following suit. The genre had its heyday between the 1950s and 1970s, with films falling either into the category of the serious social problem film or under the sexploitation label (crossing over into blaxploitation). Generic features include a relatively innocent newcomer ("new fish"), cruel or corrupt prison officials, relationships between women, shower scenes, fights or riots, and escape. Some films that occasionally verge on the pornographic may still explore serious concerns, for example, sexual exploitation by prison officials, as is the case in Jonathan Demme's *Caged Heat* (1974). For overviews of the genre and critical discussions, see also Morey; Morton; Rafter; Walters; Zalcock and Robinson. Halberstam makes brief reference to the genre in *Female Masculinity* (201–2).

Millbank analyzes representations of lesbian sexuality in the English TV series *Bad Girls* (1999–2006).

72. On the Slade School, see A. Thomas 2.

73. For a more general discussion of the challenge of distinguishing female friendships and romantic, erotic, and sexual attachments between women in the Victorian period, see Marcus.

74. Although Mayhew and Binny are listed as co-authors, Mayhew was originally meant to be the study's single author. The volume notes, "*All after page* 498 *is written by Mr. John Binny*" (x). We can assume that Mayhew was the author of the passage on female prisoners at Brixton (possibly with final corrections by Binny). According to E. P. Thompson, Mayhew "ended abruptly in mid-sentence" in part nine of *The Criminal Prisons* and went abroad (48). Binny was commissioned by the publishers, probably without Mayhew's permission (48–49n132). Humpherys writes that Mayhew's part of the study ceased upon the death of his publisher (115).

75. On collectivity through hunger striking and forcible feeding, see Corbett 150; and Green 104.

Chapter 7: Postscript

An earlier version of my readings of *Affinity* and *Alias Grace* was delivered at the "Hystorical Fictions: Women, History and Authorship" conference at the University of Wales, Swansea, in August 2003. I would like to thank Kaye Mitchell and Conny Ziegler for drawing my attention to these novels many years ago.

1. For a general overview of the genre of historical fiction, see De Groot. On women's appropriation of the genre and engagements with history more specifically, see Anderson; Heilmann and Llewellyn; Johnsen; Kohlke, "Into History"; Wallace.

2. For a detailed discussion of Robinson, see chapter 2.

3. It is beyond the scope of this chapter to discuss Atwood's exploration of Grace's Irishness. For a critical assessment of this aspect, see Lovelady, who notes "the association of Irishness with criminality" in mid-nineteenth-century Canada (190).

4. March discusses *Alias Grace* as a heteroglossic "authorial mosaic" (66).

5. Millbank's analysis of the novel focuses on the representation of lesbian desire.

6. Prior readings of *Affinity* have pointed out the novel's engagement with Jeremy Bentham's panopticon and Michel Foucault's critique of it. See especially Arias, "Female Confinement"; Llewellyn; Macpherson. Armitt and Gamble discuss Foucault alongside other texts on prison architecture relevant to the novel, such as Giovanni Battista Piranesi's engravings *Carceri d'Invenzione*.

7. McDermott and Marks were formally only tried for the murder of Kinnear.

Since they had already received a death sentence for it, another trial for the murder of Montgomery was deemed unnecessary (Atwood, Author's afterword 537).

8. On the significance of quilts and patchwork in the novel, see Delord; Elsley; Michael; Murray; Rogerson; Wilson. Atwood's own acknowledged sources on quilting include Ruth McKendry's *Quilts and Other Bed Coverings in the Canadian Tradition* (1979), Mary Conway's *300 Years of Canadian Quilts* (1976), and Marilyn L. Walker's *Ontario's Heritage Quilts* (1992) (Acknowledgements 544).

9. For a more detailed discussion of *The Moonstone*, see chapter 3.

10. Darroch analyzes the novel's engagement with nineteenth- and twentieth-century theories of traumatic memory and amnesia in detail.

11. Grace describes what she sees in the dream: "another man, someone I knew well and had long been familiar with, even as long as my childhood, but had since forgotten; nor was this the first time I'd found myself in this situation with him. I felt a warmth and a drowsy languor stealing over me, and urging me to yield, and surrender myself; as to do so would be far easier than to resist" (Atwood, *Alias Grace* 326). Other scenes of sexual harassment are hinted at on pages 38, 39, 72, 90, and 278–80. On child sexual abuse as a possible interpretation of the dream scene, see also Blanc 119; Staels 436–37.

12. For a similar discussion, see also Toron, who reads *Alias Grace* as a novel which "adds to a body of prison literature" (3) while exploring "the epistemological limits of prison narration" (1).

13. Atwood problematizes the behavior and motives of self-proclaimed "liberal-minded" (31) people like the prison governor's wife, who collects stories of "famous criminals" (29) in a scrapbook and presents Grace, who acts as her servant during the day, as one of her "accomplishments" (24) to her lady friends.

14. For a more detailed discussion of this aspect of Robinson's narratives, see chapter 2. For more on the erotic undercurrents of spiritualist circles, see chapter 4 on Susan Willis Fletcher. Other critics have discussed the influence of historical sources and figures on *Affinity*. Arias regards *Affinity* as a fictionalization of Fletcher's case, partially based on Priestley's incorrect assumption that Fletcher was imprisoned "at Tothill Fields in the 1870s" ("Female Confinement" 263)—the spiritualist in fact served her twelve-month sentence between 1881 and 1882. While Fletcher's autobiography may have been a likely source of inspiration and historical information on women's imprisonment for Waters, Arias may be overstating her case that Selina Dawes is "the fictional counterpart of Susan Willis Fletcher" (263). Waters's novel only shares a few characteristics with Fletcher's narrative; for example, Mrs. Brink bears a loose resemblance to Fletcher's antagonist, Juliet Hart-Davies, who, like Brink, communicates with her "mamma" during her private séances (Waters, *Affinity* 174). Elsewhere, in "Talking with the Dead" (90), Arias suggests, as does Spooner (354–55), that Selina is partially based on the famous medium Florence Cook, who is explicitly referenced in the novel.

15. For a discussion of Margaret's spinsterhood and the novel as a means of reconstructing the marginalized history of this form of social deviance, see R. Carroll.

16. For instances of Mrs. Prior "watching" over Margaret, see *Affinity* 30, 51, 223, 267. Aside from an engagement with Bentham and Foucault, as various critics have noted, Waters's preoccupation with the female gaze suggests a covert conversation with the women-in-prison film and the genre's more or less open allusion to lesbianism. For a brief discussion of the genre and its emphasis on "women watching other women" (Mayne 118), see chapter 6.

17. Dora's account of what she sees as Simon's "strange habit[s]" is on page 352 of *Alias Grace*.

18. In "Making Up Lost Time," Doan and Waters warn against overly romanticized, nostalgic, and homogenizing reinventions of a lesbian past, challenging the fact that "the past—which ought to proliferate with [such] differences—emerges from the [traditional] lesbian historical genre as an erotic and political continuum through which alterity can be mystically overridden" (18).

19. See also R. Carroll, who reads Margaret's unwillingness or inability to "recognize her own desires in those of the Millbank pals" as a rejection of "the criminalizing connotations which are inescapably implicated in this formation of identity," rather than being an effect of class and social difference (139).

20. For Selina's critique, see Waters, *Affinity* 112.

21. Kohlke makes a similar point regarding sexuality, suggesting that "the implication of lesbian desire in fraud and criminality inevitably reinforces outdated stereotypes of lesbianism as linked to deviance" ("Sexsation" 64).

22. Using a psychoanalytic framework, Madsen explores the dynamics of (erotic) domination in the Ruth-Selina relationship in detail.

Coda

1. For self-reflexivity in feminist criminology, see, for instance, Cain and Smart; Carlen, *Criminal Women*.

2. Nash remarks on a desire in intersectional theory "to draw on the ostensibly unique epistemological position of marginalized subjects to fashion a vision of equality" (3).

3. Carlen argues powerfully that a criminal justice system based on rehabilitation (as opposed to "reparative justice") is fundamentally flawed, as it reproduces social inequalities rather than helping to eradicate them ("Against Rehabilitation").

4. More details on the charity's work and its magazine are available on its website: http://www.womeninprison.org.uk/ (accessed 22 Jan. 2014).

5. See the charity's website: http://www.prisonerseducation.org.uk/index.php?id=104 (accessed 22 Jan. 2014).

6. The now well-established "Inside-Out" Prison Exchange Program in the United States is one example. For a detailed discussion of the "Inside-Out" approach, see Davis and Roswell; and J. Martin's special issue of the *Prison Journal*. Many others, in the United States and elsewhere, including myself, work through independently established prison-university/college partnerships. For critical accounts of such initiatives, see, for instance, Hartley and Turvey, "Reading Together" and "What Can a Book Do behind Bars?"; Jacobi; Wiltse.

WORKS CITED

Parliamentary Papers (in Chronological Order)

Report from the Select Committee on Secondary Punishments. PP 1831–32 (547) vii, 559.

Second Report from the Committee of the House of Lords on Gaols and Houses of Correction in England and Wales. PP 1835 (439) xi, 495.

First Report of the Inspectors of Prisons (Home District). PP 1836 (117) xxxv, 1.

Reports of the Directors of Convict Prisons for 1857. PP 1857–58 (2423) xxix, 49.

Parliamentary Debates

House of Commons Hansard. 2 May 1882. 3rd ser., vol. 268, col. 1942. *House of Commons Parliamentary Papers ProQuest.* Web. 30 Apr. 2014.

Public Acts

4 Geo. 4 c. 64 (An Act for Consolidating and Amending the Laws Relating to the Building, Repairing, and Regulating of Certain Gaols and Houses of Correction in England and Wales)

5 Geo. 4 c. 85 (An Act for Amending an Act of the Last Session of Parliament, Relating to the Building, Repairing, and Enlarging of Certain Gaols and Houses of Correction, and for Procuring Information as to the State of All Other Gaols and Houses of Correction in England and Wales)

2 & 3 Vict. c. 56 (An Act for the Better Ordering of Prisons)

Broadsides and Chapbooks (in Alphabetical Order)

"An Account of the Execution of Margaret Harvey." Bodleian Library, U of Oxford: John Johnson Collection; Broadsides, Murders and Executions folder 3.

"An Account of the Execution of Mary Hardcastle." Bodleian Library, U of Oxford: John Johnson Collection; Broadsides, Murders and Executions folder 3.

"The [cut off] Awful Confession of Jane Thompson, Who on Sunday Evening Last, at the Ranters' Chapel, Sheffield, Made a Full Confession of a Barbarous Murder Which She Had Committed on the Body of Her Mother." Bodleian Library, U of Oxford: John Johnson Collection; Broadsides, Murders and Executions folder 4.

"Awful Depravity: Dreadful Account of Anne Graham, Who Murdered Two of Her Own Children, and Left Another for Dead, and Who Afterwards Cut Her Own Throat, at Wigton, on the 26th Sept. 1824, during the Time Her Husband Was at Church." Bodleian Library, U of Oxford: John Johnson Collection; Broadsides, Murders and Executions folder 3.

"Dreadful Murder of Three Children by Their Mother." Bodleian Library, U of Oxford: John Johnson Collection; Broadsides, Murders and Executions folder 2.

"Dreadful Occurrence! Murder and Suicide at Wigton." Bodleian Library, U of Oxford: John Johnson Collection; Crime 1 (76). *The John Johnson Collection: An Archive of Printed Ephemera. ProQuest.* Web. 30 Apr. 2014.

"Execution of Priscilla Biggadike, at Lincoln, for the Wilful Murder of Her Husband." n.d. *Curiosities of Street Literature.* Ed. Charles Hindley. London: Reeves, 1871. 204.

"The Full Particulars of the Examination and Committal to Newgate of Annette Myers [*sic*], for the Wilful Murder of Henry Ducker, a Private in the Coldstream Guards, with a Copy of a Letter Written by the Prisoner to Deceased; And Also Other Startling Information." London, [handwritten: 1848]. British Library.

"Full Particulars of the Life, Trial, and Sentence of Mary Ann Hunt, for the Murder of Mary Stowell." London, 1847. British Library.

"The Heroes of the Guillotine and Gallows, or, the Awful Adventures of Askern, Smith and Calcraft, the Three Rival Hangmen, of York Castle, Stafford Gaol and Newgate; and Sanson, the Executioner of Paris, with His Cabinet of Murderer's Curiosities: Full of Astonishing Disclosures Concerning Their Private and Public Lives, and Startling Incidents before and after the Performance of Their Dreadful Office." *Curiosities of Street Literature.* Ed. Charles Hindley. London: Reeves, 1871.

"The Life, Trial, and Execution of Mary White." Bodleian Library, U of Oxford: John Johnson Collection; Broadsides, Murders and Executions folder 4.

"Life, Trial, Confession and Execution of Martha Browning for the Murder of Mrs. Mundell at Westminster." Bodleian Library, U of Oxford: John Johnson Collection; Broadsides, Murders and Executions large folder.

"Murder of a Child Near Measham: And Committal of the Mother for Wilful Murder." n.d. *Broadside Ballads.* Collected by the Reverend Sabine Baring-Gould. 10 vols. 1.1:149. British Library.

"The Rich and the Poor, or the Gentleman & the Bricklayer." n.d. *Broadside Ballads.* Collected by the Reverend Sabine Baring-Gould. 10 vols. 5:196. British Library.

"Shocking Case of Child Murder! The Following Is an Account of a Horrid Murder, Committed on the Body of an Infant, Which Was Discovered in a

Coal-Pit, on Sunday, April 11, 1830, near Belford." Bodleian Library, U of Oxford: John Johnson Collection; Broadsides, Murders and Executions folder 4.

"The Sorrowful Lamentation of Sarah Baker: Who Was Found Guilty of Wilful Murder at Stafford." Birmingham, UK: Pratt, n.d. Cambridge U Library, Madden Ballads 21, vol. 6, microfilm 1802, 237.

"Treason & Murder: An Account of the Behaviour and Execution of Margaret Cunningham, Alias Mason, for the Murder of Her Husband; with Remarks on Her Crime." 1807. Bodleian Library, U of Oxford: John Johnson Collection; Crime 1 (54). *The John Johnson Collection: An Archive of Printed Ephemera*. *ProQuest*. Web. 30 Apr. 2014.

Old Bailey Proceedings

Trial of Annette Meyers. Feb. 1848 (t18480228-826). *Old Bailey Proceedings Online*, version 6.0. Web. 12 July 2011.

Trial of Eliza Fenning. Apr. 1815 (t18150405-18). *Old Bailey Proceedings Online*, version 6.0. Web. 12 Aug. 2011.

Trial of Mabel Wilberforce (27). Oct. 1881 (t18811017-909). *Old Bailey Proceedings Online*, version 7.0. Web. 15 Jan. 2014.

Trial of Mary Ann Hunt. Aug. 1847 (t18470816-1797). *Old Bailey Proceedings Online*, version 6.0. Web. 12 July 2011.

Trial of Susan Willis Fletcher (32). Mar. 1881 (t18810328-406). *Old Bailey Proceedings Online*, version 6.0. Web. 5 Apr. 2011.

All Other Primary and Secondary Sources

"100 Pages Out To-morrow: The Easter Sunday *World* (Mrs. Maybrick in Bedford Reformatory)." *Evening World* 8 Apr. 1905. *Chronicling America: Historic American Newspapers*. Web. 15 Feb. 2013.

"Abolition of Capital Punishment." *Times* [London] 9 Mar. 1848: 8. *The Times Digital Archive*. Web. 10 Aug. 2012.

"Acknowledgments." *Academy* 634 (28 June 1884): 457. *British Periodicals ProQuest*. Web. 4 Feb. 2013.

Ackroyd, Peter. *Wilkie Collins*. London: Chatto and Windus, 2012. Print.

Adam, Hargrave L. *Woman and Crime*. 1912. London: Laurie, 1914. Print.

Adshead, Joseph. *Prisons and Prisoners*. London: Longman, 1845. Print.

"Advertisement." [*Female Life in Prison*]. *Athenaeum* 28 June 1862: 842. *British Periodicals ProQuest*. Web. 6 Aug. 2012.

"Advertisement." [*Female Life in Prison*]. *Athenaeum* 6 Sept. 1862: 294. *British Periodicals ProQuest*. Web. 15 Aug. 2012.

Aileen: The Life and Death of a Serial Killer. Dir. Nick Broomfield. Lafayette Films, 2003. Film.

Aileen Wuornos: The Selling of a Serial Killer. Dir. Nick Broomfield. Lafayette Films, 1993. Film.

Alber, Jan, and Frank Lauterbach, eds. *Stones of Law, Bricks of Shame: Narrating Imprisonment in the Victorian Age*. Toronto: U of Toronto P, 2009. Print.

Alexander, Lynn M. *Needlewomen in Victorian Art and Literature*. Athens, OH: Ohio UP, 2003. Print.

"The Alleged Spiritualist Fraud." *Pall Mall Gazette* 12 Apr. 1881, 2nd ed.: 8. Print.

Allen, C. J. W. *The Law of Evidence in Victorian England*. Cambridge: Cambridge UP, 1997. Print.

Altick, Richard D. *Victorian Studies in Scarlet*. London: Dent, 1972. Print.

Anderson, Linda. "The Re-imagining of History in Contemporary Women's Fiction." *Plotting Change: Contemporary Women's Fiction*. Ed. Linda Anderson. London: Arnold, 1990. 129–41. Print.

Arias, Rosario. "Female Confinement in Sarah Waters's Neo-Victorian Fiction." *Stones of Law, Bricks of Shame: Narrating Imprisonment in the Victorian Age*. Ed. Jan Alber and Frank Lauterbach. Toronto: U of Toronto P, 2009. 256–77. Print.

———. "Talking with the Dead: Revisiting the Victorian Past and the Occult in Margaret Atwood's *Alias Grace* and Sarah Waters' *Affinity*." *Estudios Ingleses de la Universidad Complutense* 13 (2005): 85–105. Print.

Armitt, Lucie, and Sarah Gamble. "The Haunted Geometries of Sarah Waters's *Affinity*." *Textual Practice* 20.1 (2006): 141–70. Print.

Arnot, Margaret L. "Gender in Focus: Infanticide in England 1840–1880." Ph.D. diss. U of Essex, 1994. Print.

Ash, Juliet. *Dress behind Bars: Prison Clothing as Criminality*. London: Tauris, 2010.

"Assize Intelligence." *Examiner* 23 July 1853; Issue 2373. *British Periodicals ProQuest*. Web. 15 Feb. 2013.

"Assize Intelligence." *Morning Chronicle* 24 July 1837; Issue 21121. *British Periodicals ProQuest*. Web. 15 Feb. 2013.

Atkinson, Juliette. *Victorian Biography Reconsidered: A Study of Nineteenth-Century "Hidden" Lives*. Oxford: Oxford UP, 2010. Print.

Atwood, Jane Evelyn. *Too Much Time: Women in Prison*. London: Phaidon, 2000. Print.

Atwood, Margaret. Acknowledgements. *Alias Grace*. London: Virago, 1997. 543–45. Print.

———. *Alias Grace*. 1996. London: Virago, 1997. Print.

———. Author's afterword. *Alias Grace*. London: Virago, 1997. 537–42. Print.

———. *In Search of Alias Grace: On Writing Canadian Historical Fiction*. Ottawa: U of Ottawa P, 1997. Print.

———. *The Servant Girl*. Dir. George Jonas. CBC (Canada), 1974. Television.

Bad Girls. Perf. Victoria Alcock, Kika Mirylees, Helen Fraser, Jack Ellis, et al. Shed Productions. ITV (UK), 1999–2006. Television.

Bakhtin, Mikhail M. *The Dialogic Imagination: Four Essays*. Ed. Michael Holquist. Trans. Caryl Emerson and Michael Holquist. Austin: U of Texas P, 1981. Print.

"Balfour on Conference." *New York Times* 23 Aug. 1895. Web. 10 Feb. 2013.

Barlow, George. *The Poetical Works of George Barlow*. Vols. 10 and 11. London: Glaisher, 1902–14. Print.

Barrish, Phillip, ed. *Cultures of Detention*. Spec. issue of *Texas Studies in Literature and Language* 50.3 (2008). *Project Muse*. Web. 18 Feb. 2013.

Barrow, Logie. *Independent Spirits: Spiritualism and English Plebeians, 1850–1910*. London: Routledge, 1986. Print.

Basham, Diana. *"The Trial of Woman": Feminism and the Occult Sciences in Victorian Literature and Society*. Basingstoke, UK: Macmillan, 1992. Print.

Beattie, J. M. *Crime and the Courts in England, 1660–1800*. Oxford, UK: Clarendon, 1986. Print.

Beetham, Margaret Rachel. *"British Workwoman (1863–1896)." Dictionary of Nineteenth-Century Journalism in Great Britain and Ireland*. Ed. Laurel Brake and Marysa Demoor. Gent, Belgium: Academia and the British Library, 2009. 80. Print.

Behlmer, George K. "Waugh, Benjamin (1839–1908)." *Oxford Dictionary of National Biography*. Oxford: Oxford UP, 2004. Web. 29 Jan. 2011.

Bender, John. *Imagining the Penitentiary: Fiction and the Architecture of Mind in Eighteenth-Century England*. Chicago: U of Chicago P, 1987. Print.

Bennett, Bridget. Introduction. *Twelve Months in an English Prison*. By Susan Willis Fletcher. Ed. Bridget Bennett. Vol. 2 of *Women, Madness and Spiritualism*. Ed. Roy Porter, Helen Nicholson, and Bridget Bennett. London: Routledge, 2003. 3–11. Print.

Bentley, David. *English Criminal Justice in the Nineteenth Century*. London: Hambledon, 1998. Print.

Berger, Courtney. "When Bad Things Happen to Bad People: Liability and Individual Consciousness in *Adam Bede* and *Silas Marner*." *Novel: A Forum on Fiction* 33.3 (2000): 307–27. *JSTOR*. Web. 20 July 2012.

Bernstein, Susan David. *Confessional Subjects: Revelations of Gender and Power in Victorian Literature and Culture*. Chapel Hill: U of North Carolina P, 1997. Print.

Biggs, Annie S. *My Life and Why I Am a Suffragette*. Croydon, UK: Croydon Citizen, 1907. 56.59/1. Copyright Museum of London. Print.

Blagg, Helen, and Charlotte Wilson. *Women and Prisons*. Fabian Women's Group Series 3. Fabian Tract 163. London: Fabian Society, 1912. Print.

Blanc, Marie-Thérèse. "Margaret Atwood's *Alias Grace* and the Construction of a Trial Narrative." *English Studies in Canada* 32.4 (2006): 101–27. *Project Muse*. Web. 20 Nov. 2010.

Blodgett, Harriet. *Centuries of Female Days: English Women's Private Diaries*. Gloucester, UK: Sutton, 1989. Print.

Bloom, Lynn Z. "'I Write for Myself and Strangers': Private Diaries as Public Documents." *Inscribing the Daily: Critical Essays on Women's Diaries*. Ed. Suzanne L. Bunkers and Cynthia A. Huff. Amherst: U of Massachusetts P, 1996. 23–37. Print.

Bodenheimer, Rosemarie. *Knowing Dickens*. Ithaca, NY: Cornell UP, 2007. Print.

Bodichon, Barbara Leigh Smith. *Women and Work*. London: Bosworth and Harrison, 1857. *JSTOR (Cowen Tracts)*. Web. 25 Feb. 2013.

Boole, Mary. "The Spiritualist Case." Letter to the editor. *Times* [London] 14 Apr. 1881. *The Times Digital Archive*. Web. 29 Apr. 2011.

Booth, William. *In Darkest England and the Way Out*. London: International Headquarters of the Salvation Army, 1890. Print.

Boswell, Charles, and Lewis Thompson. *The Girl with the Scarlet Brand*. New York: Fawcett, 1954. Print.

Bould, Geoffrey, ed. *Conscience Be My Guide: An Anthology of Prison Writings*. London: Zed, 2005. Print.

Braddon, Mary Elizabeth. *Lady Audley's Secret*. 1862. Ed. and introd. David Skilton. Oxford: Oxford UP, 1997. Print.

Bradley, A. C. "Notes on Passages in Shelley." *Modern Language Review* 1.1 (1905): 25–42. Print.

Braude, Ann. *Radical Spirits: Spiritualism and Women's Rights in Nineteenth-Century America*. Boston: Beacon, 1989. Print.

Bray, Bernard. "Letters: General Survey." *The Encyclopedia of Life Writing: Autobiographical and Biographical Forms*. Ed. Margaretta Jolly. Vol. 2. London: Fitzroy Dearborn. 551–53. Print.

British Society of Ladies for Promoting the Reformation of Female Prisoners. *Sketch of the Origin and Results of Ladies' Prison Associations, with Hints for the Formation of Local Associations*. London: Arch, 1827. Print.

Broadhead, Julian. *Unlocking the Prison Muse: The Inspirations and Effects of Prisoners' Writing in Britain*. Cambridge, UK: Cambridge Academic, 2006. Print.

Brown, Alyson. "Conflicting Objectives: Suffragette Prisoners and Female Prison Staff in Edwardian England." *Women's Studies* 31.5 (2002): 627–44. *Taylor & Francis Social Science and Humanities Library*. Web. 8 Feb. 2011.

Brown, Earl Kent. *Women of Mr. Wesley's Methodism.* New York: Mellen, 1983. Print.

Buckle, George, ed. *The Letters of Queen Victoria: A Selection from Her Majesty's Correspondence and Journal between the Years 1886 and 1901.* 3rd ser. Vol. 1: *1886–1890.* London: Murray, 1930. Print.

Bunkers, Suzanne L. "Diaries: Public *and* Private Records of Women's Lives." *Legacy: A Journal of Nineteenth-Century American Women Writers* 7.2 (1990): 17–26. Print.

———. "Reading and Interpreting Unpublished Diaries by Nineteenth-Century Women." *a/b: Auto/Biography Studies* 2.2 (Summer 1986): 15–17. Print.

Bunkers, Suzanne L., and Cynthia A. Huff. "Issues in Studying Women's Diaries: A Theoretical and Critical Introduction." *Inscribing the Daily: Critical Essays on Women's Diaries.* Ed. Suzanne L. Bunkers and Cynthia A. Huff. Amherst: U of Massachusetts P, 1996. 1–20. Print.

Burke, Carol. *Vision Narratives of Women in Prison.* Knoxville: U of Tennessee P, 1993. Print.

Caged. Dir. John Cromwell. Warner Bros., 1950. Film.

Caged Heat. Dir. Jonathan Demme. New World Pictures, 1974. Film.

Cain, Maureen, and Carol Smart. Series editors' preface. *Offending Women: Female Lawbreakers and the Criminal Justice System.* By Anne Worrall. London: Routledge, 1990. vii–viii. Print.

Caine, Barbara. "Feminist Biography and Feminist History." *Women's History Review* 3.2 (1994): 247–61. *Taylor & Francis Social Science and Humanities Library.* Web. 5 Jan. 2014.

Cairns, David J. A. *Advocacy and the Making of the Adversarial Criminal Trial, 1800–1865.* Oxford, UK: Clarendon, 1998. Print.

Cameron, Deborah. "St-i-i-i-ll Going . . . The Quest for Jack the Ripper." *Social Text* 40 (Autumn 1994): 147–54. *JSTOR.* Web. 15 Mar. 2011.

Cantor, Paul. "Stoning the Romance: The Ideological Critique of Nineteenth-Century Literature." *South Atlantic Quarterly* 88 (1989): 705–20. Print.

Carlen, Pat. "Against Rehabilitation: For Reparative Justice." *Criminal Justice Matters* 91.1 (2013): 32–33. *Taylor & Francis Journals Complete.* Web. 26 Jan. 2014.

———, ed. *Criminal Women: Autobiographical Accounts.* By Diana Christina, Jenny Hicks, Josie O'Dwyer, and Chris Tchaikovsky. Cambridge, UK: Polity, 1985. Print.

Carlen, Pat, and Chris Tchaikovsky. "Women's Imprisonment in England at the End of the Twentieth Century: Legitimacy, Realities and Utopias." *Prisons 2000: An International Perspective on the Current State and Future of Imprisonment.* Ed. Roger Matthews and Peter Francis. Basingstoke, UK: Palgrave, 1996. 201–18. Print.

Carpenter, Mary. "An Account of Visits to Gaols in India, Given at the Same Meeting, by Miss Mary Carpenter." *Address Delivered before the Reformatory Section of the Social Science Association, on the Treatment of Criminals in the Punjab, by Major G. Hutchinson, Inspector General of Police; With an Account of Visits to Prisons in Southern India, by Miss Mary Carpenter.* Bristol, UK, 1866. 14–22. Print.

———. *Juvenile Delinquents, Their Condition and Treatment.* London: Cash, 1853. Print.

———. *Our Convicts.* 2 vols. London: Longman, 1864. Print.

———. *Six Months in India.* 2 vols. London: Longmans, 1868. Print.

———. *Suggestions on Prison Discipline and Female Education in India.* London: Longmans, 1867. Print.

Carroll, David, ed. *George Eliot: The Critical Heritage.* New York: Barnes and Noble, 1971. Print.

Carroll, Rachel. "Rethinking Generational History: Queer Histories of Sexuality in Neo-Victorian Feminist Fiction." *Studies in the Literary Imagination* 39.2 (2006): 135–47. *Literature Online (LION).* Web. 6 Oct. 2010.

Cayleff, Susan E. *Wash and Be Healed: The Water-Cure Movement and Women's Health.* Philadelphia: Temple UP, 1987. Print.

"Central Criminal Court, April 7." *Times* [London] 8 Apr. 1881: 4. *The Times Digital Archive.* Web. 15 Feb. 2013.

"Central Criminal Court, April 11." *Times* [London] 12 Apr. 1881: 11. *The Times Digital Archive.* Web. 15 Feb. 2013.

"Central Criminal Court, April 12." *Times* [London] 13 Apr. 1881: 13. *The Times Digital Archive.* Web. 15 Feb. 2013.

"Central Criminal Court, Wednesday, Dec. 17." *Times* [London] 18 Dec. 1845: 7. *The Times Digital Archive.* Web. 13 Apr. 2014.

"A Chance Lost." *Owl* 5 Oct. 1883: 3. *19th Century UK Periodicals*, "New Readerships." *Gale Cengage Learning.* Web. 30 Apr. 2014.

"Charge against a Spiritualist." *Times* [London] 4 Dec. 1880: 11. *The Times Digital Archive.* Web. 15 Feb. 2013.

"Charge against a Spiritualist." *Times* [London] 29 Jan. 1881: 10. *The Times Digital Archive.* Web. 15 Feb. 2013.

Cheney, Deborah. "Dr Mary Louisa Gordon (1861–1941): A Feminist Approach in Prison." *Feminist Legal Studies* 18.2 (2010): 115–36. *SpringerLINK Contemporary (JISC Closed Consortium).* Web. 8 Feb. 2011.

Chess, Simone. " 'And I My Vowe Did Keepe': Oath Making, Subjectivity, and Husband Murder in 'Murderous Wife' Ballads." *Ballads and Broadsides in Britain, 1500–1800.* Ed. Patricia Fumerton and Anita Guerrini, with the assistance of Kris McAbee. Aldershot, UK: Ashgate, 2010. 131–47. Print.

Chevigny, Bell Gale, ed. *Doing Time: 25 Years of Prison Writing*. New York: Arcade, 1999. Print.

Chilcote, Paul Wesley, ed. *Her Own Story: Autobiographical Portraits of Early Methodist Women*. Nashville, TN: Kingswood, 2001. Print.

———. *John Wesley and the Women Preachers of Early Methodism*. Metuchen, NJ: American Theological Library Association and Scarecrow, 1991. Print.

"Child Murder at Measham." *Leeds Mercury* 29 Oct. 1873; Issue 11093. *British Newspapers 1600–1900 Gale Cengage Learning*. Web. 15 Feb. 2013.

Christie, Agatha Mallowan. *Evil Under the Sun*. 1941. London: HarperCollins, 2001. Print.

Christie, Trevor L. *Etched in Arsenic: A New Study of the Maybrick Case*. London: Harrap, 1968. Print.

Clapp-Itnyre, Alisa. "Dinah and the Secularization of Methodist Hymnody in Eliot's *Adam Bede*." *Victorians Institute Journal* 26 (1998): 40–68. Print.

Clark, Sandra. "The Broadside Ballad and the Woman's Voice." *Debating Gender in Early Modern England, 1500–1700*. Ed. Cristina Malcolmson and Mihoko Suzuki. Basingstoke, UK: Palgrave Macmillan, 2002. 103–20. Print.

Clay, Walter Lowe. *The Prison Chaplain: A Memoir of the Reverend John Clay, B.D. Late Chaplain of the Preston Gaol, with Selections from His Reports and Correspondence, and a Sketch of Prison Discipline in England*. 1855. Cambridge, UK: Macmillan, 1861. Print.

Collins, Philip. *Dickens and Crime*. 3rd ed. Basingstoke, UK: Macmillan, 1994. Print.

Collins, Wilkie. *Armadale*. 1866. Ed. and introd. John Sutherland. London: Penguin, 1995. Print.

———. "The Diary of Anne Rodway." *Household Words* 14.330 (19 July 1856): 1–7; 14.331 (26 July 1856): 30–38. *Dickens Journals Online*. Web. 30 Apr. 2014.

———. *The Fallen Leaves*. 1879. Dover, UK: Sutton, 1994. Print.

———. *The Law and the Lady*. 1875. Ed. and introd. David Skilton. London: Penguin, 1998. Print.

———. *The Legacy of Cain*. London: Chatto and Windus, 1889. Print.

———. *The Letters of Wilkie Collins*. Ed. William Baker and William M. Clarke. 2 vols. Basingstoke, UK: Macmillan, 1999. Print.

———. *The Moonstone*. 1868. Ed. J. I. M. Stewart. Harmondsworth, UK: Penguin, 1966. Print.

Collison, Philip. *The Story of Street Literature: Forerunner of the Popular Press*. London: Dent, 1973. Print.

"Commons and Mrs. Maybrick." *New York Times* 31 July 1898. Web. 10 Feb. 2013.

"The Condemned Convicts in the Provinces." *Standard*, 1 Aug. 1853; Issue 9042. *British Newspapers 1600–1900 Gale Cengage Learning*. Web. 15 Feb. 2013.

"Confession of Martha Browning." *Morning Chronicle* 24 Dec. 1845; Issue 23763. *British Newspapers 1600–1900 Gale Cengage Learning*. Web. 15 Feb. 2013.

Conley, Carolyn A. *Certain Other Countries: Homicide, Gender, and National Identity in Late Nineteenth-Century England, Ireland, Scotland, and Wales.* Columbus: Ohio State UP, 2007. Print.

"The Convicts Annette Meyers and Mary Ann Hunt." *Standard* 19 May 1848; Issue 7414. *British Newspapers 1600–1900 Gale Cengage Learning*. Web. 15 Feb. 2013.

"Convict System in England and Ireland." *Edinburgh Review* 117 (1863): 241–68. Print.

Corbett, Mary Jean. *Representing Femininity: Middle-Class Subjectivity in Victorian and Edwardian Women's Autobiographies.* New York: Oxford UP, 1992. Print.

Cowen, Zelman, and Peter Basil Carter. *Essays on the Law of Evidence.* Oxford, UK: Clarendon, 1956. Print.

Crawford, Elizabeth. "Artists' Suffrage League." *The Women's Suffrage Movement: A Reference Guide, 1866–1928.* New York: Routledge, 2001. 16–18. Print.

———. "East London Federation of Suffragettes." *The Women's Suffrage Movement: A Reference Guide, 1866–1928.* New York: Routledge, 2001. 184–85. Print.

———. "Libraries." *The Women's Suffrage Movement: A Reference Guide, 1866–1928.* New York: Routledge, 2001. 343–49. Print.

———. "Police, Prisons and Prisoners: the View from the Home Office." *Women's History Review* 14.3–4 (2005): 487–505. *Taylor & Francis Social Science and Humanities Library*. Web. 11 March 2011.

———. "Prison." *The Women's Suffrage Movement: A Reference Guide, 1866–1928.* New York: Routledge, 2001. 567–74. Print.

———. "Tyson Family." *The Women's Suffrage Movement: A Reference Guide, 1866–1928.* New York: Routledge, 2001. 691–92. Print.

———. *The Women's Suffrage Movement: A Reference Guide, 1866–1928.* New York: Routledge, 2001. Print.

Crewe, Ben. "Writing and Reading a Prison: Making Use of Prisoner Life Stories." *Criminal Justice Matters* 91.1 (2013): 20. *Taylor & Francis Journals Complete*. Web. 26 Jan. 2014.

"Criminal Calendar." *Salt Lake Daily Herald* 30 May 1882. *Chronicling America: Historic American Newspapers*. Web. 15 Feb. 2013.

Crone, Rosalind. "Reappraising Victorian Literacy through Prison Records." *Journal of Victorian Culture* 15 (2010): 3–37. *Taylor & Francis Social Science and Humanities Library*. Web. 15 Feb. 2013.

"THE CROPS.—VIENNA, Aug. 1.—From Official." *Times* [London] 21 Aug. 1854: 9. *The Times Digital Archive*. Web. 10 Aug. 2012.

Cross, Máire, and Tim Gray. *The Feminism of Flora Tristan*. Oxford, UK: Berg, 1992. Print.

Crystal Stories 1. London, 1881. British Library. Print.

Culley, Margo, ed. *A Day at a Time: Diary Literature of American Women from 1764 to the Present*. New York: Feminist P, 1985. Print.

Darroch, Heidi. "Hysteria and Traumatic Testimony: Margaret Atwood's *Alias Grace*." *Essays on Canadian Writing* 81 (Winter 2004): 103–21. Print.

Davies, Ioan. *Writers in Prison*. Oxford, UK: Blackwell, 1990. Print.

Davis, Simone Weil, and Barbara Sherr Roswell, eds. *Turning Teaching Inside Out: A Pedagogy of Transformation for Community-Based Education*. New York: Palgrave Macmillan, 2013.

Dearey, Melissa, Bethanie Petty, Brett Thompson, Clinton R. Lear, Stephanie Gadsby, and Donna Gibbs. "Prison(er) Auto/biography, 'True Crime,' and Teaching, Learning, and Research in Criminology." *Critical Survey* 23.3 (2011): 86–102. Print.

Defoe, Daniel. *Moll Flanders*. 1722. Introd. R. T. Jones. Ware, UK: Wordsworth, 2001. Print.

De Groot, Jerome. *The Historical Novel*. The New Critical Idiom. London: Routledge, 2010. Print.

Delap, Lucy, and Maria DiCenzo. " 'No One Pretends He Was Faultless': W. T. Stead and the Women's Movement." *19: Interdisciplinary Studies in the Long Nineteenth Century* 16 (2013). Web. 17 Jan. 2014. http://www.19.bbk.ac.uk/index.php/19/article/view/656.

Delord, Marie. "A Textual Quilt: Margaret Atwood's *Alias Grace*." *Études Canadiennes / Canadian Studies: Revue Interdisciplinaire des Études Canadiennes en France* 46 (1999): 111–21. Print.

Denning, Michael. *Mechanic Accents: Dime Novels and Working-Class Culture in America*. 1987. Rev. ed. London: Verso, 1998. Print.

Densmore, Helen. "The English Dreyfus Case." *Arena* 22 (July–Dec. 1899): 598–613. Print.

———. *The Maybrick Case: English Criminal Law*. London: Swan Sonnenschein, 1892. Print.

Dentith, Simon. *George Eliot*. Brighton, UK: Harvester, 1986. Print.

Despard, Charlotte, and Mabel Collins. *Outlawed: A Novel on the Woman Suffrage Question*. London: Drane, 1908. Print.

Diamond, Irene, and Lee Quinby, eds. *Feminism and Foucault: Reflections on Resistance*. Boston: Northeastern UP, 1988. Print.

Dickens, Charles. "The Author's Preface to the Third Edition." *Oliver Twist*. 1841. Ed. Kathleen Tillotson. Introd. Stephen Gill. Oxford: Oxford UP, 1999. liii–lvii. Print.

———. "The Finishing Schoolmaster." 1850. *Dickens' Journalism, Vol. 2: "The Amusements of the People" and Other Papers: Reports, Essays and Reviews, 1834–51.* Ed. Michael Slater. London: Dent, 1996. 350–56. Print.

———. "Home for Homeless Women." 1853. *Dickens' Journalism, Vol. 3. "Gone Astray" and Other Papers from Household Words 1851–59.* Ed. Michael Slater. London: Dent, 1998. 127–41. Print.

———. "Letters to the Editor of *The Times*." *Times* [London] 14 Nov. 1849: 4. 19 Nov. 1849: 5. *The Times Digital Archive.* Web. 15 Feb. 2013.

———. "Lying Awake." 1852. *Dickens' Journalism, Vol. 3. "Gone Astray" and Other Papers from Household Words 1851–59.* Ed. Michael Slater. London: Dent, 1998. 88–95. Print.

———. "A Visit to Newgate." 1836. *Sketches by Boz.* 1839. Ed. and introd. Dennis Walder. London: Penguin, 1995. 234–48. Print.

Dijkstra, Sandra. *Flora Tristan: Feminism in the Age of George Sand.* London: Pluto, 1992. Print.

Dixon, Joy. *Divine Feminine: Theosophy and Feminism in England.* Baltimore: Johns Hopkins UP, 2001. Print.

Doan, Laura, and Sarah Waters. "Making Up Lost Time: Contemporary Lesbian Writing and the Invention of History." *Territories of Desire in Queer Culture: Refiguring Contemporary Boundaries.* Ed. David Alderson and Linda Anderson. Manchester: Manchester UP, 2000. 12–28. Print.

Dobash, Russell P., R. Emerson Dobash, and Sue Gutteridge. *The Imprisonment of Women.* Oxford, UK: Blackwell, 1986. Print.

"Doctors as Torturers: The Medical Profession Exploited by the Government, Views of Medical Men." *Votes for Women: Document Pack.* Ed. Diane Atkinson. Huntingdon, UK: Elm, 1989. G1/36. Print.

Doody, Margaret Anne. "Voices of Record: Women as Witnesses and Defendants in the *Old Bailey Session Papers*." *Representing Women: Law, Literature, and Feminism.* Ed. Susan Sage Heinzelman and Zipporah Batshaw Wiseman. Durham, NC: Duke UP, 1994. 287–308. Print.

Downs, Laura. "A Reply to Joan Scott." *Comparative Studies in Society and History* 35.2 (1993): 444–51. *JSTOR.* Web. 15 Feb. 2013.

Doyle, Arthur Conan. *History of Spiritualism.* 1926. Newcastle, UK: Cambridge Scholars, 2009. Print.

Drake, Deborah, and Rod Earle, eds. *Prison Ethnography.* Spec. issue of *Criminal Justice Matters* 91.1 (2013). *Taylor & Francis Journals Complete.* Web. 26 Jan. 2014.

"Dreadful Murder of Three Children by Their Mother." *Standard* 1 June 1837; Issue 4040. *British Newspapers 1600–1900 Gale Cengage Learning.* Web. 15 Feb. 2013.

Dredge, Sarah. "Opportunism and Accommodation: The *English Woman's Journal* and the British Mid-Nineteenth-Century Women's Movement." *Women's Studies* 34 (2005): 133–57. *Taylor & Francis Social Science and Humanities Library*. Web. 15 Feb. 2013.

Duval, Elsie. "A Local Girl Suffragist's Story." Letter to the editor. *South Western Star* 16 Aug. 1912. *Papers of Elsie Duval*. Newspaper Cuttings. 7HFD/C/09. Women's Library @ LSE, London. Print.

Efforts and Reasons for the Release of Florence E. Maybrick: 1889 to 1893. London: Phelp Bros., 1893. Print.

Ek, Auli. *Race and Masculinity in Contemporary American Prison Narratives*. New York: Routledge, 2005. Print.

Eliot, George. *Adam Bede*. 1859. Introd. Robert Speaight. London: Dent, 1960. Print.

———. *The George Eliot Letters*. Vol. 3, *1859–1861*. Ed. Gordon S. Haight. New Haven: Yale UP, 1954–78. Print.

———. *The Journals of George Eliot*. Ed. Margaret Harris and Judith Johnston. Cambridge: Cambridge UP, 1998. Print.

———. "The Natural History of German Life." *Westminster Review* 66 (July 1856). *Essays of George Eliot*. Ed. Thomas Pinney. London: Routledge, 1963. 266–99. Print.

Elkins, Charles. "The Voice of the Poor: The Broadside as a Medium of Popular Culture and Dissent in Victorian England." *Journal of Popular Culture* 14 (1980): 262–74. Print.

Elliott, Dorice Williams. *The Angel Out of the House: Philanthropy and Gender in Nineteenth-Century England*. Charlottesville: U of Virginia P, 2002. Print.

Ellis, William. "The Distressed Needlewomen, and Cheap Prison Labour." *Westminster Review* 50 (1848–49): 371–94. Print.

Elmy, Elizabeth C. Wolstenholme. *The Criminal Code in Its Relation to Women: A Paper Read before the Dialectical Society, March 3rd, 1880*. Manchester, UK: Ireland, 1880. *LSE Selected Pamphlets*. *JSTOR*. Web. 22 Jan. 2014.

Elsley, Judy. "A Stitch in Crime: Quilt Detective Novels." *Uncoverings* 19 (1998): 137–53. Print.

Emsley, John. *The Elements of Murder: A History of Poison*. Oxford: Oxford UP, 2005. Print.

Erber, Nancy, and George Robb. Introduction. *Disorder in the Court: Trials and Sexual Conflict at the Turn of the Century*. Ed. George Robb and Nancy Erber. Basingstoke, UK: Macmillan, 1999. 1–11. Print.

Eustance, Claire, Joan Ryan, and Laura Ugolini, eds. *A Suffrage Reader: Charting Directions in British Suffrage History*. London: Leicester UP, 2000. Print.

Evans, Kate W. "The Cleaners of Holloway." *Holloway Jingles: Collected and Written during March and April 1912.* Coll. and ed. N. A. John. Glasgow: Glasgow Branch of the WSPU, n.d. [1912?]. 23. Print.

Everitt, Graham. "Doctors *and* Doctors." *Time* (London), 18:37 (Jan. 1888): 75–88. *British Periodicals ProQuest.* Web. 15 Feb. 2013.

"Execution of a Woman at Lincoln." *Bradford Observer* 29 Dec. 1868: 4; Issue 1879. *British Newspapers 1600–1900 Gale Cengage Learning.* Web. 15 Feb. 2013.

"Fed by Force: How the Government Treats Political Opponents in Prison; Statement of Mrs. Mary Leigh (Who Is Still in Birmingham Gaol)." *Votes for Women* 54 (1909). *Suffragette Collection Leaflets* SC13. 50.82/491. Museum of London. Print.

"Female Crime." *Lancaster Gazette, and General Advertiser for Lancashire, Westmorland, Yorkshire, &c.* 1 Nov. 1873: 3; Issue 4514. *British Newspapers 1600–1900 Gale Cengage Learning.* Web. 15 Feb. 2013.

"Female Felons." *Chamber's Journal of Popular Literature, Science and Arts* 463 (15 Nov. 1862): 310–14. *British Periodicals ProQuest.* Web. 10 Aug. 2012.

"Female Life in Prison." *Dublin Review* ns 11 (1868): 117–50. Print.

"Female Life in Prison." *Examiner* 16 Aug. 1862: 516–17. *British Periodicals ProQuest.* Web. 15 Aug. 2012.

"Female Life in Prison." *Littell's Living Age* 75 (1862): 339–53. Print.

"Female Life in Prison." *Times* [London] 23 Sept. 1862: 7. *The Times Digital Archive.* Web. 10 Aug. 2012.

Fernandez, Jean. *Victorian Servants, Class, and the Politics of Literacy.* New York: Routledge, 2010. Print.

Field, John. *Prison Discipline: The Advantages of the Separate System of Imprisonment, as Established in the New County Gaol of Reading, with a Description of the Former Prisons, and a Detailed Account of the Discipline Now Pursued.* London: Longman, 1846. Print.

F.J.L. *The Maybrick Case: A Treatise Showing Conclusive Reasons for the Continued Public Dissent from the Verdict and "Decision."* London: King, Sell and Railton, 1891. Print.

Fletcher, Susan Willis. *Twelve Months in an English Prison.* Boston: Lee and Shepard; New York: Dillingham, 1884. Ed. and introd. Bridget Bennett. London: Routledge, 2003. Print.

Flint, Kate. *The Woman Reader, 1837–1914.* Oxford, UK: Clarendon, 1993. Print.

Florence Maybrick: A Thrilling Romance. London: Purkess, 1889. Print.

Fludernik, Monika. " 'Stone Walls Do (Not) a Prison Make': Rhetorical Strategies and Sentimentalism in the Representation of the Victorian Prison Experience." *Captivating Subjects: Writing Confinement, Citizenship, and Nationhood in the Nineteenth Century*. Ed. Jason Haslam and Julia M. Wright. Toronto: U of Toronto P, 2005. 145–74. Print.

Forrester, Andrew. *The Female Detective*. London, 1864. Print.

Forsythe, William James. "Gordon, Mary Louisa (1861–1941)." *Oxford Dictionary of National Biography*. Oxford: Oxford UP, 2004. Web. 11 Feb. 2011.

———. *The Reform of Prisoners, 1830–1900*. London: Croom Helm, 1987. Print.

———. "Women Prisoners and Women Penal Officials 1840–1921." *British Journal of Criminology* 33.4 (1993): 525–40. *Oxford Journals Archive*. Web. 15 Feb. 2013.

Foucault, Michel. *Discipline and Punish: The Birth of the Prison*. 1975. Trans. Alan Sheridan. New York: Vintage, 1995. Print.

———. "Intellectuals and Power: A Conversation between Michel Foucault and Gilles Deleuze." *Language, Counter-Memory, Practice: Selected Essays and Interviews*. Ed. Donald F. Bouchard. Trans. Donald F. Bouchard and Sherry Simon. Ithaca, NY: Cornell UP, 1977. 205–17. Print.

———, ed. *I, Pierre Rivière, Having Slaughtered My Mother, My Sister and My Brother: A Case of Parricide in the 19th Century*. Trans. Frank Jellinek. Harmondsworth, UK: Penguin, 1978. Print.

———. *"Society Must Be Defended": Lectures at the Collège de France, 1975–76*. Ed. Mauro Bertani and Alessandro Fontana. Trans. David Macey. London: Lane, 2003. Print.

Franklin, H. Bruce. *Prison Literature in America: The Victim as Criminal and Artist*. Exp. ed. New York: Oxford UP, 1988. Print.

———, ed. *Prison Writings in 20th-Century America*. New York: Penguin, 1998. Print.

Fraser, Nancy. *Unruly Practices: Power, Discourse and Gender in Contemporary Social Theory*. Cambridge, UK: Polity, 1989. Print.

Friedland, M. L. "R. S. Wright's Model Criminal Code: A Forgotten Chapter in the History of the Criminal Law." *Oxford Journal of Legal Studies* 1.3 (Winter 1981): 307–46. *JSTOR*. Web. 15 Feb. 2013.

Frost, Lucy. "The Politics of Writing Convict Lives: Academic Research, State Archives and Family History." *Life Writing* 8.1 (2011): 19–33. *Taylor & Francis Social Science and Humanities Library*. Web. 15 Feb. 2013.

Frost, Lucy, and Hamish Maxwell-Stewart, eds. *Chain Letters: Narrating Convict Lives*. Carlton South, Victoria: Melbourne UP, 2001. Print.

Fry, Elizabeth. *Memoir of the Life of Elizabeth Fry: With Extracts from Her Journals and Letters*. Ed. Katharine Fry and Rachel Elizabeth Cresswell. 2 vols. London: Hatchard, 1848. Print.

———. *Observations on the Visiting, Superintendence, and Government of Female Prisoners*. London: Arch, 1827. Print.

Full Account of the Life and Trial of Mrs. Maybrick: Interesting Details of Her Earlier Life. Manchester, UK: Daisy Bank, c. 1901. Print.

Fuller, Margaret. *Woman in the Nineteenth Century and Other Writings.* Ed. and introd. Donna Dickenson. Oxford: Oxford UP, 1994. Print.

Gagnier, Regenia. *Subjectivities: A History of Self-Representation in Britain, 1832–1920.* New York: Oxford UP, 1991. Print.

Gaskell, Elizabeth. *Mary Barton.* 1848. Ed. and introd. Edgar Wright. Oxford: Oxford UP, 1998. Print.

Gass, William H. "The Art of Self: Autobiography in an Age of Narcissism." *Harper's* May 1994: 43–52. Web. 15 Feb. 2013.

Gates, Barbara T. *Victorian Suicide: Mad Crimes and Sad Histories.* Princeton, NJ: Princeton UP, 1988. Print.

Gatrell, V. A. C. *The Hanging Tree: Execution and the English People, 1770–1868.* Oxford: Oxford UP, 1994. Print.

Gaucher, Bob, ed. *Writing as Resistance: The Journal of Prisoners on Prisons Anthology (1988–2002).* Toronto: Canadian Scholars', 2002. Print.

Gay, Susan E. *John William Fletcher, Clairvoyant: A Biographical Sketch, with Some Chapters on the Present Era and Religious Reform.* London: Allen, 1883. Print.

———. *Spiritualistic Sanity: A Reply to Dr. Forbes Winslow's "Spiritualistic Madness."* London: Allen, 1879. Print.

Girls behind Bars. Narr. Timothy Spall. Dir. Michelle Friel. Friel Kean Films. BBC Scotland, 1, 8, 15 Oct. 2008. Television.

Gliddon, Katie. *Draft Autobiographical Account 1.* Papers of Katie Gliddon. 7KGG/1/4. The Women's Library @ LSE, London. Print.

———. *Papers of Katie Gliddon.* 7KGG. The Women's Library @ LSE, London. Print.

———. *Prison Diary: Letters from Holloway.* Papers of Katie Gliddon. TS 7KGG/1/1b. The Women's Library @ LSE, London. Print.

———. *Prison Diary 1.* Papers of Katie Gliddon. MS 7KGG/1/1. The Women's Library @ LSE, London. Print.

———. *Prison Diary 2.* Papers of Katie Gliddon. MS 7KGG/1/2. The Women's Library @ LSE, London. Print.

Goc, Nicola. *Women, Infanticide and the Press, 1822–1922: News Narratives in England and Australia.* Farnham, UK: Ashgate, 2013. Print.

Goldsmith, Larry. "History from the Inside Out: Prison Life in Nineteenth-Century Massachusetts." *Journal of Social History* 31.1 (1997): 109–25. *JSTOR.* Web. 28 Feb. 2011.

Gordon, Alex. "A Great Builder of the Old Three-Decker: F. W. Robinson." *Athenaeum* 21 Dec. 1901: 842. *British Periodicals ProQuest.* Web. 1 May 2014.

Gordon, Helen. *The Prisoner: A Sketch.* Letchworth, UK: Garden City, 1911. Print.

Gordon, Mary. *Penal Discipline*. London: Routledge, 1922. Print.

Graham, Anne E., and Carol Emmas. *The Last Victim: The Extraordinary Life of Florence Maybrick, the Wife of Jack the Ripper*. London: Headline, 1999. Print.

Grass, Sean. *The Self in the Cell: Narrating the Victorian Prisoner*. New York: Routledge, 2003. Print.

Gready, Paul. "Autobiography and the 'Power of Writing': Political Prison Writing in the Apartheid Era." *Journal of Southern African Studies* 19.3 (1993): 489–523. *JSTOR*. Web. 15 Feb. 2013.

Green, Barbara. *Spectacular Confessions: Autobiography, Performative Activism, and the Sites of Suffrage, 1905–1938*. Basingstoke, UK: Macmillan, 1997. Print.

Griffin, Ben. *The Politics of Gender in Victorian Britain: Masculinity, Political Culture and the Struggle for Women's Rights*. Cambridge: Cambridge UP, 2012. Print.

Grinnell, Charles E. "The Case of the Jury in the Case of Mrs. Maybrick." *Harvard Law Review* 13.6 (1900): 490–515. *JSTOR*. Web. 15 Feb. 2013.

Grogan, Susan. *Flora Tristan: Life Stories*. London: Routledge, 1998. Print.

Grundy, Isobel. "Elizabeth Heyrick (1769–1831)." *Oxford Dictionary of National Biography*. Oxford: Oxford UP, 2004. Web. 22 Jan. 2014.

Gruner, Elisabeth R. "Family Secrets and the Mysteries of the Moonstone." *Wilkie Collins*. Ed. Lyn Pykett. Basingstoke, UK: Macmillan, 1998. 221–43. Print.

Gurney, Joseph John. *Notes on a Visit Made to Some of the Prisons in Scotland and the North of England in Company with Elizabeth Fry: With Some General Observations on the Subject of Prison Discipline*. Edinburgh, UK: Constable, 1819. Print.

Halberstam, Judith. *Female Masculinity*. Durham, NC: Duke UP, 1998. Print.

Halkett, Samuel, and John Laing. "Female Life in Prison." *Dictionary of Anonymous and Pseudonymous English Literature*. New, enlarged ed. James Kennedy, W. A. Smith, and A. F. Johnson. Vol. 2. Edinburgh: Oliver and Boyd, 1926. 278. Print.

Hall, Stuart. "Notes on Deconstructing 'the Popular.'" *People's History and Socialist Theory*. Ed. Raphael Samuel. London: Routledge, 1981. 227–40. Print.

Hamilton, Gail [Mary A. Dodge]. *Gail Hamilton's Life in Letters*. Ed. H. Augusta Dodge. 2 vols. Boston: Lee and Shepard, 1901. Print.

———. *Woman's Wrongs*. 1868. New York: Arno, 1972. Print.

Hammelmann, H. A. "Review of *Five Famous Trials* by Maurice Moiseiwitsch." *Modern Law Review* 26.2 (1963): 217–18. *JSTOR*. Web. 15. Feb. 2013.

Hannam, June. "'Suffragettes Are Splendid for Any Work': The Blathwayt Diaries as a Source for Suffrage History." *A Suffrage Reader: Charting*

Directions in British Suffrage History. Ed. Claire Eustance, Joan Ryan, and Laura Ugolini. London: Leicester UP, 2000. 53–68. Print.

Harlow, Barbara. *Barred: Women, Writing, and Political Detention.* Middletown, CT: Wesleyan UP, 1992. Print.

———. "From a Women's Prison: Third World Women's Narratives of Prison." *Feminist Studies* 12.3 (1986): 501–24. *JSTOR.* Web. 15 Feb. 2013.

———. *Resistance Literature.* New York: Methuen, 1987. Print.

Harper's Bazaar. Albert R. Mann Library, Home Economics Archive: Research, Tradition and History (HEARTH), Cornell U. Web. 9 Aug. 2012. http://hearth.library.cornell.edu/h/hearth/browse/title/4732809.html.

Harrison, Brian. *Peaceable Kingdom: Stability and Change in Modern Britain.* Oxford: Oxford UP, 1982. Print.

Harrison, Shirley. *The Diary of Jack the Ripper.* London: Smith Gryphon, 1993. Print.

Hart-Davies, Juliet. "The Spiritualist Case." Letter to the editor. *Times* [London] 18 Apr. 1881. *The Times Digital Archive.* Web. 15 Feb. 2013.

Hartley, Jenny. *Charles Dickens and the House of Fallen Women.* London: Methuen, 2009. Print.

———. "Reading in Gaol." *A Return to the Common Reader: Print Culture and the Novel, 1850–1900.* Ed. Beth Palmer and Adelene Buckland. Aldershot, UK: Ashgate, 2011. 87–102. Print.

Hartley, Jenny, and Sarah Turvey. "Reading Together: The Role of the Reading Group Inside Prison." *Prison Service Journal* 183 (May 2009): 27–32. Print.

———. "What Can a Book Do behind Bars?" *Reader* 32 (Winter 2008): 60–68. Print.

Hartman, Kabi. " 'What Made Me a Suffragette': The New Woman and the New (?) Conversion Narrative." *Women's History Review* 12.1 (2003): 35–50. *Taylor & Francis Social Science and Humanities Library.* Web. 8 Feb. 2011.

Hartman, Mary S. *Victorian Murderesses: A True History of Thirteen Respectable French and English Women Accused of Unspeakable Crimes.* London: Robson, 1977. Print.

Haslam, Jason. *Fitting Sentences: Identity in Nineteenth- and Twentieth-Century Prison Narratives.* Toronto: U of Toronto P, 2005. Print.

———. Introduction. *Prisons and Prisoners.* By Constance Lytton. Peterborough, ON: Broadview, 2008. 8–39. Print.

Haslam, Jason, and Julia M. Wright, eds. *Captivating Subjects: Writing Confinement, Citizenship, and Nationhood in the Nineteenth Century.* Toronto: U of Toronto P, 2005. Print.

Hawkes, Jean. Introduction. *The London Journal of Flora Tristan, 1842, or, The Aristocracy and the Working Class of England.* By Flora Tristan. London: Virago, 1982. xiii–xlii. Print.

Hawthorne, Nathaniel. *The Blithedale Romance*. 1852. Ed. William E. Cain. Boston: Bedford, 1996. Print.

Hayward, William Stephens. *Revelations of a Lady Detective*. 1864. Transcribed, ed., and introd. Dagni Bredesen. Scholars Facsimiles & Reprints 562. Ann Arbor, MI: Scholars Facsimiles, 2010. Print.

Heidensohn, Frances, with the assistance of Marisa Silvestri. *Women and Crime*. 2nd ed. Basingstoke, UK: Macmillan, 1996. Print.

Heilmann, Ann, and Mark Llewellyn, eds. *Metafiction and Metahistory in Contemporary Women's Writing*. Basingstoke, UK: Palgrave Macmillan, 2007. Print.

Hekman, Susan J., ed. *Feminist Interpretations of Michel Foucault*. University Park: Pennsylvania State UP, 1996. Print.

Heller, Tamar. *Dead Secrets: Wilkie Collins and the Female Gothic*. New Haven: Yale UP, 1992. Print.

Henry, Joan. *Who Lie in Gaol*. London: Gollancz, 1952. Print.

———. *Yield to the Night*. London: Gollancz, 1954. Print.

Hepburn, James. *A Book of Scattered Leaves: Poetry of Poverty in Broadside Ballads of Nineteenth-Century England*. Vol. 1. Lewisburg, PA: Bucknell UP, 2000. Print.

Hertz, Neil. *George Eliot's Pulse*. Stanford: Stanford UP, 2003. Print.

Hindley, Charles, ed. *Curiosities of Street Literature*. London: Reeves, 1871. Print.

———. *The History of the Catnach Press at Berwick-upon-Tweed, Alnwick and Newcastle-upon-Tyne, in Northumberland, and Seven Dials, London (and the Two Catnachs, John & James): With Illustrations and Facsimiles*. London, 1886. Print.

Hitchcock, Tim, and Robert Shoemaker. *Tales from the Hanging Court*. London: Hodder Arnold, 2006. Print.

Hoffman, Marcelo. "Foucault and the 'Lesson' of the Prisoner Support Movement." *New Political Science* 34.1 (2012): 21–36. *Taylor & Francis Social Science and Humanities Library*. Web. 20 Dec. 2012.

Hogan, Rebecca. "Diarists on Diaries." *a/b: Auto/Biography Studies* 2.2 (Summer 1986): 9–14. Print.

———. "Engendered Autobiographies: The Diary as a Feminine Form." *Prose Studies* 14.2 (1991): 95–107. *Taylor & Francis Arts & Humanities Archive* 2012. Web. 15 Feb. 2013.

Holgate, Mike. *Agatha Christie's True Crime Inspirations: Stranger than Fiction*. Stroud, UK: History P, 2010. Print.

Holmes, Martha Stoddard, and Mark Mossman. "Disability in Victorian Sensation Fiction." *A Companion to Sensation Fiction*. Ed. Pamela K. Gilbert. Malden, MA: Wiley-Blackwell, 2011. 493–506. Print.

Holton, Sandra Stanley. *Feminism and Democracy: Women's Suffrage and Reform Politics in Britain, 1900–1918*. Cambridge: Cambridge UP, 1986. Print.

———. "Manliness and Militancy: The Political Protest of Male Suffragists and the Gendering of the 'Suffragette' Identity." *The Men's Share: Masculinities, Male Support, and Women's Suffrage in Britain 1890–1920*. Ed. Angela V. John and Claire Eustance. London: Routledge, 1997. 110–34. Print.

———. *Suffrage Days: Stories from the Women's Suffrage Movement*. London: Routledge, 1996. Print.

"Home Office Memo on Remission of Sentences and Transfer from One Division to Another." Note of an inquiry conducted by Secretary of State Gladstone. 10 Feb. 1908. HO45/11088/437465. National Archives, London. Print.

Horeck, Tanya. "From Documentary to Drama: Capturing Aileen Wuornos." *Screen* 48.2 (2007): 141–59. *Oxford Journals*. Web. 15 Jan. 2012.

Howard League for Penal Reform. "Submission to the Justice Select Committee's Inquiry on Women Offenders." Sept. 2012. Web. 24 Jan. 2014. www.howard league.org/women/.

Howe, Adrian. *Punish and Critique: Towards a Feminist Analysis of Penality*. London: Routledge, 1994. Print.

Howlett, Caroline J. "Writing on the Body? Representation and Resistance in British Suffragette Accounts of Forcible Feeding." *Bodies of Writing, Bodies in Performance*. Ed. Thomas Foster, Carol Siegel, and Ellen E. Berry. Genders 23. New York: New York UP, 1996. 3–41. Print.

H.R.D. "The Case of Annette Meyers." Letter to the editor. *Times* [London] 7 Mar. 1848: 8. *The Times Digital Archive*. Web. 15 Feb. 2013.

Huff, Cynthia A. "Reading as Re-vision: Approaches to Reading Manuscript Diaries." *Biography* 23.3 (2000): 504–23. *Project Muse*. Web. 15 Feb. 2013.

———. "Women's Letters." *The Encyclopedia of Life Writing: Autobiographical and Biographical Forms*. Ed. Margaretta Jolly. Vol. 2. London: Fitzroy Dearborn. 952–54. Print.

Huish, Robert. *The Progress of Crime, or the Authentic Memoirs of Maria Manning*. London, 1849. Print.

Humpherys, Anne. *Travels into the Poor Man's Country: The Work of Henry Mayhew*. Firle, UK: Caliban, 1977. Print.

I.C.C. "The Westminster Murder." *Times* [London] 26 Dec. 1845: 6. *The Times Digital Archive*. Web. 13 Apr. 2014.

Irving, H. B. *The Trial of Mrs. Maybrick*. Notable British Trials. London: Hodge, 1912. Print.

"It Is a Common Practice with Moralists and His-." *Times* [London] 17 Nov. 1859: 6. *The Times Digital Archive*. Web. 25 Feb. 2013.

Jackson, Mark, ed. *Infanticide: Historical Perspectives on Child Murder and Concealment, 1550–2000.* Aldershot, UK: Ashgate, 2002. Print.

———. "The Trial of Harriet Vooght: Continuity and Change in the History of Infanticide." *Infanticide: Historical Perspectives on Child Murder and Concealment, 1550–2000.* Ed. Mark Jackson. Aldershot, UK: Ashgate, 2002. 1–17. Print.

Jacobi, Tobi. "Speaking Out for Social Justice: The Problems and Possibilities of US Women's Prison and Jail Writing Workshops." *Critical Survey* 23.3 (2011): 40–54. Print.

Jacobs, Edward. "Circulating Libraries." *The Oxford Encyclopedia of British Literature.* Ed. David Scott Kastan. Vol. 2. Oxford: Oxford UP, 2006. 5–10. Print.

James, Henry. *The Bostonians.* 1886. Oxford: Oxford UP, 1984. Print.

James, Joy. *The New Abolitionists: (Neo)slave Narratives and Contemporary Prison Writings.* Albany: State U of New York P, 2005. Print.

"Jane Cameron, a Female Convict." *Reformatory and Refuge Journal* 14 (1864): 6–11. Print.

"Jennie Cameron." *Spectator* 36 (28 Nov. 1863): 2793–94. Print.

J.H.B. Jr. *Harvard Law Review* 13.3 (1899): 227–28. *JSTOR.* Web. 15 Feb. 2013.

Joannou, Maroula. "Suffragette Fiction and the Fictions of Suffrage." *The Women's Suffrage Movement: New Feminist Perspectives.* Ed. Maroula Joannou and June Purvis. Manchester: Manchester UP, 1998. 101–16. Print.

Joannou, Maroula, and June Purvis, eds. *The Women's Suffrage Movement: New Feminist Perspectives.* Manchester: Manchester UP, 1998. Print.

John, Angela V. "Men, Manners and Militancy: Literary Men and Women's Suffrage." *The Men's Share? Masculinities, Male Support, and Women's Suffrage in Britain, 1890–1920.* Ed. Angela V. John and Claire Eustance. London: Routledge, 1997. 88–109. Print.

John, Juliet. *Dickens's Villains: Melodrama, Character, Popular Culture.* Oxford: Oxford UP, 2001. Print.

Johnsen, Rosemary Erickson. *Contemporary Feminist Historical Crime Fiction.* New York: Palgrave Macmillan, 2006. Print.

Johnson, Paula C. *Inner Lives: Voices of African American Women in Prison.* New York: New York UP, 2003. Print.

Jones, Christopher J. M. *The Maybrick A to Z.* Birkenhead, UK: Countyvise, 2008. Print.

Jones, Miriam. "Fractured Narratives of Infanticide in the Crime and Execution Broadside in Britain, 1780–1850." *Writing British Infanticide: Child-Murder, Gender, and Print, 1722–1859.* Ed. Jennifer Thorn. Newark: U of Delaware P, 2003. 112–42. Print.

Jorgensen-Earp, Cheryl R. "'The Waning of the Light': The Forcible-Feeding of Jane Warton, Spinster." *Women's Studies in Communication* 22.2 (1999): 125–51. *Taylor & Francis Social Science and Humanities Library*. Web. 17 Feb. 2013.

Joseph, H. S. *Memoirs of Convicted Prisoners; Accompanied by Remarks on the Causes and Prevention of Crime*. London: Wertheim, 1853. Print.

Joyce, James. *Ulysses*. 1922. Ed. and introd. Jeri Johnson. Oxford: Oxford UP, 1993. Print.

Kaiser, Matthew. "Facing a Mirror: Philip Meadows Taylor's *Confessions of a Thug* and the Politics of Imperial Self-Incrimination." *Stones of Law, Bricks of Shame: Narrating Imprisonment in the Victorian Age*. Ed. Jan Alber and Frank Lauterbach. Toronto: U of Toronto P, 2009. 70–88. Print.

Kalikoff, Beth. *Murder and Moral Decay in Victorian Popular Literature*. Ann Arbor: UMI Research, 1986. Print.

Kean, Hilda. *Deeds Not Words: The Lives of Suffragette Teachers*. London: Pluto, 1990. Print.

Keetley, Dawn. "The Ungendered Terrain of Good Health: Mary Gove Nichols's Rewriting of the Diseased Institution of Marriage." *Separate Spheres No More: Gender Convergence in American Literature, 1830–1930*. Ed. Monika M. Elbert. Tuscaloosa: U of Alabama P, 2000. 117–42. Print.

Kenney, Annie. *Memories of a Militant*. London: Arnold, 1924. Print.

Kent, Susan Kingsley. *Sex and Suffrage in Britain, 1860–1914*. Princeton, NJ: Princeton UP, 1987. Print.

Kerr, Harriet Roberta. Letter written from Holloway Prison to Miss Mary Charlotte Tiltman (also known as Miss Mary Hessell). 23 June 1913. *Prison Letters, Police Summons, Prison Records Suffragette Collection*. MS 74.440. Copyright Museum of London. Print.

Kestner, Joseph A. "Emmuska Orczy: Lady Molly of Scotland Yard (1910)." *South Central Review* 18.3–4 (2001): 38–53. *JSTOR*. Web. 17 Feb. 2013.

———. *Sherlock's Sisters: The British Female Detective, 1864–1913*. Aldershot, UK: Ashgate, 2003. Print.

Kilgour, Raymond Lincoln. *Lee and Shepard: Publishers for the People*. Hamden, CT: Shoe String, 1965. Print.

King, Andrew, and John Plunkett, eds. *Victorian Print Media: A Reader*. Oxford: Oxford UP, 2005. Print.

King, Jeannette. *The Victorian Woman Question in Contemporary Feminist Fiction*. Basingstoke, UK: Palgrave Macmillan, 2005. Print.

Kingston, Charles. *Famous Judges and Famous Trials*. New York, 1923. Print.

———. *The Judges and the Judged*. London: John Lane, the Bodley Head, 1926. Print.

Knelman, Judith. "From Yellow Journalism to Yellowed Clippings." *Seeking a Voice: Images of Race and Gender in the 19th Century Press*. Ed. David B.

Sachsman, S. Kittrell Rushing, and Roy Morris Jr. West Lafayette, IN: Purdue UP, 2009. 277–85. Print.

——. *Twisting in the Wind: The Murderess and the English Press.* Toronto: U of Toronto P, 1998. Print.

——. "Why Can't a Woman Be More Like a Man? Attitudes to Husband-Murder 1889–1989." *Behaving Badly: Social Panic and Moral Outrage—Victorian and Modern Parallels.* Ed. Judith Rowbotham and Kim Stevenson. Aldershot, UK: Ashgate, 2003. 193–205. Print.

Kohlke, Marie-Luise. "Into History through the Back Door." *Women: A Cultural Review* 15.2 (2004): 153–66. Print.

——. "Sexsation and the Neo-Victorian Novel: Orientalising the Nineteenth Century in Contemporary Fiction." *Negotiating Sexual Idioms: Image, Text, Performance.* Ed. Marie-Luise Kohlke and Luisa Orza. Amsterdam: Rodopi, 2008. 53–77. Print.

Krueger, Christine L. "Literary Defenses and Medical Prosecutions: Representing Infanticide in Nineteenth-Century Britain." *Victorian Studies* 40.2 (Winter 1997): 271–94. *Literature Online (LION).* Web. 17 Feb. 2013.

——. *The Reader's Repentance: Women Preachers, Women Writers, and Nineteenth- Century Social Discourse.* Chicago: U of Chicago P, 1992. Print.

——. "Witnessing Women: Trial Testimony in Novels by Tonna, Gaskell, and Eliot." *Representing Women: Law, Literature, and Feminism.* Ed. Susan Sage Heinzelman and Zipporah Batshaw Wiseman. Durham, NC: Duke UP, 1994. 337–55. Print.

Kuznetsov, Edward. *Prison Diaries.* 1973. Trans. Howard Spier. Introd. Leonard Schapiro. London: Vallentine, Mitchell, 1975. Print.

Lacey, Nicola. *Women, Crime, and Character: From Moll Flanders to Tess of the D'Urbervilles.* Oxford: Oxford UP, 2008. Print.

Lamb, Wally, and the Women of York Correctional Facility. *Couldn't Keep It to Myself: Testimony from Our Imprisoned Sisters.* New York: Regan, 2003. Print.

Langbein, John H. *The Origins of Adversary Criminal Trial.* Oxford: Oxford UP, 2003. Print.

Langford, Rachel, and Russell West, eds. *Marginal Voices, Marginal Forms: Diaries in European Literature and History.* Trans. Russell West. Amsterdam: Rodopi, 1999. Print.

Larner, Christina. *Witchcraft and Religion: The Politics of Popular Belief.* Ed. and foreword Alan Macfarlane. Oxford, UK: Blackwell, 1984. Print.

"The Last Moments of Anne Boleyn, Second Wife of Henry VIII." c. 1849. Bodleian Library, U of Oxford: John Johnson Collection; Waxworks 1 (2). *The John Johnson Collection: An Archive of Printed Ephemera. ProQuest.* Web. 30 Apr. 2014.

"The Late F. W. Robinson." *Bookman: An Illustrated Magazine of Literature and Life* [New York] 14 (1902): 555. Print.

Lauterbach, Frank. "'From the Slums *to* the Slums': The Delimitation of Social Identity in Late Victorian Prison Narratives." *Captivating Subjects: Writing Confinement, Citizenship and Nationhood in the Nineteenth Century.* Ed. Jason Haslam and Julia M. Wright. Toronto: U of Toronto P, 2005. 113–43. Print.

Law, Graham, and Andrew Maunder. *Wilkie Collins: A Literary Life.* Basingstoke, UK: Palgrave Macmillan, 2008. Print.

Lawston, Jodie Michelle, and Ashley E. Lucas, eds. *Razor Wire Women: Prisoners, Activists, Scholars, and Artists.* Albany: State U of New York P, 2011. Print.

Ledger, Sally. *Dickens and the Popular Radical Imagination.* Cambridge: Cambridge UP, 2007. Print.

Lejeune, Philippe. *On Diary.* Ed. Jeremy Popkin and Julie Rak. Trans. Katharine Durnin. Honolulu: Center for Biographical Research, U of Hawai'i, 2009. Print.

Leps, Marie-Christine. *Apprehending the Criminal: The Production of Deviance in Nineteenth-Century Discourse.* Durham, NC: Duke UP, 1992. Print.

Letter to the Home Office by Governor of Holloway Prison. 28 Dec. 1911. HO144/1119/203651/66. National Archives, London. Print.

Levy, J. H. *The Necessity for Criminal Appeal as Illustrated by the Maybrick Case.* London: King, 1899. Print.

Liddington, Jill. *Rebel Girls: Their Fight for the Vote.* London: Virago, 2006. Print.

Lilley, Kate. *Prisoners and Prison Life.* Clacton-on-Sea, UK: Clacton News Company, 1912. Print.

Link, William A., and Susannah J. Link, eds. *The Gilded Age and Progressive Era: A Documentary Reader.* Malden, MA: Blackwell, 2012. Print.

Linton, Eliza Lynn. "Gone to Jail." *All the Year Round* 7.171 (2 Aug. 1862): 487–93. *Dickens Journals Online.* Web. 28 Apr. 2014.

"List of New Books." *Athenaeum* 4029 (14 Jan. 1905): 49. *British Periodicals ProQuest.* Web. 29 Apr. 2011.

"Literary Gossip." *Athenaeum* 2915 (8 Sept. 1883): 308. *British Periodicals ProQuest.* Web. 4 Feb. 2013.

Livingston, Beverly. Translator's introduction. *The Workers' Union.* By Flora Tristan. Urbana: U of Illinois P, 1983. vii–xxv. Print.

Llewellyn, Mark. "'Queer? I Should Say It Is Criminal!': Sarah Waters' *Affinity* (1999)." *Journal of Gender Studies* 13.3 (2004): 203–14. Print.

Lloyd, Jennifer. *Women and the Shaping of British Methodism: Persistent Preachers, 1807–1907.* Manchester: Manchester UP, 2009. Print.

Logan, Anne. *Feminism and Criminal Justice: A Historical Perspective.* Basingstoke, UK: Palgrave Macmillan, 2008. Print.

Lovelady, Stephanie. "'I Am Telling This to No One but You': Private Voice, Passing, and the Private Sphere in Margaret Atwood's *Alias Grace*." *Margaret Atwood: Essays on Her Works.* Ed. Branko Gorjup. Toronto: Guernica, 2008. 173–212. Print.

Low, A. Maurice. "American Affairs." *National Review* 37.217 (Mar. 1901): 75–86. *British Periodicals ProQuest.* Web. 29 Apr. 2011.

Lytton, Constance. *Prisons and Prisoners: Some Personal Experiences by Constance Lytton and Jane Warton, Spinster.* London: Heinemann, 1914. Print.

———. *Prisons and Prisoners: Some Personal Experiences by Constance Lytton and Jane Warton, Spinster.* 1914. Introd. Midge Mackenzie. London: Virago, 1988. Print.

———. *Prisons and Prisoners: Some Personal Experiences by Constance Lytton and Jane Warton, Spinster.* 1914. Ed. and introd. Jason Haslam. Peterborough, ON: Broadview, 2008. Print.

MacDougall, Alexander William. *The Maybrick Case: A Treatise on the Facts of the Case, and of the Proceedings in Connection with the Charge, Trial, Conviction, and Present Imprisonment of Florence Elizabeth Maybrick.* London: Baillière, Tindall and Cox, 1891. Print.

Macpherson, Heidi Slettedahl. "Prison, Passion, and the Female Gaze: Twentieth-Century Representations of Nineteenth-Century Panopticons." *In the Grip of the Law: Trials, Prisons and the Space Between.* Ed. Monika Fludernik and Greta Olson. Frankfurt: Lang, 2004. 205–21. Print.

Madsen, Lea Heiberg. "'Remember . . . Whose Girl You Are': Dynamics of Domination in Sarah Waters's *Affinity* (1999)." *International Journal of English Studies* 13.1 (2013): 71–92. *Gale Cengage Expanded Academic ASAP.* Web. 18 Jan. 2014.

"The Man about Town." *County Gentleman* 19 Mar. 1881: 294. *19th Century UK Periodicals*, "New Readerships." *Gale Cengage Learning.* Web. 19 Aug. 2011.

Manchester, A. H. *A Modern Legal History of England and Wales, 1750–1950.* London: Butterworths, 1980. Print.

Mangham, Andrew. *Violent Women and Sensation Fiction: Crime, Medicine and Victorian Popular Culture.* Basingstoke, UK: Palgrave Macmillan, 2007. Print.

Mapanje, Jack. *Gathering Seaweed: African Prison Writing.* Portsmouth, NH: Heinemann, 2002. Print.

March, Cristie. "Crimson Silks and New Potatoes: The Heteroglossic Power of the Object in Atwood's *Alias Grace*." *Studies in Canadian Literature* 22.2 (1997): 66–82. Print.

Marchbank, Jennifer, and Gayle Letherby. *Introduction to Gender: Social Science Perspectives*. Harlow, UK: Pearson Education, 2007. Print.

Marcus, Sharon. *Between Women: Friendship, Desire, and Marriage in Victorian England*. Princeton, NJ: Princeton UP, 2007. Print.

Marion, Kitty. "Autobiography." TS 50.82/1124. Copyright Museum of London. Print.

Marryat, Florence. *There Is No Death*. London: Griffith Farran, 1892. Print.

Martin, Bruce K. "Rescue and Marriage in *Adam Bede*." *Studies in English Literature, 1500–1900* 12.4 (1972): 745–63. *JSTOR*. Web. 18 July 2012.

Martin, Jaime, ed. *The Inside-Out Prison Exchange Program*. Spec. issue of *Prison Journal* 93.2 (2013). *Sage Premier*. Web. 6 Jan. 2014.

Martin, Randall, ed. *Women and Murder in Early Modern News Pamphlets and Broadside Ballads, 1573–1697*. Aldershot, UK: Ashgate, 2005. Print.

Martineau, Harriet. "Life in the Criminal Class." *Edinburgh Review* 122 (1865): 337–71. Print.

Maud, Constance Elizabeth. *No Surrender*. London: Duckworth, 1911. Print.

May, Allyson N. *The Bar and the Old Bailey, 1750–1850*. Chapel Hill: U of North Carolina P, 2003. Print.

Maybrick, Florence Elizabeth. "Criminal Court Procedure in England and America." *New-York Tribune Sunday Magazine* 22 Jan. 1905. *Chronicling America: Historic American Newspapers*. Web. 8 June 2011.

———. *Mrs. Maybrick's Own Story. My Fifteen Lost Years*. 1905. The State of the Prisons in Britain, 1775–1905 8. London: Routledge/Thoemmes, 2000. Print.

———. "My Year of Freedom." *New-York Tribune Sunday Magazine* 19 Nov. 1905. *Chronicling America: Historic American Newspapers*. Web. 8 June 2011.

"Maybrick Case Discussed." *New York Times* 3 Jan. 1896. Web. 17 Feb. 2013.

Mayhall, Laura E. Nym. *The Militant Suffrage Movement: Citizenship and Resistance in Britain, 1860–1930*. Oxford: Oxford UP, 2003. Print.

———. "The Rhetorics of Slavery and Citizenship: Suffragist Discourse and Canonical Texts in Britain, 1880–1914." *Gender & History* 13.3 (2001): 481–97. *NESLi2 Wiley-Blackwell Full Collection*. Web. 17 Feb. 2013.

Mayhew, Henry. *London Labour and the London Poor*. 1861–62. 4 vols. Introd. John D. Rosenberg. New York: Dover, 1968. Print.

Mayhew, Henry, and John Binny. *The Criminal Prisons of London and Scenes of Prison Life*. London: Griffin, 1862. Print.

Mayne, Judith. *Framed: Lesbians, Feminists, and Media Culture*. Minneapolis: U of Minnesota P, 2000. Print.

McClintock, Anne. *Imperial Leather: Race, Gender, and Sexuality in the Colonial Contest*. New York: Routledge, 1995. Print.

McConville, Seán. *A History of English Prison Administration, Vol. 1: 1750–1877*. London: Routledge, 1981. Print.

McDonagh, Josephine. *Child Murder and British Culture, 1720–1900.* Cambridge: Cambridge UP, 2003. Print.

———. "Child-Murder Narratives in George Eliot's *Adam Bede*: Embedded Histories and Fictional Representation." *Nineteenth-Century Literature* 56.2 (2001): 228–59. *JSTOR*. Web. 8 Aug. 2011.

McGarry, Molly. *Ghosts of Futures Past: Spiritualism and the Cultural Politics of Nineteenth-Century America.* Berkeley: U of California P, 2008. Print.

McLaren, Margaret A. *Feminism, Foucault, and Embodied Subjectivity.* Albany: State U of New York P, 2002. Print.

McNay, Lois. *Foucault and Feminism: Power, Gender, and the Self.* Boston: Northeastern UP, 1993. Print.

McWhorter, Ladelle. *Bodies and Pleasures: Foucault and the Politics of Sexual Normalization.* Bloomington: Indiana UP, 1999. Print.

Mearns, Andrew. *The Bitter Cry of Outcast London: An Inquiry into the Condition of the Abject Poor.* London: Clarke, 1883. Print.

"Measham Murder." *Leicester Chronicle and the Leicestershire Mercury* 7 Mar. 1874: 10; Issue 3372. *British Newspapers 1600–1900 Gale Cengage Learning.* Web. 17 Feb. 2013.

Meisel, Martin. *Realizations: Narrative, Pictorial, and Theatrical Arts in Nineteenth-Century England.* Princeton, NJ: Princeton UP, 1983.

Michael, Magali Cornier. "Rethinking History as Patchwork: The Case of Atwood's *Alias Grace*." *Modern Fiction Studies* 47.2 (2001): 421–47. *Project Muse.* Web. 20 Nov. 2010.

"Michael Davitt on Dreyfus." *New York Times* 16 Sept. 1899. Web. 10 Feb. 2013.

Michel, Louise. *The Red Virgin: Memoirs of Louise Michel.* Ed. and trans. Bullitt Lowry and Elizabeth Ellington Gunter. Tuscaloosa: U of Alabama P, 1981. Print.

"Midland Circuit." *Times* [London] 6 Mar. 1874: 11. *The Times Digital Archive.* Web. 17 Feb. 2013.

Millbank, Jenni. "It's about *This*: Lesbians, Prison, Desire." *Social and Legal Studies* 13.2 (2004): 155–90. *SAGE Premier.* Web. 6 Oct. 2010.

Miller, D. A. *The Novel and the Police.* Berkeley: U of California P, 1988. Print.

Miller, D. Quentin, ed. *Prose and Cons: Essays on Prison Literature in the United States.* Jefferson, NC: McFarland, 2005. Print.

Miller, Elizabeth Carolyn. *Framed: The New Woman Criminal in British Culture at the Fin de Siècle.* Ann Arbor: U of Michigan P, 2008. Print.

Mitchell, Sally. *The Fallen Angel: Chastity, Class, and Women's Reading, 1835–1880.* Bowling Green, OH: Bowling Green U Popular P, 1981. Print.

Moffat, Mary Jane, and Charlotte Painter. *Revelations: Diaries of Women.* New York: Vintage, 1975. Print.

Moodie, Susanna. *Life in the Clearings versus the Bush*. London: Bentley, 1853. Print.

"The Moonstone." *Times* [London] 3 Oct. 1868: 4. *The Times Digital Archive.* Web. 16 Apr. 2012.

Moore, George. *Esther Waters*. 1894. Ed. and introd. David Skilton. Oxford: Oxford UP, 1995. Print.

Moore, R. Laurence. *In Search of White Crows: Spiritualism, Parapsychology, and American Culture*. New York: Oxford UP, 1977. Print.

"The 'Moral Lesson' of the Gallows." *Northern Star and National Trades' Journal* 24 Jan. 1846; Issue 428. *NCSE Nineteenth-Century Serials Edition.* Web. 17 Feb. 2013.

Morey, Anne. "'The Judge Called Me an Accessory': Women's Prison Films, 1950–1962." *Journal of Popular Film and Television* 23.2 (1995): 80–87. Print.

Morgan, Steve. "Prison Lives: Critical Issues in Reading Prisoner Autobiography." *Howard Journal* 38.3 (1999): 328–40. Print.

Morland, Nigel. *This Friendless Lady: An Investigation of the Case against Florence Maybrick for the Murder of Her Husband*. London: Muller, 1957. Print.

Morrison, William Douglas. *Crime and Its Causes*. London: Swan Sonnenschein, 1891.

Morton, Jim. "Women in Prison Films." *Incredibly Strange Films*. Ed. V. Vale and Andrea Juno. London: Plexus, 1986. 151–52. Print.

Mossman, Mark. "Representations of the Abnormal Body in *The Moonstone*." *Victorian Literature and Culture* 37.2 (2009): 483–500. *Cambridge Journals Online.* Web. 17 Feb. 2013.

Mottram, William. *The True Story of George Eliot in Relation to "Adam Bede."* London: Griffiths, 1905. Print.

"Mrs. Fletcher's Story." *Literary World* 15.4 (23 Feb. 1884): 51. *Google Book Search.* Web. 17 July 2012.

"Mrs. Maybrick at Sing Sing." *New York Daily Tribune* 21 Jan. 1905: 11. *Chronicling America: Historic American Newspapers.* Web. 13 May 2011.

"Mrs. Maybrick at the Tombs." *Sun* [New York] 16 Feb. 1905: 12. *Chronicling America: Historic American Newspapers.* Web. 13 May 2011.

"Mrs. Maybrick Condemns the Sing Sing Prison." *New York Times* 21 Dec. 1906: 3. *ProQuest Historical Newspapers.* 25 Apr. 2011.

"Mrs. Maybrick's Denial." *New York Times* 18 Nov. 1904. Web. 13 May 2011.

"Mrs. Maybrick's Trip Put Off." *New York Times* 31 July 1904. Web. 13 May 2011.

"Mrs. Maybrick Talks." *New York Times* 22 Aug. 1900. Web. 13 May 2011.

"Mrs. Maybrick to Be Freed." *New York Times* 24 Mar. 1903. Web. 13 May 2011.

"Mrs. Maybrick Visits Tombs." *New York Daily Tribune* 16 Feb. 1905: 9. *Chronicling America: Historic American Newspapers.* Web. 13 May 2011.

"Mrs. Maybrick Would Forgive and Forget." *New York Times* 13 Aug. 1904. Web. 13 May 2011.

Mukherjee, Upamanyu Pablo. *Crime and Empire: The Colony in Nineteenth-Century Fictions of Crime*. Oxford: Oxford UP, 2003. Print.

Mulvey, Laura. "Visual Pleasure and Narrative Cinema." *Screen* 16.3 (1975): 6–18. *Oxford Journals*. Web. 20 Nov. 2010.

Mulvey-Roberts, Marie. "Militancy, Masochism or Martyrdom? The Public and Private Prisons of Constance Lytton." *Votes for Women*. Ed. June Purvis and Sandra Stanley Holton. London: Routledge, 2000. 159–80. Print.

Mulvey Roberts, Marie, and Tamae Mizuta, eds. *The Militants: Suffragette Activism*. London: Routledge/Thoemmes, 1994. Print.

Murray, Jennifer. "Historical Figures and Paradoxical Pattern: The Quilting Metaphor in Margaret Atwood's *Alias Grace*." *Studies in Canadian Literature / Études en Littérature Canadienne* 26.1 (2001): 65–83. Print.

Myall, Michelle. " 'Only Be Ye Strong and Very Courageous': The Militant Suffragism of Lady Constance Lytton." *Women's History Review* 7.1 (1998): 61–84. *Taylor & Francis Social Science and Humanities Library*. Web. 7 Feb. 2011.

Myerson, Joel. "Mary Gove Nichols' *Mary Lyndon*: A Forgotten Reform Novel." *American Literature* 58.4 (1986): 523–39. *JSTOR*. Web. 15 Mar. 2011.

Nash, Jennifer C. "Re-thinking Intersectionality." *Feminist Review* 89 (2008): 1–15. *JSTOR*. Web. 5 Jan. 2014.

Nayder, Lillian. "Robinson Crusoe and Friday in Victorian Britain: 'Discipline,' 'Dialogue' and Collins's Critique of Empire in *The Moonstone*." *Dickens Studies Annual* 21 (1992): 213–231. Print.

Nellis, Mike. "Prose and Cons: Offender Auto/Biographies, Penal Reform and Probation Training." *Howard Journal of Criminal Justice* 41.5 (2002): 434–68. Print.

"New Books Received." *Academy and Literature* 1708 (28 Jan. 1905): 85. *British Periodicals ProQuest*. Web. 29 Apr. 2011.

Nichols, Thomas Low. *Esoteric Anthropology: The Mysteries of Man*. From the American Stereotype Edition, revised. Malvern, UK, 1873. Print.

———. *Free Love: A Doctrine of Spiritualism; A Discourse Delivered in Foster Hall, Cincinnati, December 22, 1855*. Cincinnati, OH: Bly, 1856. *Google Book Search*. Web. 17 Feb. 2013.

———. *Journal in Jail, Kept during a Four Months' Imprisonment for Libel, in the Jail of Erie County*. 1840. New York: Arno, 1970. Print.

———. *A Memorial to the Home Secretary in Behalf of Mrs. Susan Willis Fletcher, a Spiritualist, Unjustly Condemned to Twelve Months' Imprisonment with Hard Labour: With Important Testimony Excluded upon the Trial, and Proofs*

of Perjuries Committed by the Prosecutrix. London: printed for private
circulation, 1881. *JSTOR (Cowen Tracts)*. Web. 17 Feb. 2013.

"No. 7." *Twenty-Five Years in Seventeen Prisons: The Life-Story of an Ex-Convict,
with His Impressions of Our Prison System*. London: Robinson, 1903. Print.

Nord, Deborah Epstein. *Walking the Victorian Streets: Women, Representation,
and the City*. Ithaca, NY: Cornell UP, 1995. Print.

Norgate, Gerald Le Grys. "Robinson, Frederick William (1830–1901)." Rev.
Sayoni Basu. *Oxford Dictionary of National Biography*. Oxford: Oxford UP,
2004. Web. 11 Aug 2012.

Norquay, Glenda. *Voices and Votes: A Literary Anthology of the Women's Suffrage
Campaign*. Manchester: Manchester UP, 1995. Print.

"Now Ready, in 2 Vols. 8 Vo., with Two Portraits on Steel, Facsimile of." *Times*
[London] 31 Dec. 1863: 13. *The Times Digital Archive*. Web. 3 Feb. 2013.

O'Brien, Ellen L. *Crime in Verse: The Poetics of Murder in the Victorian Era*.
Columbus: Ohio State UP, 2008. Print.

———. " 'Every Man Who Is Hanged Leaves a Poem': Criminal Poets in Victorian
Street Ballads." *Victorian Poetry* 39 (2001): 319–39. *Project Muse*. Web. 17 Feb.
2013.

Ogilvie, Marilyn, and Joy Harvey, eds. *Biographical Dictionary of Women in
Science: Pioneering Lives from Ancient Times to the Mid-20th Century*. Vol. 1.
London: Routledge, 2000. Print.

Oliphant, Margaret. "Sensation Novels." *Blackwood's Magazine* 91 (May 1862):
564–84. *The Selected Works of Margaret Oliphant, Part I: Literary Criticism
and Literary History; Vol. 1: Literary Criticism, 1854–69*. Ed. Joanne Shattock.
London: Pickering and Chatto, 2011. 245–68. Print.

O'Neill, Ellen. *Extraordinary Confessions of a Female Pickpocket, Seventeen Years
of Age, Now in the Preston House of Correction under Sentence of Transportation;
Her Serious Charge against the Factory Overlookers of Manchester; Also Her
Revelations Respecting the Conduct of the Female Factory Operatives of
Manchester; Together with Her Exploits in Preston*. Preston, UK: Drummond,
1850. Print.

"On Our Library Table." *Athenaeum* 2978 (22 Nov. 1884): 658. *British
Periodicals ProQuest*. Web. 4 Feb. 2013.

Onslow, Barbara. "The Inside Story: Crime, Convicts and Careers for Women."
Victorian Crime, Madness and Sensation. Ed. Andrew Maunder and Grace
Moore. Aldershot, UK: Ashgate, 2004. 105–18. Print.

Oppenheim, Janet. *The Other World: Spiritualism and Psychic Research in
England, 1850–1914*. Cambridge: Cambridge UP, 1985. Print.

Orange Is the New Black. Perf. Taylor Schilling, Danielle Brooks, Taryn
Manning, et al. Lionsgate Television. Netflix (USA), 2013–. Television
(Internet).

Owen, Alex. *The Darkened Room: Women, Power and Spiritualism in Late Victorian England*. London: Virago, 1989. Print.

Owen, M. E. "Criminal Women." *Cornhill Magazine* 14 (1866): 152–60. Print.

Oxley, Deborah. *Convict Maids: The Forced Migration of Women to Australia*. Cambridge: Cambridge UP, 1996. Print.

Padel, Una, and Prue Stevenson, comp. *Insiders: Women's Experience of Prison*. London: Virago, 1988. Print.

Pal-Lapinski, Piya. "Chemical Seductions: Exoticism, Toxicology, and the Female Poisoner in *Armadale* and *The Legacy of Cain*." *Reality's Dark Light: The Sensational Wilkie Collins*. Ed. Maria K. Bachman and Don Richard Cox. Knoxville: U of Tennessee P, 2003. 94–130. Print.

"Palmist Takes Poison." *Call* [San Francisco] 23 Apr. 1913: cover page. *Chronicling America: Historic American Newspapers*. Web. 16 May 2011.

Pankhurst, Christabel. *Unshackled: The Story of How We Won the Vote*. 1959. Cresset Women's Voices. London: Cresset, 1987. Print.

Pankhurst, Emmeline. *My Own Story*. 1914. London: Virago, 1979. Print.

Pankhurst, Estelle Sylvia. *The Suffragette Movement: An Intimate Account of Persons and Ideals*. 1931. London: Virago, 1977. Print.

Pankhurst, Richard. *Sylvia Pankhurst: Artist and Crusader; An Intimate Portrait*. New York: Paddington, 1979. Print.

Pankhurst, Sylvia. "The Cleaners." *Writ on Cold Slate*. London: Dreadnought, 1922. 22. Print.

———. "What It Feels Like to Be in Prison: With Some Suggestions for Reform." *Pall Mall Magazine* May 1907: 554–60. *British Periodicals ProQuest*. Web. 3 Dec. 2013.

———. "Writ on Cold Slate." *Writ on Cold Slate*. London: Dreadnought, 1922. 5. Print.

Parkes, Bessie Rayner. "Female Life in Prison." *English Woman's Journal* 10.55 (1 Sept. 1862): 1–8. *NCSE Nineteenth-Century Serials Edition*. Web. 14 Aug. 2012.

———. "What Can Educated Women Do?" *English Woman's Journal* 4.22 (1 Dec. 1859): 217–27. *NCSE Nineteenth-Century Serials Edition*. Web. 25 Feb. 2013.

Parry, Edward Abbott. *The Drama of the Law*. London, 1924. Print.

Pearsall, Ronald. *The Table-Rappers: The Victorians and the Occult*. 1972. Stroud, UK: Sutton, 2004. Print.

Peters, Sally. "Shaw's Life: A Feminist in Spite of Himself." *The Cambridge Companion to George Bernard Shaw*. Ed. Christopher Innes. Cambridge: Cambridge UP, 1998. 3–24. Print.

Pethick-Lawrence, Emmeline. *My Part in a Changing World*. London: Gollancz, 1938. Print.

Pethick-Lawrence, Frederick. "Appeal by Mr Pethick Lawrence to T. B. Silcock."
    2 Apr. 1909. HO144/904/176114. National Archives, London. Print.
"The Petting and Fretting of Female Convicts." *Meliora* 6 (1864): 45–59. Print.
Pettitt, Clare. "Legal Subjects, Legal Objects: The Law and Victorian Fiction."
    A Concise Companion to the Victorian Novel. Ed. Francis O'Gorman. Malden,
    MA: Blackwell, 2005. 71–90. Print.
PMLA 123.3 (2008). *Modern Language Association Journals*. Web. 18 Feb. 2013.
Pollack, Otto. *The Criminality of Women*. New York: Barnes, 1961. Print.
Poovey, Mary. *Making a Social Body: British Cultural Formation, 1830–1864*.
    Chicago: U of Chicago P, 1995. Print.
Powell, Kerry. "New Women, New Plays, and Shaw in the 1890s." *The
    Cambridge Companion to George Bernard Shaw*. Ed. Christopher Innes.
    Cambridge: Cambridge UP, 1998. 76–100. Print.
Priestley, Philip. *Victorian Prison Lives: English Prison Biography, 1830–1914*.
    1985. London: Pimlico, 1999. Print.
"Prison Commission's Papers." PCOM 8/228/4. National Archives, London.
    Print.
*Prison Discipline: Mrs. Elizabeth Fry and Professor Lieber (of Columbia, South
    Carolina) upon the Separate Confinement of Prisoners; From the Manchester
    Guardian of Saturday, 24th June, 1848*. Manchester, UK: Cave, 1848. Print.
Prochaska, Frank. *Women and Philanthropy in Nineteenth-Century England*.
    Oxford, UK: Clarendon, 1980. Print.
Purvis, June. " 'Deeds, Not Words': The Daily Lives of Militant WSPU
    Suffragettes in Edwardian Britain." *Women's Studies International Forum* 18.2
    (1995): 91–101. *Science Direct Freedom Collection*. Web. 17 Feb. 2013.
———. "Doing Feminist Women's History: Researching the Lives of Women in
    the Suffragette Movement in Edwardian England." *Researching Women's Lives
    from a Feminist Perspective*. Ed. Mary Maynard and June Purvis. London:
    Taylor and Francis, 1994. 166–89. Print.
———. "The Prison Experiences of the Suffragettes in Edwardian Britain."
    Women's History Review 4.1 (1995): 103–33. *Taylor & Francis Social Science
    and Humanities Library*. Web. 7 Feb. 2011.
Purvis, June, and Sandra Stanley Holton, eds. *Votes for Women*. London:
    Routledge, 2000. Print.
Pykett, Lyn. *Wilkie Collins*. Oxford: Oxford UP, 2005. Print.
Quinton, R. F. *Crime and Criminals, 1876–1910*. London: Longmans, 1910. Print.
R. "From a Reader's Note-Book." *Academy* 1288 (9 Jan. 1897): 46. *British
    Periodicals ProQuest*. Web. 29 Apr. 2011.
Radzinowicz, Leon, and Roger Hood. *A History of English Criminal Law and Its
    Administration from 1750, Vol. 5: The Emergence of Penal Policy*. London:
    Stevens, 1986. Print.

——. "The Status of Political Prisoner in England: The Struggle for Recognition." *Virginia Law Review* 65.8 (1979): 1421–81. *JSTOR*. Web. 17 Feb. 2013.

Raeburn, Antonia. *The Militant Suffragettes*. London: Joseph, 1973. Print.

Rafter, Nicole Hahn. "Prison and Execution Films." *Shots in the Mirror: Crime Films and Society*. Oxford: Oxford UP, 2000. 117–40. Print.

Ramazanoglu, Caroline, ed. *Up against Foucault: Explorations of Some Tensions between Foucault and Feminism*. London: Routledge, 1993. Print.

Ransome, Mr. H.A.V., on behalf of Irene Dallas. Feb. 1909. HO144/1032/175314/11. National Archives, London. Print.

Rendall, Jane. " 'A Moral Engine': Feminism, Liberalism and *The English-woman's Journal*." *Equal or Different: Women's Politics, 1800–1914*. Ed. Jane Rendall. Oxford, UK: Blackwell, 1987. 112–38. Print.

"Review of *Joseph Mazzini; A Memoir* by E.A.V. published by H. S. King & Co." *Englishwoman's Review of Social and Industrial Questions* ns 6 (Feb. 1875): 67–69. Print.

"The Review's Bookshop." *Review of Reviews* 31.182 (Feb. 1905): 207. *British Periodicals ProQuest*. Web. 29 Apr. 2011.

Richardson, Mary R. *Laugh a Defiance*. London: Weidenfeld and Nicolson, 1953. Print.

Rickards, Maurice. *The Encyclopedia of Ephemera: A Guide to the Fragmentary Documents of Everyday Life for the Collector, Curator, and Historian*. Ed. and comp. Michael Twyman, with the assistance of Sarah du Boscq de Beaumont and Amoret Tanner. London: British Library, 2000. Print.

Rimstead, Roxanne. "Working-Class Intruders: Female Domestics in *Kamouraska* and *Alias Grace*." *Canadian Literature* 175 (Winter 2002): 44–65. *Literature Online (LION)*. Web. 17 Feb. 2013.

Rimstead, Roxanne, and Deena Rymhs, eds. *Prison Writing / Writing Prison in Canada*. Spec. issue of *Canadian Literature* 208 (Spring 2011). *Literature Online (LION)*. Web. 18 Feb. 2013.

Robb, George. "The English Dreyfus Case: Florence Maybrick and the Sexual Double-Standard." *Disorder in the Court: Trials and Sexual Conflict at the Turn of the Century*. Ed. George Robb and Nancy Erber. Basingstoke, UK: Macmillan, 1999. 57–77. Print.

Robb, George, and Nancy Erber, eds. *Disorder in the Court: Trials and Sexual Conflict at the Turn of the Century*. Basingstoke, UK: Macmillan, 1999. Print.

Robinson, Frederick William [The Author of *Female Life in Prison, Memoirs of Jane Cameron*]. "Daisy March." *Harper's Bazaar* 14.27–30 (2–23 July 1881): 422–23, 442–43, 454–55, 470–71. Albert R. Mann Library, Home Economics Archive: Research, Tradition and History (HEARTH), Cornell U. Web. 1

May 2014. http://hearth.library.cornell.edu/h/hearth/browse/title/4732809
.html.

———— [A Prison Matron]. *Female Life in Prison*. 2 vols. London: Hurst and
Blackett, 1862. Print.

———— [A Prison Matron]. *Female Life in Prison*. 1862. New ed. rev. London:
Sampson Low, Son, and Marston, 1864. Print.

———— [By the Author of "High Church," "No Church," "Owen: A Waif," &c.].
Mattie: A Stray. 3 vols. London: Hurst and Blackett, 1864. Print.

———— [A Prison Matron]. *Memoirs of Jane Cameron, Female Convict*. 1863.
2 vols. London: Hurst and Blackett, 1864. Print.

———— [By the Author of "No Church," and "High Church"]. *Owen: A Waif*.
3 vols. London: Hurst and Blackett, 1862. Print.

———— [By the Author of "No Church"]. *Poor Humanity*. London: Hurst and
Blackett, 1868. Print.

———— [A Prison Matron]. *Prison Characters Drawn from Life with Suggestions
for Prison Government*. 2 vols. London: Hurst and Blackett, 1866. Print.

Rodensky, Lisa. *The Crime in Mind: Criminal Responsibility and the Victorian
Novel*. Oxford: Oxford UP, 2003. Print.

Rodríguez, Dylan. "Against the Discipline of 'Prison Writing': Toward a
Theoretical Conception of Contemporary Radical Prison Praxis." *Genre* 35
(Fall–Winter 2002): 407–28. *E-Duke Journals Scholarly Collection*. Web. 17
Feb. 2013.

Rogers, Helen. "The Way to Jerusalem: Reading, Writing and Reform in an Early
Victorian Gaol." *Past & Present: A Journal of Historical Studies* 205 (Nov.
2009): 71–104. Print.

Rogerson, Margaret. "Reading the Patchworks in *Alias Grace*." *Journal of
Commonwealth Literature* 33.1 (1998): 5–22. *SAGE Journals*. Web. 17 Feb.
2013.

Rolston, Simon. "Prison Life Writing, African American Narrative Strategies,
and *Bad: The Autobiography of James Carr*." *MELUS* 38.4 (2013): 191–215.
Gale Cengage Expanded Academic ASAP. Web. 26 Jan. 2014.

Rose, June. *Elizabeth Fry*. London: Macmillan, 1980. Print.

Rose, Lionel. *The Massacre of the Innocents: Infanticide in Britain, 1800–1939*.
London: Routledge, 1986. Print.

Rowbotham, Judith. "'Soldiers of Christ'? Images of Female Missionaries in Late
Nineteenth-Century Britain: Issues of Heroism and Martyrdom." *Gender &
History* 12.1 (2000): 82–106. *NESLi2 Wiley-Blackwell Full Collection*. Web. 17
Feb. 2013.

Rowbotham, Judith, and Kim Stevenson, eds. *Behaving Badly: Social Panic and
Moral Outrage—Victorian and Modern Parallels*. Aldershot, UK: Ashgate,
2003. Print.

Roy, Ashish. "The Fabulous Imperialist Semiotic of Wilkie Collins's *The Moonstone.*" *New Literary History* 24 (1993): 657–81. *JSTOR.* Web. 17 Feb. 2013.

Ryan, Bernard, with Michael Havers. *The Poisoned Life of Mrs Maybrick.* Foreword by Lord Russell of Killowen. London: Kimber, 1977. Print.

Rymhs, Deena. "'Docile Bodies Shuffling in Unison': The Prisoner as Worker in Canadian Prison Writing." *Life Writing* 6.3 (2009): 313–27. *Taylor & Francis Social Science and Humanities Library.* Web. 18 Feb. 2013.

Sanders, Andrew. "Skene, Felicia Mary Frances (1821–1899)." *Oxford Dictionary of National Biography.* Oxford: Oxford UP, 2004. Web. 30 Aug. 2012.

Sawicki, Jana. *Disciplining Foucault: Feminism, Power, and the Body.* New York: Routledge, 1991. Print.

Scheffler, Judith A. Introduction. *Wall Tappings: An International Anthology of Women's Prison Writings, 200 to the Present.* Ed. Judith A. Scheffler. Foreword by Tracy Huling. 2nd ed. New York: Feminist, 2002. xxi–xliv. Print.

———, ed. *Wall Tappings: An International Anthology of Women's Prison Writings, 200 to the Present.* 2nd ed. Foreword by Tracy Huling. New York: Feminist, 2002. Print.

Schramm, Jan-Melissa. "Is Literature More Ethical than Law? Fitzjames Stephen and Literary Responses to the Advent of Full Legal Representation for Felons." *Law and Literature.* Ed. Michael Freeman and Andrew Lewis. Oxford: Oxford UP, 1999. 417–35. Print.

———. *Testimony and Advocacy in Victorian Law, Literature, and Theology.* Cambridge: Cambridge UP, 2000. Print.

Schur, Anna. "The Poetics of 'Pattern Penitence': 'Pet Prisoners' and Plagiarized Selves." *Stones of Law, Bricks of Shame: Narrating Imprisonment in the Victorian Age.* Ed. Jan Alber and Frank Lauterbach. Toronto: U of Toronto P, 2009. 134–53. Print.

Schwan, Anne. "'Bless the Gods for My Pencils and Paper': Katie Gliddon's Prison Diary, Percy Bysshe Shelley and the Suffragettes at Holloway." *Women's History Review* 22.1 (2013): 148–67. *Taylor & Francis Social Science and Humanities Library.* Web. 17 Feb. 2013.

———. "Crime." *Dickens in Context.* Ed. Sally Ledger and Holly Furneaux. Cambridge: Cambridge UP, 2011. 301–9. Print.

———. "'Dreadful beyond Description': Mary Carpenter's Prison Reform Writings and Female Convicts in Britain and India." *European Journal of English Studies* 14.2 (2010): 107–20. *Taylor & Francis Social Science and Humanities Library.* Web. 17 Feb. 2013.

———. "Frederick William Robinson, Charles Dickens, and the Literary Tradition of 'Low Life.'" *Nineteenth-Century Radical Traditions: Essays in*

Memory of Sally Ledger. Ed. Joseph Bristow and Josephine McDonagh. New York: Palgrave Macmillan, forthcoming. Print.

———. "From 'Dry Volumes of Facts and Figures' to Stories of 'Flesh and Blood': The Prison Narratives of Frederick William Robinson." *Stones of Law, Bricks of Shame: Narrating Imprisonment in the Victorian Age.* Ed. Jan Alber and Frank Lauterbach. Toronto: U of Toronto P, 2009. 191–212. Print.

———, ed. *Reading and Writing in Prison.* Spec. issue of *Critical Survey* 23.3 (2011). Print.

Schwan, Anne, and Stephen Shapiro. *How to Read Foucault's "Discipline and Punish."* London: Pluto, 2011. Print.

Scott, Joan Wallach. "The Evidence of Experience." *Critical Inquiry* 17.4 (1991): 773–97. *JSTOR.* Web. 17 Feb. 2013.

———. *Only Paradoxes to Offer: French Feminists and the Rights of Man.* Cambridge, MA: Harvard UP, 1996. Print.

Scott, Walter. *The Heart of Midlothian.* 1818. Ed. and introd. Tony Inglis. London: Penguin, 1994. Print.

"The Seldom-at-Home Secretary and the Police." *Punch* [London] 9 July 1881: 6. *19th Century UK Periodicals,* "New Readerships." *Gale Cengage Learning.* Web. 30 Apr. 2014.

Shale, Suzanne. "Listening to the Law: Famous Trials on BBC Radio, 1934–1969." *Modern Law Review* 59.6 (1996): 813–44. *JSTOR.* Web. 17 Feb. 2013.

Shaplen, Robert. *Free Love and Heavenly Sinners: The Story of the Great Henry Ward Beecher Scandal.* London: Deutsch, 1956. Print.

Shaw, George Bernard. *Man and Superman. The Works of Bernard Shaw.* Vol. 10. London: Constable, 1930. Print.

———. *Mrs Warren's Profession.* 1898. *Plays Unpleasant.* Ed. and introd. David Edgar. London: Penguin, 2000. Print.

———. "The Unmentionable Case for Women's Suffrage." *Englishwoman* 1 (Feb.–Apr. 1909): 112–21. Print.

Shearing, Joseph [Gabrielle Margaret Vere Long]. *Airing in a Closed Carriage.* London, 1943. Print.

Shelley, Percy Bysshe. *Shelley's Poetry and Prose.* 2nd ed. Ed. Donald H. Reiman and Neil Fraistat. New York: Norton, 2002. Print.

Shepard, Leslie. *The Broadside Ballad: A Study in Origins and Meaning.* London: Jenkins, 1962. Print.

———, ed. *Encyclopedia of Occultism and Parapsychology.* Vol. 1. Detroit: Gale, 1978. Print.

———. *The History of Street Literature: The Story of Broadside Ballads, Chapbooks, Proclamations, News-Sheets, Election Bills, Tracts, Pamphlets, Cocks, Catchpennies, and Other Ephemera.* Newton Abbot, UK: David, 1973. Print.

Sherman, William H., and William J. Sheils, eds. *Prison Writings in Early Modern England*. Spec. issue of *Huntington Library Quarterly* 72.2 (2009). *JSTOR*. Web. 28 Feb. 2011.

Shoemaker, Robert B. "Print and the Female Voice: Representations of Women's Crime in London, 1690–1735." *Gender & History* 22.1 (2010): 75–91. *NESLi2 Wiley-Blackwell Full Collection*. Web. 24 Sept. 2010.

Sibly, Job. *Circumstantial Evidence: Report of the Trial of Elizabeth Fenning, Charged with Administering Poison with Intent to Murder; Whereupon She Was Found Guilty before Sir J. Silvester, the Recorder at the Old Bailey, April 11, 1815, and Suffered Death: Including All the Evidence Omitted in the Sessions Paper Report*. London: William Hone, 1819. Print.

Silver, Elaine. Introduction. *Prison Diary: Letters from Holloway*. By Katie Gliddon. TS 7KGG/1/1b. Women's Library @ LSE, London. Print.

Silver-Isenstadt, Jean. *Shameless: The Visionary Life of Mary Gove Nichols*. Baltimore: Johns Hopkins UP, 2002. Print.

"Six Years a Prisoner." *New York Times* 17 Nov. 1895. Web. 17 Feb. 2013.

Skene, Felicia. *Scenes from a Silent World, or, Prisons and Their Inmates*. 1889. New York: Cambridge UP, 2010. Print.

Smart, Carol. *Law, Crime and Sexuality: Essays in Feminism*. London: Sage, 1995. Print.

———. *Women, Crime and Criminology: A Feminist Critique*. London: Routledge, 1976. Print.

Smiles, Samuel. *Self-Help: With Illustrations of Character, Conduct, and Perseverance*. 1859. Ed., introd., and notes Peter W. Sinnema. Oxford: Oxford UP, 2002. Print.

Smith, Ann D. *Women in Prison: A Study in Penal Methods*. London: Stevens, 1962. Print.

Smith, Catherine Douglas. Petition. HO144/1032/175314/11. National Archives, London. Print.

Smith, Charles Manby. *The Little World of London; or, Pictures of London Life*. London: Hall, 1857. Print.

Smith, Roger. *Trial by Medicine: Insanity and Responsibility in Victorian Trials*. Edinburgh: Edinburgh UP, 1981. Print.

Smith, Sidonie. *A Poetics of Women's Autobiography: Marginality and the Fictions of Self-Representation*. Bloomington: Indiana UP, 1987. Print.

Smith, Sidonie, and Julia Watson. *Reading Autobiography: A Guide for Interpreting Life Narratives*. 2nd ed. Minneapolis: U of Minnesota P, 2010. Print.

Smyth, Ethel. "Mrs. Pankhurst's Treatment in Prison: Statement by Dr. Ethel Smyth." Letter to the editor. *Times* [London] 19 Apr. 1912: 6. *The Times Digital Archive*. Web. 30 Apr. 2014.

Solomon, Daisy Dorothea. *My Prison Experiences*. London: St. Clement's, 1913. Rpt. of article in *Christian Commonwealth* 25 Aug. 1909. Print.

"Spirits in Prison." *Saturday Review of Politics, Literature, Science and Art* 51:1, 329 (16 Apr. 1881): 492. *British Periodicals ProQuest*. Web. 29 Apr. 2011.

Spooner, Catherine. "'Spiritual Garments': Fashioning the Victorian Séance in Sarah Waters' *Affinity*." *Styling Texts: Dress and Fashion in Literature*. Ed. and introd. Cynthia Kuhn and Cindy Carlson. Youngstown, NY: Cambria, 2007. 351–67. Print.

Staels, Hilde. "Intertexts of Margaret Atwood's *Alias Grace*." *Modern Fiction Studies* 46.2 (2000): 427–50. *Project Muse*. Web. 20 Nov. 2010.

Stanley, Henry Morton. *In Darkest Africa, or, the Quest, Rescue and Retreat of Emin, Governor of Equatoria*. London: Sampson Low, Marston, and Searle, 1890. Print.

Stanley, Liz. "The Epistolarium: On Theorizing Letters and Correspondences." *Auto/Biography* 12.3 (2004): 201–35. Print.

Stanley, Liz, and Helen Dampier. "Simulacrum Diaries: Time, the 'Moment of Writing' and the Diaries of Johanna Brandt-Van Warmelo." *Life Writing* 3 (2006): 25–52. *Taylor & Francis Social Science and Humanities Library*. Web. 17 Feb. 2013.

"Statement Showing the Comparison between the Treatment of Prisoners under the First Division, Second Division and Rule 243A." PCOM 8/228/4. National Archives, London. Print.

Stavreva, Kirilka. "Scaffold unto Prints: Executing the Insubordinate Wife in the Ballad Trade of Early Modern England." *Journal of Popular Culture* 31.1 (Summer 1997): 177–88. Print.

Stead, W. T. "Ought Mrs. Maybrick to Be Tortured to Death?" *Review of Reviews* 6 (Oct. 1892): 390–96. Print.

Stephen, James Fitzjames. *A Digest of the Criminal Law: Crimes and Punishment*. London: Macmillan, 1877. Print.

———. *A History of the Criminal Law in England*. 3 vols. London: Macmillan, 1883. Print.

"STOCKHOLM, Dec. 9—The King has authorized the." *Times* [London] 31 Dec. 1845: 5. *The Times Digital Archive*. Web. 13 Apr. 2014.

"Stolen Brain Foils Spirits." *Dakota County Herald* 27 June 1913. *Chronicling America: Historic American Newspapers*. Web. 16 May 2011.

"Stolen Brain Foils Spirits." *North Platte* 1 July 1913. *Chronicling America: Historic American Newspapers*. Web. 16 May 2011.

Summers, Anne. "Elizabeth Fry and Mid-Nineteenth Century Reform." *The Health of Prisoners: Historical Essays*. Ed. Richard Creese, W. F. Bynum, and J. Bearn. Amsterdam: Rodopi, 1995. 83–101. Print.

———. "A Home from Home: Women's Philanthropic Work in the Nineteenth Century." *Fit Work for Women*. Ed. Sandra Burman. London: Croom Helm, 1979. 33–63. Print.

Summerscale, Kate. *The Suspicions of Mr Whicher or the Murder at Road Hill House*. London: Bloomsbury, 2008. Print.

Sutter, Gavin. "Penny Dreadfuls and Perverse Domains." *Behaving Badly: Social Panic and Moral Outrage—Victorian and Modern Parallels*. Ed. Judith Rowbotham and Kim Stevenson. Aldershot, UK: Ashgate, 2003. 159–75. Print.

Swanwick, Helena Lucy Maria. *I Have Been Young*. London: Gollancz, 1935. Print.

Sweeney, Megan. *Reading Is My Window: Books and the Art of Reading in Women's Prisons*. Chapel Hill: U of North Carolina P, 2010. Print.

Swindells, Julia. "Conclusion: Autobiography and the Politics of 'The Personal.'" *The Uses of Autobiography*. Ed. Julia Swindells. London: Taylor and Francis, 1995. 205–14. Print.

———. "Liberating the Subject? Autobiography and 'Women's History': A Reading of the Diaries of Hannah Cullwick." *Interpreting Women's Lives*. Ed. Personal Narratives Group. Bloomington: Indiana UP, 1989. 25–38. Print.

Symons, Julian. *The Blackheath Poisonings: A Victorian Murder Mystery*. London: Collins, 1978. Print.

Tarter, Michelle Lise, and Richard Bell, eds. *Buried Lives: Incarcerated in Early America*. Athens: U of Georgia P, 2012. Print.

Taylor, Jenny Bourne. *In the Secret Theatre of Home*. London: Routledge, 1988. Print.

Thackeray, William Makepeace. "Going to See a Man Hanged." 1840. *The Works of William Makepeace Thackeray, Vol. 15: The Book of Snobs; and Sketches and Travels in London*. London: Smith, 1869. 374–89. *Google Books*. Web. 3 Sept. 2012.

"This Week's Books." *Saturday Review of Politics, Literature, Science and Art* 99.2569 (21 Jan. 1905): 90. *British Periodicals ProQuest*. Web. 29 Apr. 2011.

Thomas, Alison. *Portraits of Women: Gwen John and Her Forgotten Contemporaries*. Cambridge, UK: Polity, 1994. Print.

Thomas, Ronald R. *Detective Fiction and the Rise of Forensic Science*. Cambridge: Cambridge UP, 2003. Print.

Thomas, Sue. "Scenes in the Writing of 'Constance Lytton and Jane Warton, Spinster': Contextualising a Cross-Class Dresser." *Women's History Review* 12.1 (2003): 51–71. *Taylor & Francis Social Science and Humanities Library*. Web. 7 Feb. 2011.

Thompson, E. P. "Mayhew and the *Morning Chronicle*." *The Unknown Mayhew*. Ed. and introd. E. P. Thompson and Eileen Yeo. London: Merlin, 1971. 11–50. Print.

"The Ticket of Leave System." *Quarterly Review* 113 (1863): 138–75. Print.

Tidy, Charles Meymott. *The Maybrick Case: A Toxicological Study*. London: Baillière, Tindall, and Cox, 1890. Print.

Tilghman, Carolyn M. "Autobiography, Activism, and the Carceral: An Analysis of the Prison Writing of Lady Constance Lytton." *Clio* 37.1 (2007): 69–92. *Gale Cengage Expanded Academic ASAP*. Web. 11 June 2009.

Times [London] 14 Feb. 1848: 8; col. B. *The Times Digital Archive*. Web. 17 Feb. 2013.

Todd, John. *Woman's Rights*. 1867. New York: Arno, 1972. Print.

Tomalin, Claire. *The Invisible Woman: The Story of Nelly Ternan and Charles Dickens*. London: Penguin, 1991. Print.

Toron, Alison. "The Model Prisoner: Reading Confinement in *Alias Grace*." *Canadian Literature* 208 (Spring 2011): 12–28. *Literature Online*. Web. 18 Feb. 2013.

Trahey, Jane, ed. *Harper's Bazaar: 100 Years of the American Female*. New York: Random House, 1967. Print.

"Treatment of Suffragette Prisoners since March 1st 1912." PCOM 8/228/3. National Archives, London. Print.

Tristan, Flora. *Flora Tristan's London Journal: A Survey of London Life in the 1830s*. 1840. Trans. Dennis Palmer and Giselle Pincetl. London: Prior, 1980. Print.

Trodd, Anthea. *Domestic Crime in the Victorian Novel*. Basingstoke, UK: Macmillan, 1989. Print.

Tromp, Marlene. "Spirited Sexuality: Sex, Marriage, and Victorian Spiritualism." *Victorian Literature and Culture* 31 (2003): 67–81. *Cambridge Journals Online*. Web. 30 Apr. 2011.

Tuchman, Gaye, with Nina E. Fortin. *Edging Women Out: Victorian Novelists, Publishers, and Social Change*. London: Routledge, 1989. Print.

Tyler-Bennett, Deborah. "Suffrage and Poetry: Radical Women's Voices." *The Women's Suffrage Movement: New Feminist Perspectives*. Ed. Maroula Joannou and June Purvis. Manchester: Manchester UP, 1998. 117–26. Print.

Tyson, Leonora. "A Day in Holloway." 5 Mar.–8 Mar. 1912. *Prison Letters, Police Summons, Prison Records Suffragette Collection*. SC31. 2003.46/3. Copyright Museum of London. Print.

———. *Prison Letters, Police Summons, Prison Records Suffragette Collection*. SC31. Copyright Museum of London. Print.

Uglow, Jennifer. *George Eliot*. New York: Pantheon, 1987. Print.

van Drenth, Annemieke, and Francisca de Haan. *The Rise of Caring Power: Elizabeth Fry and Josephine Butler*. Amsterdam: Amsterdam UP, 1999. Print.

van Wingerden, Sophia A. *The Women's Suffrage Movement in Britain, 1866–1928*. Basingstoke, UK: Macmillan, 1999. Print.

Vicinus, Martha. *The Industrial Muse: A Study of Nineteenth Century British Working-Class Literature*. London: Croom Helm, 1974. Print.

Voelker, Joseph C. " 'Wasn't She the Downright Villain': The Autobiography of Florence Elizabeth Maybrick." *James Joyce Quarterly* 14 (Summer 1977): 480–82. Print.

Wagner, Charles L. *Seeing Stars*. 1940. New York: Arno, 1977. Print.

Walford, Bonny. *Lifers: The Stories of Eleven Women Serving Life Sentences for Murder*. Montreal: Eden, 1987. Print.

Walkowitz, Judith R. *City of Dreadful Delight: Narratives of Sexual Danger in Late-Victorian London*. London: Virago, 1992. Print.

———. *Prostitution and Victorian Society: Women, Class, and the State*. Cambridge: Cambridge UP, 1980. Print.

Wallace, Diane. *The Women's Historical Novel*. Basingstoke, UK: Palgrave Macmillan, 2005. Print.

Walters, Suzanna Danuta. "Caged Heat: The (R)evolution of Women-in-Prison Films. *Reel Knockouts: Violent Women in the Movies*. Ed. Martha McCaughey and Neal King. Austin: U of Texas P, 2001. 106–23. Print.

Ward, Anne. *No Stone Unturned: The Story of Leonora Tyson, a Streatham Suffragette*. London: Local History Publications, 2005. Print.

Ward, Tony. "Legislating for Human Nature: Legal Responses to Infanticide, 1860–1938." *Infanticide: Historical Perspectives on Child Murder and Concealment, 1550–2000*. Ed. Mark Jackson. Aldershot, UK: Ashgate, 2002. 249–69. Print.

Waters, Sarah. *Affinity*. 1999. London: Virago, 2000. Print.

———. Interview by Lucie Armitt. *Feminist Review* 85 (2007): 116–27. *JSTOR*. Web. 6 Oct. 2010.

Watkins, John, and William Hone. *The Important Results of an Elaborate Investigation into the Mysterious Case of Elizabeth Fenning: Being a Detail of Extraordinary Facts Discovered since Her Execution, Including, the Official Report of Her Singular Trial, Now First Published, and Copious Notes Thereon; Also, Numerous Authentic Documents; An Argument on Her Case; A Memorial to H.R.H. the Prince Regent; & Strictures on a Late Pamphlet of the Prosecutor's Apothecary; with Thirty Letters, Written by the Unfortunate Girl While in Prison*. London: William Hone, 1815. Print.

Watson, Katherine D. *Poisoned Lives: English Poisoners and Their Victims*. London: Hambledon, 2004. Print.

Watts-Dunton, Theodore. "A Great Builder of the Old Three-Decker: F. W. Robinson." *Athenaeum* 14 Dec. 1901: 812–13. *British Periodicals ProQuest*. Web. 1 May 2014.

Weber, Max. *The Protestant Ethic and the Spirit of Capitalism*. 1904–5. Trans. Talcott Parsons. London: Unwin, 1971. Print.

Wesley, John. "Some Account of Sarah Peters." *Arminian Magazine* 5 (1782): 128–36. Print.

———. *The Works of the Rev. John Wesley*. Ed. Thomas Jackson. Vol. 7. London: Mason, 1829–31. Print.

West, Rebecca. *The Fountain Overflows*. 1957. Introd. Amanda Craig. London: Virago, 2011. Print.

"The Westminster Murder." *Times* [London] 24 Dec. 1845: 7. *The Times Digital Archive*. Web. 13 Apr. 2014.

Whalen, Lachlan. *Contemporary Irish Republican Prison Writing: Writing and Resistance*. New York: Palgrave Macmillan, 2007. Print.

Wiener, Martin J. *Reconstructing the Criminal: Culture, Law, and Policy in England, 1830–1914*. Cambridge: Cambridge UP, 1990. Print.

Wilde, Oscar. "The Ballad of Reading Gaol." 1898. *The Ballad of Reading Gaol and Other Poems*. London: Penguin, 2010. 1–27. Print.

Williams, Raymond. *The Country and the City*. London: Chatto and Windus, 1973. Print.

Wilson, Sharon Rose. "Quilting as Narrative Art: Metafictional Construction in *Alias Grace*." *Margaret Atwood's Textual Assassinations: Recent Poetry and Fiction*. Ed. Sharon R. Wilson. Columbus: Ohio State UP, 2003. 121–34. Print.

Wiltenburg, Joy. *Disorderly Women and Female Power in the Street Literature of Early Modern England and Germany*. Charlottesville: U of Virginia P, 1992. Print.

Wiltse, Ed. "Doing Time in College: Student-Prisoner Reading Groups and the Object(s) of Literary Study." *Critical Survey* 23.3 (2011): 6–22. Print.

Winslow, Barbara. *Sylvia Pankhurst: Sexual Politics and Political Activism*. London: UCL P, 1996. Print.

Winslow, L. Forbes. *Recollections of Forty Years*. London: Ouseley, 1910. Print.

———. *Spiritualistic Madness*. London, 1876. Print.

Wormald, Mark. "Prior Knowledge: Sarah Waters and the Victorians." *British Fiction Today*. Ed. Philip Tew and Rod Mengham. London: Continuum, 2006. 186–97. Print.

Worrall, Anne. *Offending Women: Female Lawbreakers and the Criminal Justice System*. London: Routledge, 1990. Print.

Wrench, Matilda. *Visits to Female Prisoners at Home and Abroad*. London: Wertheim, 1852. Print.

Wyndham, Percy. "Clairvoyance." *Spiritualist* 21 May 1880: 246–47. Print.

Wyner, Ruth. *From the Inside: Dispatches from a Women's Prison*. London: Aurum, 2003. Print.

XXXIII. "The Case of Annette Meyers." *Morning Post* 8 Mar. 1848: 6; Issue

23167. *British Newspapers 1600–1900 Gale Cengage Learning*. Web. 15 Feb. 2013.

Zalcock, Beverley. *Renegade Girls: Girl Gangs on Film*. London: Creation, 1998. Print.

Zalcock, Beverley, and Jocelyn Robinson. "Inside Cell Block H: Hard Steel and Soft Soap." *Continuum* 9.1 (1996): 88–97. Print.

Zedner, Lucia. *Women, Crime, and Custody in Victorian England*. Oxford, UK: Clarendon, 1991. Print.

INDEX

"counter-discourse of prisoners," 200n11

Crewe, Ben: *Criminal Justice Matters*, 200n8

Criminal Evidence Act, 106

cross-class relationships, 87, 89, 137–38; women's prisons, 117, 122, 147, 151, 167–77, 179, 182, 196

Cunningham, Margaret, 27

Dampier, Helen, 225n26

Davitt, Michael, 131

Defoe, Daniel, 42; *Moll Flanders*, 8, 50

de Haan, Francisca, 11, 202n29

Denning, Michael, 206n16

Densmore, Emmet, 133, 140

Densmore, Helen, 122, 129, 131, 135, 137, 139, 140, 222n20, 222n24

Despard, Charlotte: *Outlawed*, 162, 221n15

Dickens, Charles, 10, 23, 27, 42, 45–46, 50, 64, 78, 102, 108, 137, 211n26, 214n18; *All the Year Round*, 59; and Eliot, 218n35; *Great Expectations*, 209n5; "Home for Homeless Women," 66, 77, 80, 81; *Household Words*, 81, 206n21, 212n35; "Lying Awake," 206n21; "No Thorough-fare," 212n34; *Oliver Twist*, 18, 24; prison novels, 226n33; *Sketches by Boz*, 18; travels with Collins, 215n24; Urania Cottage, 81, 83, 212n35

Dijkstra, Sandra, 203n37

Doan, Laura: "Making Up Lost Time," 232n18

Dodge, Mary Abigail. *See* Hamilton, Gail

Donnithorne, Arthur, 71

double standard of morality, 110, 117, 118, 121, 126, 159, 217n23

Drake, Deborah: *Prison Ethnography*, 200n8

Du Cane, Edmund, 15

Ducker, Henry: "The Full Particulars of the Examination and Committal to Newgate of Annette Myers [*sic*], for the Wilful Murder of Henry Ducker, a Private in the Coldstream Guards," 33

Duval, Elsie, 168

Earle, Rod: *Prison Ethnography*, 200n8

Eliot, George, 10, 90, 91, 106, 108, 226n33; *Adam Bede*, 2, 11, 19, 68, 69, 70–78, 88, 89, 196, 202n29, 212n37, 213nn1–3, 213nn7–8, 214n12, 214n15, 214n17; view of art, 68

Engels, Friedrich, 17, 203n37

Evans, Elizabeth Tomlinson, 71–72, 73, 213n4, 213n7; employment, 213n8

Evans, Kate: "The Cleaners of Holloway," 170

Evans, Samuel, 72

Everitt, Graham, 93–95, 111

experience, concept of, 200n10, 225n21

Fabian Women's Group Series, 199n5

Fenning, Eliza, 32, 33, 136, 137, 207n25, 207n27, 222n27

Fenton, W. Hugh, 152

Field, John: *Prison Discipline*, 51, 52, 201n16, 210n19

first-person accounts, 2, 21, 22, 28, 34, 35, 37, 42, 50, 59, 74, 170, 172, 192, 195

Fletcher, John William, 92–93, 99, 105, 109, 110, 114, 116, 216n16, 216n18, 217n22; death, 119–20, 219n53; disappearance of brain, 119–20,

Gladstone, Herbert, 152

Gladstone, William, 130, 131

Gliddon, Katie: cross-class relations, 167–71, 172–77; Holloway, 150–51, 179, 218n45, 224n14, 225nn23–27; hunger strikes, martyrdom, and narrating imprisonment, 181–83; politics of the gaze, 177–81, 182; reading and writing at Holloway, 156–58; reading practices at Holloway, 158–62; regret of Stead drowning, 228n61; religious language, 229n66; secret prison diary, 150–51, 155–56, 162–63, 165, 166, 167–71, 172–78, 223n6, 224n15, 226n31, 226n36, 228n62, 229n69; suffragette, 116, 182–83, 223n3, 227n40

Goldsmith, Larry, 200n12

Gordon, Helen, 162–63

Gordon, Mary, 17–18, 152, 204n41; *Penal Discipline*, 18

Graham, Anne: "Awful Depravity," 35

Grass, Sean, 210n19; *The Self in the Cell*, 6

Great Yarmouth Gaol, 8, 202n25, 214n9

Green, Barbara, 150, 162, 178, 180, 224n18

Groupe d'Information sur les Prisons (GIP), 5, 201n13

Gruner, Elisabeth R., 81

Gurney, Joseph John: *Notes on a Visit*, 202n29

Gurneyism, 202n29

Gwilt, Lydia, 78

Hall, Stuart, 26

Hamilton, Gail, 125–26, 130–31, 143, 221n11; *Woman's Wrongs*, 99

hangings, 24, 32, 204n1; public, 27, 29

Harcourt, William, 101, 217n22, 217n28, 219n49

Hardcastle, Mary: "Account of the Execution of Mary Hardcastle," 38–39, 208n40

Harrison, William, 100

Hart-Davies, Juliet Anne Theodora, 92, 104–5, 108, 109–11, 112, 113, 115, 215n1, 231n14

Hartley, Jenny, 212n35, 233n6; *Charles Dickens and the House of Fallen Women*, 81

Hartman, Kabi, 169, 173–74

Hartman, Mary, 128, 132, 219n5

Harvey, Margaret: "An Account of the Execution of Margaret Harvey," 208n40

Haslam, Jason, 149–50, 170

Hawkins, Judge, 92, 103, 108, 114, 217n31

Hawthorne, Nathaniel: *The Blithedale Romance*, 95

Hayward, Stephens: *Revelations of a Lady Detective*, 44

Heller, Tamar, 80

Hennell, Sara Sophia, 75, 213n7

Henry, Joan: *Who Lie in Gaol*, 2, 199n3; *Women in Prison*, 199n3; *Yield to the Night*, 2

Heyrick, Elizabeth, 203n36

Hitchcock, Tim, 9

Hoare, Samuel, 202n29

Hogan, Rebecca, 155, 167

Holloway Prison, 150, 152, 153–54, 155, 217n30, 225n22, 226n30, 226n35, 227n40, 228n56; cross-class relations, 167–77; female prisoners and the politics of the gaze, 177–81; hunger strikes, martyrdom, and

Mayhew, Henry (*continued*)
the London Poor, 58; remuneration of writers, 205n10

Mayne, Fanny, "The Literature of the Working Classes," 206n18

Mayne, Judith, 178

Mazzini, Giuseppe, 162, 226nn35–36; "Young Italy," 160, 161

McConville, Seán, 203n32, 210n23

McDermott, James, 185, 230n7

McDonagh, Josephine, 73, 212n37, 213n3

McGeary, James (Dr. Mack), 92, 216n3

McKendry, Ruth: *Quilts and Other Bed Coverings in the Canadian Tradition*, 231n8

McKenna, Reginald, 153

Mearn, Andrew: *The Bitter Cry of Outcast London*, 94

Methodists, 11, 76; prisoner visitation, 71, 72–73, 75, 202n25, 203n36, 214n15; split, 214n9

Meyers, Annette, 207n31; "The Full Particulars of the Examination and Committal to Newgate of Annette Myers [*sic*], for the Wilful Murder of Henry Ducker, a Private in the Coldstream Guards," 33–34

Michel, Louise, 109

Mill, John Stuart, 162; *On Liberty*, 226n33; *On the Subjection of Women*, 226n33

Millbank, Jenni, 179, 228n71, 230n5, 232n19

Millbank Prison, 16, 45, 46, 53, 59, 189, 190, 191, 192; 1857 report, 202n27; employee salaries, 210n23; lesbianism, 210n22, 229n71, 232n19

Miller, D. A., 78; *The Novel and the Police*, 200n12

Miller, Elizabeth Carolyn, 219n5

Moffat, Mary Jane, 151

Moodie, Susanna: *Life in the Clearings versus the Bush*, 188–89

Moore, George: *Esther Waters*, 42, 66

Moore, R. Laurence, 95–96

Morgan, John, 205n10

Morris, William: *News from Nowhere*, 226n33

Morrison, William Douglas, 128

Morton, Francis, 92

Morton, Levi P., 129

Mukherjee, Upamanyu Pablo, 78–79, 84, 86, 214n20

Mulvey, Laura: "Visual Pleasure and Narrative Cinema," 177

"The Narrow Way," 158, 159–60

Nash, Jennifer C., 199n6, 232n2

National Association of Lady Visitors, 15

National Association of Spiritualists, 216n19

National Society for the Prevention of Cruelty against Children (NSPCC), 172

Nayder, Lillian, 78, 89, 214n20, 215n27

Nesbitt, Mary, 176–77

Newgate novels, 23, 24

Newgate Prison, 16, 72, 80, 103, 202n18, 204n40, 217n30; first matron, 14; Fletcher, 103, 116, 218n48; Fry, 11, 12, 44, 189–90, 204n40; Tristan visits, 16, 17, 211n28, 218n48. *See also* Ainsworth, William Harrison; Fletcher, John William; Lancaster, John, 72; Ordinary of Newgate's Accounts; Weldon, Georgina

"Newgate School of fiction," 24

Nichols, Mary Sargeant Gove, 100, 115, 119, 218n26; "water cure," 117

Nichols, Thomas Low, 102, 115, 126, 217n28, 218n46, 219n49; *Esoteric Anthropology*, 101; *Herald of Health*, 118; *Journal in Jail*, 102; *Memorial to the Home Secretary in Behalf of Mrs. Susan Willis Fletcher*, 101, 102; "water cure," 117

NSPCC. *See* National Society for the Prevention of Cruelty against Children

O'Brien, Ellen, 26, 28, 30, 222n28

O'Connor, Patrick, 206n21

Old Bailey, 9, 33, 91, 92, 103, 104, 107, 108

Oliphant, Margaret, 209n5

O'Neill, Ellen: *Extraordinary Confessions of a Female Pickpocket*, 201n16

Ordinary of Newgate's Accounts, 8, 202n18

Owen, Alex, 103, 109

Owen, M. E., 44

Oxford Gaol, 18

Pacha, Arabi, 107, 115

Painter, Charlotte, 151

Palgrave, Francis Turner: *Golden Treasury of English Verse*, 226n29

Pankhurst, Christabel, 155, 228n55

Pankhurst, Emmeline, 152, 155, 161, 162, 204n40, 223n8, 224n12; compared to a pope by Gliddon, 229n66

Pankhurst, Sylvia, 151, 170; "The Cleaners," 170; founder of the East London Federation of Suffragettes (ELFS), 228n55; launched the

Women's Dreadnought paper, 228n55; "Sketches at Holloway," 171, 228n56; "What It Feels Like to Be in Prison," 170; "Writ on Cold Slate," 149, 163; *Writ on Cold Slate*, 228n57

Parkes, Bessie Rayner, 44, 49, 58, 60

Parry, Edward Abbott, 124

paternalism, 41, 54, 113, 114, 126

Paul, James, 205n4

Peel, Robert, 202n26

penny dreadfuls, 206n18, 212n32

Pentonville Prison, 14

Peters, Sarah, 72, 202n25, 213n6

Pethick-Lawrence, Emmeline, 152, 159, 174, 178, 224n12; *My Part in a Changing World*, 160

philanthropy, 77, 81, 104, 202n29; Christian, 62; female, 2, 11, 15, 15, 16, 116–19, 174, 188, 189, 190, 192, 203n34, 203n36; fraudulent, 78; middle class, 61

poisoning, 23, 72, 123, 128; arsenic, 124

Poovey, Mary, 42

Preston House of Correction, 201n16

Priestley, Philip, 231n14; *Victorian Prison Lives*, 8

Prior, Margaret, 189, 232n16

Prison Commission, 18, 153

Prison Department of the Home Office, 153

Prisoner's Aid Society, 45

Prisoners' Counsel Act, 9, 105, 206n14

Prisoners' Education Trust, 197; website, 199n7

Prisoner's Temporary Discharge for Ill-Health Bill (Cat and Mouse Act), 154, 182, 228n62

prison ethnography, 200n8

prison literacy, 5, 197, 200n9